INTRODUCTION TO HOMELAND SECURITY:

UNDERSTANDING TERRORISM WITH AN EMERGENCY MANAGEMENT PERSPECTIVE

WILEY PATHWAYS

INTRODUCTION TO HOMELAND SECURITY:

UNDERSTANDING TERRORISM WITH AN EMERGENCY MANAGEMENT PERSPECTIVE

DAVID A. MCENTIRE, PH.D.
University of North Texas

WILEY

John Wiley & Sons, Inc.
New York • Chichester • Weinheim • Brisbane • Toronto • Singapore

PUBLISHER	Anne Smith
PROJECT EDITOR	Brian B. Baker
DEVELOPMENT EDITOR	Laura Town
SENIOR EDITORIAL ASSISTANT	Tiara Kelly
COPYEDITOR	Camelot Editorial Services
PRODUCTION MANAGER	Micheline Frederick
PRODUCTION EDITOR	Kerry Weinstein
CREATIVE DIRECTOR	Harry Nolan
ART DIRECTOR	Jeof Vita
COVER DESIGNER	Hope Miller
PHOTO EDITOR	Sarah Ascione
COVER PHOTO	©Noah Berger/AP/Wide World Photos

This book was set in Times New Roman by Aptara Inc.

To order books or for customer service, please call 1-800-CALL WILEY (225-5945).

ISBN 978-0-470-12752-0

10 9 8 7 6 5 4 3 2

For Mason, Madison, Kailey, and Ashley
and the future of children everywhere

Dr. David A. McEntire is an Associate Professor in the Emergency Administration and Planning (EADP) Program in the Department of Public Administration at the University of North Texas. He teaches emergency management and homeland security courses in both the undergraduate and graduate programs. His academic interests include emergency management theory, international disasters, community preparedness, response coordination, terrorism, and vulnerability reduction.

Dr. McEntire has received several Quick Response Grants (funded by the National Science Foundation through the Natural Hazards Center at the University of Colorado) which allowed him to conduct research on disasters in Peru, the Dominican Republic, Texas, New York, and California. Dr. McEntire is the author of *Disaster Response and Recovery* (Wiley) and the editor of *Disciplines, Disasters and Emergency Management* (C.C. Thomas). His research has also been published in *Public Administration Review*, the *Australian Journal of Emergency Management, Disasters*, the *International Journal of Mass Emergencies and Disasters, Journal of Emergency Management, Journal of the Environment and Sustainable Development, Sustainable Communities Review, International Journal of Emergency Management, Towson Journal of International Affairs, Journal of the American Society of Professional Emergency Planners*, and the *Journal of International and Public Affairs*. His articles in *Disaster Prevention and Management* have received Highly Commended and Outstanding Paper Awards.

Dr. McEntire completed an instructor guide for the Federal Emergency Management Agency, and he is a contributing author to the *Handbook of Disaster Research* and the *Handbook of Disaster Management*. He also has a chapter in *Emergency Management,* a book published by the International City/County Management Association.

Dr. McEntire has received grants to conduct terrorism response training for FEMA in Arkansas and Oklahoma. He has been a contributing author for a study of Texas Homeland Security Preparedness for the Century Foundation as well as two IQ Reports for the International City/County Management Association. McEntire has presented papers in Mexico and Norway, at the National Science Foundation, at the National Academy of Sciences, and at the Higher Education Conference at FEMA's Emergency Management Institute in Emmitsburg, Maryland. He is a member of Congressman Michael C. Burgess's Homeland Security Advisory Board and the Fire Protection Publications Advisory Board. He has reviewed books for Delmar Learning and is on the editorial staff for the *Journal of Emergency Management*.

Dr. McEntire is a former Coordinator of the EADP program and is currently serving as the Ph.D. Coordinator in the Department of Public Administration. Prior to coming to the University of North Texas in the Fall of 1999, he attended the Graduate School of International Studies at the University of Denver. While pursuing his degree, he worked for the International and Emergency Services Departments at the American Red Cross.

Contact information:
P.O. Box 310617
Denton, Texas 76203-0617
mcentire@unt.edu
(940) 565-2996

Today's students have different goals, different life experiences, and different academic backgrounds, but they are all on the same path to success in the real world. This diversity, coupled with the reality that these learners often have jobs, families, and other commitments, requires a flexibility that our nation's higher education system is addressing. Distance learning, shorter course terms, new disciplines, evening courses, and certification programs are some of the approaches that colleges employ to reach as many students as possible and help them clarify and achieve their goals.

The *Wiley Pathways* program, a suite of services and content created especially for career colleges, community colleges, and continuing education institutions, is designed to help you address this diversity and the need for flexibility. *Wiley Pathways* content puts a focus on the fundamentals to help students grasp the subject, bringing them all to the same basic understanding. Content from the *Wiley Pathways* program has an emphasis on teaching job-related skills and practical applications of concepts with clear and professional language. The core competencies and skills help students succeed in the classroom and beyond, whether in another course or in a professional setting. A variety of built-in learning resources allow the students to practice what they need to perform and help instructors and students gauge students' understanding of the content. These resources enable students to think critically about their new knowledge and apply their skills in any situation.

Our goal with *Wiley Pathways* is to celebrate the many students in your courses, respect their needs, and help you guide them on their way.

LEARNING SYSTEM

To meet the needs of working college students, *Wiley Pathways* uses a learning system based on Bloom's Taxonomy. Key topics in *Wiley Pathways Introduction to Homeland Security* are presented in easy-to-follow chapters. The text then prompts analysis, evaluation, and creation with a variety of learning aids and assessment tools. Students move efficiently from reviewing what they have learned, to acquiring new information and skills, to applying their new knowledge and skills to real-life scenarios.

Using this learning system, students not only achieve academic mastery of Homeland Security *topics*, but they master real-world *skills* related to that content. The learning system also helps students become independent learners, giving them a distinct advantage in the field, whether they are just starting out or seeking to advance in their careers.

ORGANIZATION, DEPTH, AND BREADTH OF THE TEXT

Modular Format

Research on college students shows that they access information from textbooks in a non-linear way. Instructors also often wish to reorder textbook content to suit the needs of a particular class. Therefore, although *Wiley Pathways* proceeds logically from the basics to increasingly more challenging material, chapters are further organized into sections that are self-contained for maximum teaching and learning flexibility.

Numeric System of Headings

Wiley Pathways uses a numeric system for headings (e.g., 2.3.4 identifies the fourth subsection of Section 3 of Chapter 2). With this system, students and teachers can quickly and easily pinpoint topics in the table of contents and the text, keeping class time and study sessions focused.

Core Content

United States disaster policy has witnessed an ever-present history of tension among the security and emergency management points of view. From the late 1940s through the year 2000 there has been recurring disagreement about the priority given to conflict events versus other types of hazards. Two events have recently elevated the stakes in this debate and created urgency for finding some sort of consensus about future priorities.

On the one hand, 9/11 underscored the fact that the threat of terrorism needs to be been taken seriously by disaster scholars and emergency managers. No one should pretend that the world is the way it once used to be. On the other hand, Hurricane Katrina reminded homeland security officials that they must not disregard human vulnerability to natural hazards. The frequency of natural disasters is simply too great to ignore and their impact is getting worse over time.

With these observations in mind, it is the opinion of this author that both homeland security and emergency management priorities will need to be addressed in the future. The possibility of terrorism involving weapons of mass destruction remains fairly low, but the consequences of such attacks would indeed be overwhelming. Terrorism has been given the lion's share of public support in recent years, but this attention should not be allowed to overshadow the essential function and contributions of emergency management.

Unfortunately, policy makers have created a substantial divide between the homeland security and disaster communities. Politicians may have over-reacted to 9/11 and their decisions all but destroyed the well-functioning, but not perfect, emergency management system in the 1990s. This has caused many ill-feelings among emergency managers toward the military personnel and the law enforcement profession, which is not a good situation when one considers the fact that terrorists have vowed to kill Americans everywhere (including at home).

This book, *Introduction to Homeland Security: Understanding Terrorism with an Emergency Management Perspective*, aims to lay a foundation which could assist in spanning the readily apparent chasm between the disaster and terrorism communities. Its focus on terrorism may help to educate those who do not yet understand the need to prepare for this expanding threat. Its concentration on emergency management will remind homeland security officials that reinventing of the wheel is not only unnecessary, but problematic.

Of course, taking this middle ground could result in increased antagonism between the different parties. It is also possible that the author has not adequately portrayed the specific details pertinent to all of the actors involved in the broad and interdisciplinary array of homeland security and emergency management activities. Nevertheless, it is the author's hope that this work will educate those working in each area and help promote a synergy of effort.

Chapter 1, "Understanding a New National Priority: 9/11, Homeland Security, and Emergency Management," examines the enormous impact of the terrorist attacks on 9/11 on world history, defines homeland security, and supplements homeland security with an emergency management perspective, thereby offering a broad view of how to deal with terrorist attacks.

Chapter 2, "Identifying Terrorism: Ideologically Motivated Acts of Violence," identifies the numerous definitions and perspectives of terrorism, comparing how these are both alike and dissimilar, and also looks at the connections among terrorism and other types of disasters.

Chapter 3, "Recognizing the Causes of Terrorism: Differing Perspectives and the Role of Ideology," explores what motivates people to participate in terrorism, paying special attention to how historical conflicts, mistakes in foreign policy, and extreme levels of poverty may impel some to engage in terrorist attacks.

Chapter 4, "Comprehending Terrorists and Their Behavior: Who They Are and What They Do," assesses the nature of individual terrorists and those associated with groups and states, and identifies how they finance operations, communicate with secret codes, and carry out attacks.

Chapter 5, "Uncovering the Dynamic Nature of Terrorism: History and Change over Time," explores why terrorism initially emerged, how it evolved in other nations, and ways it has manifested in the United States.

Chapter 6, "Evaluating a Major Dilemma: Terrorism, the Media, and Censorship," looks at the difficult relationship between terrorism and the media, how to predict how reporters view terrorism, and the drawbacks and limitations of censorship.

In Chapter 7, "Contemplating a Quandary: Terrorism, Security, and Liberty," you learn why, as a participant in homeland security, it is imperative that you assess the trade-offs between security and rights and why terrorism exploits the tension between them.

Chapter 8, "Preventing Terrorist Attacks," addresses the root causes of terrorism and explores primary ways of preventing attacks, like promoting laws that prohibit terrorism and punish those who support it, protecting all points of entry into the United States, and relying on human and other sources of intelligence to apprehend terrorists before they strike.

Chapter 9, "Protecting against Potential Attacks: Threat Assessment and Security Enhancement," looks at the benefits of mitigation practices, such as working with others to assess threats posed to critical infrastructure, key assets, and soft targets, as well as differentiating between structural and non-structural mitigation methods.

In Chapter 10, "Preparing for the Unthinkable: Readiness for Terrorism," we learn that preparing for terrorism is one of the central responsibilities in homeland security. In order to help your community become ready for possible terrorist attacks, you will need to be familiar with the executive orders and legislation issued by the president and congress, and set the foundation for preparedness by creating an advisory council, passing ordinances, acquiring monetary resources, and establishing an EOC.

Chapter 11, "Responding to Attacks: Important Functions and Coordination Mechanisms," examines effective ways to react to terrorist attacks, including the numerous functions involved, such as the protection of first responders and the decontamination of the victims of terrorist attacks.

Chapter 12, "Recovering from Impacts: Short-term and Long-term Measures," addresses the variety of recovery measures that need to be performed after a terrorist attack takes place, including declaring a disaster or state of emergency, addressing mass fatality issues, disposing of debris, and providing emotional support for those who have been emotionally impacted by the event.

In Chapter 13, "Looking toward the Future: Forthcoming Challenges and Opportunities," discusses how as a participant in homeland security, it is imperative that you prepare for the future and comprehend the impacts of dirty bombs, radiological dispersion devices, and the possible devastation that may result if nuclear weapons are acquired and used by terrorists.

PRE-READING LEARNING AIDS

Each chapter of *Wiley Pathways Introduction to Homeland Security* features a number of learning and study aids, described in the following sections, to activate students' prior knowledge of the topics and orient them to the material.

Do You Already Know?

This bulleted list focuses on *subject matter* that will be taught. It tells students what they will be learning in this chapter and why it is significant for their careers. It also helps students understand why the chapter is important and how it relates to other chapters in the text.

The online assessment tool in multiple-choice format not only introduces chapter material, but it also helps students anticipate the chapter's learning outcomes. By focusing students' attention on what they do not know, the self-test provides students with a benchmark against which they can measure their own progress. The Pre Test is available online at www.wiley.com/college/mcentire.

What You Will Find Out and *What You Will Be Able To Do*

This bulleted list emphasizes *capabilities and skills* students will learn as a result of reading the chapter and notes the sections in which they will be found. It prepares students to synthesize and evaluate the chapter material and relate it to the real world.

WITHIN-TEXT LEARNING AIDS

The following learning aids are designed to encourage analysis and synthesis of the material, support the learning process, and ensure success during the evaluation phase.

Introduction

This section orients the student by introducing the chapter and explaining its practical value and relevance to the book as a whole. Short summaries of chapter sections preview the topics to follow.

In the Real World

These boxes tie section content to real-world organizations, scenarios, and applications. Engaging stories of professionals and institutions—challenges they faced, successes they had, and their ultimate outcome.

Homeland Security in Action

These margin boxes point out places in the text where professional applications of a concept are demonstrated. An arrow in the box points to the section of the text and a description of the application is given in the box.

For Example

These margin boxes highlight documents and web sites from real companies that further help students understand a key concept. The boxes can reference a figure or the Toolkit found at the end of each chapter.

Career Connection

Case studies of real people in the field depicting the skills that helped them succeed in the professional world. Each profile ends with a list of "Tips from the Professional" that provide relevant advice and helpful tools.

Pathway to. . .

This boxed section provides students with how-to or step-by-step lists helping them to perform specific tasks.

Summary

Each chapter concludes with a summary paragraph that reviews the major concepts in the chapter and links back to the "Do You Already Know" list.

Key Terms and Glossary

To help students develop a professional vocabulary, key terms are bolded when they first appear in the chapter and are also shown in the margin of page with their definitions. A complete list of key terms with brief definitions appears at the end of each chapter and again in a glossary at the end of the book. Knowledge of key terms is assessed by all assessment tools (see below).

Toolkit

An end-of-chapter appendix that contains relevant documents and examples from real companies.

EVALUATION AND ASSESSMENT TOOLS

The evaluation phase of the *Wiley Pathways* learning system consists of a variety of within-chapter and end-of-chapter assessment tools that test how well students have learned the material and their ability to apply it in the real world. These tools also encourage students to extend their learning into different scenarios and higher levels of understanding and thinking. The following assessment tools appear in every chapter of *Wiley Pathways*.

Self-Check

Related to the "Do You Already Know" bullets and found at the end of each section, this battery of short-answer questions emphasizes student understanding of concepts and mastery of section content. Though the questions may be either discussed in class or studied by students outside of class, students should not go on before they can answer all questions correctly.

Understand: What Have You Learned?

This online Post Test should be taken after students have completed the chapter. It includes all of the questions in the Pre Test so that students can see how their learning has progressed and improved. The Post Test is available online at www.wiley.com/college/mcentire.

Apply: What Would You Do?

These questions drive home key ideas by asking students to synthesize and apply chapter concepts to new, real-life situations and scenarios.

Be a Homeland Security Professional

Found at the end of each chapter, "Be a. . ." questions are designed to extend students' thinking and are thus ideal for discussion or writing assignments. Using an open-ended format and sometimes based on Web sources, they encourage students to draw conclusions using chapter material applied to real-world situations, which fosters both mastery and independent learning.

INSTRUCTOR AND STUDENT PACKAGE

Wiley Pathways Introduction to Homeland Security is available with the following teaching and learning supplements. All supplements are available online at the text's Book Companion Web site, located at www.wiley.com/college/mcentire.

Instructor's Resource Guide

The Instructor's Resource Guide provides the following aids and supplements for teaching a Homeland Security course:

- **Text summary aids:** For each chapter, these include a chapter summary, learning objectives, definitions of key terms, and answers to in-text question sets.
- **Teaching suggestions:** For each chapter, these include at least three suggestions for learning activities (such as ideas for speakers to invite, videos to show, and other projects), and suggestions for additional resources.

PowerPoints

Key information is summarized in ten to fifteen PowerPoints per chapter. Instructors may use these in class or choose to share them with students for class presentations or to provide additional study support.

Test Bank

The test bank features one test per chapter, as well as a mid-term and two finals—one cumulative and one non-cumulative. Each includes true/false, multiple-choice, and open-ended questions. Answers and page references are provided for the true/false and multiple-choice questions, and page references are given for the open-ended questions. Tests are available in Microsoft Word and computerized formats.

ACKNOWLEDGMENTS

I express appreciation to those individuals who have made substantial contributions to *Introduction to Homeland Security*. I am indebted first and foremost to Laura Town and Brian Baker (two editors at Wiley) for their critical assessment of the text and their useful recommendations for improvement. I am also grateful to the other members of the Wiley staff who helped format the text, find pictures, and create the index for the entire document.

I am likewise appreciative of several outside reviewers for their beneficial suggestions on earlier versions of the manuscript. This includes:

- Vincent J. Doherty, Naval Postgraduate School
- David W. Lewis, University of Maryland
- Scott D. Lassa, Milwaukee Area Technical College.

While I am solely responsible for the content of this book, I am thankful for their valuable insights and unique perspectives. Their areas of expertise and years of experience have undoubtedly assisted me during the publication process.

Finally, I would be remiss if I did not recognize the many scholars and practitioners that I have come across during my involvement in this field. Your knowledge and professionalism have not only helped to educate me about terrorism and disasters, but you have also helped me to identify the significant need for homeland security and emergency management functions in our society. More importantly, I am cognizant that your persistent efforts will enable our nation to reduce vulnerability and increase our ability to react effectively when exigency exists. For this I am truly thankful.

David A. McEntire, Ph.D.

FOREWORD

In the United States, and indeed in many places around the world, terrorism has gained prominence as a principal threat to safety and well-being. While many of us in the emergency and disaster community are concerned that the emphasis on terrorism has displaced attention from more likely and possibly more destructive natural hazards, we also know that the threat is significant, and that terrorist attacks can be launched anywhere and with any degree of destructive force. Thus the threat must be evaluated in terms of likelihoods, needs, priorities, capabilities, and vulnerabilities. Yet the ambiguous character of this threat—so difficult to quantify or to relate to a place, even in the most general terms—presents a unique public-policy challenge. Moreover, each of us is affected personally—each of us is aware of this threat and feels its effects as we tiptoe in our socks at the airport or surrender our toothpaste to security personnel.

Tackling this challenge demands knowledge, but because the challenge is so multidimensional, that knowledge must be wide-ranging and comprehensive. David McEntire addresses that need in this volume, which is in equal parts a literature review, a historical survey, and a management guide for meeting homeland security needs. McEntire sets the current challenge in local and global contexts; he leads the reader through the origins and varied manifestations of terrorism across time, nations, and cultures; he considers the threat of terrorism in light of implications for security and for liberty; and he introduces the institutional framework and technical resources for anticipating terrorist acts and responding to their effects.

This book is important for another reason: the September 11 attacks destabilized people's understanding of safety. But terrorist events also destabilized officials' expectations of how people are supposed to respond to security policies, such as in sensitive facilities. Some of us can remember the surliness and antagonism of airport screening agents, ordering around passengers whose knowledge of where to stand and when to move was suddenly obsolete. Airports, complex systems of procedures and technology, weren't designed for the kinds of demands suddenly placed on them. The significance is that policy shifts, even those intended to increase our safety, can be startling and disorienting and add to the public sense of tension and menace.

Policymakers need principles, ideas, and guidance from several disciplines that can be the foundation for good decision making. David McEntire supplies these in this book, which emerges from his popular courses on terrorism and homeland security. Hundreds of students have taken these courses and brought his analysis and insight into diverse public and private organizations. But I'm sure that Dr. McEntire will not object if I suggest that reading *Introduction to Homeland Security* is only an important first step in the emergency manager's response to terrorist threats. Policymakers grappling with public safety concerns must strive for an elusive balance of decisiveness, sensitivity, vigilance, and wisdom. These qualities are up to the readers of this book to develop.

James Kendra
Emergency Administration and Planning Program
Department of Public Administration
University of North Texas

BRIEF CONTENTS

CONTENTS

UNDERSTANDING A NEW NATIONAL PRIORITY

9/11, Homeland Security, and Emergency Management

Do You Already Know?

- Why we should be concerned about future terrorist threats
- How to define homeland security
- Why many fields, including emergency management, can help deal with terrorist attacks

For additional questions to assess your current knowledge on homeland security, go to **www.wiley.com/college/mcentire**

What You Will Find Out	What You Will Be Able To Do
1.1 The importance of the terrorist attacks of 9/11	• Recall the events of 9/11
1.2 The growing threat of terrorism	• Understand why terrorism occurs
1.3 The nature of homeland security	• Compare and contrast the different missions of homeland security
1.4 The disciplines involved in emergency management and homeland security	• Assess why many disciplines, such as emergency management, help practitioners respond to terrorist threats

INTRODUCTION

If you are interested or involved in dealing with the threat of terrorism, it is imperative that you understand the fundamental principles of homeland security. The following book has the purpose of helping you achieve this goal. While reading this introductory chapter you will learn how the terrorist attacks on September 11, 2001 changed the world and opened up a new era in history. You will gain an understanding of the growing threat of terrorism and the numerous reasons why this problem should be addressed in the future. You will be able to discuss the mission and scope of homeland security along with the challenges it currently faces. The importance of approaching homeland security from a holistic perspective is then mentioned, enabling you to recognize why emergency management must form an integral part of efforts to deal with terrorism. The chapter concludes with a preview of the remaining material presented in this textbook.

1.1 9/11: A WAKE-UP CALL

9/11:
The terrorist attacks involving hijacked planes against the United States that occurred on September 11, 2001.

Al Qaeda:
An extreme Islamic fundamentalist terrorist organization.

September 11, 2001, ushered in a new era in world history. Henceforth, **9/11** will forever be remembered as the terrorist attacks involving hijacked planes against the United States.

After years of planning, a number of hijackers affiliated with Osama bin Laden and **Al Qaeda** (an extreme Islamic fundamentalist organization) boarded four commercial planes on this date to initiate a massive campaign of terror against the United States. American Airlines Flight 11, departing from Boston to Los Angeles, was overtaken by men with box cutters or other sharp instruments. It was then deliberately flown into the North tower of World Trade Center in New York City. United Airlines Flight 175, also departing from Boston to Los Angeles, was diverted and used as a missile to kill people working in the South tower of the World Trade Center. Within minutes, America Airlines Flight 77, departing from Dulles to Los Angeles, was crashed into the Pentagon in Arlington, Virginia. Another plane, United Airlines Flight 93, departing from Newark to San Francisco, was also hijacked. By this time, passengers on board became aware of other incidents and attempted to take back the aircraft. A short time later, the plane was deliberately flown into the ground in an empty field southeast of Pittsburgh.

The brave efforts of the passengers on Flight 93 amounted to a symbolic victory for the United States. Nevertheless, the hijackers succeeded in their goal of bringing attention to their hatred of Western culture and disapproval of American foreign policy. At least 266 passengers and crew were killed in the orchestrated attacks. Over 2,500 more people died in the subsequent collapses of the World Trade Center towers in New York and the fire at the Pentagon in Virginia. In addition to the loss of life, America encountered fear and economic disruption on an unprecedented scale. **Terrorism**—the use or

Terrorism:
The use or threat of violence to support ideological purposes.

threat of violence to support ideological purposes—had certainly captured the attention of the United States.

When informed of the situation, President Bush ordered any additional hijacked planes be shot down should they be encountered. He also requested the grounding of all other flights to prevent further loss of life and damage. Fire fighters, police officers, paramedics, hospital personnel, and government officials immediately began to address the needs of the terrorists' victims. Volunteers, businesses, and numerous local, state, and federal agencies also arrived to consider how they would address long-term rebuilding activities. When flights resumed a few days later, new measures were taken at U.S. airports to minimize the probability of similar events in the future.

After determining who was responsible for these attacks, U.S. troops were sent into Afghanistan to topple the Taliban. The **Taliban** is the name of the government which provided a safe haven for Al Qaeda. Intelligence efforts were also augmented and a massive manhunt was underway to find Osama bin Laden, the leader of the Al Qaeda terrorist network. In time, Congress passed numerous laws to repel terrorist activity by improving border control, increasing public security, and promoting readiness for future terrorist plots. Elected officials, public servants, law enforcement agencies, corporations, and many others are now working together to prevent further terrorist attacks or react effectively should they occur.

The above narrative describing 9/11 brings up three important questions that will be addressed in the remainder of this book:

- What is terrorism?
- Why and how does terrorism occur?
- What can and should be done to deal with it in an effective manner?

Taliban:
The name of the government which provided a safe haven for Al Qaeda.

SELF-CHECK

1. Terrorism may be described as the pursuit of ideological purposes through violent means or the threat of violence. True or False?
2. 9/11 is the name given to the terrorist attacks on the World Trade Center and the Pentagon. True or False?
3. The 9/11 attacks involved:
   (a) Explosives
   (b) Guns
   (c) Hijacked airplanes
   (d) Hand grenades
   (e) None of the above
4. Why did 9/11 change the world?

1.2 A GROWING THREAT

The events of 9/11 shocked people everywhere since they were unprecedented in terms of impact and publicity. However, these terrorist attacks were not the first to occur in the United States or around the world. Nor will they be the last ones to take place in our country or elsewhere.

If you pick up a national or international newspaper on any given day, you will probably find several articles discussing the rising menace of terrorism. Headlines frequently highlight possible threats and recent attacks:

- Terrorists Infiltrate the United States
- Man Attempts to Detonate Shoe on Plane
- Aviation Security Still Weak
- Oregon Professor Charged with Terrorism
- Sea-born Cargo a Likely Target
- Eco-terrorism Occurs in California
- Officials Detain Man after Filming Chicago Bridge
- Explosives Missing in Georgia
- Agro-terrorism a Real Possibility
- Industrial Security Still Lacking
- Pipelines Targeted in Possible Attack
- Cruise Ship Receives Threatening Letter
- Bombs Obliterate Spanish Resort
- Australia Weary about Potential Terrorists
- Plot Busted in Pakistan
- Bus Ripped Apart by Blast in London
- Children Taken Hostage in Russia
- Cartoon of Mohamed Inflames Terrorists in Europe
- Iran Seeks Nuclear Weapons
- Terrorists Set Sights on 2012 Olympics

Recognizing these perceived threats and actual terrorist activity, many conclude that politically motivated acts of violence will be more common in the future. In a study undertaken by the U.S. Senate Foreign Relations Committee in 2004, security experts were asked to estimate the possibility of major attacks around the world (Associated Press, 2005). It was believed that the risk of an attack involving nuclear, biological, chemical, or radiological weapons is 70 percent over the coming decade. Commenting on the Committee's report, Senator Richard Lugar, R-Ind, stated "The bottom line is this: For the foreseeable future, the United States and other nations will face an existential threat from . . . terrorism."

There are numerous reasons why we may witness additional and more deadly attacks in the future:

- Prior conflicts among nation-states persist, and patience to resolve them is growing thin (e.g., the creation of Israel has resulted in ongoing tensions in the Middle East).
- The end of the Cold War resulted in the resurgence of deep-seated ethnic or political rivalries (e.g., Chechnya desires autonomy and independence from Russia).
- Western forms of economic development have not materialized in many nations around the world and poverty may be associated with terrorist activities (e.g., the poor nations fifty years ago are predominantly the poor countries today and they are breeding grounds for terrorist organizations).
- Citizens are frustrated with the harsh conditions of dictatorship or the unresponsiveness of certain democratic governments (e.g., they desire political change and think that their needs are not being met in an expeditious manner).
- Some religious and social movements have become more extreme over time (e.g., fundamentalist Muslims and other interest groups want change now and are willing to promote it through violent behavior).
- U.S. military power and involvement in Iraq has angered many Arabs (e.g., those in the Middle East view American presence as a new form of colonialism).
- It is extremely difficult for intelligence analysts to know who the "enemy" is (e.g., how can one pinpoint a terrorist when they often blend into the crowd?).
- Technology and education will allow terrorists to develop and use more sophisticated weapons (e.g., household chemicals can be used to make bombs).
- We cannot protect all of the potential targets that the terrorists could attack (e.g., government buildings, ports, shopping malls, schools).
- Training and preparedness for terrorism response is inadequate (e.g., we do not know enough about how to deal with poisonous substances used by terrorists).

Should more and worse terrorist attacks occur as predicted, the United States can expect increased loss of life, financial losses in the billions, social disruption, dramatic political changes, and other negative consequences. The attacks on 9/11 killed nearly 3,000 people. With more sophisticated weapons, it is not out of the realm of possibilities to have casualties in the hundreds of thousands or even millions. September 11 resulted in around $40 billion in

IN THE REAL WORLD

Bin Laden's War Against the United States

Terrorists like Osama bin Laden have declared war against western nations. He and his followers disapprove of the foreign policy of the United States in the Middle East and they declare it is the responsibility of all Muslims to attack the "infidels." Reports from intelligence analysts indicate that terrorist groups are working hard to launch new attacks in the United States and elsewhere around the world. Most experts believe that they may be successful in the future.

losses. Had New York been leveled by a nuclear weapon, the cost would be unimaginable. September 11 halted air travel and negatively impacted the economy. Future attacks may be geared toward increased impacts on people's way of life. September 11 resulted in a massive transformation of government and the introduction of new laws pertaining to security, travel, and immigration. Further changes might be undertaken if terrorists strike again in the United States. All of this is to say that terrorism is now recognized as a feature of our time that cannot be discounted or ignored.

SELF-CHECK

1. There are very few reports of terrorism threats in newspapers. True or False?
2. Terrorism is not a growing threat. True or False?
3. Reasons to be concerned about terrorism include:
    (a) Resurgence of ethnic rivalries
    (b) Poverty in many nations around the world
    (c) More extreme religious attitudes
    (d) Availability of weapons
    (e) All of the above
4. Will we have more attacks in the future? If so, why?

1.3 THE NATURE OF HOMELAND SECURITY

The foregoing discussion indicates the need for what is now known as "homeland security." Discussions about this field did not begin after 9/11. For instance, President Clinton acknowledged the threat of terrorism after a number of attacks were initiated in the 1990s. President Bush created an office to assess the growing threat of terrorism after his election. However,

Homeland security:
A concerted national effort to prevent terrorist attacks within the United States, reduce America's vulnerability to terrorism, and recover from and minimize the damage of attacks that do occur.

Department of Homeland Security (DHS):
A newly created organization which aims to prevent terrorist attacks or react to them effectively.

homeland security moved to the forefront of policy after 9/11. The events of this day revealed the reality of what was heretofore unthinkable.

When it was initially conceived by national leaders, **homeland security** was defined as "a concerted national effort to prevent terrorist attacks within the United States, reduce America's vulnerability to terrorism, and recover from and minimize the damage of attacks that do occur" (Office of Homeland Security 2002, 2). While this definition captures the essence of current efforts to deal with terrorism, consensus on the term is not universal. For instance:

- *Citizens believe homeland security refers to the federal agency in charge of preventing terrorist attacks in the United States.* The **Department of Homeland Security (DHS)** is a newly created organization comprised of over 170,000 employees from 22 federal agencies. Its mission is to prevent terrorist attacks and react to those that may occur.

- *Elected officials view homeland security as a policy framework.* Its purpose is to organize "the activities of government and all sectors of society to detect, deter, protect against, and if necessary, respond to domestic attacks such as 9/11" (Kamien 2006, xli).

- *Scholars see homeland security as an area of study.* It is considered a multi- or inter-disciplinary research endeavor that involves academic fields such as international relations, criminal justice, public administration, and even medicine.

- *Practitioners regard it to be a function or functions performed in response to the terrorist threat.* In this sense, homeland security deals with intelligence gathering, border control, airport security, fire suppression, public health, and emergency medical care.

- *The military asserts that homeland security is its new priority in the post-cold war era.* Since relations between the United States and Russia improved dramatically in the late 1980s, attention in national security is now directed toward individual terrorists, terrorist organizations, and those states that support terrorism.

Even though homeland security means different things to different people, there are several points of agreement. First, homeland security, according to the National Strategy for Homeland Security, entails six essential missions. These include:

- **Mission Area 1: Intelligence and Warning.** One goal of homeland security is to identify possible terrorist attacks before they occur. This eliminates surprises and permits the implementation of protective measures if potential targets can be identified.

- **Mission Area 2: Border and Transportation Security.** Another purpose of homeland security is to prevent the infiltration of terrorists into the

United States. Protecting our land, water, and air transportation systems from attack is also a major objective of homeland security.

- **Mission Area 3: Domestic Counterterrorism.** This aim focuses on interdicting terrorist activity and prosecuting those who fund or engage in terrorism. The goal here is to thwart terrorist plans and apprehend those involved in attacks against America.

- **Mission Area 4: Protecting Critical Infrastructure and Key Assets.** This strategy desires to defend vital buildings, roadways, utilities, technology, etc. Steps must also be taken to prevent attacks against important monuments, valued industries, and national symbols (e.g., the Statue of Liberty).

- **Mission Area 5: Defending against Catastrophic Threat.** The intention of this mission is to prevent the proliferation of dangerous weapons. Homeland security also intends to quickly detect and deal with the impact of major attacks.

- **Mission Area 6: Emergency Preparedness and Response.** The final priority of homeland security is to plan, train, and equip police, fire, and paramedics to react successfully to terrorism. There is also a need to promote recovery with the assistance of disaster specialists.

Homeland security is therefore a major undertaking that requires a comprehensive approach against the threat of terrorism.

A second widely held view is that homeland security requires integrated efforts on the part of many people. According to Richard Falkenrath, an expert on international conflict:

> Men and women from dozens of different disciplines—regional experts, terrorism analysts, law enforcement officials, intelligence officers, privacy specialists, diplomats, military officers, immigration specialists, customs inspectors, specific industry experts, regulatory lawyers, doctors and epidemiologists, research scientists, chemists, nuclear physicists, information technologists, emergency managers, firefighters, communications specialists, and politicians, to name a few—are currently involved in homeland security (in Kamien 2006, xxvi).

In other words, there are a variety of participants in homeland security. Some may represent the government at local, state, and national levels. Many municipals and states now have homeland security agencies like the Department of Homeland Security. Others will assist from the business and non-profit communities. Corporations play a huge role in transportation and shipping, while organizations like the American Red Cross help to educate the public about terrorism preparedness. Even citizens may fulfill homeland security functions by notifying officials of potential terrorist activity. Although much of homeland security activity occurs within the domestic arena, the assistance of national and international organizations is also required. National intelligence agencies may share information about terrorists operating abroad and the United Nations may pass resolutions on how the international community should confront terrorism.

Federal Emergency Management Agency (FEMA): The national organization in charge of disaster management.

A third area of agreement is that tensions have resulted from or re-emerged due to homeland security initiatives. The most visible examples concern the problems homeland security has produced for those responsible for dealing with disasters. For example, the **Federal Emergency Management Agency (FEMA)**—the national organization in charge of disaster management—lost much of its budget and autonomy when it was integrated into the newly created Department of Homeland Security.

Much of the operating funds from FEMA's small budget (by federal standards) were poured into the Department of Homeland Security to cover startup costs, and the ability of this disaster organization to influence the direction of policy was severely hampered. FEMA, which had cabinet level status in a prior administration, also saw its direct ties to the president severed when its director was placed under DHS. Furthermore, FEMA's interest in all types of hazards, disaster prevention programs, and even certain preparedness functions were overlooked. Under the Department of Homeland Security, terrorism seemed to take precedence over all other concerns, and efforts to counter other types of disasters were neglected. The heavy military and law-enforcement approach to homeland security also had an impact upon inter-agency collaboration. Information sensitivities as well as command and control top-down communication structures hindered coordination across organizations horizontally and among governments vertically.

Morale at FEMA started to deteriorate under these conditions, and many knowledgeable disaster professionals retired or switched careers as a result. Other tensions also exist among DHS and the public health community. Such problems were in part responsible for the slow and disjointed response to Hurricane Katrina in the fall 2005. Neither FEMA nor DHS officials could effectively coordinate important post-disaster functions such as mass care, sheltering, and evacuation. After several congressional investigations into these failures, efforts are now being made to correct them. In particular, there is growing recognition that homeland security cannot focus on the threat of terrorism alone or without the help of organizations like FEMA. In fact, the mission of DHS was adapted in 2007 to include a greater emphasis on all types of disasters and the importance of preparedness.

Finally, homeland security has had mixed results during its short existence. On the one hand, the United States has been successful through the end of 2007 in preventing further terrorist attacks on the homeland. Efforts in this area are to be commended because several terrorist plots against Americans have been foiled. This, probably more than any other factor, is a major achievement against terrorism. On the other hand, the Department of Homeland Security is going through several growing pains because of its newness and the enormous challenges pertaining to its mission. For instance, there have been numerous allegations that the money devoted to homeland security lacks careful controls to prevent fraud, waste, and abuse. At least some of the money designated for homeland security has not gone to legitimate purposes. Stories abound of communities using homeland security

IN THE REAL WORLD

The National Response Plan

After 9/11, the government developed a new strategy for dealing with terrorist attacks. Rather than building upon the prior federal response plan, a new plan was created. The National Response Plan (NRP) added layers of bureaucracy to federal response operations and obfuscated responsibility for numerous disaster functions. The plan was criticized as it was being created and especially after it failed dramatically in Hurricane Katrina. Part of the problem was a result of placing too much attention on terrorism and downplaying other types of hazards. The director of FEMA also lacked direct ties to the president, which hindered communication. The challenges that have resulted indicate why the Federal Emergency Management Agency should be more involved in homeland security policies. This is because FEMA plays the lead role in preparing for and coordinating post-disaster responses. Fortunately, efforts are being made to clarify agency tasks in all types of disasters. The National Response Framework is a new document that intends to correct the weaknesses of the NRP.

money to buy dump trucks, polo shirts and other items unrelated to terrorism. Other problems, like border control, do not seem to have been resolved yet. For these reasons, the impact of homeland security is somewhat inconclusive. Of course, it is necessary to recognize that it is not easy to access what success means in the context of homeland security. This is because you cannot always publicize threats or evaluate attacks that do not happen.

SELF-CHECK

1. Homeland security is defined as an effort to prevent terrorist activity, reduce vulnerability, and recover from attacks. True or False?
2. Everyone views homeland security in the same way. True or False?
3. The goals of homeland security are to:
    - (a) Gather intelligence
    - (b) Protect borders and infrastructure
    - (c) Prepare for major catastrophes
    - (d) Answers a, b and c
    - (e) Answers a and b only
4. Why it important to take a broad view of homeland security?
5. Has homeland security been effective thus far? Why or why not?

1.4 DISCIPLINES INVOLVED IN HOMELAND SECURITY AND THE EMERGENCY MANAGEMENT PROFESSION

If you are to work in homeland security, you must be aware that this field is a combination of many areas of study including international relations, criminal justice, public administration, and public health among others. These fields and others offer important insights into terrorism and for homeland security.

International relations:
A discipline and profession that deals with the conflicts among nation states and non-state actors (e.g., why terrorism occurs and what governments are doing about it).

Criminal justice:
A discipline and profession interested in intelligence gathering, terrorist investigation, prosecution, border control, and other security measures.

Public administration:
A discipline and profession that directs attention to the formation policy and the best organization to deal with difficult societal problems.

Public health:
A discipline and profession that concentrates on understanding diseases and how to treat them (e.g., identifying how to react from a medical standpoint to the use of nuclear, biological, chemical or radiological weapons).

- **International relations** focus on the conflicts among nation states and non-state actors. It identifies why terrorism occurs and what governments are doing about it.
- **Criminal justice** is interested in intelligence gathering, terrorist investigation, and prosecution. It also has relation to border control and other security measures.
- **Public administration** directs attention on the formation and implementation of policy. It also helps to identify the best form of organization to deal with difficult societal problems.
- **Public health** concentrates on understanding diseases and how to treat them. It plays an important role in preparing for terrorists' use of nuclear, biological, chemical, or radiological weapons.

Other academic disciplines are also important to the study of homeland security. Anthropology enables an understanding of the culture of terrorism. Sociology facilitates comprehension of human behavior in crisis situations. Political science and law address policy making and human rights issues, which are vital as democratic governments fight terrorism. Journalism permits comprehension of terrorists' use of the media for increased publicity. Engineering provides valuable advice on protecting buildings and critical infrastructure from possible attacks. The physical sciences permit discussion of nuclear material, chemical reactions, and biological processes. As these and other fields are vital to homeland security, this book will approach the subject of terrorism from a holistic perspective. Emergency management plays an especially important role in homeland security.

1.4.1 The Role of Emergency Management

Emergency management:
A discipline and profession that addresses how to prevent or react successfully to various types of disasters.

Emergency management specifies how to prevent or react successfully to various types of disasters. It includes four functional phases described as the life cycle of disaster: mitigation, preparedness, response and recovery. Each of these concepts is important for the study of terrorism and the homeland security profession.

Mitigation:
Activity that attempts to avoid disasters or minimize negative consequences.

Prevention:
Counter-terrorism operations such as intelligence gathering and preventive strike activity.

Protection:
Anti-terrorism operations such as improved building design, enhanced security, infrastructure protection.

Preparedness:
Readiness measures in anticipation of a disaster.

Response:
The immediate reaction to an emergency situation, like a terrorist attack.

Recovery:
Long-term activities to rebound after disasters or terrorist attacks.

Crisis management:
A law enforcement function that concentrates on identifying, anticipating, preventing and prosecuting those involved in terrorism.

Consequence management:
An emergency management function that stresses planning, emergency medical response and public health, disaster relief, and restoration of communities.

Civil defense:
The government's initiative to prepare communities and citizens to react effectively to a nuclear exchange during the Cold War.

Mitigation is activity that attempts to avoid disasters or minimize negative consequences. Mitigation is closely associated with two terms in homeland security:

- **Prevention,** or counter-terrorism operations such as intelligence gathering and preventive strike activity, and

- **Protection,** which is anti-terrorism operations such as improved building design, enhanced security, and infrastructure protection.

There are three other important phases in emergency management. **Preparedness** includes readiness measures in anticipation of a disaster. Planning, training, and exercises are examples of preparedness initiatives. **Response** is the immediate reaction to an emergency situation like a terrorist attack. In homeland security, response refers most often to evidence collection and emergency medical care functions. **Recovery** refers to long-term activities to rebound after disasters or terrorist attacks. It includes emotional recovery as well as rebuilding with future hazards and threats in mind.

Since its inception, homeland security has focused most of its attention on prevention, protection and prosecution activities. These activities have been labeled as **crisis management**. Homeland security has downplayed, however, the need for preparedness, response and recovery operations. These are known as **consequence management**. While it is imperative to perform crisis and consequence management functions, there is growing realization that they should not be treated as isolated activities. Doing so only leads to coordination difficulties. In addition, while it is crucial to stress prevention, protection and prosecution measures, the assumption that this will be possible 100 percent of the time must be avoided. For these reasons, emergency management must become an increasingly vital component of homeland security.

Emergency management has a long history of dealing with a plethora of natural, technological, and man-made disasters. It has generated excellent recommendations for dealing with conflict and collective stress situations (Drabek 1986). What is more, scholars such as Bill Waugh (2001) and David McEntire (2001) indicate the close relation between terrorism and emergency management. Others also see unique ties among emergency management and homeland security (Bullock et. al. 2005).

In spite of this close relation, homeland security has not drawn sufficiently from the research and practice of emergency management. This has created many challenges for homeland security. Some of today's problems are reminiscent of those during the civil defense era (Alexander 2002). **Civil defense** is the name given to the government's initiative to prepare communities and citizens to react effectively to nuclear war against the Soviet Union. The primary focus of the Cold War was on responding to

EMERGENCY MANAGEMENT

Definition, Vision, Mission, Principles

Definition

Emergency management is the managerial function charged with creating the framework within which communities reduce vulnerability to hazards and cope with disasters.

Vision

Emergency management seeks to promote safer, less vulnerable communities with the capacity to cope with hazards and disasters.

Mission

Emergency management protects communities by coordinating and integrating all activities necessary to build, sustain, and improve the capability to mitigate against, prepare for, respond to, and recover from threatened or actual natural disasters, acts of terrorism, or other man-made disasters.

Principles

Emergency management must be:

Comprehensive — emergency managers consider and take into account all hazards, all phases, all stakeholders and all impacts relevant to disasters.

Progressive — emergency managers anticipate future disasters and take preventive and preparatory measures to build disaster-resistant and disaster-resilient communities.

Risk-driven — emergency managers use sound risk management principles (hazard identification, risk analysis, and impact analysis) in assigning priorities and resources.

Integrated — emergency managers ensure unity of effort among all levels of government and all elements of a community.

Collaborative — emergency managers create and sustain broad and sincere relationships among individuals and organizations to encourage trust, advocate a team atmosphere, build consensus, and facilitate communication.

Coordinated — emergency managers synchronize the activities of all relevant stakeholders to achieve a common purpose.

Flexible — emergency managers use creative and innovative approaches in solving disaster challenges.

Professional — emergency managers value a science and knowledge-based approach based on education, training, experience, ethical practice, public stewardship and continuous improvement.

nuclear weapons with a top-down, military, command and control approach. Natural and technological hazards as well as collaboration with others were not given serious consideration during this period. Homeland security officials have made similar mistakes in recent years. Those in charge of

Homeland Security Advisory System (HSAS): The nation's method for warning the population of potential and unfolding terrorist attacks.

policy initially focused almost exclusively on terrorism and favored a law enforcement or paramilitary approach. Leaders failed to recognize that the United States is prone to many different types of hazards (Mileti 1999). Homeland security also ignored to its own peril the research which suggests that coordination with others is of paramount importance if responses to disasters are to be successful (Auf der Heide 1987).

The most vivid example of homeland security's mistakes was the **Homeland Security Advisory System (HSAS)**. The HSAS is the nation's method for warning the population of potential and unfolding terrorist attacks. It illustrates an unwillingness to consult with the emergency management community or incorporate its lessons learned from prior disasters. For instance, research on disasters in emergency management provides solid advice for improved warning functions (McEntire 2007, 121). Warnings have to be clear, consistent and credible. They must also help people understand exactly what they are supposed to do when disasters and terrorist attacks occur.

In contrast to these recommendations, many argue that HSAS lacks clarity as well as specific and useful information for citizens (Knight 2005; Aguirre 2004). For example, what is implied when the threat level is raised

Figure 1-1

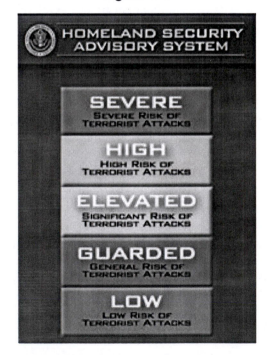

The Homeland Security Advisory System has not adequately warned citizens about what to do if a terrorist attack should occur.

from yellow to orange? Does it mean an attack has occurred? How should citizens react? Why does a change in color status help promote successful responses? Because the HSAS is not based on the emergency management literature, it has difficulty in successfully providing answers to these questions. The HSAS has therefore been the focus of many jokes on late night television. It reveals that emergency management is an important discipline for homeland security.

1.4.2 Important Terminology

Hazard:
The physical or other agent(s) that may trigger or initiate disaster events and processes.

While emergency management knowledge can help in many areas, one of the greatest potential contributions to homeland security is in reference to this profession's views about hazards, vulnerability, and risk. The term **hazard** was introduced by geographers and it almost always refers to physical or other agents that may trigger or initiate disaster events and processes (Alexander 2002, 29). While hazards such as an earthquake, industrial plant explosion, or terrorist attack are real and menacing, focusing on them excessively can create many problems for those involved in homeland security and emergency management. For instance, giving priority to hazards often leads to dramatic and detrimental shifts in policies as we have recently seen with the almost exclusive emphasis on terrorism (Waugh 2004). Placing ultimate priority on hazards likewise downplays human role and responsibility in all types of disasters (McEntire 2005). Since we cannot eliminate or control all extreme events, there is growing recognition that vulnerability is a stronger determinant of disaster than the hazards themselves (Alexander 2006, 2; Cutter 2005, 39). For these and other reasons, many recommend moving from an "agent centered approach" to one that gives greater attention to a broad conceptualization of vulnerability (Perry 2006, 9; Weichselgartner 2001).

Vulnerability:
A high degree of disaster proneness and/or limited disaster management capabilities.

As defined in the research literature, **vulnerability** implies a high degree of disaster proneness and/or limited disaster management capabilities. One school of thought suggests that vulnerability is the likelihood of a disaster occurring and that individuals or the community as a whole will experience negative impacts from hazards (e.g., injuries, death, property damage, financial losses, social disruption, etc.). There are several scholars that accept this viewpoint (Anderson 1995, 41; Bolin and Stanford 1998, 9; Boullè, Vrolijks and Palm 1997, 179; Maskrey 1989, 1; Mitchell 1999, 296; Salter 1997–98, 28; Wisner et. al. 1994, 11).

Another perspective on vulnerability relates to capacity or capability. This way of thought centers on the ability or inability of people and social systems to anticipate, prevent, prepare for, cope with, respond to, or recover from the impact of a hazard. It is also supported by many researchers (Schroeder 1987, 33; Warmington 1995, 1; Vasta 2004, 10–11; Wisner et. al. 2004, 11). Vulnerability is thus regarded as a multi-faceted concept that the literature almost always conveys it in terms of proneness and capabilities (Chambers 1989; Comfort et. al. 1999; Pelling and Uitto 2001; Watts and Bohle 1993).

Hazards and vulnerability are closely associated with the concept of risk. Some scholars assert that hazards and vulnerability are determinants of risk, or the likelihood of occurrence (Mileti 1999). Others assert that risk deals with exposure to disaster agents or possible losses (Alexander 2002). The truth of the matter is that risk is determined by both of these variables. **Risk** is therefore a measure of probability and consequences. The concept of risk permits an understanding of what can happen and how bad it could be. Although we struggle to know how much weight to give to probability versus consequences, the notion of risk is valuable to the emergency management community.

Interestingly, this same framework of risk can also be applied to terrorism and homeland security. For instance, limited intelligence, porous borders, and weak security are factors that must be corrected if the probability of attacks is to be minimized. Furthermore, limited prevention and preparedness abilities will likely increase the consequences of attacks during response and recovery operations. Probabilities and consequences thus seem to be extremely important concepts for both the emergency management and homeland security professions. Consequently, this book will approach terrorism from the themes of probability and consequences.

Risk:
A measure of probability and consequences.

IN THE REAL WORLD

Risk and 9/11

The attacks on 9/11 clearly illustrated the risk facing the United States. Terrorists had managed to enter the United States in virtually an unnoticed manner. They trained for their attacks in American flight schools and managed to smuggle box cutters onto planes. Once the hijackings were underway, a system was not fully in place to interdict the airplanes. After the aircraft were flown into the World Trade Center, fire fighters and police had a difficult time communicating with each other. Many died because information could not be shared among agencies. After the buildings collapsed, it took some time before different pieces of intelligence could be utilized to determine who was responsible for the attacks and how they were funded. September 11 showed that a variety of efforts are needed to minimize the probability of attack and successfully deal with their consequences.

SELF-CHECK

1. International relations and criminal justice are related to homeland security. True or False?

2. There is not a close relationship between homeland security and emergency management. True or False?

3. Vulnerability implies:
    (a) An ability to deal with terrorism effectively
    (b) A high degree of proneness and limited capabilities
    (c) A low degree of proneness and enhanced capabilities
    (d) That terrorism will not occur
    (e) That we can respond successfully

4. What is meant by the terms "probability" and "consequences"?

SUMMARY

In this chapter, you have examined the enormous impact of the terrorist attacks on 9/11 on world history. You have identified evidence that suggests that further attacks will take place against us in the future. The chapter defined homeland security—a concerted national effort to prevent terrorist attacks within the United States, reduce America's vulnerability to terrorism, and recover from and minimize the damage of attacks that do occur. It also discussed the mission of homeland security and the need for a holistic framework. By supplementing homeland security with an emergency management perspective, you will be better able to deal with the probability and impacts of terrorist attacks.

ASSESS YOUR UNDERSTANDING

UNDERSTAND: WHAT HAVE YOU LEARNED?

 Go to **www.wiley.com/college/mcentire** to assess your knowledge of homeland security.

SUMMARY QUESTIONS

1. Why were the terrorist attacks on 9/11 so significant? Explain how this event has had an impact on American way of life.

2. In Section 2 of this chapter, there is list of reasons why we may witness a greater number of more violent attacks in the future. Please pick a terrorist attack found in today's current events and explain it in terms of one or more of the reasons listed in Section 2.

3. Discuss what the response to a terrorist attack could look like with successful collaboration between citizens, cities, states, nonprofits, businesses and the federal government. How would it be different if there was no collaboration?

4. State the importance of "probability" and "consequences" in homeland security. How do these ideas tie back into the concept of vulnerability?

5. Osama bin Laden and Al Qaeda were responsible for the 9/11 terrorist attacks. True or False?

6. The 9/11 hijackers flew the four hijacked planes into the world trade center buildings. True or False?

7. Terrorism is not an important topic in today's world. True or False?

8. Scholars, elected officials, military personnel, practitioners, and citizens have a common view of homeland security. True or False?

9. Corporations and non profits do not play an important role in homeland security. True or False?

10. Emergency management addresses the prevention of and reaction to different types of disasters. True or False?

11. The Homeland Security Advisory System does a good job of informing citizens on how to take action in a heightened threat stage. True or False?

12. There is an important relationship between emergency management and homeland security. True or False?

13. A community that has a low degree of disaster proneness and sufficient access to resources has a high degree of vulnerability. True or False?

14. What government is responsible for supporting the 9/11 attacks?

    (a) Hamas

    (b) The Taliban

(c) Hezbollah

(d) China

15. In 2004, the U.S. Senate Foreign Relations Committee predicted a _____ chance that there will be an attack using nuclear, biological, chemical, or radiological weapons in the coming decade.

   (a) 50%

   (b) 85%

   (c) 70%

   (d) 30%

16. Included in the National Strategy for Homeland Security's six missions are:

   (a) Border and Transportation Security.

   (b) Extensive Academic Research on Terrorism.

   (c) Defending against Catastrophic Threat.

   (d) a and c.

17. Since the formation of the Department of Homeland Security:

   (a) the United States has been successful at preventing further terrorist attacks through 2007.

   (b) there have been no allegations that money devoted to homeland security lacks controls to prevent fraud, waste, and abuse.

   (c) the Department of Homeland Security has positively impacted FEMA's ability to perform effectively.

   (d) all of the above.

18. Emergency management deals with

   (a) natural disasters only.

   (b) technological disasters only.

   (c) all types of disasters including terrorist attacks.

   (d) terrorist attacks only.

19. Homeland security involves which of the following disciplines?

   (a) International relations

   (b) Criminal justice

   (c) Public administration

   (d) All of the above

20. Which of the following increase vulnerability to terrorism?

   (a) Secure borders

   (b) Limited Intelligence

   (c) Preparedness

   (d) Both b and c

BE A HOMELAND SECURITY PROFESSIONAL

Explaining Homeland Security

You work for the Department of Homeland Security as a public information officer. During an interview, you noticed that the press is struggling to understand what homeland security is. How would you define it to them? What is the mission of homeland security? How could you describe it as a function or agency? What else could you say to help them understand this concept?

Educating City Council

As the lead member of the local homeland security office, you have been assigned to speak in front of the city council to defend your budget. You must clearly state why it is important to have lots of resources at your disposal. Make a case as to why terrorism is a significant threat and why the city council needs to take it seriously.

Tensions in Homeland Security

Homeland security illustrates some tensions between a law enforcement and emergency management perspective. Explain why both viewpoints are needed, and how their goals may complement one another.

KEY TERMS

9/11	The terrorist attacks involving hijacked planes against the United States that occurred on September 11, 2001.
Al Qaeda	An extreme Islamic fundamentalist terrorist organization.
Civil defense	The government's initiative to prepare communities and citizens to react effectively to a nuclear exchange during the Cold War.
Consequence management	An emergency management function that stresses planning, emergency medical response and public health, disaster relief, and restoration of communities.
Criminal justice	A discipline and profession interested in intelligence gathering, terrorist investigation, prosecution, border control, and other security measures.
Crisis management	A law enforcement function that concentrates on identifying, anticipating, preventing and prosecuting those involved in terrorism.
Department of Homeland Security (DHS)	A newly created organization which aims to prevent terrorist attacks or react to them effectively.
Emergency management	A discipline and profession that addresses how to prevent or react successfully to various types of disasters.
Federal Emergency Management Agency (FEMA)	The national organization in charge of disaster management.
Hazard(s)	The physical or other agent(s) that may trigger or initiate disaster events and processes.
Homeland security	A concerted national effort to prevent terrorist attacks within the United States, reduce America's vulnerability to terrorism, and recover from and minimize the damage of attacks that do occur.
Homeland Security Advisory System (HSAS)	The nation's method for warning the population of potential and unfolding terrorist attacks.
International relations	A discipline and profession that deals with the conflicts among nation states and non-state actors (e.g., why terrorism occurs and what governments are doing about it).
Mitigation	Activity that attempts to avoid disasters or minimize negative consequences.

Preparedness	Readiness measures in anticipation of a disaster.
Prevention	Counter-terrorism operations such as intelligence gathering and preventive strike activity.
Protection	Anti-terrorism operations such as improved building design, enhanced security, and infrastructure protection.
Public administration	A discipline and profession that directs attention to the formation policy and the best organization to deal with difficult societal problems.
Public health	A discipline and profession that concentrates on understanding diseases and how to treat them (e.g., identifying how to react from a medical standpoint to the use of nuclear, biological, chemical or radiological weapons).
Recovery	Long-term activities to rebound after disasters or terrorist attacks.
Response	The immediate reaction to an emergency situation, like a terrorist attack.
Risk	A measure of probability and consequences.
Taliban	The name of the government which provided a safe haven for Al Qaeda.
Terrorism	The use or threat of violence to support ideological purposes.
Vulnerability	A high degree of disaster proneness and/or limited disaster management capabilities.

REFERENCES

Aguiree, Benigno E. (2004). "Homeland Security Warnings: Lessons Learned and Unlearned." *International Journal of Mass Emergencies and Disasters* 22: 103–115.

Alexander, David. (2002). *Confronting Catastrophe*. Oxford University Press, New York.

Alexander, David. (2006). "Globalization of Disaster: Trends, Problems and Dilemmas." *Journal of International Affairs* 59 (2): 1–24.

Anderson, M. B. (1995). "Vulnerability to Disaster and Sustainable Development: A General Framework." Pp. 41–60 in Munasinghe, M., Clarke, C. (eds). *Disaster Prevention for Sustainable Development: Economic and Policy Issues*. International Decade for Natural Disaster Reduction/ World Bank.

Associated Press. (2005). "Study: 50% Chance of Major Attack in Next 5 Years." *USA Today*. June, 23.

Auf der Heide, Erik. (1989). *Disaster Response: Principles of Preparation and Coordination*. Mosby: St. Louis, MO.

Bolin, R. and Stanford, L. (1998). *The Northridge Earthquake: Vulnerability and Disaster*. Routledge: New York.

Boulle, P., Vrolijks, L., and Palm, E. (1997). "Vulnerability Reduction for Sustainable Urban Development." *Journal of Contingencies and Crisis Management* 5: 179.

Bullock, Jane A., George D. Haddow, Damon Coppola, Erdem Ergin, Lissa Westerman, Sarp Yeletaysi. (2005). *Introduction to Homeland Security*. Butterworth-Heinemann: New York.

Chambers, R. (1989). "Editorial Introduction: Vulnerability, Coping, and Policy." *IDS Bulletin* 2 (2): 1–7.

Comfort, L., Wisner, B., Cutter, S., Pulwarty, R., Hewitt, K., Oliver-Smith, A., Wiener, J., Fordham, M., Peacock, W., and Krimgold, F. (1999). "Reframing Disaster Policy: The Global Evolution of Vulnerability Communities." *Environmental Hazards* 1: 39–44.

Cutter, Susan. (2005). "Are We Asking the Right Question?" Pp. 39–48 in Perry, Ronald W. and E. L. Quarantelli. *What is a Disaster? New Answers to Old Questions*. Xlibris, Philadelphia.

Drabek, Thomas E. (1986). *Human System Responses to Disaster: An Inventory of Sociological Findings*. Springer-Verlag: New York.

Kamien, David. (Ed.). (2006). *The McGraw-Hill Homeland Security Handbook*. McGraw Hill, New York.

Knight, Andrew J. (2005). "Alert Status Red: Awareness, Knowledge and Reaction to the Threat Advisory System," *Journal of Homeland Security and Emergency Management*: 2 (1) Article 9. Available at: www.bepress.com/jhsem/vol2/iss1/9.

Maskrey, A. (1989). *Disaster Mitigation: A Community Based Approach. Development Guidelines*, No. 3. Oxfam: Oxford, England.

McEntire, D. A. (2004). "Tenets of Vulnerability: An Assessment of a Fundamental Concept." *Journal of Emergency Management* 2 (2): 23–29.

McEntire, David A. (2000). *Sustainability or Invulnerable Development? Justification for a Modified Disaster Reduction Concept and Policy Guide.* University of Denver, Denver.

McEntire, David A. (2005). "Revisiting the Definition of 'Hazard' and the Importance of Reducing Vulnerability." *Journal of Emergency Management* 3 (4): 9–11.

McEntire, David A. (2007). *Disaster Response and Recovery: Strategies and Tactics for Resilience.* Wiley: New York.

Mileti, Dennis S. (1999). *Disasters by Design: A Reassessment of Natural Hazards in the United States.* Joseph Henry Press, Washington, D.C.

Mitchell, James K. (1999). *Crucibles of Hazard: Megacities and Disasters in Transition.* James K. Mitchell, ed., United Nations University Press, Tokyo.

Office of Homeland Security. (2002). *National Strategy for Homeland Security.* Washington, D.C.

Pelling, M., Uitto, J. I. (2001). "Small Island Developing States: Natural Disaster Vulnerability and Global Change." *Environmental Hazards* 3: 49–62.

Perry, Ronald W. (2006). "What is a Disaster?" Pp. 1–15 in Rodriguez, Havidán, E. L. Quarantelli, and Russell R. Dynes. *Handbook of Disaster Research.* Springer, New York.

Salter, J. (1997/98) "Risk Management in the Emergency Management Context." *Australian Journal of Emergency Management* 12 (4).

Schroeder, R. A. (1987). *Gender Vulnerability to Drought: A Case Study of the Hausa Social Environment.* University of Wisconsin: Madison.

Vasta, K. S. (2004). "Risk, Vulnerability, and Asset-based Approach to Disaster Risk Management." *International Journal of Sociology and Social Policy* 24 (10/11).

Waugh, William L. (2004). "The 'All-hazards' Approach Must Be Continued." *Journal of Emergency Management* 2 (1): 11–12.

Warmington, V. (1995). *Disaster Reduction: A Review of Disaster Prevention, Mitigation and Preparedness.* Reconstruction and Rehabilitation Fund of the Canadian Council for International Cooperation: Otttowa.

Watts, M. J. and Bohle, H. G. (1993). "The Space of Vulnerability: The Causal Structure of Hunger and Famine." *Progress in Human Geography* 17: 43–67.

Waugh, William L. (2001). "Managing Terrorism as an Environmental Hazard." Pp. 659–676 in Farazmand, Ali (ed.) *Handbook of Crisis and Emergency Management.* Marcel Dekker: New York.

Weichselgartner, J. (2001). "Disaster Mitigation: The Concept of Vulnerability Revisited." *Disaster Prevention and Management* 10 (2): 85–94.

Wisner, B., Blaikie, P., Cannon, T., and Davis, I. (2004). *At Risk: Natural Hazards, People's Vulnerability and Disasters.* Routledge: New York.

2

IDENTIFYING TERRORISM
Ideologically Motivated Acts of Violence

Do You Already Know?

- How to define terrorism
- The common characteristics of terrorism
- Types of terrorism
- The relation of terrorism to other disasters

 For additional questions to assess your current knowledge on terrorism, go to **www.wiley.com/college/mcentire**

What You Will Find Out	What You Will Be Able To Do
2.1 The different definitions of terrorism that various government agencies use	• Define terrorism
2.2 The characteristics of terrorism	• Recognize the characteristics of terrorism
2.3 The types of terrorism	• Comprehend the different types of terrorism
2.4 The relationship between terrorism and other disasters	• Compare and contrast conflict disasters with consensus disasters

INTRODUCTION

If you work in homeland security, the first and most important step for you to reduce the probabilities and consequences of terrorism is to understand what this phenomenon is. This chapter provides several definitions of terrorism, and compares the similarities and differences among the divergent views. You will then assess the common characteristics of terrorism, thereby helping you determine if certain activity can be considered as such phenomena. The types of terrorism are then covered in order to help you discover its numerous manifestations. Finally, the chapter explores the relationship between terrorism and other types of disasters.

2.1 DEFINING TERRORISM

There are literally hundreds of definitions of terrorism but little agreement on a single concept capturing the essence of what the term actually means. Much of the difficulty in defining terrorism is a result of the fact that the term is emotionally charged and laden with value judgments. It is a common adage that "one person's terrorist in another person's freedom fighter" (Martin 2003, 22). A case in point is the U.S. patriots seeking independence from Britain in the late 1700s. Did the activities of these citizens during the revolutionary war constitute terrorism? Those in England and in the new world certainly had different perspectives on this question. The British viewed the Boston Tea Party and the unconventional combat tactics as terrorist activities, whereas the Americans regarded them as a form of protest or method to level the playing field against the better trained and equipped red coats.

The problem of defining terrorism continues today among practitioners and scholars alike. For instance, the United States government has developed several definitions of terrorism:

Department of State (DOS):
The government agency in charge of diplomatic relationships among nations.

- **The Department of State (DOS)** is the government agency in charge of diplomatic relationships among nations. It asserts terrorism is "premeditated, politically motivated violence perpetrated against noncombatant targets by sub-national groups or clandestine agents, usually intended to influence an audience."

Department of Defense (DOD):
The government agency responsible for the military.

- The **Department of Defense (DOD)** is the government agency responsible for the military. It declares that terrorism is "The calculated use of violence or the threat of violence to inculcate fear, intended to coerce or to intimidate governments or societies in the pursuit of goals that are generally political, religious or ideological."

Federal Bureau of Investigation (FBI):
The government agency that concentrates on the enforcement of United States law.

- The **Federal Bureau of Investigation (FBI)** is a government agency that concentrates on the enforcement of United States law. It states that terrorism is "The unlawful use of force against persons or property to intimidate or coerce a government, the civilian population, or any segment thereof, in the furtherance of political or social objectives."

- The Department of Homeland Security, in one of its planning documents, describes terrorism as "Any activity that (1) involves an act that (a) is dangerous to human life or potentially destructive of critical infrastructure or key resources; and (b) is a violation of the criminal laws of the United States or of any State or other subdivision of the United States; and (2) appears to be intended (a) to intimidate or coerce a civilian population; (b) to influence the policy of a government by intimidation or coercion; or (c) to affect the conduct of a government by mass destruction, assassination, or kidnapping" (DHS 2004, 73).

Each of these definitions reflects the unique mission and perspective of the sponsoring agency. The DOS takes an international view and concentrates attention on non-state actors around the world. The DOD recognizes that terrorism impacts national security and has the objective of influencing foreign policy. The FBI reveals that terrorism is illegal since their violent behavior is not permitted under the law. Finally, the DHS focuses heavily on the destruction of critical infrastructure. While each definition provides an important view of terrorism, it is important to recognize the benefit of a holistic perspective. Any single definition may limit our understanding of the phenomena and therefore hinder efforts to deal with the threat of terrorism.

Scholars have also described terrorism in divergent ways. Brian Jenkins (1984) calls "terrorism the use or threatened use of force designed to bring about a political change" (in White 2002, 8). Walter Laqueur (1987, 72) says "terrorism constitutes the illegitimate use of force to achieve a political objective by targeting innocent people" (in White 2002, 8). And Cindy Combs believes that terrorism "is the synthesis of war and theater, a dramatization of the most proscribed kind of violence—that which is perpetrated on innocent victims—played out before an audience in the hope of creating a mood of fear, for political purposes" (2000, 8).

The differences among these definitions are likewise noteworthy. Jenkins accepts the threat of force as terrorism, whereas Laqueur and Combs do not. The definitions by Laqueur and Combs focus on non-combatants as victims. Their inclusion of innocent people reiterates that governments are not the only targets selected by terrorists. Furthermore, Combs implies that the media is utilized to broadcast messages to further the aims and intentions of terrorism. Fear is mentioned in some of the definitions and not in others. Only one stresses the influence of ideology on terrorism (an issue that will be taken up in Chapter 3), even though this seems to have a significant role in this type of violent activity.

Although there are clearly distinct ways of looking at terrorism, the definitions provided above share remarkable similarities. All acknowledge the use or threat of force and the goal of obtaining specific purposes or objectives. At the same time, none recognize the disruption of society that occurs because of terrorism. This is ironic in that terrorism may adversely impact government policies (e.g., with the creation of new laws), business activities (e.g., due to computer viruses), and citizen behavior (e.g., as a result of the reluctance to travel). Disruption is therefore another major goal of terrorists.

SELF-CHECK

1. There are many different definitions of terrorism. True or False?
2. Definitions do not reflect the values of missions of different people and organizations. True or False?
3. In Combs definition of terrorism, the term "theater" implies:
    (a) The location of the terrorist attack
    (b) The widespread publicity of an attack
    (c) The importance of national security
    (d) The disruption caused by terrorism
4. Compare and contrast the different definitions of terrorism.

2.2 COMMON CHARACTERISTICS OF TERRORISM

Taking all of the above definitions and considerations into account, we may conclude that there are a number of crucial components of terrorism. Terrorism is often:

- **An act of disruption, violence or the threat of violence.** It is not like a protest, a sit in, or a strike with a picket line. Instead, it involves illegitimate activities that are not sanctioned by law. Terrorism creates many social, political, and economic problems for targeted populations, societies, and the international community. Some of the means of terrorism may include the use of guns or bombs.

- **Performed by an individual, group, or state that espouses an ideology.** Terrorism results from unique ways of looking at the world that rationalize their behavior. For instance, terrorism often neglects or subverts negotiation, diplomacy, and democratic processes.

- **Conducted against governments or citizens as targets and an audience.** Certain people may be injured, killed, or otherwise affected by terrorism.

But terrorism also intends to spread adverse impact far beyond those who were immediately targeted in attacks. Victims may be produced directly or indirectly by terrorism.

- **Accompanied with fear and coercion.** Terrorism relies on shock, outrage, horror, discouragement, and intimidation to impel some sort of activity on the part of its victims. This includes both those targeted and the audience observing the attacks.

- **Directed toward the attainment of goals and objectives.** Terrorism may have the aim of promoting political independence, social justice, human rights, environmental protection, religious freedoms or dominance, and other objectives (e.g., free reign of drug cartels or the halting of abortions).

When phenomena have most or all of these traits, you may have increasing confidence that the activity is terrorism. Conversely, if these features are not present, the incident in question cannot be considered in this light.

SELF-CHECK

1. Terrorists have a goal that is associated with their violent activity. True or False?
2. Only groups are involved in terrorism. True or False?
3. Which of the following is not a common characteristic of terrorism?

    (a) An act of disruption or violence
    (b) Performed by someone who espouses an ideology
    (c) Accompanied with fear
    (d) A strike at the company office

4. Restate why terrorists target innocent citizens.

2.3   TYPES OF TERRORISM

In spite of common qualities, terrorism may take on unique forms at any given time. Feliks Gross, an expert on terrorism in Russia and Eastern Europe, affirms that terrorism manifests itself in five different ways (1990, 8). These include mass terror, dynastic assassination, random terror, focused terror, and tactical terror.

Mass terror:
Terrorism by the government in power against its own citizens.

- **Mass terror** is terrorism by the government in power against its own citizens. This is a situation in which the ruling regime suppresses the opposition to maintain control. The efforts of Saddam Hussein and his

Republican Guard fall into this category. The Iraqi leaders used poison gas on the Kurds in the Northern part of the country, and killed or imprisoned anyone who dared to speak out against the dictatorship and military in this nation.

Dynastic assassination:
The murder of the head official in government.

- **Dynastic assassination** is the murder of the head official in government. Some may assert that the shooting of President Lincoln falls into this category. After shooting this leader, Booth shouted "Sic semper tyrannis," which translated means "Thus always to tyrants."

Random terror:
An attack on large numbers of people wherever they gather.

- **Random terror** is an attack on large numbers of people wherever they gather. The coordinated attacks on Spanish trains on March 11, 2004, are an example of random terror. These blasts killed nearly 200 people and injured over 2,000 others.

Focused terror:
Terrorism directed toward a specific group of people deemed as the enemy.

- **Focused terror** is terrorism directed toward a specific group of people deemed as the enemy. The Polish Underground, an organization that opposed German occupation during World War II, practiced focused terror. They detonated explosives at a café where Nazi officers dinned (Combs 2000, 9).

Tactical terror:
The use of attacks against the government for revolutionary or other purposes.

- **Tactical terror** is the use of attacks against the government for revolutionary or other purposes. The 1995 bombing of the Murrah Federal Building in Oklahoma City by Timothy McVeigh is an example of tactical terror.

Besides the five types of terrorism described by Gross, it may be necessary to add other important categories. You are probably aware of the frequent terrorist attacks on American troops in Iraq. These events frequently involve

Figure 2-1

Attacks on streets or open markets are examples of random terror.

Guerilla:
Spanish term for little war which is an armed protest of occupying forces.

Asymmetrical warfare:
Terrorist attacks on the part of the militarily weak against those who are powerful.

Domestic terrorism:
Terrorism that occurs within a single country.

International terrorism:
Terrorism that spans two or more nations.

a sudden and surprise strike with small arms or bombs and a quick retreat. How would you describe this type of terrorism? Many suggest that this is guerilla warfare. **Guerilla** is a Spanish term for little war which is an armed protest of occupying forces (Simonsen and Spindlove 2000, 35). Guerilla warfare is similar to **asymmetrical warfare**, which implies terrorist attacks on the part of the militarily weak against those who are powerful.

Terrorism has also been categorized in other ways. **Domestic terrorism** is terrorism that occurs within a single country. The release of nerve gas on March 19, 1995, in a subway by the Japanese religious group Aum Shinrikyo is an example of this type of terrorism. **International terrorism**, on the other hand, is terrorism that spans two or more nations. This is terrorism that is initiated by individuals, groups, or the government within one country and targets the people or the leaders of another. The bombing of the USS Cole in Yemen on October 12, 2000, can be considered international terrorism.

Although classifying terrorism as being domestic or international in origin or scope is helpful, it is not always so clear cut. Sometimes it is difficult to determine where an attack was instigated as well as the extent of the incident. The bombings of two Russian planes on August 24, 2004, by a Chechen field commander and the October 12, 2002, Bali bombings in Indonesia by Jammah Islamiyah are examples of this dilemma. Attacks took place in these countries but included terrorists and victims from many other nations around the world.

There are similar overlaps with all of the above categories of terrorism. For instance, the bombing by McVeigh was tactical terror, but it could also be described as asymmetrical warfare and domestic terrorism. In contrast, the warfare in Iraq is focused and international in scope, and not just a guerilla variant. Therefore, caution should be used when classifying terrorism into distinct alternatives.

IN THE REAL WORLD

Classifying the Attacks on 9/11

Suppose you were working as a CIA analyst when the World Trade Center was bombed on February 26, 1993. Ramzi Yousef, along with nine other Arab Islamic terrorists, devised a plan to park a van full of urea nitrate-fuel in the underground garage of the North Tower. Their goal was to destroy the foundation of Tower One so that this building would collapse onto Tower Two. Although their intentions ultimately failed, the bomb did kill six people and injured more than 1,000. If you had to write an after-action report on this attack, how would you classify it? Is there more than one way to look at it?

SELF-CHECK

1. All terrorist attacks manifest themselves in the same fashion. True or False?

2. Tactical terror is the shooting of the president. True or False?

3. Which type of terrorism is implemented by the government to control citizens?

   (a) Focused terror
   (b) Mass terror
   (c) International terrorism
   (d) Random terror

4. Differentiate among the five types of terrorism proposed by Gross.

2.4 RELATION OF TERRORISM TO OTHER DISASTERS

Conflict disaster:
A socially disruptive and divisive event that involves a riot or some type of warfare.

Consensus disaster:
A socially disruptive event such as an earthquake that brings the community together.

Some scholars, such as Quarantelli (1993), assert that terrorism is a "conflict disaster" and that it is qualitatively different from "consensus disasters." A **conflict disaster** is an event that involves a riot, violence, or some type of warfare. It often illustrates division within or across societies. A **consensus disaster**, on the other hand, is an event like an earthquake or tornado that brings the community together. Quarantelli asserts that a major difference between these two types of events is that conflict disasters include a person or group that is intentionally trying to inflict harm or distress on others. In contrast, a consensus disaster is characterized by the community working together to solve mutual challenges. According to Quarantelli, the first type of disaster divides society while the other unites it.

Quarantelli's study raises an interesting question about how to classify terrorism. Is terrorism a conflict disaster or a consensus disaster? Gary Webb (2002) provides evidence that social behavior in terrorism is very similar to consensus disasters. As an example, he declares that there is very little panic in most consensus disasters and that people also acted rationally in spite of major challenges on 9/11. He relays the fact that police and fire personnel are reliable in virtually all disasters and that no one abandoned their post after the World Trade Center was attacked. Webb also states that response is characterized by improvisation in disasters, and this was certainly the case as organizations adapted to difficult circumstances in New York City. While his research recognizes the need for additional studies on terrorism, Webb asserts that their defining features of 9/11 are remarkably similar to consensus disasters.

Figure 2-2

September 11 has features of both conflict and consensus disasters. It was initiated by international terrorists, but unified American sentiment.

Research by Lori Peek and Jeannette Sutton (2003) likewise seems to illustrate that terrorism does not always fall easily into the conflict category. They discuss six hypotheses to make their argument:

- **Proposition 1:** Both social and antisocial behavior occurred after 9/11. In most disasters, people forget prior divisions in society and they work jointly to reach important goals. This behavior was evident on 9/11 since people helped one another evacuate the World Trade Center towers and donated blood to help potential victims. However, there was also some intolerance and hostility toward Muslims and others of Arab descent after the attacks in 2001.

- **Proposition 2:** People experienced negative consequences owing to 9/11. In consensus disasters, most people do not suffer any lengthy psychological disturbances or health repercussions. Preliminary evidence suggests that this was not the case with the attacks on New York City. Many people experienced post-traumatic stress and depression, and emergency personnel developed respiratory problems due to the dust debris they encountered from the collapsed buildings.

- **Proposition 3:** The response to 9/11 was made more difficult due to continuing security concerns. During consensus disasters, organizations often struggle to accomplish the monumental tasks that they are required to meet. After the attacks on the World Trade Center, air, water, and road transportation systems were shut down. In addition, control over the disaster area was strictly guarded in case further attacks were to occur. These measures complicated efforts to respond to the disaster.

- **Proposition 4:** Political change was dramatic after 9/11. Most consensus disasters do not often result in massive transformations in society. This was not the case after the 2001 terrorist attacks. New legislation was quickly devised and passed, and the government underwent a massive transformation to deal with homeland security issues. These changes were impressive in terms of speed and scope.

- **Proposition 5:** Preparing for terrorism involves measures beyond consensus type disasters. Natural and technological disasters require planning, training, and exercises. Terrorist attacks such as 9/11 introduce a new complication in that it is very difficult to anticipate and predict where the next attack will occur. In this sense, it could be more challenging to prepare for terrorism than consensus type disasters.

- **Proposition 6:** Long-term change will be a defining feature of the 9/11 attacks. Most disasters do not impact or influence societies in any significant way. The events in New York seem to have resulted in substantial financial loss and unemployment, created disagreement about rebuilding plans, and led to the implementation of new security measures around the nation.

Based on these six propositions, Peek and Sutton therefore believe that terrorism is a complex phenomenon that exhibits features of both conflict and consensus type disasters.

McEntire and his colleagues accept the findings from Webb as well as Peek and Sutton. They state that "managing the threat of terrorism is both similar to and different from the management of other types of disasters" (McEntire et. al. 2002, 1). On the one hand, those involved in planning for or reacting to terrorism must be able to perform functions that are routine to almost any disaster. This would include warning the population, evacuating the affected area, sheltering impacted residents, and providing emergency medical care as needed.

On other hand, terrorism poses new challenges that have not been experienced by emergency management personnel in the past. For instance:

- Intelligence gathering is a new and important task for terrorism prevention.
- Planning in homeland security must give a great amount of emphasis to the military, the FBI, and public health.

- Response operations will incorporate law functions (e.g., investigation).
- Recovery may be lengthy or impossible if an area has been contaminated by deadly radiation or harmful chemicals.

The nature of terrorism complicates traditional emergency management operations and makes working harmoniously in homeland security imperative. Even though you might generally expect people to behave as they do in consensus disasters, we probably do not have sufficient evidence to predict with full certainty how they will react to terrorist events that are unfamiliar (e.g., a biological attack).

SELF-CHECK

1. Terrorism is always exactly like any other type of disaster. True or False?

2. A conflict disaster is often characterized by a riot or some type of violent behavior. True or False?

3. Which of the following is true about the 9/11 terrorist attacks:
   (a) There was no indication of antisocial behavior afterwards.
   (b) It resulted in new laws and significant changes in government.
   (c) Security measures did not impact response operations.
   (d) Muslims were not the target of hatred or discrimination.

4. Quarantelli asserts that terrorism is a conflict disaster. Support or critique this proposition.

SUMMARY

In this chapter you learned that one of the first steps to addressing the probability and consequences of terrorism is to comprehend what this phenomenon is. After reviewing numerous definitions about this complicated concept, you compared how the various perspectives are both alike and dissimilar. The prevalent features of terrorism were revealed, which will enable you to appraise if terrorism has occurred or is about to take place. Although there are recurring features of terrorism, this should not imply that every situation is similar. There are many different types of terrorism. In this chapter, you also examined the connections among terrorism and other types of disasters. Based on the evidence provided, it appears that terrorism has features of both conflict and consensus type disasters.

ASSESS YOUR UNDERSTANDING

UNDERSTAND: WHAT HAVE YOU LEARNED

 Go to **www.wiley.com/college/mcentire** to assess your knowledge of terrorism.

SUMMARY QUESTIONS

1. What is meant by the adage "one person's terrorist is another person's freedom fighter?" How does this complicate the process of defining terrorism?

2. It is suggested that terrorism is directed towards both victims and an audience. How do these means, in the view of terrorists, impact their ability to reach their goals and objectives?

3. There are many different classifications for terrorist activity. Why is it so difficult to put a terrorist attack into one specific category?

4. Briefly discuss terrorism in terms of conflict disasters and consensus disasters. What are some examples of how terrorist attacks take on characteristics of both kinds of disasters? Are all terrorist acts the same?

5. Definitions of terrorism are all objective and free of value judgments. True or False?

6. Terrorists only want to affect those directly impacted by the attack. True or False?

7. Feliks Gross says that terrorism manifests itself in five different ways: mass terror, tactical terror, focused terror, dynastic assassination, and random terror. True or False?

8. Guerilla warfare is the opposite of asymmetrical warfare. True or False?

9. It can be difficult to determine whether a terrorist attack is categorized as domestic or international. True or False?

10. Consensus disasters involve some kind of conflict or warfare. True or False?

11. According to Peek and Sutton's Proposition 4, it is not common for extreme political and societal changes to occur after a disaster. True or False?

12. All of the following agencies have established definitions for terrorism except:

(a) the Department of Defense.

(b) the Department of Homeland Security.

(c) the Department of Housing and Urban Development.

(d) the Department of State.

13. The definition of terrorism provided by the Department of Homeland Security emphasizes:

(a) the destruction of important infrastructure.

(b) the illegal nature of terrorism.

(c) terrorisms' effects on foreign policy.

(d) the role of non-state actors in the terrorist event.

14. Which of the following best describes "random terror?"

(a) Terrorism by a government against its citizens

(b) Terrorism against a group of people who are considered the enemy

(c) Terrorism used for revolutionary purposes

(d) A terrorist attack on a large group of people in a gathering place

15. Each of the following is a crucial component of the definition of terrorism except:

(a) an act of disruption, violence or the threat of violence.

(b) always carried out on a large scale, using many people.

(c) accompanied with fear and coercion.

(d) directed toward the attainment of goals and objectives.

16. Which of the following definitions best describes guerilla warfare?

(a) Large military attack

(b) Small, planned military attacks on those who are less powerful

(c) Armed protest of occupying forces

(d) Anticipated attacks from terrorists

17. Which of the following is not an aspect of a consensus disaster?

(a) It brings the community together.

(b) It often takes the form of a natural disaster.

(c) It is socially disruptive.

(d) It involves a person or group intentionally causing harm to others.

BE A HOMELAND SECURITY PROFESSIONAL

Defining Terrorism in a Public Document

You have been assigned to write the strategic plan for the police department. Your boss wants you to discuss terrorism and homeland security. How would you define terrorism? Is it similar to or different than other types of illegal behavior? How so?

Writing a Report on Terrorism

As an analyst for the FBI, you have been asked to write a report denoting the common characteristics of terrorism and the different manifestations it has over time. The report will be given to members of congress who oversee national security issues. What would you include in your statement?

Assessing Terrorism and Disasters

While attending a conference on homeland security, you observe disagreement among scholars and practitioners regarding terrorism. Some suggest that it is similar to natural and technological disasters while others state that it has the defining features of conflict events. Could you make a comment that would satisfy both sides of the argument? What would you say?

KEY TERMS

Asymmetrical warfare	Terrorist attacks on the part of the militarily weak against those who are powerful.
Conflict disaster	A socially disruptive and divisive event that involves a riot or some type of warfare.
Consensus disaster	A socially disruptive event such as an earthquake that brings the community together.
Department of Defense (DOD)	The government agency responsible for the military.
Department of State (DOS)	The government agency in charge of diplomatic relationships among nations.
Domestic terrorism	Terrorism that occurs within a single country.
Dynastic assassination	The murder of the head official in government.
Federal Bureau of Investigation (FBI)	The government agency that concentrates on the enforcement of United States law.
Focused terror	Terrorism directed toward a specific group of people deemed as the enemy.
Guerilla	Spanish term for little war which is an armed protest of occupying forces.
International terrorism	Terrorism that spans two or more nations.
Mass terror	Terrorism by the government in power against its own citizens.
Random terror	An attack on large numbers of people wherever they gather.
Tactical terror	The use of attacks against the government for revolutionary or other purposes.

REFERENCES

Combs, Cindy C. (2000). *Terrorism in the Twenty-First Century*. Prentice Hall: New Jersey.

Department of Homeland Security. (2004). *National Response Plan*. DHS: Washington, D.C.

Gross, Feliks. (1990). *Political Violence and Terror in Nineteenth and Twentieth Century Russia and Eastern Europe*. Cambridge University Press: New York.

Kamien, David. (Ed.). (2006). *The McGraw-Hill Homeland Security Handbook*. McGraw Hill, New York.

Maniscalco, Paul M. and Hank T. Christen. (2002). *Understanding Terrorism and Managing the Consequences*. Prentice Hall: New Jersey.

Martin, Gus. (2003). *Understanding Terrorism: Challenges, Perspectives and Issues*. Sage Publications: Thousand Oaks, CA.

McEntire, David A. (2005). "Revisiting the Definition of 'Hazard' and the Importance of Reducing Vulnerability." *Journal of Emergency Management* 3 (4): 9–11.

McEntire, David A. (2007). *Disaster Response and Recovery: Strategies and Tactics for Resilience*. Wiley: New York.

McEntire, David A., Robie J. Robinson and Richard T. Weber. (2002). *Managing the Threat of Terrorism*. IQ Report. 33 (12). ICMA: Washington, D.C.

Office of Homeland Security. (2002). *National Strategy for Homeland Security*. Washington, D.C.

Peek, Lori A. and Jeannette N. Sutton. (2003). "An Exploratory Comparison of Disasters, Riots and Terrorist Attacks." *Disasters* 27 (4): 319–335.

Quarantelli, E. L. (1993). "Community Crises: An Exploratory Comparison of the Characteristics and Consequences of Disasters and Riots." *Journal of Contingencies and Crisis Management* 1 (2): 67–78.

Simonsen, Clifford E. and Jeremy R. Spindlove. (2000). *Terrorism Today: The Past, The Players, The Future*. Prentice Hall: New Jersey.

Waugh, William L. (2001). "Managing Terrorism as an Environmental Hazard." Pp. 659–676 in Farazmand, Ali (ed.) *Handbook of Crisis and Emergency Management*. Marcel Dekker: New York.

Webb, Gary R. (2002). "Sociology, Disasters, and Terrorism: Understanding Threats of the New Millennium." *Sociological Focus* 35 (1): 87–95.

White, Jonathan R. (2002). *Terrorism: An Introduction*. Wadsworth: Belmont, CA.

3

RECOGNIZING THE CAUSES OF TERRORISM

Differing Perspectives and the Role of Ideology

Do You Already Know?

- Why historical grievances, foreign policy, and poverty relate to terrorism
- How various political variables are associated with terrorism
- If religion and culture are causes of terrorism
- The role of ideology in terrorism

 For additional questions to assess your current knowledge on homeland security, go to **www.wiley.com/college/mcentire**

What You Will Find Out	What You Will Be Able To Do
3.1 Frequently cited causes of terrorism	• Evaluate the most frequently mentioned causes of terrorism
3.2 Political causes of terrorism	• Differentiate among the numerous political origins of terrorist attacks
3.3 Cultural and religious causes of terrorism	• Predict how terrorism may be influenced by culture and religion
3.4 The ideology of terrorism	• Appraise the impact of ideology on the phenomena of terrorism

INTRODUCTION

If you are to reduce the likelihood and impact of terrorism it is necessary to understand its causes so you may take steps to alleviate them. Ian Lesser asserts that terrorism "has systemic origins [or root causes] that can be ameliorated" (1999, 127). You should therefore recognize that historical conflicts, foreign policy, and poverty may aggravate terrorism. Internal political factors, culture, and religion may also influence those who implement terrorist attacks. While there are many possible causes of terrorism, you must pay special attention to the role of ideology. People's beliefs always have significant bearing on terrorism.

3.1 FREQUENTLY MENTIONED CAUSES

You've probably wondered what drives people to engage in terrorist attacks. It is commonly said that there are perhaps as many causes of terrorism as there are terrorists. Some of the frequent explanations deal with historical grievances, foreign policy decisions, and poverty. Each of these will be explained in turn.

3.1.1 Historical Grievances

One perspective of why terrorism occurs focuses on historical grievances. The assertion here is that small initial conflicts among different groups of people have been perpetuated and aggravated over time. There is ample evidence to support this claim, and the Middle East provides a strong case in point.

There have been continual conflicts between Arabs and the Jews in that part of the world. The historical narrative in the Bible is full of such struggles and it records numerous violent acts among different groups of people. Numbers 25: 1, 6–8 reveals how Phineas killed an Israelite man and a Midianite woman who were involved in illicit sexual relations. In Joshua 10: 1–14 we learn that Joshua attacked the city of Hazor, killed all of the inhabitants, burned the buildings, and took all of the remaining livestock.

Later on, there were wars in the Middle East as Christians tried to spread their beliefs during the crusades. The **Crusades** were wars endorsed by the Pope to recapture the Holy Land of Jerusalem from the control of **Muslims**—those following the prophet Muhammad and adhering to the religion of Islam. These wars, which had religious and another motivations, took place between 1100 A.D. and 1300 A.D. Because of the intolerance and cruelty exhibited in the crusades, Christians were opposed by those espousing Islam. Nevertheless, the Christians pushed back Muslims, who lost their empire and leadership in science, art, and trade.

Crusades:
Wars between 1100 and 1300 A.D. endorsed by the Pope to recapture the Holy Land of Jerusalem from the control of Muslims.

Muslims:
People who follow the prophet Muhammad and adhere to the religion of Islam.

Figure 3-1

Israeli police officers confront Israeli Arabs during a demonstration near the Prime Minister's office in Jerusalem Wednesday, December 8, 1999. Many Arabs oppose the establishment of Israel in the Middle East.

Holocaust:
The extermination of Jews by the Nazi regime during World War II.

In time, other events would add to the frustration of those residing in the Middle East. During World War II, the German leader, Adolf Hitler, denounced the Jews and desired to eradicate those professing this faith from Europe. This resulted in the **Holocaust**, the extermination of approximately six million Jews by the Nazi regime. Recognizing the plight of the Jews, the United Nations established the state of Israel in 1948. Israel was created with the purpose of serving as a safe haven for Jews. Unfortunately, this move of compassion intensified a long-standing dispute over territory that is sacred to both Jews and Muslims (see figure 3-1). Conflict and terrorism have been prevalent features of this part of the world for centuries. Both sides claim self-defense against the enemy aggressor. It seems as if terrorism has been omnipresent in the Middle East.

3.1.2 U.S. Foreign Policy

Another explanation for terrorism focuses on the foreign policy decisions of the United States. Under this view, American activities abroad are to blame for the terrorist attacks against the United States. Many Islamic terrorists have made this explicit in his justification for their aggression against the United States.

For instance, Osama bin Laden says he and his followers are justified for attacking Americans for at least six reasons. He asserts that the United States:

1. *Does not understand the history and desires of Middle Eastern countries.* The United States does not recognize the preference of Muslims for **theocracy**, a government run by clerics in the name of God.

Theocracy:
A government run by clerics in the name of God.

2. *Participates in colonialism in the area and is involved in exploitative policies.* The United States has military bases in Saudi Arabia, and he declares our reliance on oil has caused us to meddle in the affairs of sovereign nations.

3. *Supports puppet governments that are repressive regimes.* Saddam Hussein was an ally of the United States during the Iran-Iraq war, and he was a brutal leader.

4. *Founded the state of Israel and continues to fund their military capability.* This resulted in the loss of Arab land and is regarded to pose a threat to neighboring countries.

5. *Neglects human rights.* Palestinians assert they have fewer political rights than their Israeli counterparts.

6. *Sends American troops to the Middle East.* This desecrates sacred land and is associated with increased conflict and war.

Many of bin Laden's claims appear to have merit, but others might be considered debatable or even hypocritical. It is true that people in the United States do not fully comprehend the Middle East. America does rely heavily on oil from the Middle East. The United States did support Saddam Hussein as a means to counter the military threat posed by Iran after this country experienced revolution and sanctioned the taking of hostages from the U.S. embassy. At the same time, the intention of America and other nations to find a safe haven (i.e., the state of Israel) for persecuted Jews after World War II was understandable. The democracy in America provides more freedoms and rights to its citizens than do theocratic governments (i.e., women may not have the same political status of men in some Arab nations). Also, bin Laden was allied with the Taliban, a Sunni government which restricted the rights of women and oppressed the Hazara (Shia) minority.

In spite of the above observations, U.S. foreign policy may certainly influence the degree of terrorist activity around the world. Paul Pillar states that "most of the issues underlying . . . terrorism are to be found overseas" and that decisions on how to prevent or react to terrorism "must be formulated as an integral part of broader U.S. foreign policy" (2001, 10).

3.1.3 Poverty

Relative poverty:
State where some people are less wealthy than their fellow citizens or peers in other countries.

Absolute poverty:
State in which people lack so many resources that they cannot even meet basic necessities such as food, clothing, and shelter.

Another common causal explanation for terrorism is poverty. It is painfully evident poverty abounds around the world. But poverty is not equally found in all societies. This brings up the notion of **relative poverty**, meaning that some people are less wealthy than their fellow citizens or peers in other countries. In contrast, **absolute poverty** implies that people lack so many resources that they cannot even meet basic necessities such as food, clothing, and shelter. In this case, the deprivation and want are so significant that life is full of misery, illness, and even death. Unfortunately, there are millions around the world that fall into this later category. For instance, 1.1 billion people make only US$370 annually. It is possible that this number could grow in the future, particularly in Africa (Weatherby et. al. 2000, 14).

The causal link between poverty and terrorism has been noted by many people including scholars and the leaders of various countries. It is reported that "the head of the World Bank even proclaimed that terrorism will not end until poverty is eliminated" (Francis 2002, 1). The argument here is that people become frustrated with their impoverished conditions and that they express their aggravation through violent activity including terrorism.

There is evidence that seems to support this viewpoint. Alberto Abadie notes that "much of the modern-day transnational terrorism seems to generate from grievances against rich countries" (Lozada 2005, 1). However, it is important to remember that not all poor people engage in terrorism. In addition, per capita income is not always associated with terrorism. Research reveals that "protest, violence, and even terrorism can follow either a rising or declining economic tide" (Krueger and Maleckova in Francis 2002, 1). Regardless, poverty does need to be addressed and it is a logical explanation for the occurrence of terrorism.

SELF-CHECK

1. Historical events may lead to terrorism. True or False?
2. Osama bin Laden promotes terrorism because U.S. foreign policy:
   (a) disavows support of puppet governments.
   (b) places U.S. troops in the Middle East.
   (c) does not support Israel.
   (d) benefits poor countries.
3. Why would poor people be involved in terrorism?

3.2 POLITICAL CAUSES

Terrorism has an inherent relation to political disagreements. It may also result from the nature of political systems, functions, and structures. Conflict over priorities, the inability of political systems to adapt, the performance of government, and the structural arrangements of the ruling regime may all impact the possibility of terrorist attacks.

3.2.1 Politics

Politics:
The authoritative allocation of values and resources in society.

Disagreement about politics is a possible reason for terrorism. **Politics** refers to the authoritative allocation of values and resources in society (Easton 1953). Politics therefore refers to the process of determining who gets what in a community or nation through the creation and enforcement of law. Since there are often conflicting views on values (such as what constitutes "good government?") and because designing and running an effective government is inherently a political process, disputes and even conflict may occur.

Any reading of early and modern political thought would likely reveal numerous suggestions on how to best govern societies. For some, the establishing of good government is based on acquiring knowledge, creating and enforcing beneficial laws, and promoting justice. While most people would agree with these recommendations, there are other points of significant disagreement.

For instance, some assert that majority rule should be promoted while others believe the rights of minorities must be guaranteed. Political equality is espoused by many as a way to ensure that all viewpoints are taken into consideration, yet others believe that some individuals are better suited to shape public policy because of their education, leadership, and communication skills. Armed revolution against corrupt leaders is regarded as plausible method for the foundation of good government by certain groups, but a divergent view is that order and stability are necessary to promote safety and security. Another disagreement centers on the contributions of leaders and citizens. One perspective is that wise elected officials will promote good government. Another school of thought is that it is citizen involvement that makes politics legitimate.

The major implication of this explanation is that values and what constitutes good government are issues of considerable debate. This being the case, then it is to be expected that conflict might occur. In other words, if individuals or groups do not feel that their values and priorities are given attention, then it follows that they could engage in violent activity to increase the chance that their preferences will be sufficiently recognized. For instance, if a person feels that environmental degradation is wrong and that society is not protecting natural resources, then there is a possibility that he or she may act violently against those who profit from such activity. There have been many cases where extreme environmentalists have burned SUVs on dealers' lots as a way to protest their poor gas mileage.

3.2.2 Political Systems

Political system:
A governing process that operates in a self-contained environment.

Another thought about terrorism is based on the ability of political systems to adapt and change. A **political system** is a governing process which operates in a self-contained environment (e.g., a national territory) (see figure 3-2). David Easton (1953), one of the most recognized political scientists in the United States, suggests that political systems are comprised of inputs (i.e., taxes and demands for service), decision making processes (i.e., debates about proposed pieces of legislation), and outputs (i.e., policy choices and government programs). Easton also notes that political systems are influenced by feedback, meaning that the inputs, decision-making processes, and outputs can change over time and adjust to new needs and preferences. In Easton's view, this feedback loop is essential for the successful performance of political systems. In other words, if the political system does not adapt to unfolding situations, it will fail.

Applying this model to terrorism, we may conclude that terrorism may result when political systems do not react to the preferences of citizens. An example would be the desire of people to own a gun. If the system is viewed as not protecting citizen rights to possess weapons, then some may become disgruntled and engage in acts of terrorism as a result. The Viper Militia in Arizona is a group that attempted to engage in terrorism due to concerns over weapons rights. Its members plotted to blow up several federal offices in Arizona in 1996, but they were caught before the plans could be implemented (Hoffman 1998, 109).

Figure 3-2

Political Systems

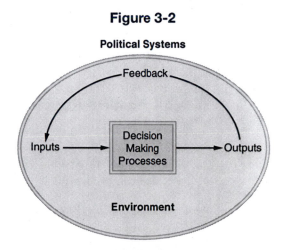

Without sufficient feedback and adaptation, a political system may be affected by terrorism.

3.2.3 Political Functions

A closely related view is that the functioning of government may also have an impact on conflict, including terrorism. Work in this area is similar to the research by Easton, and it has been espoused by Gabriel Almond and James S. Coleman. In their book, *The Politics of the Developing Areas*, Almond and Coleman suggest that we need to examine how government works (1960). In particular, they note that the most important functions government performs include system requirements, inputs, outputs, and maintenance.

System requirements:
Functions that must be established to maintain the operation of a political system.

- **System requirements** are functions that must be established to maintain the operation of a political system. They include routinization of the way things are done (e.g., elections and policy debates), integration of parts (e.g., political parties working together), and goal attainment (e.g., the satisfying of wants).

Input functions:
Activities that influence priorities in the political system.

- **Input functions** are activities that influence priorities in the political system. This includes interest articulation (e.g., agenda setting) and interest aggregation (e.g., formation of political parties).

Output functions:
Activities emanating from the political system.

- **Output functions** are activities emanating from the political system. They incorporate rule making (e.g., policy decisions), rule application (i.e., policy enforcement), and rule adjudication (e.g., judicial decisions about policy).

Maintenance:
The feedback function of the political system.

- **Maintenance** is the feedback function of the political system. It is composed of socialization (e.g., teaching rules of appropriate political behavior), political recruitment (e.g., the joining of interest groups), communication (e.g., calling your senator or state of the union speeches by the President), and symbolism (e.g., a parade to increase pride and trust).

Applying this theoretical perspective to terrorism, we might conclude that political systems that do not perform these functions to a certain standard would be prone to attack. For instance, if a person does not believe law adequately protects animals in medical testing, then he or she may be more inclined to engage in terrorism against the government.

3.2.4 Political Structure

Structure:
The organizational relationships within the political system.

A fourth political explanation for terrorism is related to the structure of government in society. **Structure** refers to the organizational relationships within the political system. There are at least four different political structures that can be identified.

Group competition model:
A model of politics that asserts interest groups interact with or counteract one another in their attempt to sway government policy.

- The **group competition model** asserts that interest groups interact with or counteract one another in their attempt to sway government policy. Some might assert that the United States is an example of this particular perspective.

Economic class model:
A model that suggests a division of society based on the amount of wealth one possesses.

Political elite model:
A model in which the leaders are ruling over the masses.

Corporatist model:
A model that stresses the integration of various components of society into the state government.

- The **economic class model** suggests a division of society based on the amount of wealth one possesses (e.g., upper, middle and lower classes). Depending on your viewpoint, the United States or Latin American countries might also been seen in this light.

- The **political elite model** is a situation where the leaders are ruling over the masses. Iraqi citizens, under the control of Saddam Hussein and his Republican Guard, would fall under this category.

- The **corporatist model** stresses the integration of various components of society into the government (e.g., close ties to business, churches, clubs, etc.). Germany, during World War II, would be a logical example of this model.

The implication of the political structure argument is that certain forms of government will experience violence in different ways. For instance, if a special interest organization feels its needs are not being met in the group competition model, then it might participate in terrorism. In 2006, some Muslims in France burned McDonald's restaurants due to a law that would allow the company to fine them for violating corporate policy. In another case, if one class is being exploited economically by another, then terrorism may result. The Tupamaros, a revolutionary organization in Uruguay, engaged in terrorism to nationalize economic resources and distribute them according to their preference. The political elite and corporatist models may be accompanied by state sponsored terrorism against its own citizens (or terrorist activity on the part of the citizens against the government). Joseph Stalin used violence as a way to maintain his power over the masses in

IN THE REAL WORLD

State Terrorism in Russia

Although the Russian revolution of 1917 had the goal of promoting economic equality, it soon became apparent that a dictatorship had been formed. Vladimir Lenin promoted the Bolshevik take over, and his government began to repress those who voiced opposition. Many artists, intellectuals, and clergy soon became targets of the new regime. When Lenin died, Joseph Stalin took over as the absolute ruler in the Soviet Union. He was the communist leader from 1929 to 1953. During his tenure, Stalin also ruled with an iron fist. He introduced new laws to crack down on those who dissented. His secret police executed thousands and sent millions to labor camps. It is estimated that he killed 800,000 people. Approximately 1.5 million people died due to the extreme conditions of the labor camps. This experience seems to suggest that authoritarian or totalitarian political structures, where an elite group rules over the citizens, may be closely associated with mass terror.

Russia and Francisco Franco executed many opponents of his fascist regime after the Spanish Civil war.

SELF-CHECK

1. Because politics is about competing values, it is not associated with terrorism. True or False?

2. Which part does Easton believe is essential to a political system?
   (a) Inputs
   (b) Outputs
   (c) Feedback loop
   (d) Decision making

3. If the government always met the needs of individuals, would terrorism occur? Can the government meet all citizen needs?

4. Is terrorism related to political structure? How so?

3.3 CULTURAL AND RELIGIOUS CAUSES

Culture:
The lifestyle of groups, including their shared history, language, religion, and moral system.

Religion:
The beliefs and practices espoused by those sharing a common spiritual faith.

Other potential reasons for terrorism focus on culture and religion. **Culture** is the lifestyle of groups based on their shared history, language, religion, and moral system. **Religion** is the beliefs and practices espoused by those sharing a common spiritual faith. Both culture and religion are assumed to be related to terrorist activity and there is ample literature on these subjects.

3.3.1 Cultural Dimensions of Terrorism

One of the most well-known discussions about the impact of culture comes from Samuel Huntington, an American political scientist. In 1993, he wrote at article in *Foreign Affairs* describing how the world had changed when the Cold War ended. He states that the conflicts of the past were a result of (1) kings seeking power, safety, or wealth, (2) nations seeking territory or sovereignty, and (3) governments seeking to promote democracy or communism around the world. In the future, Huntington believes conflict will revolve around culture.

Huntington asserts that there are numerous civilizations around the world (e.g., Western, Confucian, Japanese, Islamic, African, Hindu, Slavic, Latin American). Although there are conflicts within these civilizations, he is more concerned about the possibility that some of the world's civilizations may oppose western culture because the United States is so powerful militarily, economically, and politically. Others may counter American values because of its individualism, constitutional government, human rights, and democracy. Huntington affirms that conflict could result from this "clash of civilizations."

Others including Benjamin Barber have followed up on this theme. In his book *Jihad vs. McWorld*, Barber asserts that the tribal values of certain cultural groups (e.g., Islamic fundamentalists) are diametrically opposed to those who espouse the western capitalist economic system (e.g., symbolized by the fast-food chain McDonalds). The differences of opinion are reasons for conflict today. In particular, those people opposing globalization "argue the virtues of ancient identities, sometimes in the language of bombs" (Barber 1992, 5). Barber declares that "the aim of many of these small-scale wars is to redraw boundaries, to implode states and re-secure parochial identities. . . . War . . . [is also] an emblem of identity, an expression of community, and an end in itself" (1992, 5).

Huntington and Barber bring up some intriguing points about the cultural dimensions of terrorism. In particular, is certainly clear that there are significant disagreements about culture and that acts of violence have emanated because of opposing traditions and viewpoints. The Basques in Spain have created a terrorist organization known as the ETA (Euskadi ta Askatasuna). Their desire is political separatism in order to protect their language and other cultural attributes and interests.

3.3.2 The Role of Religion in Terrorism

Religion has also been cited as a reason why conflict occurs and there appears to be a unique relationship among faith and terrorism (Juergensmeyer 1993; Hoffman 1995). Terrorism has occurred by those professing Christian, Jewish, Muslim, and other faiths.

Terrorism in the name of Christianity has taken place many times in history. In Ireland, Catholics and Protestants have used "religion to identify people with politics" (White 2002, 57). Terrorists on both sides have used their faith as the means to promote Irish independence or continue national association with the United Kingdom. Terrorism in the name of Christianity has also occurred elsewhere.

Terrorists in the United States have at times intertwined Christianity with racist or anti-government overtones. *The Turner Diaries*, written by a white supremacist named William Pierce (1978), discusses the fictitious story of a man who joins a terrorist organization. The man learns about God's alleged plan for a pure race and becomes violent toward others as a result. Timothy McVeigh was influenced by this book. Although he did not appear to be racist, it is alleged that he learned how to bomb the Murrah Federal building in Oklahoma City in 1995 while reading this work. He and other people have relied on such teachings to reinforce their hatred toward the government.

According to Jonathan White, groups including Aryan Nations, Posse Comitatus, and the American Institute of Theology have adopted a religious view that whites are superior to other races. He states that "Christian identity is strongly anti-Semitic, claiming that humans originated from two seed lines. Whites are direct descendants from God, while Jews originated from an illicit sexual union between the devil and the first white woman. Non-white races evolved from animals and are categorized as sub-humans. Identity Christians believe that biblical covenants apply only to the white race and that Jesus of Nazareth was not a Jew, but "the white Israelite son of God" (White 2002, 59). It is unfortunate that people advocate such attitudes and that they try to legitimize terrorism as a result.

There are also terrorists associated with the Jewish faith. Rabbi Meir Kahane was an American cleric who was deeply offended by the violence against Jews in Israel. He created the Jewish Defense League as a way to ensure the survival of the Israeli state. He states that God made a covenant with Abraham to maintain biblical lands. Kahane's followers were involved in terrorist attacks in the United States in the 1960s. Although he was later assassinated, his son established a new organization (named Kahane Chair) to carry out similar missions. One member killed 12 Muslims in a mosque in 1994.

Today, the major threat of religious terrorism comes from Muslim extremists. Many of the Islamic terrorists support **Wahhabism**, a very stringent and legalistic religious movement which attempts to ensure the purity of the Muslim faith with no deviations whatsoever. There are many fundamentalists that engage in terrorism under the banner of this doctrine. For instance, Hezbollah means the "Party of God" while the Mujahadeen are known as "holy fighters" in Afghanistan. **Hamas** is the name for the Islamic Resistance Movement. It is an offshoot of the Muslim Brotherhood and was founded in 1925 to denounce the national borders drawn up by colonial powers from Europe. Their desire is to oppose the creation of the Jewish state and unify all Arabs under a pure Islamic government. They are willing to kill anyone who supports peace.

The term Jihad is often used to describe terrorism that is influenced by the Islamic fundamentalists. **Jihad** actually means an internal struggle to pursue righteousness or a war of self-defense. However, terrorists, such as Osama bin Laden, have altered this term to encourage his followers to engage in a "holy war" against non-believers or infidels. He says in his **fatwa** (a religious edict) that it is the individual duty of every Muslim to fight against Israel and murder Americans everywhere.

Terrorism is not confined to Christian, Jewish, or Islamic religions, however. Shoko Asahara, the leader of Japan's Aum Shinrikyo (Supreme Truth), stated he had been called as a messenger for God. After returning from a trip to the Himalayas, he prophesied that Armageddon would occur at the end of the 1900s and that only a divinely appointed race would survive in Japan. His religious views mixed Buddhism and Hinduism along with strong anti-American sentiment. On March 20, 1995, his followers used Sarin gas to attack commuters on five subways. The attacks had the purpose of delaying police investigation into the groups' acquisition of deadly chemical weapons (Hoffman 1998, 126).

In each of these cases, followers of religion use terrorism as a tool and claimed to act in God's name. Under these circumstances, "believers must

Wahhabism:
A stringent and legalistic movement that attempts to ensure the purity of the Muslim faith with no deviations whatsoever.

Hamas:
The name for the Islamic Resistance Movement, an offshoot of the Muslim Brotherhood founded to denounce the national borders drawn up by colonial powers in Europe.

Jihad:
Literally means an internal struggle to pursue righteousness or a war of self-defense, but has been used by terrorists to denote an offensive attack.

Fatwa
A religious edict.

IN THE REAL WORLD

The Emergence of the Irish Republic Army

During the Protestant reformation, King Henry VIII separated himself from the Catholic Church and created the Church of England. About the same time, the king's daughter, Elizabeth, sanctioned the creation of the Ulster Plantation in Ireland, which resulted in the displacement of many of the Catholic inhabitants. Many of the Irish Catholics who lost their land eventually perished because of malnourishment. This, coupled with a new law passed in 1801 (the Act of Union) to join Ireland under the United Kingdom, created serious tensions between Irish Catholics and Protestants from England. Witnessing the plight of their kin, many of the Irish who had migrated to the United States created the Irish Republican Brotherhood (IRB). Although the IRB had the intention of helping relatives in their old country, it soon became apparent that Irish independence was desired. The IRB mutated into a revolutionary organization, its members traveled back to Ireland, and they later became known as the Irish Republican Army (IRA). Its founder, Michael Collins, used religion as a way to recruit members to fight the British Protestants. The IRA was responsible for many bombings in Ireland and England in the 1970s and 1980s. Although various peace accords have been signed between England and the terrorists, attacks have continued. Terrorism continues to have close ties to religion in Ireland today, although it is less common than in the past.

identify with a deity and believe they are participating in a struggle to change history. They must also believe in cosmic consequences; that is, the outcome of the struggle will lead to a new relationship between good and evil. When they feel the struggle has reached a critical stage, violence may be endorsed and terrorism may result" (White 2002, 52).

SELF-CHECK

1. According to Samuel Huntington, culture will be the major source of conflict in the future. True or False?

2. According to bin Laden, Jihad refers to:

   (a) Internal struggle
   (b) Holy war
   (c) Fatwa
   (d) Wahhabism

3. Do all Christians, Jews, and Muslims support terrorist attacks?

3.4 IDEOLOGY

Based on the above discussion, we may conclude that historical grievances, poverty, foreign policy, political factors, culture, and religion are
often associated with terrorism. Nevertheless, it is obvious that these
variables cannot always be considered as the only or motivating "cause"
of terrorist phenomena. For instance, not all poor people participate in
terrorism. Ineffective political systems do not always produce terrorists.
Not all Muslims attack the United States, even if many disagree with its
foreign policy or culture. It accordingly appears that there must be an
additional reason as to why terrorism occurs. Gus Martin suggests that
while "not all extremists become terrorists, some do cross the line to
engage in terrorist violence. For them, terrorism is a calculated strategy.
It is a specifically selected method that is used to further their cause"
(2003, 56). Ideology is therefore a plausible explanation for the occurrence of terrorism.

Ideology:
A set of beliefs related
to values, attitudes, ways
of thinking, and goals.

The word ideology is based on the prefix "idea." An **ideology** is consequently a set of beliefs related to values, attitudes, ways of thinking and
goals (Plamenatz 1970). In other words, ideologies are comprehensive theoretical viewpoints that often recommend certain types of political action.
They are often referred to as "secular religions." Ideologies have their roots
in early political philosophy from notable intellectuals such as Socrates,
Plato, and Aristotle. But the term ideology did not appear until the late
1700s when a man named Destutt de Tracy attempted to discredit the political institutions in France. He claimed that the king was not divinely appointed and argued that the government did not represent the interests of the
people. Destutt de Tracy's ideology opened up the possibility of political
change in France. This was one of the first examples of how ideology is
used for political purposes.

3.4.1 Understanding Ideologies

Ideologies cover a broad range of subjects and may be related to numerous
questions (MaCridis and Hulliung 1996):

- What is truth how can it be pursued?
- What makes political authority or a political system legitimate?
- Should individual rights be promoted or should the majority rule?
- Is it more important to espouse political freedoms or economic
  equality?
- Is it better to acquire wealth or protect the environment?
- Should you follow the laws of men or God's commandments?

Ideologies therefore serve several purposes. They help promote understanding and they simplify a complex world. Ideologies facilitate communication among individuals, and generate identity and emotional fulfillment in groups. Ideologies are used as tools by leaders and provide guidelines for the behavior of followers. An ideology not only endorses certain viewpoints (while rejecting others), but it also helps to mobilize people in the accomplishment of goals and priorities. Ideologies can therefore be very powerful motivators in the lives of their adherents.

Although all ideologies share many similarities, they differ in dramatic ways. Ideologies may discourage change, promote revolution, or accept incremental reform (MaCridis and Hulliung 1996). They may unite some groups and cause divisions with others. Roy MaCridis and Mark Hulliung (1996, 16–17) suggest that ideologies may be assessed on five bases:

Scope:
The subjects covered by an ideology.

Coherence:
The internal logic of an ideology.

Pervasiveness:
How long an ideology has been in existence.

Extensiveness:
How many people share a particular ideology.

Intensiveness:
The strength of attachment to an ideology.

Cognitive dimension:
The knowledge and beliefs of ideology.

Affect dimension:
Specific emotions that are generated in conjunction with an ideology.

Valuation dimension:
The norms and judgments of an ideology.

Program dimension:
Conjure up the plans and actions to support the goals of an ideology.

Social base dimension:
The individuals or groups that espouse an ideology.

1. **Scope:** What subjects does the ideology cover? Does it focus on human rights or environmental issues?

2. **Coherence:** Does the internal logic make sense? In other words, does the ideology contradict itself?

3. **Pervasiveness:** How long has it been in existence? Is it a relatively new ideology like feminism, or has it been prevalent for centuries?

4. **Extensiveness:** How many people share that particular belief? What is the number of people that support it?

5. **Intensiveness:** What is the strength of attachment? Are people casually associated with the ideology or are they fully committed to their particular beliefs?

3.4.2 Ideological Dimensions and Terrorism

According to Mostafa Rejai, an Indian scholar, there are five dimensions that are integral to any ideology (1991). Rejai states that all ideologies have a **cognitive dimension.** This refers to the knowledge and beliefs of the ideology. Ideologies are related to the **affect dimension**—specific feelings or emotions that are generated in conjunction with beliefs. The **valuation dimension** deals with the norms and judgments of the ideology. **Program dimension** conjure up the plans and actions to support goals. The **social base dimension** refers to the individuals or groups that espouse the ideology.

These dimensions are useful to understand the ideologies associated with terrorism. Terrorists like Osama bin Laden have unique attitudes about the world (e.g., he sees the United States as a problem and asserts that its influence needs to be countered). He has strong sentiments to a particular issue (e.g., a desire to retain a pure version of Islam). Osama bin Laden is passionate about values and preferences (e.g., he is willing to injure others or even kill himself if that is required). He also develops methods to accomplish his objectives (e.g., training and operational planning are needed to carry out attacks). Osama bin Laden also has a clearly identified group that supports his ideology (e.g., Al Qaeda members endorse violence while most Muslims prefer peace).

There is no shortage of ideologies that may be related to terrorism. Some conservative ideologies are associated with political regimes that engage in violence to maintain the power of the ruling elite. In contrast, a liberal ideology may endorse terrorism as the means to expand rights to individuals and citizens. Some terrorists favor nationalistic movements, thereby attempting to promote a group with a particular culture, ethnicity, or language. Terrorism may have a relation to Marxist ideology. In this case, some people denounce capitalism and see revolution as a way to promote economic equality. Other ideologies, like fascism and Nazism, sanction terrorism in order to expand a nation or promote racial superiority. At times, extreme conservationists engage in terrorism to avert global environmental degradation. Religious beliefs may be used by some people to endorse terrorism and counter the advances of secular society. Others, like anarchists and post-modernists, question all types of authority structures and accept violence as a way to protect individual freedoms. When you understand these ideological sources of conflict, you are in a better position to start dealing with the causes and consequences of terrorism.

IN THE REAL WORLD

Terrorist Ideology and Abortions

People have engaged in terrorist activities to halt abortions in the United States. The ideology of these individuals and groups has all of the elements identified by Mostafa Rejai. The cognitive dimension of their belief is that abortion is wrong and that this practice has increased dramatically since it was legalized. A feeling of deep sorrow for the loss of these babies is the affect dimension of this ideology. The preference to protect the life of all children is the value dimension. With this in mind, some terrorists have relied on a program of violence against doctors to halt abortions. The social base of this ideology is comprised of certain fundamentalist Christians. While many of those adhering to Christianity oppose abortions, they are not willing to kill others to stop them from doing so. Being able to detect those people who endorse ideological positions in extreme ways could help you identify potential terrorists.

SELF-CHECK

1. Ideology is not related to beliefs, ideas, or attitudes. True or False?
2. Marxism is an ideology. True or False?
3. Which is not one of the five dimensions of ideologies suggested by Mostafa Rejai?
   (a) Program
   (b) Cognitive
   (c) Affect
   (d) Coherence
4. Think of the terrorist attacks that have occurred in recent history. Can you identify the ideology of the terrorists in each case?

SUMMARY

If you are to reduce the probability of terrorism it is imperative that you understand what motivates people to participate in this type of behavior. You discovered that historical conflicts, mistakes in foreign policy, and extreme levels of poverty may impel some to engage in terrorist attacks. You learned that political systems, functions, and structures are often associated with terrorism. Diverse cultures and extreme religious beliefs may also be used by terrorists to engage in violent or disruptive activity. While all of these variables may influence terrorist behavior, it is likely that ideology is a better predictor of terrorism. People's beliefs seem to play a large role in terrorism. Once you recognize this fact, you can identify terrorists and take other measures to prevent future attacks.

ASSESS YOUR UNDERSTANDING

UNDERSTAND: WHAT HAVE YOU LEARNED

 Go to **www.wiley.com/college/mcentire** to assess your knowledge of the causes of terrorism.

SUMMARY QUESTIONS

1. You are the public information officer for the Department of Homeland Security. The media wants to know why terrorism occurs. List at least five causes of terrorism and evaluate which explanation makes the most sense.

2. If you were in charge of U.S. foreign policy, what causes of terrorism should you be aware of?

3. You are a scholar with expertise in terrorism. While appearing on the news show *60 Minutes*, you are questioned about the political systems and terrorism. Diagram the components of a political system and explain how the feedback loop relates to terrorism.

4. As a FBI analyst, your job is to identify potential terrorists. Predict why some people may use Christian, Jewish, and Islamic faith to justify terrorism.

5. There have been continual conflicts in the Middle East. True or False?

6. Absolute poverty implies that everyone in the country is poor or lacks resources. True or False?

7. There is considerable disagreement about what constitutes good government. True or False?

8. The economic class model is not related to terrorism. True or False?

9. Language is an aspect of culture but not moral belief systems. True or False?

10. Terrorism has only been undertaken by those professing the Islamic faith. True or False?

11. The intensiveness of an ideology may have a direct bearing on terrorism. True or False?

12. The wars committed by Christians against the Muslims were known as:
    (a) Crusades.
    (b) Wahhabism.
    (c) Fatwas.
    (d) Holocaust.

13. An environment that has inputs, decision processes, outputs, and feedback is known as a:

(a) maintenance.

(b) structure.

(c) political system.

(d) corporatist model.

14. What is the religious movement that adheres to a strict interpretation of Islam?

(a) Fatwa

(b) Wahhabism

(c) Marxism

(d) *The Turner Diaries*

15. The cognitive dimension of an ideology refers to:

(a) feelings.

(b) norms and judgments.

(c) plans and actions.

(d) knowledge and beliefs.

16. According to bin Laden, Al Qaeda is justified in attacking America because the United States:

(a) supports Israel.

(b) distrusts Israel.

(c) distrusts puppet governments.

(d) is opposed to colonialism.

BE A HOMELAND SECURITY PROFESSIONAL

Briefing the President

You are a political advisor with expertise in homeland security. The President has asked you to brief him/her on the causes of terrorism. What would you say? What are the differing perspectives on this matter? Which one(s) is/are most important?

Promoting Cultural Understanding

You are the Secretary of State, and it is your job to improve relations among groups and nations internationally. An important aspect of your position is to foster cultural understanding. Explain how this might ease the occurrence of terrorism around the world. Do you think it would be possible to eliminate culture as a cause of terrorism? Why or why not?

Assignment: Understanding Ideology

Write a paper about the impact of ideology on terrorism. Be sure to discuss what an ideology is, what the common characteristics of ideologies are, and the types of ideologies that may lead to violence.

KEY TERMS

Absolute poverty	State in which people lack so many resources that they cannot even meet basic necessities such as food, clothing, and shelter.
Affect dimension	Specific emotions that are generated in conjunction with an ideology.
Cognitive dimension	The knowledge and beliefs of the ideology.
Coherence	The internal logic of an ideology.
Corporatist model	A model that stresses the integration of various components of society into the state government.
Crusades	Wars between 1100 and 1300 A.D. endorsed by the Pope to recapture the Holy Land of Jerusalem from the control of Muslims.
Culture	The lifestyle of groups, including their shared history, language, religion, and moral system.
Economic class model	A model that suggests a division of society based on the amount of wealth one possesses.
Extensiveness	How many people share a particular ideology.
Fatwa	A religious edict.
Group competition model	A model of politics that asserts that interest groups interact with or counteract one another in their attempt to sway government policy.
Hamas	The name for the Islamic Resistance Movement, an offshoot of the Muslim Brotherhood founded to denounce the national borders drawn up by colonial powers in Europe.
Holocaust	The extermination of Jews by the Nazi regime during World War II.

Ideology	A set of beliefs related to values, attitudes, ways of thinking, and goals.
Input functions	Activities that influence priorities in the political system.
Intensiveness	The strength of attachment to an ideology.
Jihad	Literally means an internal struggle to pursue righteousness or a war of self-defense, but has been used by terrorists to denote an offensive attack.
Maintenance	The feedback function of the political system.
Muslims	People who follow the prophet Muhammad and adhere to the religion of Islam.
Output functions	Activities emanating from the political system.
Pervasiveness	How long an ideology has been in existence.
Political elite model	A model in which the leaders are ruling over the masses.
Political system	A governing process that operates in a self-contained environment (e.g., a national territory).
Politics	The authoritative allocation of values and resources in society.
Program dimension	Conjure up the plans and actions to support the goals of an ideology.
Programs dimension	The plans and actions to support goals.
Relative poverty	State where some people are less wealthy than their fellow citizens or peers in other countries.
Religion	The beliefs and practices espoused by those sharing a common spiritual faith.
Scope	The subjects covered by an ideology.
Social base dimension	The individuals or groups that espouse an ideology.
Structure	The organizational relationships within the political system.
System requirements	Functions that must be established to maintain operation of a political system.
Theocracy	A government run by clerics in the name of God.
Valuation dimension	The norms and judgments of an ideology.
Wahhabism	A stringent and legalistic movement that attempts to ensure the purity of the Muslim faith with no deviations whatsoever.

REFERENCES

Almond, Gabriel A. and James S. Coleman. (1960). *The Politics of the Developing Areas*. Princeton University Press: Princeton, NJ.

Barber, Benjamin. (1992). "Jihad vs. McWorld." *The Atlantic*. March. www.theatlantic.com/doc/print/199203/barber.

Barber, Benjamin. (1996). *Jihad vs. McWorld: How Globalism and Tribalism Are Reshaping the World*. Ballantine Books, New York.

Easton, David. (1953). *The Political System*. Alfred P. Knopf: New York.

Francis, David R. (2002). "Poverty and Low Education Don't Cause Terrorism." *The NBER Digest*, September, 1–2.

Hoffman, Bruce. (1995). "Holy Terror: The Implications of Terrorism Motivated by a Religious Imperative." *Studies in Conflict and Terrorism*. 18: 271–284.

Hoffman, Bruce. (1998). *Inside Terrorism*. Columbia University Press: New York.

Huntington, Samuel P. (1993). "The Clash of Civilizations." *Foreign Affairs* 72 (3): 22–49.

Juergensmeyer, Mark. (1993). *The New Cold War? Religious Nationalism Confronts the Secular State*. University of California Press: Berkeley, CA.

Lesser, Ian O. (1999). "Countering the New Terrorism: Implications for Strategy." In Lesser, Ian O., Bruce Hoffman, John Arguilla, David Ronfeldt, and Michele Zanini. *Countering the New Terrorism*. Rand, Santa Monica, CA.

Lozada, Carlos. (2005). "Does Poverty Cause Terrorism?" *The NBER Digest*, May, 1.

Martin, Gus. (2003). *Understanding Terrorism: Challenges, Perspectives, and Issues*. Sage Publications: Thousand Oaks, CA.

McCridis, Roy C., and Mark L. Hulliung. (1996). *Contemporary Political Ideologies: Movements and Regimes*. HarperCollins: New York.

Pierce, William (aka Andrew MacDonald). (1978). *The Turner Diaries*. National Vanguard Books: Hillsboro, WV.

Plamenatz, John. (1970). *Ideology*. Praeger: New York.

Pillar, Paul R. (2001). *Terrorism and U.S. Foreign Policy*. Brookings Institution Press: Washington, D.C.

Rejai, Mostafa. (1991). *Political Ideologies: A Comparative Approach*. M.E. Sharpe: New York.

Weatherby, Joseph N., Randal L. Cuikshanks, Emmit B. Evans, Jr., Reginald Gooden, Earl De Huff, Richard Kranzdorf, Dianne Long. (2000). *The Other World: Issues and Politics of the Developing World*. Longman: New York.

White, Jonathan R. (2002). *Terrorism: An Introduction*. Wadsworth, Belmont, CA.

4

COMPREHENDING TERRORISTS AND THEIR BEHAVIOR
Who They Are and What They Do

Do You Already Know?

- How to classify terrorists based on their intentions
- The common attitudes and personality traits of terrorists
- The similarities and differences among terrorist organizations
- The operational tactics used by terrorists

 For additional questions to assess your current knowledge of terrorists and their behavior, go to **www.wiley.com/college/mcentire**

What You Will Find Out	What You Will Be Able To Do
4.1 Examples of individuals, groups, and states involved in terrorism	• Classify terrorists based on their intentions
4.2 The common attitudes and personality traits of terrorists	• Critique stereotypical views about terrorists
4.3 The similarities and differences among terrorist organizations	• Predict terrorist behavior
4.4 Operational tactics of those engaging in terrorism	• Anticipate how terrorists plan and carry out attacks

INTRODUCTION

If you are to reduce the probability and consequences of terrorism, it is imperative that you comprehend who terrorists are and how they operate. In this chapter, you will examine terrorists, whether they are acting alone or in conjunction with others. You will learn how to categorize terrorists based on personality traits, and evaluate their similarities and differences. By assessing the behavior of terrorists, you will be able to recognize how they recruit and train members, support their activities financially, and plan and carry out attacks.

4.1 TERRORISTS AND TERRORIST ORGANIZATIONS

Who is a terrorist? What groups are involved in terrorism? These are important questions that must be addressed by those involved in homeland security. Some terrorists are well known, while others are not. Certain proponents of terrorism have given up their violent activities, while other organizations remain heavily involved in attacks at the current time. Numerous examples of terrorists can be given. The list seems to grow each day.

George Habash:
Founder of the militant Popular Front for the Liberation of Palestine (PFLP) and a terrorist who opposes Israel. He sponsored many airline hijackings in the 1970's and 1980's.

George Habash is an example of an individual terrorist. He was born in Palestine to a wealthy family in 1925. Although he was a medical doctor, he was influenced by Marxist thought. In addition, he also opposed Israel and the involvement of the United States in the Middle East. He felt that Arabs were justified in attacking the Jews in order to regain Palestinian lands. Habash planned one of his most notable terrorist acts in history: the hijacking of a Trans World airliner (from Beruit to Jordan). Security at airports has never been the same since that attack.

Japanese Red Army (JRA):
A left-wing terrorist organization that emerged in the 1960s to protest U.S. military presence in Japan after World War II, the war in Vietnam, and capitalism.

Another example of terrorism is from the **Japanese Red Army (JRA)**, an organization that emerged in the 1960s. Its members protested the presence of the U.S. military in Japan after World War II, disapproved of the Vietnam War, and rejected capitalism. Its first terrorist operation was in 1970, when it hijacked an airplane headed to North Korea. This extreme left-wing organization has been involved in attacks in the Middle East, Italy, and in Japan. Its activity has waned in recent years.

Libya:
A country in Northern Africa that heavily supported terrorism in the 1980s.

Countries may also be supporters of terrorist activity. For instance, **Libya** is a nation in Africa that has been sympathetic to the Palestinian cause in Israel. Under the direction of Muammar Qadhafi, this nation was involved in the 1986 La Belle discotheque bombing in Berlin. It also was responsible for the Pan Am Flight 103 bombing over Lockerbie, Scotland, in 1988. This attack killed 270 people. Because of sanctions imposed by the United Nations and the threat of retaliation from the United States after 9/11, Libya has dramatically reduced its involvement in terrorism in recent years.

**Theodore "Ted"
Kaczynski:**
Terrorist known as the
"Unabomber" who opposed
technological advances.

As can be seen from these examples, terrorists may be individuals, groups, or states. Examples of individual terrorists include Richard Baumhammers (a neo-Nazi who attacked people in Pennsylvania in April 2000) and Ramzi Yousef (the ringleader of the World Trade Center bombing in 1993). **Theodore "Ted" Kaczynski** also comes to mind

IN THE REAL WORLD

The Unabomber Manifesto

1. The Industrial Revolution and its consequences have been a disaster for the human race. They have greatly increased the life-expectancy of those of us who live in "advanced" countries, but they have destabilized society, have made life unfulfilling, have subjected human beings to indignities, have led to widespread psychological suffering (in the Third World to physical suffering as well) and have inflicted severe damage on the natural world. The continued development of technology will worsen the situation. It will certainly subject human beings to greater indignities and inflict greater damage on the natural world, it will probably lead to greater social disruption and psychological suffering, and it may lead to increased physical suffering even in "advanced" countries.

2. The industrial-technological system may survive or it may break down. If it survives, it MAY eventually achieve a low level of physical and psychological suffering, but only after passing through a long and very painful period of adjustment and only at the cost of permanently reducing human beings and many other living organisms to engineered products and mere cogs in the social machine. Furthermore, if the system survives, the consequences will be inevitable: There is no way of reforming or modifying the system so as to prevent it from depriving people of dignity and autonomy.

3. If the system breaks down the consequences will still be very painful. But the bigger the system grows the more disastrous the results of its breakdown will be, so if it is to break down it had best break down sooner rather than later.

4. We therefore advocate a revolution against the industrial system. This revolution may or may not make use of violence: it may be sudden or it may be a relatively gradual process spanning a few decades. We can't predict any of that. But we do outline in a very general way the measures that those who hate the industrial system should take in order to prepare the way for a revolution against that form of society. This is not to be a POLITICAL revolution. Its object will be to overthrow not governments but the economic and technological basis of the present society.

when discussing individual terrorists. Known as the Unabomber, Kaczynski opposed technology and even wrote a manifesto decrying advances in this area. His attacks were aimed mainly at university professors and corporate leaders. He was responsible for at least 15 bombings around that United States that killed three people and injured 22 others. Individuals who act alone are sometimes described as **lone-wolf terrorists**.

Lone-wolf terrorists:
Individual terrorists who act alone.

Besides individual terrorists, there are literally hundreds of groups and organizations involved in violence around the world. Examples include Abu Nidal, the Armed Forces of National Liberation, the Democratic Front for the Liberation of Palestine, the Earth Liberation Front, the German Red Army Faction, Hamas, the Irish National Liberation Army, the Liberation Tigers of Tamil Elaam, and the Revolutionary Armed Forces of Colombia. There are obviously too many terrorist groups to mention.

Abu Sayef:
An Islamic separatist group in the Philippines that desires an independent state in Mindanao.

Abu Sayef is a powerful terrorist organization in the Philippines. Abu Sayef is an Islamic separatist group that desires an independent state in Mindanao. As a splinter group of the Moro National Liberation Front, it opposes any type of colonialism or foreign involvement in the Philippines. Abu Sayef has been involved in kidnappings and has used its hostages to acquire lucrative ransoms from family members or their employers (i.e., large international corporations).

Iran:
A state in the Middle East that denounces the United States, promotes anti-western propaganda, and has a long history of participation in terrorism.

Many states have also been involved in terrorism including Syria and the Sudan. Iraq has likewise been associated with terrorism. Although Iraq was not responsible for 9/11, it too provided arms, funding, safe haven, and diplomatic assistance to terrorists. **Iran** is another state in the Middle East that has a long history of participation in terrorism. After it underwent a revolution sponsored by Ayatollah Khomeini, this country increasingly denounced the United States and promoted anti-western propaganda. It has since provided funds to terrorist organizations like Hezbollah. In addition, the Shia government in Iran had a role in attacks on foreign embassies and on the Marine barracks in Beirut during the 1980s. Most recently, evidence suggests that Iran is providing bombs to terrorists who are trying to destabilize Iraq. Both the United States and the United Nations are concerned that Iran is currently trying to develop nuclear weapons.

Abu Musab al-Zarqawi:
A Sunni terrorist responsible for many atrocities in Iraq, including the beheading of American businessman Nicolas Berg.

Terrorists often have unique forms of organization. At times, they may be under the direction of a single individual. For instance, many terrorists in Iraq support the ideology and vision promoted by **Abu Musab al-Zarqawi**. Al-Zarqawi was a Sunni terrorist who was responsible for many atrocities in Iraq, including the beheading of an American businessman named Nicolas Berg. Terrorists groups may also have a central headquarter. As an example, **Al Qaeda** actually means the "base." This term refers to the location from

Al Qaeda:
A well-known terrorist organization whose name refers to the "base"—the location from which its supporters attacked the Soviet Union to free Afghanistan.

which Muslim soldiers coordinated the fight against the Soviet Union in the late 1980s.

Cell:
A terrorist branch or unit operating in locations away from the organization's headquarters.

At other times, terrorists have **cells** (or branches with members) around the world. For instance, Jamaah Islamiya is an Islamic terrorist organization that has presence in Malaysia, Singapore, and Indonesia. In contrast, it is believed that Khifa has had units in New York, Chicago, Pittsburgh, and Tucson. Terrorist organizations may also interact one with another. For instance, Al Qaeda has consulted with Jamaah Islamiya. The Red Army Faction was likewise trained by other terrorists in the Middle East. Today, terrorists are increasingly decentralized and transform themselves to avoid detection. There are also many splinter groups with similar ideologies. Both the IRA and PLO have produced scores of different terrorist groups over time, especially when disagreements arise regarding the organizations' policy positions (e.g., willingness or unwillingness to negotiate and compromise).

4.1.1 Classifying Terrorists

Individuals, groups, states, or cell-oriented terrorists may be classified in one of three ways. Frederick Hacker (1976), a doctor who later became an expert in hostage negotiation, suggests that terrorists may be labeled as criminals, crusaders, or crazies:

Criminal:
A terrorist that seeks personal gain through illegal means (e.g., drugs or crime).

Crusader:
A terrorist that promotes high moral goals (e.g., Islamic fundamentalists).

Crazy:
A terrorist that is regarded to be psychologically disturbed (e.g., Ted Kaczynski).

- A terrorist that is a **criminal** seeks personal gain. Abu Sayef is an example of a criminal terrorist organization. Today, it seems to be more interested in making money through extortion and less motivated by its initial founding goals of national independence.

- A **crusader** is a terrorist that promotes high moral goals. Examples of this type of terrorist include left-wing groups seeking economic or political equality, right-wing groups desiring to limit government interference in their lives, and environmental groups attempting to protect the earth's resources. Nationalist groups seeking separatism, or religious groups trying to promote their beliefs and impose them on others are also examples from this category.

- A terrorist that is a **crazy** is regarded to be psychologically disturbed. For instance, Ted Kaczynski might be regarded as falling into this type of terrorist since the reasoning for his attacks is not logical to others.

Of course, it is important to recognize that some terrorists may exhibit elements of all three classifications. Thus, it is not always easy to distinguish among criminals, crusaders, and crazies. In the words of one scholar, "[t]he categories are not mutually exclusive; any terrorist group could contain a variety of these . . . types" (White 2002, 25).

Figure 4-1

Some individuals, like Eric Rudolph pictured above, use terrorist tactics to achieve moral objectives.

IN THE REAL WORLD

Saddam Hussein's Al-Anfal Attacks on the Kurds

While Saddam Hussein reigned with his Ba'ath Party in Iraq, he implemented state terrorism to rid his nation of the Kurdish people (Martin 2003, 104). He dropped chemical weapons on villages in Northern Iraq to hinder their quest for political autonomy. The mustard gas and nerve agents produced a yellow cloud and smelled like onions. When people breathed the smoke, they would fall to the ground and blood would spew from their mouths. Between 50,000 and 100,000 died, and 2.5 million Kurds were displaced. This series of attacks, which occurred in 1988, was named Al-Anfal. It is reported to have been given this title in reference to revelations given by the Prophet Mohammed after his first great victory. The scripture allegedly advised the Prophet to kill unbelievers when necessary. It is an example of a crusader-type attitude that is common among many terrorists today.

SELF-CHECK

1. Terrorists always act alone. True or False?

2. Which of the following countries has supported terrorist attacks in Iraq?

   (a) Sudan
   (b) Syria
   (c) Iran
   (d) Sri Lanka

3. Into what three categories does Hacker classify terrorists?

4.2 PERSONAL CHARACTERISTICS OF TERRORISTS

Regardless of how terrorists are classified, it is apparent that they all share remarkable similarities. For example, in the *Language of Violence*, Edgar O'Balance (1979) states that terrorists are often dedicated, brave, and stoic. Terrorists are willing to sacrifice their time, energy, possessions, and lives for what they believe in. They are calm in light of the possibility of being subjected to prison, torture, or even death. Terrorists also lack emotions and show no pity or remorse for the victims of their attacks.

Beyond these characteristics, terrorists have other similarities among their belief systems (Combs 2000, 39). These include the following:

- **Terrorists see the world simplistically in terms of right and wrong.** They may not accept the complexity of issues or recognize the positive and negative aspects of alternative points of view. For instance, they might have a negative perception of capitalism only and fail to acknowledge any possible benefits from this type of economic system.

- **Terrorists are disturbed by the current situation.** They are disappointed by societal problems and are able to identify what should be changed. As an example, Islamic fundamentalists assert that Western culture is responsible for the secularization of Arab societies.

- **Terrorists have a unique image of themselves.** They feel that they are in a morally superior position to others. Terrorists are self-regarded to be the means for change and improvement. For instance, a terrorist who opposes abortions may view himself or herself as a messenger from God.

- **Terrorists identify the enemy and have strong feelings against them.** They frequently place blame and discredit those they regard to be at fault. Extreme nationalists dehumanize those of other ethnic groups as a way to mobilize action and limit guilt. They view others as enemies, collateral damage, or instruments of change. It is alleged that Michael Collins (IRA founder) stated after killing fourteen men: "They were undesirables by whose destruction the very air is made sweeter" (Taylor 1958, 17).

- **Terrorists believe their actions are justified.** Recognizing their inferior position in terms of numbers or strength as well as their inability to work through democratic processes, terrorists are willing to promote their goals through illegal means. Violence brings attention to their plight and speeds up the resolution to problems. For those participating in violence for religious reasons, terrorism may even bring salvation. Before his execution, Paul Hill stated that he expected a great reward in heaven for killing a doctor who performs abortions.

4.2.1 Distinct Differences

Although terrorists have several common personality traits, they do not fall into a simple profile. Divergence can be seen in terms of age, gender, education, and economic status.

Most terrorists are younger adults in their twenties. However, this trend is not always accurate. During the 1970s, many of the terrorists captured in Ireland were as young as 12 years old. Arab terrorist groups today also include a large number of teenagers in their ranks. There are older terrorists that contradict prevalent expectations, however. For instance, Osama bin Laden was in his mid-forties when the 9/11 attacks occurred. Thus, with regard to age, it might be wise to state that the leaders tend to be older, while those who implement attacks are younger.

The typical terrorist is often regarded to be male. Men have traditionally been involved in the dangerous activities of planning and carrying out terrorist attacks. However, women have always played a significant support role in terrorism, and some have participated in spying and actual operations (Griset and Mahan 2003). There have also been many females involved in terrorism in Germany (i.e., Baader-Meinhof gang and Red Army Faction). In addition, about half of the terrorists in Sri Lanka (i.e., Tamil Tigers) are girls or women, and they are particularly deadly in their craft. Therefore, while most terrorists are men, you should not expect that this will always the case.

The educational status of terrorists is in question, too. Many terrorists are well-educated, obtaining degrees in difficult subjects such as engineering, chemistry, or computer science. In fact, several of the leaders of Al Qaeda earned college degrees in the United States and elsewhere. Not all terrorists are highly educated, though. Many of the terrorists in the Middle East receive basic education in schools known as **Madrasahs**. These institutions appear to indoctrinate orphan students in extreme Islamic thought, as occurs in some remote areas of Pakistan. Other terrorists may lack any formal type of education whatsoever.

Madrasahs:
Schools in Pakistan and elsewhere that at times indoctrinate students in extreme Islamic thought.

It is sometimes difficult to predict how economic class relates to terrorism. Some terrorists, like Abu Nidal, were born into the lap of luxury. Others rejected their parents' middle class lifestyle in the 1960s to fight for economic equality. Today, many of the terrorists around the world are poor and lack the basic necessities of life. Osama bin Laden is an exception to this rule. He is an extremely rich terrorist who acquired money from a number of oil and construction industries his family owned. Thus, "it remains true that to generalize about the 'typical' terrorist can be very difficult with any degree of accuracy" (Combs 2000, 51).

Figure 4-2

Many, but not all, terrorists are young. During a march organized by the Afghan Defense Council (a Muslim religious group based in Pakistan), Friday, October 5, 2001, in Rawalpindi, near Islamabad, Pakistan, a boy holds a pistol. Thousands of demonstrators shouted anti-American slogans and support of Osama bin Laden.

IN THE REAL WORLD

Rearing Terrorists in the Middle East

Socialization into the world of terrorism is a common practice among many of the terrorists in the Middle East. Children are brought up to support terrorist organizations like Hamas and Hezbollah. Children attend parades that celebrate militancy, and they are taught at an early age to fire guns and use knives. Children dress in camouflage uniforms and proudly wave the colors or flags of their terrorist organization. Cartoons illustrate the blessings of violence and songs extol the virtue of terrorist heroes. Under these circumstances, it is no wonder that the ultimate goal in life for children is to die as a martyr. This is one reason why terrorism is proving to be the enduring problem of our time.

SELF-CHECK

1. Terrorists are not willing to sacrifice for their cause. True or False?
2. Terrorists often see themselves as the means for change. True or False?
3. Terrorists:
    (a) are always young.
    (b) are not always male.
    (c) are never rich.
    (d) are always educated.
4. How are all terrorists similar?

4.3 THE BEHAVIOR AND TACTICS OF TERRORISTS

To a certain extent, terrorist activities are predictable. Terrorists are involved in propaganda, recruiting, financing, and training. They also acquire false documents, travel, seek safe haven, use code words and secret communications, plan attacks, and search for weapons. Eventually, terrorists also launch attacks against their enemies.

4.3.1 Propaganda

If you are to work in homeland security, you must know that terrorists actively promote their ideological goals (Martin 2003). For instance, the

Al Jazeera:
A TV station based in Qatar that is popular in the Middle East and used to disseminate terrorist information.

Palestinian Islamic Jihad has a "manifesto." This policy document rejects any peaceful solution to the Palestinian cause and lays out the objective of destroying Israel and ending western influence in the Middle East. The document has been circulated widely among countries in the area and the media is often used to publicize such interests. **Al Jazeera** is the most widely viewed TV station in the Middle East. Based in Qatar, Al Jazeera is often used as the vehicle to disseminate information. Terrorists use it to call for the end of Western occupation in the Middle East and encourage viewers to "cut the head off of the snake" (destroy the United States). Material on this station often shows video of attacks (actual or recreated) as well as terrorist training activities. In other cases, members of Al Qaeda swear loyalty to Osama bin Laden and film a martyrdom statement. Videos of these terrorists are then mass produced and given to people in Saudi Arabia, Yemen, and elsewhere. By doing so, young men and women are told about the benefits of terrorism. In one case, a 16-year-old terrorist apprehended in Israel said, "A river of honey, a river of wine, and 72 virgins. Since I have been studying the Quran, I know about the sweet life that waits me there" (Daraghmeh 2004, 27a).

4.3.2 Recruiting

Terrorists also attempt to recruit new members (Combs 2000). They may seek out other individuals or groups that have similar ideologies (e.g., anti-government groups, anti-American groups). For this purpose, the terrorists may use well developed Web sites to share their views with others. In different cases, terrorists seek out students at universities who often have idealistic views of the world. Such people are sought since they are aware of the world's problems, have specific technical knowledge sets, and desire change. Military personnel are also in high demand because they have understanding of how to use weapons or manufacture explosives. Crooked law enforcement officers are other ideal terrorists, especially if they help the terrorists to operate with impunity.

Terrorists may also be recruited at prisons. One New York correctional official said that "our prisons are stuffed full of people who have a hatred of the prison administration, a hatred towards America and have nothing but time to seethe about it" (Associated Press 2002). An example is Jose Padilla (a.k.a. Abdullah Al-Muhajir). Padilla was thrown in jail after pulling a gun on another driver in the United States. Padilla then converted to Islam while in prison and traveled to Afghanistan and Pakistan in late 1990s. He was arrested in May 2002 for conspiring to kill American's abroad.

Research suggests that some of those who are recruited into terrorist organizations often join to fill unmet emotional needs (Gerwehr and Daly 2006, 85). It has been illustrated that individuals who adhere to terrorist ideology are dissatisfied, disillusioned, and lack strong family ties. Before recruitment, they often have no value system, but desire clarity of purpose instead of ambiguity.

Once the terrorists are recruited, they are then interrogated extensively to ensure their loyalty. Terrorists are asked questions such as: What brought you to Afghanistan? How did you hear about us? What attracted you to the cause? How did you travel here? What is your educational or professional background? These inquiries not only help filter out spies, but they also determine the usefulness of new recruits.

4.3.3 Financing

Terrorist groups also seek to obtain financial resources to support their activities (Emerson 2006). At times, terrorist organizations may appear to resemble large corporations. Cindy Combs has researched this issue and she concludes that terrorism is a "big business" (2000). Two groups seem to illustrate her point very well.

One such organization is Irish Northern Aid (NORAID), which was established by Michael Flannery in 1969. This organization had headquarters in the Bronx (New York City) at 273rd East and 194th Street. Its goal was to assist the Irish Republican Army through fundraising. On several occasions it sponsored dinners, thereby raising between $20,000–30,000 in cities around the United States. James Adams, one expert on terrorism, asserts that "[f]rom the onset of modern terrorism in Northern Ireland in 1969, the United States has played a key role in its support. The enormous Irish-American population has always felt a strong sentimental attachment to the 'old country,' and this has been translated into a steady stream of cash and guns to the IRA, which has, in part, enabled them to survive" (in Combs 2000, 95).

Another example is the Palestinian Liberation Organization (PLO). Its office is in Damascus, where it has a bank of computers and accountants and other employees from MIT and Harvard. Much of its funds were acquired through dairy and poultry farms as well as cattle ranches or duty-free stores in airports. The PLO has invested in stocks on Wall Street. Money acquired from these transactions is stored in bank accounts in Switzerland and Germany, or passed through the Arab Bank for Economic Development. Combs asserts that this organization would be on the Fortune 500 list if it were a company (2000, 90). In 1993, it was worth an estimated $8–$10 billion. According to a National Criminal Intelligence Service report Terrorists may also obtain money from their involvement in the drug trade. There is historically a close connection between terrorism and narcotics. In fact, the word assassin comes from Arabic term *hashashin*—one who eats or is addicted to hashish (Combs 2000, 18). This term is in reference to the recipients of drugs from Muslim leaders in exchange for terrorist acts against the crusaders. Marco Polo noted this behavior in his travels to the Middle East. The close relation of drugs to terrorism has continued throughout history.

During the 1980s, it was reported that "Lebanese hashish helps to pay for everything from hijacking and bombing spectaculars in Europe and the Middle East to a simmering revolt by Muslim insurgents in the Philippines" (U.S. News and World Report 1987, 36–37). More recently, Al Qaeda operatives were caught with drugs in the Persian Gulf. In December 2003, United States investigators found 54 bags of hashish weighing 70 pounds each. Al Qaeda also sells opium to finance their terrorist operations. In another situation, 600 kilos of heroin were traded to buy stinger missiles in a case that included suspects from Chicago and New York. The Sendero Luminoso is a Peruvian terrorist organization that makes money from cocaine production. As these examples attest, narcoterrorism is described by *U.S. News and World Report* as "the unholiest of alliances, a malevolent marriage between two of the most feared and destructive forces on modern society—terror and drugs" (1987).

Money for terrorism may also come from other illegal activities. The Red Army Faction in Germany robbed banks and automobiles. In the United States, Ahmed Ressam (the LAX bomber) stole the chemicals that were used in his explosives. Al Qaeda has relied on African clans' production of conflict diamonds to raise money. These gemstones are also used to buy weapons for terrorists in Liberia. Child trafficking supports Jamah Islamia and Abu Sayef. Corrupt charities, such as the Haramain Islamic Foundation, are used to support terrorism. Counterfeiting of perfume, software, and music CDs has also been undertaken to raise money. Cigarette smuggling (from states with low taxes/prices to states with higher taxes/prices) resulted in $8 million in profits for terrorists. Nearly $100,000 of this was sent to Hezbollah to purchase stun guns, night vision equipment, and other devices (Emerson 2006, 217).

Terrorists may also get their financial resources from individuals or governments. Osama bin Laden received a large inheritance from his father. He also owned several construction companies. A significant proportion of Al Qaeda's operating budget (perhaps up to $30 million annually) came from bin Laden, and he used some of this to pay off the Taliban government for safe harbor. Shoko Asa Hara, a terrorist in Japan, also played a large financing role for his organization. Aum Shinrikyo was able to acquire money from the sale of books and computers. In other cases, states have sponsored terrorism. During the 1980s, Libya frequently provided terrorists with monetary resources. Terrorists therefore seem to be able to raise or acquire significant amounts of funds for their operations.

4.3.4 Training

Terrorists seek to educate themselves and others about their deadly craft. In 1986, there was an international terrorist congress in Germany. Five hundred people attended, including terrorists from France, Ireland, Portugal,

Spain, and Latin America (Combs 2000, 89). There have also been conferences in the United States. One event was in 1990 in Dallas, Texas. It is reported to have hosted more radical Muslims under one roof than any other event in history (Reeve 2002, 224). Such events reiterate the need that terrorists have to bring in attendees to discuss the best methods for accomplishing their goals through violence.

Training camps are also favored by terrorists. There have been terrorist training camps in Cuba, Bulgaria, Czechoslovakia, East Germany, Lebanon, Libya, North Korea, South Korea, and Syria. The Mes Aynak training camp is located in an abandoned copper mine in Afghanistan. At secluded locations such as this, terrorists may participate in advanced commando courses. They may be taught how to raise money, recruit others, gather tactical information, disguise themselves, travel discretely, fit into a foreign culture, read maps, and understand cryptology. At other training locations, they may be taught to speak English or German and be introduced to weapons manufacturing. Some training facilities help terrorists use knives by butchering sheep or implement gas attacks on dogs.

In many of these training camps, terrorists will be given kits, manuals, or literature to educate them further (Griset and Mahan 2003, 196). Documents found at training camps include sections on how to acquire and make chemical explosives as well as the best location to place charge on bridges and overpasses. An Al Qaeda manual that was obtained illustrates how terrorists may enter the United States through Canada. It also suggested that terrorists avoid hanging out at radical mosques, use cash only for expenditures, and rely on public Internet access to send emails. Terrorists are also advised in manuals to use pay phones to communicate or throw away cells phones once they are used. The materials collected from Ramzi Yousef (a mastermind in the 1993 World Trade Center bombing) included bomb making instructions, false identification documents, videos denouncing the US, and guidance for terrorist operations.

4.3.5 False Documents, Travel, and Safe Haven

Terrorists often seek to obtain fraudulent documents, they travel frequently, and they seek protection among sympathizers (9/11 Commission, 2004). For instance, Al Qaeda had an office in the Kandahar airport. Personnel in this facility helped some of its members obtain Yemeni passports. They were able to substitute photos and add or erase entry stamps. Terrorists can also submit false paperwork in an attempt to acquire visas. Mohammed Atta told U.S. officials that he lost his old passport. Because he was worried about visa stamps from Pakistan, he ordered a new passport. This allowed him to enter the United States with ease prior to 9/11.

As terrorists go about their activities, they travel frequently. Khalid Sheikh Mohammed (another person who knew about the 9/11 attacks) visited

India, Indonesia, and Malaysia. Other terrorists have been known to journey between Afghanistan and the United States. Terrorists have also traveled through Iran, which neglected to stamp passports. As terrorists travel, they will seek safe haven. Both Sudan and Afghanistan provided sanctuary bases for Osama bin Laden. Weak countries with remote areas are attractive to terrorist organizations because of the protection they provide. When terrorists enter enemy territory, they are picked up by associates and taken to homes or apartments where food, shelter, and other necessities of life can be met.

4.3.6 Code Words and Secret Communications

In order to avoid detection, terrorists are very cautious about their communications. When discussing the timing to pick up bomb, one terrorist told his colleague that they were in the "ninth month of pregnancy." In another situation, a bin Laden supporter in Yemen said his impending "marriage" would be a "surprise." This was in reference to an attack that was being planned. However, leaders do not always tell terrorists everything about operations. For instance, bin Laden wanted to limit the information implementors possessed in case they were caught. Terrorists may also use the Internet to communicate. In March 2001, Al Qaeda used hidden script on Web pages. Known as steganography, this technique allows terrorists to hide maps, photos, and letters in chat rooms or pornographic sites. Louis Freeh, former director of the FBI, says "uncrackable encryption is allowing terrorists—Hamas, Hazbollah, Al-Qaeda and others—to communicate about their criminal intentions without fear of outside intrusion" (Thetford 2001, 252).

4.3.7 Planning

Terrorists spend a great deal of time planning attacks (9/11 Commission 2003). In researching possible targets, terrorists may rely on the Internet and open-source records (e.g., library or government documents), insider information (e.g., knowledge from employees), electronic equipment (e.g., police scanners or phone taps), or physical surveillance (e.g., casing a location) (Pluchinsky 2006).

Terrorists are therefore meticulous planners. In 1994, Khalid Sheikh Mohammed designed the Manila air plot. He and other terrorists intended to bomb 12 U.S. jets over the Pacific Ocean during a two-day span. They started casing flights and purchased timers and nitrocellulose to make bombs. Fortunately, the Philippine government discovered the plot and was able to thwart it.

Terrorists involved in the embassy bombings in Africa in 1998 used state of the art video cameras for reconnaissance purposes. They obtained

Figure 4-3

Terrorists spend a lot of time planning attacks, as was the case in the twin African Embassy bombings.

this equipment from dealers in China and Germany. The terrorists were interested in traffic patterns, building construction, and occupancy rates to inflict maximum casualties. The 9/11 plot was discussed seven or eight years before it actually occurred. It was initially supposed to have about 10 planes, but was scaled back to due to complexity. Nevertheless, the terrorists involved in the 9/11 attacks cased flights to determine the best time to hijack the planes. They also went to flight school in the United States so they could maneuver the aircraft.

An important function of planning is to find a symbolic date or location for when and where terrorist attacks should take place (Martin 2003). For example, the 1995 bombing of the Murrah Federal Building in Oklahoma City took place on the anniversary of disturbing events in Waco, Texas. In this case, Timothy McVeigh chose this date because he was frustrated with the way the ATF and FBI dealt with the Branch Davidians. The targets on 9/11 were not selected by chance. Their airlines—American Airlines and United Airlines—had reference to America and the United States. The World Trade Center was also the heart of Western capitalist economy and the Pentagon signified the strength of the U.S. military. Although Flight 93 never arrived at its intended location, many believe it was headed for the White House or the Capitol Building (the political leadership of the country). Meticulous planning and choice of targets by terrorists adds to death tolls, damage, and social disruption.

4.3.8 Obtaining Weapons

Sometime before, during, or after terrorists plan attacks they will also acquire weapons (Martin 2003). These may range from simple devices to advanced military armaments. Such weapons may impact one or a few people, or even hundreds and thousands. For instance, mace, pepper spray, box cutters, or small knives were used on some of the passengers and crew on 9/11. In other cases, terrorists obtain and use pistols and light artillery. Guns and rocket propelled grenades are also commonly used by terrorists. Incendiary devices (e.g., Molotov cocktails that start fires) are used when destruction of property is desired.

Terrorists have been increasingly interested in weapons of mass destruction **(WMDs)**, which will be discussed in depth later on in the book. Common acronyms for WMDs are NBC or CBRNE. **NBC** stands for nuclear, biological, and chemical weapons. CBRNE is currently a more recognized acronym because it is more comprehensive. **CBRNE** stands for chemical, biological, radiological, nuclear, or explosive devices. Some weapons of mass destruction may include typical household cleaning agents that have been mixed into hazardous or unstable combinations.

Terrorists may also try to find military weapons such as mustard gas or nerve agents. It is reported that the Japanese terrorists, Shoka Asa Hara, spent an estimated $30 million to make anthrax. Biological agents include pathogens, toxins, or viruses. Larry Wayne Harris, a member of the Aryan Nation, tried to acquire this type of weapon in 1995. He was arrested in Arizona and was caught with plague in a container in the glove box of his car. Radiological weapons are devices that contain and emit alpha, beta, or gamma emitting material. Radiological material has been lost at a number of industrial or medical facilities, and terrorists are believed to be associated with some of these reports. A nuclear weapon is far different than a radiological weapon. Nuclear weapons are large bombs created by fusion or fusion processes. They can decimate entire cities. It is reported that bin Laden was working with a Sudanese military officer to purchase weapons grade uranium. Explosive devices are bombs. Improvised explosive devices **(IEDs)**, like pipe bombs, are increasingly sought by insurgents in Iraq. They can pierce armor and kill or maim soldiers.

WMDs:
Acronym for weapons of mass destruction.

NBC:
Acronym for nuclear, biological, and chemical weapons.

CBRNE:
Acronym for chemical, biological, radiological, nuclear, or explosive devices.

IED:
Acronym for improvised explosive device.

4.3.9 Initiating Acts of Civil Disorder or Terrorism

Once terrorists plan attacks and obtain weapons, they will then launch attacks (Pluchinsky 2006). There have been numerous cases where individuals have mailed letters with white powdery substances. These hoaxes and threats instill fear and intend to disrupt society. At other times, sabotage is preferred. This includes virus attacks through computer programs. In Oregon in 1984 the Rajneeshee cult sprayed salmonella on a salad bar at a restaurant. Seven hundred people were made ill as the group was testing its ability to influence the outcome of approaching local elections.

Terrorists also hijack planes or sea-going vessels. As everyone is aware, the 9/11 attacks, which resulted in so much destruction in New York and Virginia, began with the takeover of aircrafts. Hostage taking and kidnapping is a frequent ploy of terrorists. Some hostages are used for ransom or killed if the demands of terrorists are not met. Other victims of attacks are murdered through assassinations and ambushes. Yitzak Rabin, a Prime Minister of Israel, was shot to death. Arson is another frequent choice of terrorists, and it has been used to intimidate members of black religious congregations. Bombings are the most prevalent type of attack, however. They account for nearly 75 percent of attacks. In one case, Al Qaeda terrorists pretended to be reporters. They met with Ahmed Shah Massoud (a Northern Alliance leader in Afghanistan) and killed him with a bomb. Bombings have taken place at abortion clinics, the World Trade Center (in 1993), the Marriot hotel in Indonesia, U.S. embassies in Africa, and the USS Cole in the Middle East. Such attacks are often initiated by suicide bombers. These terrorists wear or carry explosive that they detonate around others. It may be a matter of time before these attacks occur in the United States.

While weapons of mass destruction have not been used often, terrorists did use sarin gas in an attack on the subway in Tokyo in 1995. More recently, terrorists have started using chemicals such as chlorine in their bombings in Iraq. If they survive attacks, terrorists will survey the success of their operations before fleeing the scene. After the first WTC bombing in 1993, Ramzi Yousef fled to Pakistan. He remained there for two years until he was caught by special agents from the Federal Bureau of Investigation.

IN THE REAL WORLD

Operations of the Tamil Tigers

The Tamil Tigers seek independence in North Eastern Sri Lanka. When India gained autonomy at the end of World War II, both the Sihala and Tamil ethnic groups shared political authority. In 1955, pro-Sihala policies were implemented, and the Tamils became disgruntled at their loss of power. After assassinating the Sihala leader in 1959, the Tamil Tigers emerged as a serious terrorist threat. They easily recruited members of their ethnic group to participate. Funding was obtained through bank robberies. Training camps were founded in India, and members of the organization received instructions from terrorists in the Middle East. The Tamil Tigers have built a navy to attack Indian fleets. In 1991 they killed the Indian prime minister. The Tamils prefer bombings and suicide attacks, tactics utilized to this day.

SELF-CHECK

1. Terrorists want to recruit others, but they are also careful who they allow to join with them. True or False?

2. Training does not appear to be a major priority of terrorists. True or False?

3. Terrorists:

   (a) often obtain false documents.
   (b) do not travel frequently.
   (c) spend little time planning attacks.
   (d) do not prefer explosives.

4. Why do terrorists select some targets over others?

SUMMARY

Understanding who terrorists are and how they operate is extremely important if you are to reduce prospect of terrorist attacks. In this chapter, you have assessed the nature of individual terrorists and those associated with groups and states. You have acquired information about common personality traits as well as the significant differences among terrorists. Your review of terrorist behavior has enabled you to identify how they finance operations, communicate with secret codes, and carry out attacks. Such knowledge is imperative if you are to work successfully in homeland security.

ASSESS YOUR UNDERSTANDING

UNDERSTAND: WHAT HAVE YOU LEARNED

 Go to **www.wiley.com/college/mcentire** to assess your knowledge of terrorists and their behavior.

SUMMARY QUESTIONS

1. Pick a terrorist attack not mentioned in this chapter and describe it based on the following criteria:

    (a) What was the terrorist act?

    (b) Was it performed by an individual or group?

    (c) Would the terrorist(s) be classified as a criminal, crusader, or crazy? Why?

2. Using the same terrorist attack you picked for the previous question, describe what personal characteristics the person or group involved in the act has in common with other terrorists described in this chapter. Are there differences? If so, what are they?

3. Terrorist groups often recruit new members to grow their organization and increase their influence. What groups of people do terrorists often recruit? What are some reasons why people join terrorist groups? What happens once they are recruited?

4. Why is it important for us to understand the various behaviors and tactics of terrorist groups? Using the information in the chapter, describe how we can use information on terrorist groups to help monitor and suppress terrorist activity.

5. The Japanese Red Army is a terrorist organization that supports capitalism. True or False?

6. Libya, an African country, was responsible for the bombing of Pan Am Flight 103. True or False?

7. Individuals who commit terrorist acts are sometimes referred to as lone-wolf terrorists. True or False?

8. Abu Sayef is an Islamic separatist group that wants to increase foreign involvement in the Philippines. True or False?

9. Terrorist groups may be lead by a single individual, a headquarters station, or several cells throughout the world. True or False?

10. Terrorists often see the world as a complicated place with many different interpretations of what is right and wrong. True or False?

11. Terrorists groups avoid using the Internet as a means of communication. True or False?

12. Which of the following statements does **not** accurately describe Meir Kahane?

    (a) He was a Jewish rabbi.

    (b) He founded the Jewish Defense League.

    (c) He founded the Palestinian Jihad.

    (d) He was assassinated in 1990.

13. Theodore "Ted" Kaczynski was known for his:

    (a) opposition to technology and studies in this field.

    (b) loyalty to professors and corporate leaders.

    (c) collaboration with terrorist organizations.

    (d) efforts to combat terrorist activity.

14. All of the following states have a history of involvement in sponsoring terrorism **except**:

    (a) Iran.

    (b) Syria.

    (c) Sudan.

    (d) France.

15. Left-wing groups that seek economic or political equality through terrorist acts are an example of what kind of terrorist group?

    (a) Criminals

    (b) Careless

    (c) Crusaders

    (d) Crazies

16. Terrorist groups use all of the following techniques to raise funds **except**:

    (a) drug sales and other illegal activities.

    (b) mass mail-outs to households.

    (c) using organized "big business" techniques.

    (d) funding from individuals and governments.

17. CBRNE stands for:

    (a) chemical, biological, radiological, nuclear, or explosive devices.

    (b) chemical, biological, radiological, nuclear, or expensive devices.

    (c) catastrophic, biological, radiological, nuclear, or explosive devices.

    (d) catastrophic, biological, radiological, nuclear, or expensive devices.

18. Bombings account for what percentage of terrorist attacks?

(a) 25%

(b) 50%

(c) 75%

(d) 80%

BE A HOMELAND SECURITY PROFESSIONAL

Common Terrorist Characteristics

You are an analyst with the FBI. Your boss would like you to write a report on common terrorist profiles. How could you describe terrorists? In what ways could you classify them?

Similarities and Differences Among Terrorists

Write a three-page paper about the personal characteristics of terrorists. Be sure to discuss how terrorists are similar and different. Mention why it is important to understand who terrorists are.

Looking for Terrorists

You work as a member of a terrorist task force in law enforcement in local government. Your job is to identify potential terrorists before they launch attacks. What type of behavior are you looking for? Explain at least five activities that you would want to consider.

KEY TERMS

Abu Musab al-Zarqawi	A Sunni terrorist responsible for many atrocities in Iraq, including the beheading of American businessman Nicolas Berg.
Abu Sayef	An Islamic separatist group in the Philippines that desires an independent state in Mindanao.
Al Jazeera	A TV station based in Qatar that is popular in the Middle East and used to disseminate terrorist information.

Al Qaeda	A well-known terrorist organization whose name refers to the "base"— the location from which its supporters attacked the Soviet Union to free Afghanistan.
CBRNE	Acronym for chemical, biological, radiological, nuclear, or explosive devices.
Cell	A terrorist branch or unit operating in locations away from the organization's headquarters.
Crazy	A terrorist that is regarded to be psychologically disturbed (e.g., Ted Kaczynski).
Criminal	A terrorist that seeks personal gain through illegal means (e.g., drugs or crime).
Crusader	A terrorist that promotes high moral goals (e.g., Islamic fundamentalists).
George Habash	Founder of the militant Popular Front for the Liberation of Palestine (PFLP) and a terrorist who opposes Israel. He sponsored many airline hijackings in the 1970's and 1980's.
IED	Acronym for improvised explosive device.
Iran	A state in the Middle East that denounces the United States, promotes anti-western propaganda and has a long history of participation in terrorism.
Japanese Red Army (JRA)	A left-wing terrorist organization that emerged in the 1960s to protest U.S. military presence in Japan after World War II, the war in Vietnam, and capitalism.
Libya	A country in Northern Africa that heavily supported terrorism in the 1980s.
Lone-wolf terrorists	Individual terrorists who act alone.
Madrasahs	Schools in Pakistan and elsewhere that at times indoctrinate students in extreme Islamic thought.
NBC	Acronym for nuclear, biological, and chemical weapons.
Theodore "Ted" Kaczynski	Terrorist known as the "Unabomber" who opposed technological advances.
WMDs	Acronym for weapons of mass destruction.

REFERENCES

9/11 Commission. (2003). *The 9/11 Commission Report: Final Report of the National Commission on Terrorist Attacks Upon the United States.* W.W. Norton and Company: New York.

Associated Press. (2002). "Prisons are Breeding Ground for Terrorists." *Fox News*. Wednesday, June 12. www.foxnews.com/story/0,2933,55068,00.html

Combs, Cindy C. (2000). *Terrorism in the Twenty-First Century*. Prentice Hall: New Jersey.

Daraghmeh, Ali. (2004). "Family: Teen Exploited for Bomb Mission." *Dallas Morning News*. Friday, March 26, 27a.

Gerwehr, Scott and Sara Daly. (2006). "Al Qaida: Terrorist Selection and Recruitment." Pp. 73–89 in Kamien, David G. (Ed.) *The McGraw-Hill Homeland Security Handbook*. McGraw-Hill: New York.

Griset, Pamala L., and Sue Mahan. (2003). *Terrorism in Perspective*. Sage: Thousand Oaks, CA.

Hacker, Frederick J. (1976). *Crusaders, Criminals, Crazies: Terror and Terrorism in Our Time*. Norton: New York.

Martin, Gus. (2003). *Understanding Terrorism: Challenges, Perspective, and Issues*. Sage: Thousand Oaks, CA.

O'Balance, Edgar O. (1979). *The Language of Violence: The Blood Politics of Terrorism*. Presidio: San Rafael, CA.

Pluchinsky, Dennis A. (2006). "A Typology and Anatomy of Terrorist Operations." 365–390 in Kamien, David G. (Ed.) *The McGraw-Hill Homeland Security Handbook*. McGraw-Hill: New York.

Reeve, Simon. (2002). *The New Jackals: Ramzi, Yousef, Osama bin Laden, and the Future of Terrorism*. Northeastern University Press: Lebanon, NH.

Taylor, Rex. (1958). *Michael Collins*. Hutchinson: London.

Thetford, Robert T. (2001). "The Challenge of Cyberterrorism." Pp. 239–257 in Hogan, Lawrence J. (Ed.). *Terrorism: Defensive Strategies for Individuals, Companies and Governments*. Amlex, Inc.: Frederick, Maryland.

U.S. News and World Report. (1987). "Narcotics: Terror's New Ally." May 4. 36–37.

White, Jonathan. (2002). *Terrorism: An Introduction*. Wadsworth: Belmont, CA.

5

UNCOVERING THE DYNAMIC NATURE OF TERRORISM

History and Change over Time

Do You Already Know?

- The early history of terrorism
- How terrorism has evolved in other countries
- How terrorist affacks have affected the United States
- The differences between traditional and modern terrorism

 For additional questions to assess your current knowledge of the dynamic nature of terrorism, go to **www.wiley.com/college/mcentire**

What You Will Find Out	What You Will Be Able To Do
5.1 The early history of terrorism	• Synthesize the factors influencing the appearance of terrorism
5.2 The manifestation of terrorism in other countries	• Assess the evolution of terrorism in other countries
5.3 The experience of terrorism in the United States	• Evaluate the impact of terrorism in the United States
5.4 The differences between traditional and modern terrorism	• Judge how terrorism has changed over time

INTRODUCTION

One of the best ways to decrease the chances and consequences of terrorism is to understand how it has evolved over time. Terrorism has probably always existed in one form or another, but it has changed throughout history. In this chapter, you will learn how the use of violence, fear, and philosophy has impacted the emergence of terrorism. You will also acquire an understanding of the dynamic nature of terrorism around the world and be able to describe the history of terrorism in the United States. Finally, this chapter will help you defend the assertion that terrorism is different today than it was in prior decades. Understanding the dynamic nature of terrorism is imperative for anyone working in homeland security. Recognizing how terrorism has changed over time may help you to anticipate what to expect in the future.

5.1 THE APPEARANCE OF TERRORISM

Violence with an eye toward creating fear among an enemy has occurred repeatedly throughout history. The examples of warriors painting their faces, brandishing weapons, and yelling loudly at their opponents are too numerous to mention. In such cases, this activity could be regarded as effort to dissuade the violent intent of the adversary. Averting conflict was the goal of engaging in such behavior. If hostilities did break out, ruthlessness was made painfully evident to illustrate the consequences of combating the victor. Those from the opposing tribe were killed, and their lifeless bodies were displayed visibly for everyone to see. For instance, bodies were hung from trees and skulls placed on poles. In addition, homes were burned, property and cattle were taken, women were raped, and children were enslaved. This was a vivid message regarding the strength of the prevailing party. In this sense, the fear associated with war is somewhat similar to that associated with terrorism. However, the two cannot be considered synonymous.

Violent activities undertaken with the goal of obtaining ideological objectives—which is an integral aspect of terrorism—can be traced back to at least the philosophers of the Roman and Greek republics (Combs 2000, 18). Aristotle was a famous Greek philosopher who lived from 384 to 322 B.C. He asserted that killing despotic rulers could be completely justified. If such leaders failed to serve the interests of the people, they should be eliminated. Others felt similarly. For example, when Brutus killed Roman emperor Julius Caesar, Cicero observed "there can be no such thing as fellowship with tyrants, nothing but a bitter feud is possible . . . [Such] monsters . . . should be severed from the common body of humanity" (in Griset and Mahen 2003, 2). Thus, from ancient times, people have rationalized terrorism based on their perception of the actions of others, suggesting that it is "just" and necessary.

Gunpowder Plot:
An attempted terrorist attack in 1605 against King James I and other leaders of Parliament to reinstate Catholic involvement in England.

In addition, assassinations of political leaders, as the previous paragraph indicates, have been a prevalent form of terrorism throughout history. For example, in 1605, Guy Fawkes was caught in an attempt to murder King James I and other leaders of the British Parliament (Griset and Mahan 2003). The cause of his **"Gunpowder Plot"** was a disagreement between the King Henry VIII and Pope Clement VII. King Henry desired an annulment of his marriage to Catherine in order to wed Anne Boleyn. Because the Pope did not grant this request, King Henry denounced Catholicism and created the Church of England. Monasteries were closed and cathedrals were taken over by those loyal to the king. Catholics were suppressed in England and lost their ability to worship as they saw fit.

Fawkes and others were angry with these circumstances. They desired to reinstall the Pope as the religious head of England by blowing up the Palace of Westminster. When the king was notified of the scheme, Fawkes was immediately captured. He and the other conspirators were drawn and quartered by galloping horses in front of the public gathered at Westminster.

Enlightenment:
A period in history when a new way of looking at social, political, and economic structures emerged.

While Fawkes' attempt to kill the king may be regarded as an act of terrorism, the word "terrorism" did not appear until the Enlightenment. The **Enlightenment** was a period in history when a new way of looking at the world emerged. For instance, advances in scientific knowledge offered an alternative to the religious explanations of nature in that period. Improvements in communications and travel increased the sharing of ideas within and across nations. As these and other changes took place, the divine appointment of kings was subsequently questioned. Common people began to demand political rights and freedoms. Democratic governments began to emerge as a result. The feudal economic system gave way to capitalism. Sociopolitical structures were altered. This transformation is evidenced by such events as the independence movement in the United States (1775–1783) and the French Revolution (1789–1795).

The revolutionary war in North America resulted from the questioning of the religious authority of the King as well as taxation without representation. It was successful in that it only required a transfer of power from the King in England to the elite in America. In contrast, the ambitions in France were loftier in that middle classes desired to oust reigning nobility. However, those seeking "liberty, equality, and fraternity" could not accomplish their goals. The Jacobin party acquired control of France and began to repel the revolutionary movement. During this period, an estimated 20,000 persons were killed by France's Committee of Public Safety. The state sponsored violence against its own citizens is what Edmond Burke and others called the **"Reign of Terror."** Marie Antoinette was one of the most notable casualties in this conflict. She was beheaded on October 16, 1793.

Reign of Terror:
A period during the French Revolution where an estimated 20,000 persons were killed by France's Committee of Public Safety.

SELF-CHECK

1. In many ways, violence, fear, and terrorism have always existed. True or False?

2. When did the word "terrorism" appear?
   (a) During Aristotle's time
   (b) In medieval times
   (c) During the enlightenment
   (d) Long after the American revolutionary war

3. Discuss why Guy Fawkes wanted to kill King James I.

5.2 THE EVOLUTION OF TERRORISM ABROAD

Terrorism has changed dramatically since the enlightenment. The history of terrorism is not simple or linear. Instead, the evolution of terrorism is complex, and numerous manifestations of violent activity have coexisted at times. However, this history is best understood when considered as an unfolding transformation.

Terrorism took on distinct forms as the nineteenth century got underway. In the late 1700s, Napoleon Bonaparte gained control of France and then began to spread his empire to the rest of Europe. His armies were well trained, staffed, and equipped. Nevertheless, the Spanish attempted to repel Napoleon's invasions in 1808. Hit-and-run tactics were common in this war for liberation. Spanish resistance was aided by the support of the British military. **Nationalist movements** like this have been common in many parts of the world. They have led to numerous terrorist acts in the Middle East, Ireland, and India. These types of terrorist attacks have had significant impacts. For instance, World War I was triggered on June 28, 1914. A nineteen-year-old member of the Black Hand (a Serbian terrorist organization) opposed the Austro-Hungarian Empire. He was therefore recruited to assassinate the Archduke Franz Ferdinand. Terrorism with nationalistic overtones has been evident in many countries ever since. This includes the countless and cruel acts in the Balkan region (i.e., Yugoslavia) and in African nations (e.g., Rwanda) during the 1990s.

Anarchists—those opposing specific governments or all governments—also launched numerous terrorist attacks in the 1800s. In Russia, men like Michail Bakunin sought to dismantle the czarist state. He and others disapproved of the government and desired a major transformation of society. As a means to accomplish his goal, he advocated the selective killing of Russian officials. Sergei Nachaev, another Russian, also recommended that terrorism be used in his publication, *Revolutionary Catechism*.

Nationalist movements:
Efforts on the part of a group or nation to obtain political independence and autonomy.

Anarchists:
Those opposing specific governments or all governments.

He stated that the anarchist must "have one single thought, one single purpose: merciless destruction. With this aim in view, tirelessly and in cold blood, he must always be prepared to kill with his own hands anyone who stands in the way of achieving his goals" (Venturi 1966, 366). In 1879, Zemiya I Volva (a terrorist organization known as the Will of the People) was created in Russia. This group used terrorism often as a form of political protest against the ruling elite (Combs 2000, 25).

Fascism:
An ideology which promotes the uniting of citizens in support of the state.

In the early and mid 1900s, fascist governments were involved in terrorist attacks against their own citizens. **Fascism** is an ideology which promotes the uniting of citizens in support of the state. It is a right wing movement aimed at protecting government interests. Fascist regimes existed in Spain under Francisco Franco and Italy under Benito Mussolini. Of course, the most egregious use of force against the populous occurred in Germany. Adolf Hitler killed an estimated six million Jews during the Holocaust. Others, including the Aryan Nations today, have been influenced by Hitler's hatred toward those of Jewish descent.

Communism:
An ideology that sympathizes with the poor and downtrodden, and attempts to do away with private property.

In the mid to late 1900s, **communism** was a driving force of terrorism. Communism is an ideology that sympathizes with the poor and down trodden. It attempts to do away with private property and exploitative class relations. Communists have commonly been involved in terrorism in Latin America. During the Cold War, the United States supported many military dictators in an attempt to halt Russian political influence in the area. As a result, many peasants and intellectuals began to attack the governments they saw as illegitimate in the 1960s, 1970s, and 1980s.

One example was from Maximo Hernández in El Salvador. He ruled with an iron fist and persecuted anyone suspected of having ties with Russia. In some cases, he forced alleged communists to dig ditches which were then filled when they were executed. A few historians assert that the U.S. Marines were stationed offshore in case their assistance in the effort was needed. One of the prominent leftists of the time, Farabundo Marti, was put to death during the purge known as the Matanza (the killing). This resulted in the creation of the Farabundo Martí Liberation Front. The FMLF was involved in guerilla-type activities in El Salvador until a peace accord was signed with the government in 1992.

There have been many other terrorist organizations that have fought for economic justice including the Zapatisa National Liberation Army in Mexico and the Rebel Armed Forces in Guatemala. The Morazanist Patriotic Front, Sandinistas, Revolutionary Armed Forces were other left-wing terrorist organizations in Honduras, Nicaragua, and Colombia respectively. Bolivia, Chile, Uruguay, Argentina, and Brazil have also witnessed many terrorist attacks in the name of communism. The Shining Path and Tupac Amaru Revolutionary Movement (TARM) have similar ideologies in Peru. They desire to rid their country of outside imperial influence. TARM was responsible for the assassination of General Enrique López Albújar.

In the 1970s and 1980s, state-sponsored terrorism was common in the Middle East (Combs 2000). For instance, Syria provided help for the Marine barracks bombing in 1983. It supported terrorists who delivered a truck bomb against U.S. forces in Lebanon, killing 241 soldiers. This nation was also involved in bombings in France and plane hijackings. It has frequently provided training and safe haven for terrorists operating in the area. In addition to Syria, Sudan has supported many terrorist groups. In the 1990s, it was the home of Osama bin Laden and his followers. Because of international pressure, however, Al Qaeda was asked to leave and this terrorist organization took up residence in Afghanistan. The Taliban, the ruling government in Afghanistan, allowed bin Laden to use the country as a terrorist headquarter. In return, bin Laden paid these leaders to permit their presence and operation in this country. Terrorists have often benefited from states that support their ideological objectives. Both terrorists and states in the Middle East oppose Israel and the United States for political and religious reasons.

Islamic fundamentalists: Individuals or groups of Muslims that violently oppose Israel and the United States.

Today, it is widely believed that the major threat of international terrorism comes from radical **Islamic fundamentalists**. Israel has been dealing with such violence for decades, but the groups opposing the Jews and the United States have been growing in number, political strength, and operational sophistication. Russia has also been dealing with attacks from similar groups who desire independence in Chechnya. There are many other Islamic fundamentalist organizations throughout the Middle East, Europe, and in nations such as the Philippines and Indonesia. Arab and Muslim extremists are now viewed as the most dangerous terrorists because of events like 9/11, the bombing of trains in Spain in 2004, and the attacks on buses and subways in England in 2005. Such extremists appear to have no reservations about dying as martyrs for their cause.

This brief history of terrorism abroad generates at least two lessons for those involved in homeland security. First, terrorism has been manifested in different ways over time. On some occasions, citizens rose up against governments. There have been countless cases where political leaders have been assassinated by those who have felt mistreated. Later on, states engaged in terrorism against their own people. Russia has a deplorable history of state sponsored terrorism. So does Cambodia. It is believed that Pol Pot (the leader of the Khmer Rouge in Cambodia) killed as many as two million people from 1975 to 1978. He accomplished this through executions, starvation, and the grueling conditions of forced labor (Simensen and Spindlove 2000, 227). Terrorism has also been related to nationalistic and communistic movements. States have sponsored terrorist groups over time, and a major threat today emanates from radical Islamic fundamentalists around the world.

A second point to be recognized is that terrorism often breeds violent counter-terrorism activity. Terrorism in France, Spain, Russia, Latin America, and other parts of the world has often resulted in long-standing conflicts among those promoting and opposing terrorism. For instance, the civil war in El Salvador lasted from 1980 to 1992. It resulted in the death of 75,000 people and displaced millions. The perception that violence is an effective solution to ideological disagreements cannot always be supported with evidence. In most cases, it has only brought more problems to those seeking a better way of life. Terrorism creates a vicious cycle of violence (Combs 2000, 24).

IN THE REAL WORLD

Chechen Terrorism in Russia

When the Soviet Union disintegrated at the end of the Cold War, pent-up ethnic tensions and rivalries began to emerge. Many Chechens disliked Russian involvement in the political decisions that affected them and desired increased independence. In addition, Chechens share greater affinity for Islamic tradition than do their Russian counterparts, and this has been a notable source of conflict among the two groups. Because of continued presence and influence of Russia over the affairs of this nation, Chechens have launched numerous terrorist attacks against them. On August 24, 2004, two passenger aircraft departing from Moscow were blown up in coordinated terrorist attacks. The explosive hexogen was used to bring down the planes. The bombing resulted in the death of 89 passengers and crew members. It is believed that two females from the Islambouli Brigades and a Chechen field commander were responsible for the attack.

SELF-CHECK

1. World War I was initiated in part due to a terrorist attack. True or False?

2. Which ideology was not involved in the early development of terrorism?

   (a) National liberation
   (b) Anarchism
   (c) Environmentalism
   (d) Communism

3. What are some of the major lessons we learn from terrorism in other nations?

5.3 TERRORISM AND THE UNITED STATES

It is imperative that those involved in homeland security realize that terrorism is not just a foreign problem. Certain historians believe that United States citizens and its government have participated in terrorism. For instance, it is asserted that the war tactics used against the British during the American Revolution bear close relation to those of terrorists. Others suggest that the U.S. government sponsored terrorism abroad while it fought communism during the Cold War. It is alleged that the United States spent $7 million dollars to finance opposition groups to destabilize the leftist government in Chile. The CIA is even reported to have been involved—directly or indirectly—in an attack on Rene Schneider, a commander of the Chilean Army. Evidence also suggests that the United States tried to assassinate Fidel Castro from 1961 to 1962. **Operation Mongoose**, as it was known, involved an attempt to kill the Cuban leader with a poisoned cigar. In another case, it is believed that the United States tried to hire Castro's former girlfriend to kill him. This plot was also unsuccessful. Politicians at the time claimed that Castro was threatening the security of the United States. Cuba had close ties to the Soviet Union and Castro accepted the placement of Russian missiles in this Caribbean nation. Others scholars argue that the United States was not engaged in terrorism, but violence for geo-political purposes. This case reiterates that it is not always easy to define what terrorism is.

Operation Mongoose:
An attempt by the United States to kill Cuban leader Fidel Castro with a poisoned cigar.

Although the United States may or may not have been involved in terrorism as a participant, it has definitely been the target of terrorism throughout its history. For instance, the **Molly Maguires** were one of the many organizations involved in terrorism in this country after it was founded. The Mollies, as the organization was commonly known, was a group of citizens that joined together in Ireland to dispute the treatment of tenants by landlords. At times, their protests were violent in nature. In the early 1800s, many members of this group migrated to the United States and settled in Pennsylvania. Feeling that they were being treated unfairly in the coal mines of this area, they began to engage in acts of violence. They killed many of the mine superintendents in protest. The situation became so bad in the 1870s that Franklin Gown, president of the Philadelphia and Reading Railroad, told detectives that they were "to remain in the field until every cut-throat has paid with his life for the lives so cruelly taken" (Lejeune 2001, 208). Nineteen members of the Molly Maguires were therefore killed in the late 1800s.

Molly Maguires:
A group of Irish citizens that joined together to dispute the treatment of coal mine workers in the United States.

Disputes over workers rights and compensation also led to other terrorists acts in large cities across the United States (Lejeune 2001, 208). In 1886, labor unions requested an eight-hour work day. They felt the existing and strenuous work hours were unreasonable. As strikes and picketing took place in Chicago, skirmishes broke out among police and rioters. One person was shot and killed in the riot. A few days later, a protest was held to denounce the death. When police tried to disperse the crowed, a bomb was detonated. Eight police officers died in the blast. Bombs were also set off elsewhere to protest political and economic issues. On September 16, 1920, in New York City, a horse drawn carriage was taken near J. P. Morgan's building on Wall Street. Its deadly cargo resulted in thirty-five people being killed and hundreds more injured. The perpetrators, who were believed to have Bolshevist or anarchist leanings, were never apprehended.

Ku Klux Klan (KKK):
A white supremacist group that has been involved in terrorism in the United States since the Civil War.

The **Ku Klux Klan (KKK)**, a white supremacist group, has also been involved in terrorism in the United States. The Ku Klux Klan emerged after the Civil War era (Simonsen and Spindlove 2000, 40). Six Confederate veterans were talking around a fireplace one night in Tennessee in the late 1800s and decided to create a secret society. After coming to agreement on a name to represent the group, they disguised themselves in sheets and rode through the town on horseback. The regalia they wore had gained so much attention that the KKK adopted white hooded clothing as a symbol of the organization. In time, more people joined, and the KKK began to threaten blacks. This behavior was particularly evident in the early and mid-1990s. Hate speech soon turned to terrorism, and the KKK was involved in "hanging, acid branding, tar-and-feathering, torture, shooting, stabbing, clubbing, firebranding, castration and other forms of mutilation" (Simonsen and Spindlove 2003, 41–42). Thousands of African Americans have been killed or attacked by members of the KKK. Fortunately, such activities have waned dramatically in recent years. But this type of activity has yet to be eliminated. Current Neo-Nazi groups also share much of the KKK ideology. They desire to establish a white controlled government in the United States.

Figure 5-1

The United States has had to deal with terrorist organizations. Members of the Church of the American Knights of the Ku Klux Klan march around the Madison County Courthouse in Canton, Mississippi, Saturday, May 29, 1999.

During the 1950s, 1960s, and 1970s, terrorists in the United States also came from the political left. They identified with Marxist class struggles or desired equal rights. These terrorists planted bombs in public areas, police stations, and military bases (Griset and Mahan 2003, 87). Some groups during this time protested the Vietnam War. Others, like the Symbionese Liberation Army (SLA), had utopian visions for society. They desired a unified populous based on cooperative economic institutions. The SLA was responsible for several bank robberies, kidnappings, and assassinations. The **Black Panthers**, in contrast, sought revenge for the mistreatment of African Americans by the KKK. Their activities have become less notable over time, although there was a resurgence of violence at the end of the twentieth century.

Black Panthers:
An organization comprised of African Americans to revenge the actions of the KKK and other white supremacists.

In the 1970s and early 1980s, much of the terrorist activity in the United States came from Puerto Rican terrorists. The **Armed Forces of National Liberation (FALN)** emerged in 1974. Their goal was to obtain liberation of Puerto Rico and they were willing to utilize violent means if necessary. The FALN was responsible for at least 100 bombings in the United States in the mid- to late 1970s. Since that time, many other Puerto Rican groups were formed and have launched attacks against the United States. "Between 1982 and 1994, approximately 44 percent of terrorist incident committed in the United States and its territories are attributed to Puerto Rican terrorist groups" (Lejeune 2001, 211).

Armed Forces of National Liberation (FALN):
A Puerto Rican terrorist organization seeking liberation of Puerto Rico from the United States.

In the 1980s and 1990s, terrorism was associated with many different advocacy issues. Some right-wing terrorist organizations opposed the government. They disliked taxes as well as United States' involvement in the United Nations. Other conservative groups wanted to protect rights to own firearms, or they opposed Jews and homosexuals. People like Eric Rudolph have also been involved in terrorism to stop abortions. Rudolph bombed abortion clinics and Olympic Park in Atlanta during the 1996 summer games. Numerous people were killed or injured as a result. There are also terrorists who used violence in the 1990s to promote animal rights or environmental conservation. For instance, terrorists have attacked research facilities that conduct tests on animals. They are concerned about cruel procedures in meat packing facilities as well. The **Animal Liberation Front** was founded in 1976 and is a terrorist organization that opposes cruelty to animals. The **Earth Liberation Front**, founded in 1992, is a terrorist organization that opposes environmental degradation.

Animal Liberation Front:
A terrorist organization that opposes cruelty to animals.

Earth Liberation Front
A terrorist organization that opposes environmental degradation.

Auto dealers have consequently been targets of arson and bombings because of the low gas mileage of their trucks and SUVs. New neighborhood developments have likewise been vandalized or set ablaze to discourage the destruction of forests (for wood) or the expansion of urban sprawl. "Earth Now, one militant environmental group in the United States, rationalized that if it was necessary to kill people to save the trees, then they would be justified in killing people" (Combs 2000, 43).

All of these cases illustrate that the United States has been affected by terrorism long before the first World Trade Center attack in 1993, the bombing of the Murrah Federal Building in 1995, or the 9/11 attacks in 2001. It is also evident that terrorists in the United States come from diverse ideological interests as well. These facts illustrate the complicated nature of terrorism today.

SELF-CHECK

1. The United States is not believed to have been involved in terrorism. True or False?

2. The Black Panthers may have emerged due to the activities of the KKK. True or False?

3. Which terrorist organization emerged due to concerns over workers' rights?

    (a) Molly Maguires

    (b) The KKK

    (c) The Armed Forces of National Liberation

    (d) Animal Liberation Front

4. Explain how terrorism has manifested itself in different ways over time in the United States.

5.4 TERRORISM TODAY

Another important requisite for dealing effectively with terrorism is to be aware of how different current terrorism is as compared to the past. In recent years, notable alterations in the manifestation of terrorism have become evident. Scholars such as Veness (2001), Hoffman (2001), Kegley (2003), and Jenkins (2008) have explored how terrorism has changed in recent years. They cite numerous examples of significant alterations, including the following:

• In the past, terrorists were organized hierarchically. Organizations such as the PLO often had a clear leader and an identified chain of command. *Today, terrorists around the world (and regardless of issue orientation) organize in a diffuse manner and are cell-oriented.* A cell is a semi-autonomous terrorist organization that may be loosely affiliated with other terrorist groups. Current terrorism therefore resembles a network of many groups that operate in a loosely coordinated fashion. In other words, direction among terrorists may or may not always emanate from a central headquarter.

- Terrorists were frequently supported by states in prior years. Governments like Libya or Syria provided sanctuary and financial assistance to those engaging in terrorism. Many terrorists, such as Hamas and Hezbollah, continue to work closely with governments now. However, *many terrorists have become more independent in terms of raising funds*. They launch attacks with or without approval from governments that sanction such behavior. In addition, Aum Shinrikyo, a Japanese terrorist group, acquired money through religious and corporate donations.

- In former years, it was easier to distinguish between crime and terrorism. The differences between theft and assassinations were more readily apparent. *Currently, it is more challenging to make a distinction between criminal and terrorist activities.* Many terrorist groups rely on crime to raise money, and some organizations that were founded on terrorist aspirations now promote extortion for financial gain (e.g., left-wing groups in Latin America or the Philippines).

- Citizens of the United States have typically perceived that terrorism is a problem in a very limited geographic area. *Terrorism has traditionally been viewed as a feature of the Middle East or, to a lesser extent, Europe.* Nonetheless, terrorism has been prevalent in the United States throughout its history, and 9/11 brought the reality of international terrorism home. Terrorism is also making significant headway in South Asia. No place appears to be immune.

- Historically, terrorists desired goals such as liberty, national independence, or political stability. They used violence as a way to promote freedom or strengthen government control over the masses. *At the moment, the mission of terrorists is more messianic in orientation.* There is a desire to "save" the world from abortions, environmental degradation, or the evils of Western civilization. Extreme Christian groups, the Environmental Liberation Front, and Al Qaeda come to mind as examples of these types of terrorist organizations. Of course, each of these groups has their own strategies and tactics to promote their messianic objectives.

- Terrorists were somewhat cautious about their statements in the past and did not always want to take responsibility for their harsh words or activities. They may have tried to avoid being ridiculed and held accountable for their actions. *Terrorists have more vocal and defiant attitudes today.* While all terrorists are not alike, many publicly denounce their enemies and take credit for their violent and disruptive behavior. Al Qaeda is one of many organizations that publicly denounce the United States as the "great Satan." They do not hesitate to take credit for their actions.

- Twenty years ago, terrorists desired to share their ideological goals and messages with the public at large. *More recently, terrorists such as*

Hamas or Hezbollah give greater attention to sharing their message in detail with their sympathizers. Their goal is to improve recruitment for sustained operations. Terrorists recognize that they need backing if they are to be successful in the future.

- Since its birth, terrorism has largely been related to the assassination of specific leaders for clearly defined purposes. By "taking out" individual politicians (e.g., Yitzhak Rabin), the hope was to advance a particular political or ideological agenda. *Today, terrorists are increasingly willing to target citizens.* The belief is that citizens will subsequently cave in to terrorist demands and help to promote the change terrorists desire.

- Terrorists have always been willing to kill others when it advanced their cause. Violence was seen as a "logical" means for goal attainment. While terrorists have periodically engaged in suicide attacks, the practice has been given more legitimacy in the late 1900s and early 2000s. *Terrorists from the Middle East and elsewhere are increasingly willing to kill themselves in the process of taking the lives of others.*

- Terrorist activities in the past were relatively small. Attacks killing more than a handful of individuals were, for the most part, rare. *Terrorism, especially international terrorism, is more deadly today.* Many attacks kill more than a dozen and there are others that have extinguished the life of hundreds and even thousands. Terrorism in Africa, the 9/11 attacks, or events in Spain, Russia, and England all suggest more deaths as compared to the past.

- Terrorist attacks a few decades ago were relatively simple and limited in terms of impact. A conventional explosive was used to kill the occupants of a single building. In contrast, *terrorists today employ novel techniques in attacks and their objectives or more grandiose.* Planes used as missiles, the intentional disruption of urban infrastructure, and adverse effect on the economy are sophisticated methods utilized in modern terrorism. **Cyber-terrorism**—the use of computers to plan or launch attacks—is an example of the use of technology by modern terrorists. Pluschinsky suggests that "a cyber-attack involves digitally targeting a computer information system so as to destroy, damage, or steal data and thereby disrupt or disable telecommunications, health, transportation, finances, utilities, food distribution, and other critical infrastructure systems. The primary target of a cyber-attack is information, but such attacks can ultimately cause casualties, depending on the system targeted" (2006, 367).

Cyber-terrorism
The use of computers to plan or launch attacks.

- Terrorists in earlier decades were relatively easier to track and capture. They were not always careful about their communications and were less than meticulous about leaving evidence that could be used for prosecution. *Terrorists are now more elusive.* They utilize technology (e.g., calling cards or the Internet) to minimize detection. They often blend into the community, or hide in countries with weak governments and in isolated areas that cannot be reached easily. As an example, Osama bin Laden is believed to be operating from remote locations in either Afghanistan or Pakistan. These obscure activities create serious challenges for those trying to thwart terrorism.

As a participant in homeland security, you should be aware of these changes and their potential impact on your profession. It is imperative that you recognize that terrorism is not static, but ever-changing and likely to morph in unique ways in the future. You must anticipate unique and more consequential attacks from diverse terrorist organizations. Uncertainty and complexity are the characteristics of terrorism today.

IN THE REAL WORLD

Terrorism and Technology

Terrorists now increasingly exploit technology to carry out their attacks (Thetford 2001). In 1998, the Tamil Tigers sent repeated emails to the Sri Lankan embassies to disrupt the activities of this government. During the Gulf War in 1990, "High Tech for Peace," a group of Dutch hackers, asked Iraqi agents if they would pay $1 million (USD) to disrupt communications among bases in the U.S. and military units in Saudi Arabia. There have been other instances of foreigners or high school students accessing sensitive computers (e.g., 911 systems, NASA, and Pentagon). Many terrorist groups also use encryption techniques on the Internet to hide their secret communications. James Kallstrom, a chief of engineering at the FBI laboratory in Virginia states that "In the old days . . . Fort Knox was the symbol of how we protected things of great value: we put them in buildings with thick walls and concrete. We put armed guards at the doors, with sophisticated multiple locks and locking bars. We could even build a moat and fill it with alligators . . . [Today] we are not equipped to deal with . . . [cyber-terrorism], both in the government and [in] private industry" (in Thetford 2001, 243–44).

SELF-CHECK

1. Terrorists today are organized hierarchically. True or False?
2. Terrorism is a problem in the Middle East only. True or False?
3. Which is not a feature of modern terrorism?
   (a) Terrorists are individually sponsored.
   (b) Terrorists attack key individuals only (e.g., politicians).
   (c) Terrorists work harder to recruit members.
   (d) Terrorism is more complex today than in the past.
4. List three ways that terrorism has changed in recent years.

SUMMARY

In this chapter, you have been exposed to the dynamic history of terrorism. You have gained a better comprehension of how terrorism emerged. You have seen how terrorism evolved in other nations, and how it has been manifest in the United States. In addition, you have increased your knowledge about the differences between terrorism in the current century as compared to the past. If you are to be successful in minimizing the possibility and effects of future attacks, it is imperative that you are aware how terrorism changes over time.

ASSESS YOUR UNDERSTANDING

UNDERSTAND: WHAT HAVE YOU LEARNED

 Go to **www.wiley.com/college/mcentire** to assess your knowledge of the dynamic nature of terrorism.

SUMMARY QUESTIONS

1. How did the Enlightenment change the way people saw their role in society? How did it change the way they viewed their leaders? What is one reason for the increased violence and the creation of the term "terrorism" during the Enlightenment?

2. Describe the difference between the violence mentioned in Section 1 of the chapter and the terrorist attacks we see today.

3. The chapter makes clear the fact that terrorism is used both by groups acting against established organizations and groups connected with government organizations. Why is it important that we understand both kinds of terrorism? Provide one example of a terrorist group rising against an established organization or government and one example of a terrorist group supported by a government organization.

4. There are several examples of different terrorist groups that have acted within the United States. What common threads run throughout these groups? Why is it important to understand these commonalities?

5. This chapter lists twelve ways in which terrorism has changed and evolved. Why is it important for those working in homeland security to understand these changes? What does the evolution of terrorism tell us about terrorism in the future?

6. The fear created by warriors painting their faces, brandishing weapons, and yelling loudly at their opponents is synonymous with terrorism. True or False?

7. The word "terrorism" appeared during the Enlightenment. True or False?

8. Communism is an ideology that sympathizes with the poor and downtrodden. True or False?

9. Today, it is widely held that the Black Panthers are an increasingly dangerous group. True or False?

10. Operation Mongoose was an attempt to assassinate Saddam Hussein. True or False?

11. The Ku Klux Klan was formed in Tennessee. True or False?

12. A cell is a completely autonomous terrorist group with no affiliation to other terrorist groups. True or False?

13. Anarchists are those people who:

(a) want a communist nation.

(b) oppose specific or all governments.

(c) fight for a democratic state.

(d) think that government is not doing enough.

14. Syria is known for all of the following **except**:

(a) being sympathetic to U.S. Marines.

(b) bombing barracks in Lebanon.

(c) bombings in France.

(d) plane hijackings.

15. Which of the following individuals was **not** in some way associated with the "Gunpowder Plot"?

(a) Pope Clement VII

(b) King Henry VIII

(c) Sarah Elizabeth

(d) Anne Boleyn

16. Each of the following groups or individuals were a present during the "Reign of Terror" **except**:

(a) the Jacobin party.

(b) Marie Antoinette.

(c) France's Committee of Public Safety.

(d) the Spaniards.

17. The Molly Maguires were:

(a) a Scottish group opposed to the religious state.

(b) an American group opposed to immigration.

(c) an Irish group supporting the elite of Ireland.

(d) an Irish group that disputed the treatment of tenants by landlords.

18. Which of the following groups would be likely to set fire to ski resorts in Colorado?

(a) Earth Liberation Front

(b) Black Panthers

(c) Molly Maguires

(d) The Armed Forces of National Liberation

19. All of the following are characteristics of today's terrorist groups **except**:

  (a) some rely on crime for money.

  (b) terrorism is only considered a feature of the Middle East.

  (c) the practice of suicide attacks is seen as more legitimate.

  (d) terrorist activity is carried out on a larger scale.

BE A HOMELAND SECURITY PROFESSIONAL

The Emergence of Terrorism

You are a historian who has been hired as a consultant by the CIA. Your job is to write a two-page brief about the birth of terrorism. What could you say about the emergence of terrorism and its manifestations in the 1700s and 1800s?

History of Terrorism Abroad or in the United States

Write a three-page paper describing the evolution of terrorism abroad or in the United States. Be sure to describe how it has changed over time.

Differences Between Modern and Traditional Terrorism

As a local emergency manager or employee in homeland security, your job is to anticipate terrorist attacks in your community. Could the knowledge about the differences between modern and traditional terrorism help you in your job? How so?

KEY TERMS

Anarchists	Those opposing specific governments or all governments.
Animal Liberation Front	A terrorist organization that opposes cruelty to animals.
Armed Forces of National Liberation (FALN)	A Puerto Rican terrorist organization seeking liberation of Puerto Rico from the United States.
Black Panthers	An organization comprised of African Americans to revenge the actions of the KKK and other white supremacists.
Communism	An ideology that sympathizes with the poor and downtrodden and attempts to do away with private property.
Cyber-terrorism	The use of computers to plan or launch attacks.
Earth Liberation Front	A terrorist organization that opposes environmental degradation.
Enlightenment	A period in history when a new way of looking at social, political, and economic structures emerged.
Fascism	An ideology which promotes the uniting of citizens in support of the state.
Gunpowder Plot	An attempted terrorist attack in 1605 against King James I and other leaders of Parliament to reinstate Catholic involvement in England.
Islamic fundamentalists	Individuals or groups of Muslims that violently oppose Israel and the United States.
Ku Klux Klan (KKK)	A white supremacist group that has been involved in terrorism in the United States since the Civil War.
Molly Maguires	A group of Irish citizens that joined together to dispute the treatment of coal mine workers in the United States.
Nationalist movements	Efforts on the part of a group or nation to obtain political independence and autonomy.
Operation Mongoose	An attempt by the United States to kill Cuban leader Fidel Castro with a poisoned cigar.
Reign of Terror	A period during the French Revolution where an estimated 20,000 persons were killed by France's Committee of Public Safety.

REFERENCES

Combs, Cindy C. (2000). *Terrorism in the Twenty-First Century*. Prentice Hall: New Jersey.

Griset, Pamala L. and Sue Mahan. (2003). *Terrorism in Perspective*. Sage Publications: Thousand Oaks, CA.

Hoffman, Bruce. (2001). "Change and Continuity in Terrorism." *Studies in Conflict and Terrorism* 24: 417–428.

Jenkins, Brian Michael. (2008). "The New Age of Terrorism." Pp. 23–31 in Howard, Russell D. and James J. F. Forest. *Weapons of Mass Destruction and Terrorism*. McGraw Hill: New York.

Kegley, Charles W. Jr. (2003). *The New Global Terrorism: Characteristics, Causes, Control*. Prentice Hall, New Jersey.

Lejeune, Peter H. B. (2001). "History and Anatomy of Terrorism." Pp. 203–238 in Hogan, Lawrence J. (Ed.). *Terrorism: Defensive Strategies for Individuals, Companies, and Governments*. Amlex, Inc.: Frederick, MD.

Pluchinsky, Dennis A. (2006). "A Typology and Anatomy of Terrorist Operations." Pp. 365–390 in Kamien, David G. *The McGraw-Hill Homeland Security Handbook*. McGraw Hill: New York.

Simensen, Clifford E. and Jeremy R. Spindlove. (2000). *Terrorism Today: The Past, The Players, the Future*. Prentice Hall: New Jersey.

Thetford, Robert T. (2001). "The Challenge of Cyberterrorism." Pp. 239–257 in Hogan, Lawrence J. (Ed.). *Terrorism: Defensive Strategies for Individuals, Companies, and Governments*. Amlex, Inc.: Frederick, MD.

Veness, David. (2001). "Terrorism and Counterterrorism: An International Perspective." *Studies in Conflict and Terrorism* 24: 407–416.

Venuri, F. (1966). *Roots of Revolution: A History of the Populist and Socialist Movement in the Nineteenth Century*. Norton: New York.

6

EVALUATING A MAJOR DILEMMA
Terrorism, the Media, and Censorship

Do You Already Know?

- How the media has changed over time
- Why terrorists utilize the media
- How the media benefits from terrorist activity
- Why the reporting of terrorist attacks concerns the government
- The drawbacks of media censorship

 For additional questions to assess your current knowledge of the dilemmas associated with terrorism, the media, and censorship, go to **www.wiley.com/college/mcentire**

What You Will Find Out	What You Will Be Able To Do
6.1 How the media has changed over time	• Compare and contrast the positive and negative features of modern news coverage
6.2 Why terrorists utilize the media	• Predict advantages terrorists receive from media publicity
6.3 What the media gains from terrorist activity	• Evaluate reasons for media coverage of terrorist attacks
6.4 Why the government is concerned about the reporting of terrorist attacks	• Assess why reporting is of concern to government officials
6.5 The drawbacks of censorship	• Critique the possibility of media censorship in the United States

INTRODUCTION

An important way for you to reduce the impact of terrorism is to comprehend the role of the media in this type of violent activity. You must evaluate how the media has changed over time, as well as the complicated relationships among terrorists and the media. It is also imperative that you recognize what the government desires from the media, in addition to the drawbacks of censorship or self-censorship. Finding an appropriate way to deal with the media is one of the greatest challenges facing you and others in homeland security.

6.1 CHANGES IN THE MEDIA OVER TIME

To adequately understand the nature of terrorism today, it is imperative that you recognize how the media has changed over time. Up until the mid- to late 1700s, there were no unofficial outlets for news. Information was distributed (and sometimes even fabricated) by the king or political party in power. This resulted in a great deal of control over the sharing of information. News also traveled slowly. It was transmitted by horse, rail, or telegraph. But the dissemination of news was limited due to geographical distances. The lack of education also limited the demand for information. People could not always read or understand what was being distributed.

Although authoritarian governments still control information in certain countries around the world, things have changed dramatically for the media over the past few centuries and even in recent decades (Hoffman 1998, 136). The establishment of democratic governments and the rise of capitalism have resulted in the appearance of additional news sources. Media organizations now determine what the news is and convey it to an increasingly educated public citizenry. Furthermore, technological innovations have reduced the time it takes to share information around the world. Television, cable TV, satellite dishes, Internet, email access, and cell phones with mini-camcorders have revolutionized the media. Getting news to the public once took months, weeks, or days. Now, the sharing of information is measured in hours or seconds. News that was only given to people in large urban and developed communities is now accessible to anyone around the world. Such changes have had dramatic consequences. On the positive side, we are more aware of what is going on around the world and we can quickly share information with one another. On the negative side, new technologies and the media can be fully exploited by terrorists.

SELF-CHECK

1. Prior to the 1800s, most news came from the king or ruling elite. True or False?
2. Information traditionally traveled slowly around the world because of limitations in travel or communications. True or False?
3. What type of technology has not transformed the media in recent years?
    (a) Television
    (b) The typewriter
    (c) Satellite dishes
    (d) The Internet
4. What are the pros and cons of the modern media?

6.2 TERRORISTS AND THE MEDIA

It is increasingly accepted as fact that terrorism and the media have an extremely close relationship. Indeed, terrorists are heavily dependent on the media in our modern era. To realize their ideological goals, terrorists want to increase legitimacy for their cause, shock as many people as possible, and instill widespread fear. Terrorists also desire to increase visibility (for monetary support and recruiting purposes) and destabilize the enemy (by illustrating that the government cannot cope effectively with attacks). In the mind of terrorists, the best way for them to reach their desired objectives is to rely on the assistance of reporters.

One of the most vivid examples of this occurred during the 1972 Munich Olympics. In an attempt to reverse real or perceived injustices against Palestinians, **Black September**—an operational unit of the Al-Fatah terrorism organization—launched an attack against Israeli athletes participating in the international games (Simonsen and Spindlove 2000, 140). Decrying the eviction of the PLO from Jordanian training camps in September 1970, Abu Iyad (head of the Palestinian intelligence network) and his followers entered the Olympic Village and immediately killed two members of the Israeli team. Using the threat of AK-47 assault rifles to keep remaining the hostages at bay, the terrorists then demanded the release of 234 Palestinians held in Israeli jails. The large global audience that had tuned into the Olympics became very interested in the unfolding drama. Terrorists thought this would be the key for putting sufficient pressure on the Israeli government to acquiesce to their demands. The state of Israel gained sympathy from those watching the events unfold and decided not to release the prisoners. Nevertheless,

Black September:
An operational unit of the Al-Fatah terrorism organization that initiated the terrorist attacks on Israeli athletes at the Munich Olympic games in 1972.

Figure 6-1

The media was used extensively by terrorists in the 1972 Olympics. Here, an Arab terrorist extends his hand as he talks with another terrorist, leaning from upper window, during discussions with Munich chief of police Manfred Schreiber, far left, and West German interior minister Hans-Dietrich Genscher on September 5, 1972.

Israeli leaders did allow the terrorists to fly by helicopter to Furstenfeldburk Airport. Even though these and other terrorists were hunted down and killed, this event illustrated the potential impact of the media in negotiations.

Since then, the media has increasingly been seen as an important tool at the disposal of terrorists. For instance, after taking hostages at OPEC headquarters in Vienna in 1975, Carlos "the Jackal" waited for the media to arrive before exiting the building with his kidnapped oil ministers (Hickey 1976, 6). While 52 American hostages were being held at the American Embassy in Tehran in 1979, the mob outside only began to shake their fists, burn flags, and denounce President Carter when a Canadian Broadcasting Company showed up at the scene (Hoffman 1998, 142). In order to increase public relations, the Irish Republic Army "historically included close relationships with the print and broadcast media" (Martin 2003, 281). Ted Kaczynski likewise sent his 35,000 word manifesto against technology to the *Washington Post* and the *New York Times*. This document, denouncing development and the U.S. government, was published in 1995 (Griset and Mahan 2003, 132).

Osama bin Laden also uses the media to promote Al Qaeda's agenda. In the late 1990s, bin Laden was interviewed by Western reporters. He told them that America would be attacked if it did not withdraw its troops from the Middle East and stop supporting puppet governments in the area. On 9/11, Al Qaeda relied on the morning news broadcasts and large international media organizations in New York to publicize the lengths it was willing to go to force the United States to cave in to its demands. In recent years, bin Laden and other Al Qaeda leaders have encouraged sympathizers to acquire weapons of mass destruction and use them against Americans or their interests, regardless of their location around the world. Thus, it is evident that the media is viewed as a significant means for reaching terrorist aims.

Brian Jenkins, a well-known RAND Corporation researcher, states "terrorists want a lot of people watching and a lot of people listening. . . . Terrorists choreograph dramatic incidents to achieve maximum publicity, and in that sense, terrorism is theater" (1985, A4). He also asserts "terrorism is violence for effect—not primarily, and sometimes not at all for the physical effect on the actual target, but rather for its dramatic impact on an audience" (Jenkins 1978, 101). Others agree with Jenkins. For instance, Walter Laquer believes the "media are a terrorist's best friend." Frederick Hacker declares emphatically that "[i]f the mass media [organizations] did not exist, terrorists would have to invent them!" (see Combs 2000, 128).

IN THE REAL WORLD

Terrorism on TV

On June 14, 1985, three Lebanese terrorists hijacked TWA Flight 847 going from Athens to Rome. The plane was initially flown to Beirut, Lebanon, and it then made several trips between Beruit and Algeria. During the 16-day ordeal, nearly 500 reports on nightly news programs (CBS, ABC, NBC) were devoted to the event. The terrorists skillfully used the media to publicize their cause, and they even attempted to charge networks for a tour of the plane and interviews with them. The broadcasts ended up creating enough pressure on the U.S. government to negotiate with the terrorists. All on board the plane were released when 756 Shi'a terrorists were released from prison in Israel. Gus Martin believes "the hijackers masterfully manipulated the world's media" (2003, 294).

SELF-CHECK

1. The media helps give terrorists visibility. True or False?

2. Osama bin Laden never speaks with Western media because he regards them to be infidels. True or False?

3. Which terrorist attack was among the first to exploit international media?
   (a) Tehran hostage crisis
   (b) The OPEC hostage crisis
   (c) The Munich Olympic massacre
   (d) 9/11

4. Why is the media regarded to be the terrorist's "best friend"?

6.3 THE MEDIA AND TERRORISM

According to former British Prime Minister Margaret Thatcher, the media provides "the oxygen of publicity on which [terrorists] depend" (in Hoffman 1998, 142). But the media also stands to gain much from terrorism and ideologically motivated attacks on others. In particular, the media desires to make "the news entertaining enough to 'sell'" (White 2003, 257).

Fortunately for the media, terrorist attacks offer a dramatic presentation that keeps viewers riveted. Terrorism is associated with violence, heroic responses, and unusual consequences. These are only a few of the features that keep people glued to their televisions, encourage them to stay tuned to the radio, or impel them to return to the Internet or newspaper. Ratings are important and, therefore, the media exploits terrorism to its advantage. In other words, the media broadcasts terrorist attacks to maintain or increase their standings in the competitive news world.

Of course, the media does present a timely and accurate portrayal of the news to keep society informed on important events (Perl 1997, 7). The media may also play a positive role in the resolution of some terrorist conflicts. For instance, some hostages feel that reporters helped keep politicians interested in their plight until their situation could be peacefully resolved (Hoffman 1998, 147). However, media involvement in terrorism is not without drawbacks.

One of the major problems created by the media concerns their interference in counter-terrorism operations. For instance, as the FBI was making final preparations to raid the Branch Davidian compound due to weapons violations in Waco, Texas, the media told David Koresh of the FBI's impending plans. This intensified the Branch Davidian's fear of the government and may have augmented the violence that broke out on February 28, 1993. Ten people (both FBI agents and Branch Davidians) died during the exchange of gunfire, and

Figure 6-2

The media played a significant role in the outcome of the Branch Davidian standoff. Here, flames engulf the Branch Davidian compound on April 20, 1993, in Waco, Texas.

this resulted in a 51 day standoff between the two opposing parties. Another 79 Branch Davidians died when the FBI launched tear gas into the building and fires engulfed the entire edifice.

Another excellent case in point concerns the Hanafi siege that occurred in Washington, D.C., on March 9–11, 1977 (Combs 2000, 135–136). Twelve gunmen took over three buildings in an attempt to force the release of convicted murderers and protect the sacred name of the Prophet Mohammad. In the process, two people were killed and another 149 were taken hostage. During the ordeal, the media complicated negotiations with the terrorists. One reporter who communicated with the terrorists said the police were preparing to attack. Another called the terrorist leader and stated that the police were trying to trick him. This terrorist then selected ten hostages for execution. He did not carry through with the threat, however, because the police agreed to defuse the situation by removing sharpshooters. Nevertheless, the participation of the media slowed down and even reversed negotiations. One of the hostages (who happened to also be a reporter) said this about the media's mistakes during the take over:

As hostages, many of us felt that the Hanafi takeover was a . . . high impact propaganda exercise programmed for the TV screen, and for the front pages of newspapers around the world. Beneath the resentment and the anger of my fellow hostages toward the press is a conviction gained that the news media and terrorism feed on each other, that the news media and particularly TV, create a thirst for fame and recognition. Reporters do not simply report the news. They help create it. They are not objective observers, but subjective participants (Schmid and de Graff 1982, 172).

Besides complicating negotiations and rescues, the media may also exacerbate terrorism in other ways. For instance, by giving terrorists airtime, reports may help the terrorists appear more powerful than they are actually are. In addition, continued coverage of terrorist attacks could create emotional problems for viewers. As an example, numerous children suffered from nightmares after repeatedly witnessing the World Trade Center towers collapse in media reports after 9/11. Alex Schmid offers other perspectives about the negative impact of the media on the occurrence of terrorist attacks:

Social learning theory:
Observing terrorist attacks in the news may generate similar type of behavior among others.

Disinhibition hypothesis:
Violence portrayed by the media may weaken the inhibition of others to participate in terrorism.

Arousal hypothesis:
Media reports on terrorism can increase people's interest in acting aggressively.

Built-in escalation hypothesis:
More deadly and visible attacks are required to get equal media coverage in the future.

- **Social learning theory:** Observing terrorist attacks in the news may be the first step in generating similar type of behavior among others (e.g., people learn from what they see).
- **Disinhibition hypothesis:** Violence portrayed by the media may weaken the reticence of others to participate in terrorism (e.g., people become immune to the violence of terrorism).
- **Arousal hypothesis:** Media reports on terrorism can increase people's interest in acting aggressively (e.g., terrorism may be seen as a legitimate way to accomplish goals).
- **Built-in escalation hypothesis:** More deadly and visible attacks in the future are required to get the same amount of media coverage as in the past (in Combs 2000).

IN THE REAL WORLD

The Achille Lauro Incident

In 1985, the Palestine Liberation Front hijacked an Italian cruise ship, the *Achille Lauro*. Their goal was to exchange passengers for 50 Palestinian terrorists imprisoned in Israel. During the incident, a terrorist killed a man who was confined to a wheelchair and dumped his body into the Mediterranean Sea. The United States announced a $250,000 reward for anyone who could provide information that would lead to the arrest of the leader Abul Abbas. The government struggled in its attempt to bring Abbas to justice. However, the media was able to contact him for an exclusive interview on NBC's news program. Although some viewed the interview as tasteless, others claimed it was indeed of interest to the American people. This was an excellent case of the symbiotic relationship among terrorists and the media (Hoffman 1998, 144).

SELF-CHECK

1. The Hanafi hostage crisis illustrates how the media worked to effectively deal with terrorism. True or False?

2. Social learning theory implies that people will mimic the behavior they see on TV. True or False?

3. Which of the following concepts describes why people become complacent about terrorism in the media?
   (a) Social learning theory
   (b) Disinhibition hypothesis
   (c) Arousal hypothesis
   (d) Built-in escalation hypothesis

4. Explain why terrorism is appealing to the media and those interested in the news.

6.4 GOVERNMENT AND THE MEDIA

According to an editorial in the journal *Terrorism and Political Violence*, "the relationship between publicity and terror is indeed paradoxical and complicated. Publicity focuses attention on a group, strengthening its morale and helping to attract recruits and sympathizers. But publicity is pernicious to the terrorist groups too. It helps an outraged public to mobilize its vast resources, and produces information that the public needs to pierce the veil of secrecy all terrorist groups require" (Rapoport 1996, viii). This complex relationship is convoluted further because the government also has an interest in using the media to defeat terrorism.

Raphael Perl, a specialist in foreign affairs, believes that the government has several requests of the media before, during, and after terrorist attacks (1997, 5–6). Government leaders generally desire to do the following:

- Gain information about possible terrorist attacks (if those plans exist).

- Separate the terrorists from the media in order to deny them a public platform.

- Obtain information about terrorists if the media is aware of the location where hostages are being kept.

- Have the media present terrorists as criminals who devalue life and ignore international or national laws.

- Diffuse the crisis through the accurate dissemination of public information, rather than contribute to an already tense situation.
- Avoid emotional stories as media reports may place extreme pressure on officials to negotiate with terrorists.
- Withhold information that may notify terrorists of pending counter-terrorism or rescue operations.
- Avert the sharing of details about intelligence gathering or successful operations.
- Seek media cooperation in holding back evidence that could be used for future prosecution.
- Boost the image of their agencies by controlling leaks to the press and avoiding undue criticism.

As can be seen, the government is very concerned about media involvement in terrorism. This is because "terrorists learn their tactics and copy methods from the mass media. Media coverage also serves as a motivation for terrorism. The most serious outcome is that violence seems to increase during media coverage. The mass media have become the perfect instrument of violent communication" (White 2002, 262). How can this major problem be addressed? Two choices are available, but neither is totally desirable or achievable. The first is to have the government censor the media. The second is to have the media control its own broadcasts.

SELF-CHECK

1. The relationship between terrorism and the media is straightforward. True or False?

2. Which is not a reason why the government is concerned about the media's involvement in terrorism?

   (a) They don't want the media to make money.
   (b) The media could share evidence that might hurt the prosecution of terrorists.
   (c) The media may have information about forthcoming terrorist attacks.
   (d) Emotional stories could cause officials to react to terrorism prematurely.

3. Why would the government worry about the media discussing intelligence operations?

6.5 CENSORSHIP AND SELF-CENSORSHIP

Censorship:
The withholding, banning, or altering of information the media shares with the public.

One of the ways to limit the negative aspects of media coverage is to implement some form of government censorship. **Censorship** is the withholding, banning, or altering of information the media shares with the public. Censorship is forbidden by law in United States. In fact, the First Amendment to the Constitution states that "Congress shall make no law . . . abridging the freedom of speech, or of the press." Nevertheless, there have been cases where censorship has occurred in our history and elsewhere. During World War II, the amount and type of information about the conflict was controlled by the government. This had the purpose of maintaining unity at home and confusing Germans about U.S. war plans. Also, in the first Gulf War, the U.S. government denied immediate access of reporters in war zones (presumably for their own safety). Britain has been particularly adept at restraining media coverage of terrorism. On some occasions, the media in the United Kingdom could not broadcast interviews or statements by members of the Irish Republican Army.

While this type of activity is extremely controversial, some scholars suggest that restrictions on news coverage may be necessary in emergency conditions. "Lives hang in the balance during hostage crises. . . . Reporting and the freedom to report are not the only critical concerns in such crises: The impact of the media on the event, and media interference with police operations, have also become central issues" (White 2002, 263).

The issue of censorship is far from being settled, however. Besides being in conflict with our democratic ideals for government, censorship probably does nothing to stop terrorist activity. In fact, prohibiting the freedom of speech or of the press may actually augment terrorism. This is because people will not have a voice to express concerns about government policies or highly contentious debates. People have shown a tendency over time to engage in violence if they feel their political values are not being heeded by elected officials. Chechen rebels feel, for example, that Russia has limited their freedom over the press. Although censorship is possible to some degree and at different times, it will probably never completely occur in the west because of our interest in a free society.

Self-censorship:
Media control over their reporting of news to the public.

The other option for dealing with terrorism is to have the media take more stringent measures to control their reporting of news to the public. In some ways, **self-censorship** is in the interest of news organizations. Terrorists often see reporters as pawns of their enemies, and therefore seek to silence their opposition to terrorist ideology and violent behavior. Also, killing reporters is an additional way that terrorists spread fear among the population.

Reporters participate in a very dangerous profession. The Committee to Protect Journalists says 63 journalists were killed around the world in 2007. While a portion of these deaths were due to accidents, many resulted from assassinations. Hot spots for attacks on journalists include countries such as Algeria, Nigeria, Russia, Turkey, Syria, and Zaire. Drug Cartels in Mexico and Colombia are also quick to kill journalists who point out corruption in the government. Reporters and media organizations are also targeted in the United States. A week after the 9/11 attacks, unidentified terrorists sent letters laced with anthrax spores to Tom Brokaw as well as ABC News, CBS News, the *New York Post*, and the *National Enquirer*. Although Brokaw was not harmed, five people died and seventeen others were infected by the disease.

Daniel Pearl:
A reporter with the *Wall Street Journal* who was killed by terrorists in Karachi, Pakistan.

One of the most notable cases of this concerns **Daniel Pearl**. Pearl was a reporter with the *Wall Street Journal*. He was investigating Richard Reid (the shoe bomber) and possible ties between Al Qaeda and Pakistan's intelligence service. On January 23, 2002, he went to interview a suspected terrorist. In the process, a group calling itself the National Movement for the Restoration of Pakistani Sovereignty kidnapped Pearl. They demanded, among other things, the release of terror detainees in Guantanamo Bay, Cuba. The terrorists also stated that they would kill Pearl if the United States did not meet their request. On February 1, 2002, Khalid Sheikh Mohammed decapitated Pearl in Karachi, Pakistan. His death was captured on video and released with the comment that such actions would occur repeatedly if the United States

Figure 6-3

Terrorists captured Daniel Pearl and killed him for his reports about Al Qaeda and Pakistan.

did not give in to the terrorists' request. The media refused to air this brutal murder and the demands of the terrorists. In time, Ahmed Omar Saeed Sheikh and three other suspects were charged with murder in March 2002.

Unfortunately, most of the slayings of reporters remain unsolved crimes. In Latin America, it is estimated that "95 percent of the 155 killings, 1,109 known beatings, 49 kidnappings, and 205 terrorist acts against media installations . . . tallied for the last seven years have gone unpunished" (Marks 1995, 9). Other media personnel are frequently threatened verbally or jailed for long periods of time. As an example, China has more journalists in prison than any other Asian country.

With the above in mind, one would assume that reporters and media organizations would want to limit their involvement in controversial subjects like terrorism. This is not necessarily the case. The media wants desperately to protect citizens' right to public information. In addition, a failure to report the news results in lower ratings in a very competitive media market. Although committees among media organizations have been and can be formed to police news reporting, disagreement about what should or should not be reported is prevalent.

Reporters therefore do their job in spite of potential threats or disagreement about content. Horria Saihi, an Algerian TV producer, states "I know what awaits me in the end is a bullet in the head, but what kills me more is censorship. That would be symbolic death" (Marks 1995, 9). Others agree that any form of censorship is an attack on liberty. Cindy Combs states, "[w]hen a democratic society, in panic and anger, abandons one of the cherished principles of law that make it democratic, the society has inflicted on itself a greater wound than the terrorists could achieve, were they to bomb a hundred buildings" (2000, 131). Knowing what to do in regards to the media's involvement in terrorism remains problematic at best.

IN THE REAL WORLD

The Case of Terry Anderson

Terry Anderson was a reporter stationed in Beirut in 1985. He was snatched from his car and held for seven years by Islamic fundamentalists. When freed, he later stated, "[i]f there ever was a sense that journalists should be given some sort of immunity, it is long gone" (Marks 1995, 1). As Anderson's comments indicate, people in the media now recognize that they may be kidnapped, beaten, or killed for their comments about terrorism.

SELF-CHECK

1. Amendments to the constitution protect freedom of the press. True or False?

2. Censorship has never occurred in democratic countries. True or False?

3. Which reporter was kidnapped and killed in Pakistan?
   (a) Richard Reid
   (b) Daniel Pearl
   (c) Tom Brokaw
   (d) Dan Rather

4. Why would the media want to censor its reporting of terrorist activity?

SUMMARY

One of the greatest dilemmas you will face in homeland security is in regards to the relationship between terrorism and the media. Because the media can relay information around the world in a matter of minutes, you should be aware of the reasons why terrorists desire to publicize their activities. If you are to anticipate how the government should interact with the media, it is imperative that you are able to predict how reporters view terrorism. Although you may need to monitor the information you give to the media during a terrorist attack, you should be aware of the drawbacks and limitations of censorship.

ASSESS YOUR UNDERSTANDING

UNDERSTAND: WHAT HAVE YOU LEARNED?

 Go to **www.wiley.com/college/mcentire** to assess your knowledge of the dilemmas associated with terrorism, the media, and censorship.

SUMMARY QUESTIONS

1. Explain why terrorists are able to have an impact on countries far away from the actual attack. Be sure to list at least three reasons.

2. Many scholars, including Brian Jenkins, state that "terrorism is theater." What is meant by this comment? How do terrorists use "theater" to get their message across?

3. What were some of the problems created by the media during the Hanafi siege? How was this resolved?

4. Raphael Perl states that the government is interested in media reports of terrorism for at least ten reasons. List three of them.

5. Censorship of the media is a controversial strategy for dealing with terrorism. Explain why this is the case, and be sure to discuss advantages and disadvantages of curtailing news to the public.

6. News that once traveled slowly can now travel around the world in minutes or seconds. True or False?

7. One of the reasons why terrorists want to have media coverage is to show the inability of government to deal with their attacks. True or False?

8. Red October is the name of the terrorist group that killed Israeli athletes in the 1972 Olympic Games in Germany. True or False?

9. Terrorism is regarded to be "theater" because it is directed toward an audience and not just actual victims. True or False?

10. The media has no interest in terrorist attacks. True or False?

11. People are interested in terrorist attacks because of their drama and suspense. True or False?

12. The government wants the media to portray terrorists as criminals. True or False?

13. Censorship is the withholding, banning, or altering of information the media shares with the public. True or False?

14. We are likely to see full censorship of the media in the future in the United States. True or False?

15. Which terrorist sent a manifesto to the media to complain about modern technology?

    (a) Osama bin Laden

    (b) Timothy McVeigh

    (c) Ted Kaczynski

    (d) Khalid Sheikh Mohammed

16. Which of the following is not one of Osama bin Laden's demands issued through the media?

    (a) Withdraw U.S. troops from the Middle East

    (b) Limit pollutants into the environment

    (c) Stop supporting corrupt puppet governments

    (d) Have Muslims acquire and use nuclear weapons against the United States

17. If a terrorist is successful in reaching his or her goals with the help of the media, others may be likely to engage in similar behavior. This is known as:

    (a) the arousal hypothesis.

    (b) the disincentive hypothesis.

    (c) the built-in escalation hypothesis.

    (d) the inflammatory hypothesis.

18. Why is the government interested in how the media conveys news about terrorism?

    (a) Because terrorists do not care about media reports about attacks.

    (b) Because the government can never provide any details about what is happening.

    (c) Because the media makes too much money off of terrorism.

    (d) Because the media never helps the government after terrorist attacks.

BE A HOMELAND SECURITY PROFESSIONAL

Covering a Terrorist Attack

You are a reporter for CNN. You have just been notified that a terrorist is holding hostages in a shopping mall in Phoenix, Arizona. The terrorist group called you to ask someone to relay their grievances. They decry U.S. involvement in the United Nations and are threatening to kill people if international polices are not reconsidered. Your boss wants you to conduct the interview. What are the drawbacks and potential dangers of doing this?

Public Information Officer

As the public information officer for the Department of Homeland Security, your job is to ensure that the government's perspective of terrorism is shared with the media. A bomb has just been detonated in California, and an environmental group is claiming responsibility for the destruction at a petrochemical plant. What are some of the issues or comments you would like the media to address as they cover this attack?

Your Views About Censorship

Write a two-page paper about censorship of the media in relation to terrorist activities. Be sure to discuss why censorship might be considered, as well as its advantages and disadvantages.

KEY TERMS

Arousal hypothesis	Media reports on terrorism can increase people's interest in acting aggressively.
Black September	An operational unit of the Al-Fatah terrorism organization that initiated the terrorist attacks on Israeli athletes at the Munich Olympic games in 1972.
Built-in escalation hypothesis	More deadly and visible attacks are required to get equal media coverage in the future.
Censorship	The withholding, banning, or altering of information the media shares with the public.
Daniel Pearl	A reporter with the *Wall Street Journal* who was killed by terrorists in Karachi, Pakistan.
Disinhibition hypothesis	Violence portrayed by the media may weaken the inhibition of others to participate in terrorism.
Self-censorship	Media control over their reporting of news to the public.
Social learning theory	Observing terrorist attacks in the news may generate similar type of behavior among others.

REFERENCES

Combs, Cindy C. (2000). *Terrorism in the Twenty-First Century*. Prentice Hall: Upper Saddle River, New Jersey.

Committee to Protect Journalists. www.cpj.org/

Griset, Pamala L. and Sue Mahan. (2003). *Terrorism in Perspective*. Sage Publications: Thousand Oaks, CA.

Hickey, Neil. (1976). "Terrorism and Television." *TV Guide*, 31 July, Radnor, Pennsylvania.

Hoffman, Bruce. (1998). *Inside Terrorism*. Columbia University Press: New York.

Jenkins, Brian. (1978). "High Technology Terrorism and Surrogate War: The Impact of New Technology on Low-Level Violence." In Eds. Elliott, K. D. and L. K. Gibson, *Contemporary Terrorism: Selected Readings*. International Association of Chiefs of Police: Gaithersburg, MD.

Jenkins, Brian. (1985). "Terrorism Found Rising, Now Almost Accepted." *Washington Post*, December 3, A4.

Marks, Alexandra. (1995). "Reporters at Risk: War and Lawlessness Increasingly Turn Foreign Correspondents into Targets." *Christian Science Monitor*, November 10, pp. 1, 10–11.

Perl, Raphael F. (1997). "Terrorism, The Media, and The Government: Perspectives, Trends, and Options for Policy Makers." http://usinfo.state.gov/topical/pol/terror/crs.htm

Rapoport, David. (1996). "Editorial: The Media and Terrorism: Implications of the Unabomber Case." *Terrorism and Political Violence*, 8 (1): viii.

Schmid, A. P. and J. de Graff. (1982). *Violence as Communication: Insurgent Terrorism and the Western New Media*. Sage: Beverly Hills, CA.

Simonsen, Clifford E. and Jeremy R. Spindlove. (2000). *Terrorism Today: The Past, The Players, The Future*. Prentice Hall: Upper Saddle River, New Jersey.

White, Jonathan R. (2003). *Terrorism: An Introduction*. Thomson/Wadsworth: Belmont, CA.

7

CONTEMPLATING A QUANDARY
Terrorism, Security, and Liberty

Do You Already Know?

- The difference between terrorism and war
- Why security and freedom are important
- How prevention against terrorism can impact liberty
- How rights can be protected in spite of terrorism

For additional questions to assess your current knowledge of the relationship of terrorism to security and liberty, go to **www.wiley.com/ college/mcentire**

What You Will Find Out	What You Will Be Able To Do
7.1 How terrorism is different than war	• Appraise how security and liberty may be at odds with one another
7.2 Why security and freedom are important priorities	• Argue why security is necessary
7.3 Ways that liberty is adversely impacted by efforts to prevent terrorist attacks	• Evaluate reasons why more people are concerned about liberty today
7.4 How rights can be protected in spite of terrorism	• Predict ways to secure the nation against terrorism while also maintaining rights

INTRODUCTION

One of the major difficulties you will have in homeland security concerns the proper relationship between security and liberty. If you are to devise and implement policies that will minimize terrorist attacks you must be able to appraise why these values are desired in democracies such as the United States. You must be able to critically evaluate the probability of terrorism and estimate the negative impact that this may have on rights and freedoms. Above all, you must select policies that limit the threat of terrorism but maintain liberty as a cherished principle.

7.1 WAR, TERRORISM, AND LAW

All countries desire to ensure their security from external or internal threats. Such threats may come from enemy nations or from those who would subvert or overthrow political leaders. If the government is unable to defend its citizens or itself from these aggressors, it could logically cease to exist. For this reason, many declare the need to recognize potential enemies and, if required, take measures to protect the country against them. However, not all threats are alike. War and terrorism both involve violent behavior, but these types of conflict are distinct in very fundamental ways.

Fighting in a traditional conflict against another nation may be a difficult challenge, but the enemy is typically identifiable. In most cases, the government of the opposing forces issues a formal statement of war and soldiers are clearly identified with their own matching uniforms. The location of the battle is often distinguishable and efforts are usually made to fight within Geneva Convention rules. The **Geneva Conventions** are a set of internationally accepted laws pertaining to the conduct of war. They were initiated in Europe by Henry Dunant in 1863 after he witnessed the depressing lack of medical treatment for wounded soldiers at the Battle of Solferino in 1859. He believed both sides of any conflict have a responsibility to care for the injured. Dunant was responsible for the development of international law on the humane treatment of soldiers.

Geneva Conventions:
A set of internationally accepted laws pertaining to the conduct of war.

Since this time, the conventions have undergone numerous changes. One of the most notable revisions of the Geneva Convention occurred after World War II. The United Nations felt that citizens should not be targeted in war because they have no way of protecting themselves. Signatory nations have therefore established moral guidelines to limit the most disturbing aspects of war. Nearly 200 countries have declared their support of the Geneva Convention.

Terrorism is unlike the national conflicts mentioned above. First, the perpetrator of a terrorist attack is not always distinguishable to others. Terrorists may be foreigners or citizens of the victim country. Second, terrorists do not typically wear uniforms which denote their intent to engage in conflict. Instead, they may be dressed as an ordinary person in order to carry out their attacks in a covert manner. Terrorists also disregard the Geneva Conventions. Although they may kill soldiers in attacks, they also prefer to target civilians in order to increase fear and publicity. It is this aspect that makes terrorism so deplorable.

The unique attributes of terrorism presents major challenges to democratic governments and the law under which they operate. One of the greatest struggles facing those involved in homeland security is to protect the United States from terrorism while also maintaining the rights we enjoy. For instance, "the Constitution weighs heavily in both sides of the debate over national security and civil liberties" (Rosenzweig 2006, 1020). The President

Figure 7-1

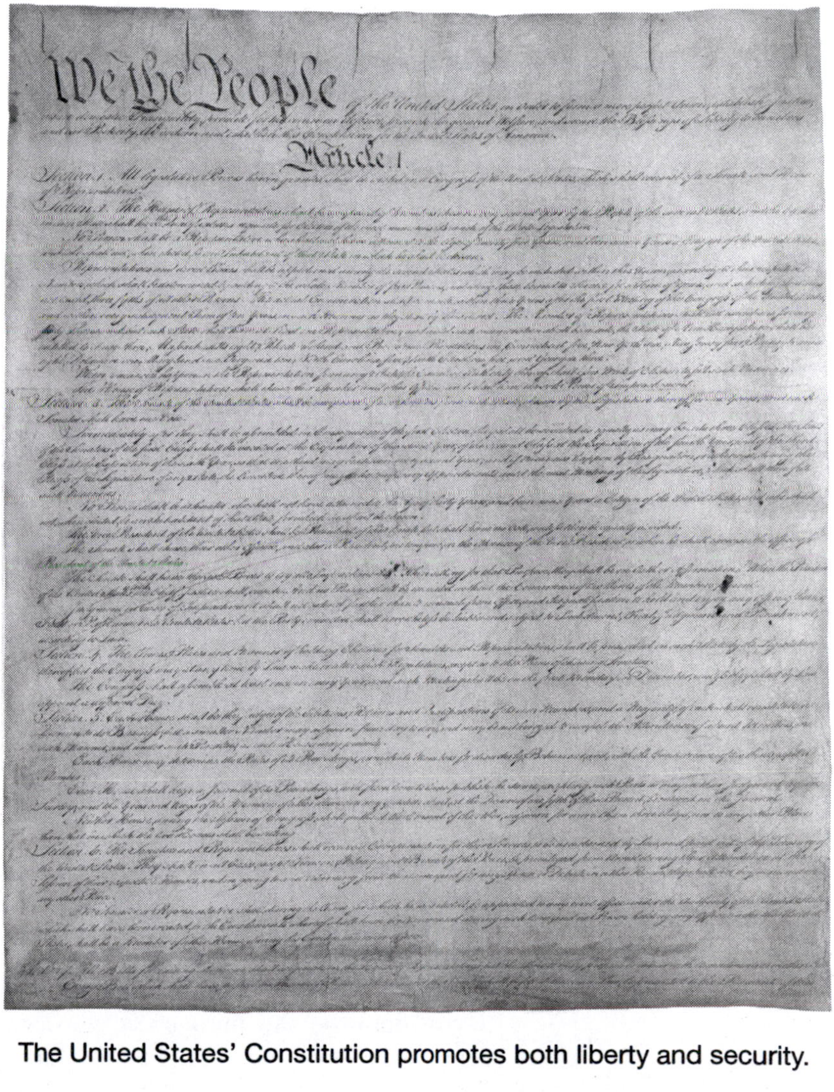
We the People

Article. I

The United States' Constitution promotes both liberty and security.

and Congress must take steps to protect the nation against terrorist attacks. These leaders are also obligated to implement policies that do not infringe upon citizens' freedoms.

Some scholars and practitioners see little or no conflict between these important priorities. For instance, K. A. Taipale states:

> Within the public discourse, concerns about domestic security and civil liberties are often asserted as competing and potentially incompatible policy interests requiring the achievement of some tolerable state of balance. Implicitly in this notion of balance is the smuggled assumption of a dichotomous rivalry in which security and liberty are traded one for another in a zero-sum political game. But the notion is misleading, for there is no fulcrum—as is implicitly in the metaphor of a balance—at which the correct amount of security and liberty can be achieved. Rather, security and liberty are dual obligations of civil society, and each must be maximized (2006, 1009).

Others, however, are quick to point out conflicting goals rather than values that can be achieved in harmonious fashion. Justin Hood observes that "our history has shown us that insecurity threatens liberty. Yet if our liberties are curtailed, we lose the values that we are struggling to defend" (Murphy 2006, 1047). Jonathan White asks a question that may be difficult to answer: "is there a point where civil liberties can be curtailed in the name of public safety?" (White 2002, 275). These issues and inquiries illustrate there is an uneasy relationship among security and liberty. Unfortunately, "terrorism exploits this tension" (Badey 2008, 123).

SELF-CHECK

1. War and terrorism are alike in almost every way. True or False?
2. The Geneva Convention is a law that specifically prohibits terrorism. True or False?
3. The Constitution:
    (a) ignores security.
    (b) supports liberty only.
    (c) sees security and liberty as important priorities.
    (d) denounces liberty.
4. As a type of conflict, what are the unique attributes of terrorism?

7.2 SECURITY AND LIBERTY

One school of thought asserts that security is an extremely important objective. People holding this view acknowledge that national protection has become even more important since the attacks against the United States in

2001. For instance, a spokeswoman for the Department of Justice states that "Sept. 11th has forced the entire government to change the way we do business. . . . Our No. 1 priority right now is to prevent any further terrorist attacks" (in Griset and Mahan 2003, 285).

Others provide evidence of the current scope of the threat and indicate that it is becoming more severe over time. Rosenzweig's research reveals:

- 70,000 terrorists were trained in Afghanistan before the United States deposed the Taliban.
- The State Department has compiled a list of at least 100,000 known-terrorists around the world.
- Jemaah Islamiyah, a terrorist organization in Indonesia, has 3,000 members and it is still growing.
- As many as 5,000 Al Qaeda operatives could be present in the United States.
- "Virtually every terrorism expert in and out of government believes that there is a significant risk of another attack" (2006, 1022).

Furthermore, views that favor security recognize the negative impact of terrorism. Because of weapons of mass destruction, terrorists today may kill hundreds, thousands, or even millions of people. Attacks will adversely affect the economy and disrupt our way of life in the process as well. Along these lines, another assertion is that taking drastic measures to counter terrorism may be unavoidable. One intelligence chief for the Department of Homeland Security believes "things are changing, and this change is happening because [attacks] can be brought to us that we cannot afford to absorb. We can't deal with them, so we're going to . . . do something ahead of time to preclude them. Is that going to change your lives? It already has" (Murphy 2006, 1047). In this light, combating terrorism is seen as a crucial moral responsibility—perhaps a goal that is even more important than the protection of civil liberties. It is better to forego a few rights, the argument goes, than to suffer the negative consequences of terrorism.

Others disagree vehemently. It is reported that Ben Franklin once stated that those who give up liberty for security, deserve neither. His argument is that the loss of rights would inevitably lead to insecurity; stable governments can only be brought about when citizens' liberty is guaranteed. Under this perspective, our rights are as valuable—or even more important—than security.

According to this viewpoint, many people feel that the government has gone too far in its attempt to ensure security against terrorism (Demmer 2004, 149). For instance:

- Critics of the government's . . . policy have long argued that lawmakers overrate terrorist threats to achieve their political goals, with the result that civil liberties are sacrificed (Griset and Mahan 2003, 282).

Figure 7-2

Benjamin Franklin declared that those who give up liberty for security deserve neither.

- The American Civil Liberties Union states "If we give up our freedoms, the terrorists win" (Murphy 2006, 1047).
- A movement has emerged that might be called anti-antiterrorism. Its argument is that certain steps being taken domestically against potential terrorist attacks are too intrusive and threaten civil liberties (Rosenzweig 2006, 1013).

The view favoring rights has gained a great deal of attention in recent years. However, Paul Rosenzweig, an adjunct professor at George Mason University, lists several reasons why it cannot be blamed solely on the aftermath of 9/11. He states that the liberty view has become more popular due to:

- **A more activist court.** The judicial system in the last 40 years has tended to overturn executive branch actions and congressional decisions.
- **A more partisan Congress.** Congressional investigative authority has expanded oversight of the President's power.
- **Investigative journalism.** Reporters have increasingly focused on activities that some might want to out of the public light.
- **Public interest groups.** Organizations like the American Civil Liberties Union are heavily involved in public information and litigation actions.
- **Technology.** Computers and the Internet have augmented people's ability to monitor the government.
- **Greater awareness of civil liberties.** Citizens are more educated about rights than ever before.

Thus, the perspective favoring liberty downplays the focus on security, and remains a popular paradigm to this day.

IN THE REAL WORLD

Physical Security vs. Civil Liberties

Paul Rosenzweig, an adjunct professor in the George Mason University School of Law, states that some people believe physical security is becoming more important than civil liberties (2006, 1023). He uses a hypothetical case of placing 10 alleged terrorists in prison. In the past, people in the United States generally accepted the rule that it is "better 10 terrorists go free than one innocent be mistakenly punished." Today, because of the high costs of terrorism, more people believe it is better to punish 10 alleged terrorists even if only one of them is actually guilty. This is because the potential for a terrorist attack increases if the guilty are released back into the general population. Such cases show the difficulty of balancing security and liberty in the United States.

SELF-CHECK

1. There are less than 10,000 terrorists around the world. True or False?
2. Some people believe that security is more important than liberty, but others believe the reverse is also true. True or False?
3. Ben Franklin stated:
    (a) law makers exaggerate the threat of terrorism.
    (b) if we give up our liberties, the terrorists win.
    (c) combating terrorism is a crucial moral responsibility.
    (d) those who give up liberty for security, deserve neither.
4. Explain why the anti-antiterrorism movement has gained momentum in recent years.

7.3 CASES AND CONSIDERATIONS

As can be seen, people feel strongly about both security and liberty. At times, these political values have been in direct conflict with one another. By trying to ensure security, policy makers have implemented decisions which have had dramatic repercussions on liberty. Rosenzweig (2006) as well as Griset and Mahan (2003) provide several examples from history:

• When the Civil War broke out in the United States, President Abraham Lincoln declared that anyone guilty of disloyal practices would be imprisoned.

Writ of habeas corpus:
A law protecting citizens from unlawful imprisonment.

Red Scare:
Senator McCarthy's fear of communist infiltration into the United States.

Freedom of speech:
People are allowed to express their opinions, even when they criticize the government.

Freedom of religion:
People cannot be denied their right to worship according to the dictates of their own conscience.

Right to assemble:
People are permitted to join in politically motivated gatherings.

Right to bear arms:
Guns can be purchased and owned without government interference.

Those convicted could not seek redress through the **writ of habeas corpus** (a law protecting citizens from unlawful imprisonment).

- During World War I, over 2,000 people were locked up because of their opposition to the global conflict. This eliminated virtually all anti-war sentiment in the United States.
- After Pearl Harbor was attacked in World War II, President Franklin D. Roosevelt signed Executive Order 9066. This allowed him to gather more than 110,000 people of Japanese decent and "relocate" them in detention centers in the Western/Pacific region of the United States (see figure 7-3).
- In 1953, Senator Joseph McCarthy raised fear of Russian infiltration into the United States. Under the banner of the **"Red Scare,"** his permanent investigations subcommittee sent numerous directors and actors to prison for alleged involvement in communism.

Such incidents have led Geoffrey Stone to suggest that "in time of war . . . we respond too harshly in our restriction of civil liberties, and then, later, regret our behavior" (in Rosenweig 2006, 1017).

Liberty may also be limited when terrorism is taken into account. For example, citizens of the United States are guaranteed:

- **Freedom of speech.** They are allowed to express their opinions, even when they criticize the government or others.
- **Freedom of religion.** They cannot be denied their right to worship according to the dictates of their own conscience.
- **Right to assemble.** People are permitted to join in politically motivated gatherings.
- **Right to bear arms.** Guns can be purchased and owned without government interference.

While these are all liberties that Americans enjoy and desire, they do present thorny questions for those engaged in creating homeland security policies. What if people are inciting terrorist attacks as they talk to others? What should be done with a religious group that promotes terrorism? What if meetings have the purpose of planning attacks? What if weapons will be used by terrorists to kill others?

The rights sustained by American political values could therefore run counter to efforts to stop terrorism. Should liberties be curtailed to promote security? Or, must liberty be treasured more than security? These are not just historical, hypothetical, or philosophical predicaments. We are facing very difficult choices today regarding security and liberty. A variety of recent examples can be given:

- After 9/11, the federal government immediately began to investigate the status of immigrants and visitors (mostly from Arab and Muslim nations)

Figure 7-3

During World War II, over 100,000 people of Japanese descent were relocated to detention centers due to security concerns.

in the United States. Over 1,000 foreigners were detained and some of them were charged for involvement in the attacks on America, expired visas, or miscellaneous violations (e.g., traffic tickets). Although this action may have prevented other attacks, some people suggest that the racial profiling and detentions were illegal (Griset and Mahan 2003, 285).

- As U.S. forces captured Taliban soldiers and Al Qaeda members in Afghanistan, they sent many of them to prisons at Guantanamo Bay, Cuba. Many were held for indefinite periods without being charged of formal crimes. If evidence warrants further investigation, prisoners are tried in military tribunals that lack juries and civilian oversight. These efforts have reduced the number of "enemy combatants" around the world, but seem to reject our own laws pertaining to illegal seizures and fair trials.

- The State of Florida declined to issue a driver's license to a woman who did not want to remove the veil over her face when pictures were being taken (Long 2003). The woman sued and claimed religious discrimination. Howard Marks, the woman's attorney, states "There is no public safety issue here with Sultanna Freeman, none whatsoever. Sometime when there are fears and prejudices in our country, we react and . . . go overboard. We go too far. We infringe on the liberties we are fighting for; the liberties that make us the American Society." Judge Janet C. Thorpe disagrees with the lawsuit: "If you rule for the plaintiff, someday a man will present himself to a driver license office and demand a license, without a photo, based upon his religious convictions. You may have to give it to him, but we will not know if his objectives are sincere or peaceful, or if they are terrible until it is too late." Both comments are justified—but difficult to reconcile in light of the other.

- A professional emergency management organization in one state wrote Congress about its fear of sensitive public information getting into the hands of terrorists. The letter declares: "Over the past several years, government agencies across the state have been assessing our vulnerability to natural disasters and, more recently, terrorist attacks. Unfortunately, these assessments, if publicly disclosed, can provide a road map for a person or groups intent on destroying government facilities, disrupting government services and, in some cases, causing injury and death. Such assessments are now available upon request under provisions of the Open Government Act. In addition to the assessments, other critical information is available which has the same potential to be used against the interests of governments and their constituents. This includes items such as: detailed engineering drawings of facilities such as dams, power plants and government buildings; detailed response plans and procedures; and network diagrams for information management and telecommunications systems. . . . We propose that the Open Government Act be amended to allow officials to deny access to certain, carefully defined classes of information such as those described previously. Our goal is to restrict public access to sensitive emergency plans and information that might be valuable to persons attempting to mount an attack." Such limitations seem perfectly logical in light of the terrorist threat. However, are there potential dangers in amending the Open Government Act?

There are perhaps no simple resolutions to the difficult situations discussed above. For such reasons success is not to be achieved by giving security preference over liberty or by elevating liberty concerns over the goal of security. Instead, both values should be carefully weighed against the other, and decisions should be fluid and never set in stone. Paul Rosenzweig affirms "one possible lesson from history is that we should not be utterly unwilling to adjust our response to liberty and security for the sake of counterterrorism, since we have the capacity to manage that adjustment, and to readjust it as necessary" (2006, 1020).

Others have also provided recommendations for ensuring liberty even while we address threats to security. In a statement before Congress, Richard Ben-Veniste and Slade Gorton of the National Commission on Terrorist Attacks on the United States, state that "The test is a simple but important one. The burden of proof should be on the proponents of the measure to establish the power or authority being sought would in fact materially enhance national security, and that there will be adequate supervision of the exercise of that power or authority to ensure the protection of civil liberties. If additional powers are granted, there must be adequate guidelines and oversight to properly confine their use" (Murphy 2006, 1048).

Laura Murphy, Director of the Washington Legislative Office of the ACLU, says we need to apply additional tests (2006, 1049–1051):

- Do the costs of liberty outweigh the potential benefits to public safety?
- Will the measure call for, or result in, discrimination based on religion, ethnicity, race, or other group characteristics?
- Is the measure properly tailored to the desired mission, or could it result in unintended and possibly abusive consequences?
- Will the public react negatively to the measure?

If the answers to these questions are in the affirmative, Murphy recommends that the considered action be rejected in favor of less severe alternatives.

Thus, logic and evidence implies that security may require some limitations on liberty. The threat of terrorism is significant and should be taken seriously. Nonetheless, liberty should not be fully sacrificed on the security altar. One of the reasons why we should be extremely careful is because there is circumstantial evidence that terrorists are likely to

IN THE REAL WORLD

Treatment of Detainees at Guantanamo Bay

After an investigation of the prison facility at Guantanamo Bay, Cuba, the FBI described the treatment of enemy combatants captured in Afghanistan or elsewhere (Ackerman 2008, 124). At times, detainees had insufficient water or food. Others had been chained to the wall and had urinated or defecated on themselves. The temperature of interrogation rooms was set either too cold or too hot. Detainees were exposed to loud music by Lil' Kim and Eminen or repeated videos of a Meow Mix commercial. Each of these incidents was authorized by Pentagon guidelines. Such cases raise challenging questions for those involved in homeland security. If such techniques could prevent a terrorist attack, would they be justified? Is it ever correct to limit people's rights and liberties? Can a proper balance between security and liberty be found? If so, how? This is a very contentious issue. Some assert that the loss of rights does nothing to prevent terrorism and it may actually promote it. Others declare that many lives have been saved by making security the top priority. It is likely that this debate will continue into the future.

emanate from politically repressed societies. In addition, a failure to appreciate the importance of rights may create the terrorism we are trying to counter. If we deny rights to others, we run the risk of creating more enemies in the future. Lhaj-Thami Breze, President of the Union of Islamic Organizations in France, states "The majority of Muslims want to practice their religion in peace and in total respect of the laws. But, when you persecute, when you make fun of, when you refuse, when you don't respect beliefs, what is the consequence? The consequence is radicalization" (Associated Press 2004). Also, if domestic rights are severely eroded in the name of homeland security, there is the chance that citizens in the United States may rise up violently against their own government. Both possibilities should be avoided.

 SELF-CHECK

1. There have been no wars that have resulted in the loss of liberties. True or False?

2. Law in the United States protects the right to assemble, and terrorists could use this right to meet to plan out attacks. True or False?

3. The search for communists after World War II was known as:

   (a) the writ of habeas corpus.
   (b) the Red Scare.
   (c) the Japanese interment.
   (d) Executive Order 9066.

4. What are some tests that could help to protect rights as we fight the war on terrorism?

SUMMARY

As a participant in homeland security, it is imperative that you assess the trade offs between security and rights. You must know why terrorism exploits the tension between these two important priorities. You should be aware of the menacing threat of terrorism as well as the reasons why freedoms should not be eliminated. Because there are historical and current events that illustrate the delicate balance between security and freedoms, you must educate yourself about the consequences of homeland security policies. Most importantly, you should find ways to protect security while minimizing the loss of liberty. Striving for both objectives is most likely to reduce the possibility of future terrorist attacks.

ASSESS YOUR UNDERSTANDING

UNDERSTAND: WHAT HAVE YOU LEARNED?

 Go to **www.wiley.com/college/mcentire** to assess your knowledge of the relationship of terrorism to security and liberty.

SUMMARY QUESTIONS

1. Why is terrorism different than war?

2. What are some of the reasons why security is important after 9/11?

3. List three reasons why an appreciation for liberty and rights has increased in recent years.

4. Has there ever been a time when liberty has been curtailed in the name of security? If so, discuss this case.

5. Discuss how the right to assemble can be abused by terrorists. Does this create a dilemma for policy makers?

6. One professional emergency management organization proposed to limit public access to sensitive government information. Why was this recommendation made?

7. What are five tests that can help us to protect rights as we attempt to augment security?

8. Governments take measures to protect themselves from outside aggressors, otherwise they may cease to exist. True or False?

9. The President and Congress have no responsibility to protect citizen freedoms and rights. True or False?

10. Security has become a much greater priority since 9/11. True or False?

11. There are no known international terrorists in the United States. True or False?

12. Some government leaders feel their most important responsibility is to protect the nation from further attacks. True or False?

13. During the Civil War, President Lincoln did not send people to prison if they were involved in disloyal practices. True or False?

14. The right to bear arms implies that people can purchase and own guns without government interference. True or False?

15. U.S. citizens are guaranteed freedom of religion. This could create a difficult choice for policy makers if people use their beliefs to incite terrorist attacks. True or False?

16. What is the name of the international laws that were created to protect soldiers?

    (a) The Stafford Agreement

    (b) The Hague Convention

    (c) The Geneva Convention

    (d) The Paris Accords

17. According to the American Civil Liberties Union, "if we give up our freedoms:

    (a) we are most likely to win the war on terrorism."

    (b) the terrorists win."

    (c) we will not be able to prevail against terrorism."

    (d) the terrorists will not be able to prevail against terrorism."

18. A more activist court implies:

    (a) congressional investigative authority has expanded.

    (b) reporters increasingly focus on rights.

    (c) citizens are more aware of their liberties.

    (d) the judicial system has overturned executive decisions.

19. During World War II, President Roosevelt:

    (a) sent 110,000 Japanese Americans to relocation centers.

    (b) sent many Hollywood actors and directors to prison.

    (c) stopped all anti-war sentiment.

    (d) rescinded the writ of habeas corpus.

20. The State of Florida:

    (a) does not want to give sensitive information to the public.

    (b) did not give a license to a woman who refused to remove her veil.

    (c) held Arab and Muslims who were here illegally.

    (d) took the U.S. government to court because it violated the writ of habeas corpus.

BE A HOMELAND SECURITY PROFESSIONAL

The Threat of Terrorism

You have been asked to testify before Congress about the need for new laws to protect our nation. What evidence could you use to describe the threat we are facing?

The Importance of Rights

As a member of a Congressional committee on terrorism, you are concerned about rights and liberties. What questions could you ask those who are proposing more stringent security measures?

The Geneva Conventions and Terrorism

Read a book or search the Internet for information about the Geneva Convention. Write a two-page essay describing the relation between the Geneva Convention and the treatment of terrorists.

KEY TERMS

Freedom of religion	People cannot be denied their right to worship according to the dictates of their own conscience.
Freedom of speech	People are allowed to express their opinions, even when they criticize the government.
Geneva Conventions	A set of internationally accepted laws pertaining to the conduct of war.
Red Scare	Senator McCarthy's fear of communist infiltration into the United States.
Right to assemble	People are permitted to join in politically motivated gatherings.
Right to bear arms	Guns can be purchased and owned without government interference.
Writ of habeas corpus	A law protecting citizens from unlawful imprisonment.

REFERENCES

Ackerman, Spencer. (2008). "Island Mentality." Pp. 124–128 in Badey, Thomas J. *Homeland Security.* McGraw-Hill: Dubuque, IA.

Associated Press. (2004). "Head Scarf Ban Backlash Warning." CNN.Com, February 10, www.cnn.com/2004/WORLD/europe/02/10/france. headscarves.ap.

Badey, Thomas J. (2008). *Homeland Security.* McGraw-Hill: Dubuque, IA.

Demmer, Valerie L. (2004). "Civil Liberties and Homeland Security." Pp. 149–152 in Badey, Thomas J. (Ed.). *Homeland Security.* McGraw-Hill/Dushkin: Guilford, CT.

Griset, Pamala L. and Sue Mahan. (2003). *Terrorism in Perspective.* Sage: Thousands Oaks, CA.

Long, Phil. (2003). "State: ID Photo is Security Issue." *The Miami Herald.* May 30. www.miami.com.mld.miamiherald/news/state/5972523.htm.

Murphy, Laura W. (2006). "Principled Prudence: Civil Liberties and the Homeland Security Practitioner." Pp. 1045–1062 in Kamien, David G. (Ed.). *The McGraw-Hill Homeland Security Handbook.* McGraw-Hill: New York.

Rosenzweig, Paul. (2006). "Thinking about Civil Liberty and Terrorism" Pp. 1013–1030 in Kamien, David G. (Ed.) *The McGraw-Hill Homeland Security Handbook.* McGraw-Hill: New York.

Taipale, K. A. (2006). "Introduction to Section 12" Pp. 1009–1012 in Kamien, David G. (Ed.). *The McGraw-Hill Homeland Security Handbook.* McGraw-Hill: New York.

White, Jonathan R. (2002). Terrorism: An Introduction. Wadsworth: Belmont, CA.

8

PREVENTING TERRORIST ATTACKS

Root Causes, Law, Intelligence, Counter-terrorism, and Border Control

Do You Already Know?

- The difficulty of addressing root causes of terrorism
- The laws that aim to stop terrorist attacks
- How information is acquired about potential terrorists
- Benefits and drawbacks of counter-terrorism
- Methods to enhance border control

 For additional questions to assess your current knowledge of measures to prevent terrorist attacks, go to **www.wiley.com/college/mcentire**

What You Will Find Out	What You Will Be Able To Do
8.1 The importance and difficulty of addressing the root causes of terrorism	• Describe ways to minimize people's desire to attack the United States
8.2 Laws that aim to stop terrorist attacks	• Evaluate the nature of policies designed to prevent terrorism
8.3 The cycle used to acquire information about terrorists and potential attacks	• Plan ways to acquire intelligence about potential terrorists
8.4 The benefits and drawbacks of counter-terrorism activities	• Critique the need for and impact of preemptive strikes against terrorist enemies
8.5 Methods to enhance border control	• Synthesize the variety of steps Kthat can be taken to protect the border

INTRODUCTION

As a participant in homeland security, one of your principle objectives is to prevent terrorist attacks against the United States. For this reason, it will be imperative that you take several steps to minimize the probability of terrorism. One such measure is to eliminate, if possible, grievances that result in terrorist attacks. You should also be aware of and support laws that proscribe terrorist activity. Another requirement is to anticipate terrorist intentions through intelligence gathering methods. At other times, the military may need to be deployed in counter-terrorism operations abroad. Programs must also be initiated to prevent the infiltration of terrorists into the United States. Each of these measures may help to halt terrorist attacks now and in the future.

8.1 ADDRESSING ROOT CAUSES

According to certain scholars, the current approach in the name of homeland security (i.e., the war against terrorism in Iraq) has been ineffective and even counter-productive (Lustick 2007). Instead of advocating an aggressive military response to terrorism, war protestors as well as journalists and politicians around the world often assert that the United States should do its best to reverse the root causes of terrorism through other means (Shakil-ur-Rahman 2007). According to this view, one of the most important, but currently under-utilized, activities to prevent terrorism is to eliminate terrorists' motivations to commit terrorist attacks. As noted in Chapter 3, it is believed that terrorism will occur more frequently when abject poverty prevails, when political freedoms are limited, when human rights are ignored, and when alternate viewpoints or groups of people are not respected. Jonathan Lash, a reporter for *Science Magazine*, states "the compound of poverty, powerlessness, lack of opportunity, and injustice is volatile" (2001, 1789). U.S. Foreign policy decisions, in the opinion of President Mohammad Khatami of Iran, may also lead to opposition against America and further terrorist attacks around the world (CNN 2001). Such perspectives hold the opinion that there are many things that must be changed if the number of terrorist attacks is to be diminished in the future.

For instance, the head of the World Bank stated that "terrorism will not end until poverty is eliminated" (as cited by Francis 2002). It is also suggested that people have an innate desire to participate in and influence political decisions. Others assert that the United States must protect the human rights of everyone around the world—and not just American citizens. A common perception in the Middle East is that terrorism would be minimized if the West shows consideration to Muslim values. There is also a belief that terrorism could be reduced if the United States and Israel avoid unfair treatment of Arabs (i.e., they claim to support liberty but Palestinians feel they are denied freedoms and a political voice) (Abu-Amara 2002).

The idea of addressing such root causes is both controversial and difficult. American corporations will oppose many practices that limit free trade or curtail profits. The expanding of democracy to other nations may actually augment the attacks we are trying to prevent because it is viewed as a threat to the theocratic governments which exist in some nations. Human rights of potential victims can run in opposition to those of terrorists (e.g., is it alright to kill potential terrorists that others may be spared?). Countries in the Middle East may misunderstand America's intentions to increase political freedoms everywhere. It is true that Israel has held elections for Arab-Israelis and the United States is attempting to establish a state to protect Palestinian people. However, the violence shown toward Israel and the United States may augment security measures taken against Palestinians and Muslims. There are likewise some root causes that the United States may not be able to control. As an example, children in some countries are often taught to hate Americans and are brought up in a culture of violent behavior (Leiter 2002). It may be virtually impossible to reverse such attitudes when they are ingrained at such a young age.

Regardless of the severity of these challenges, it would be advisable that the United States government recognize that it must do more to address root causes if homeland security is to be enhanced. Failing to do so will only lead to a more protracted conflict with individual terrorists and the groups and nations that support them. Reaching out to moderate Muslims in a partnership may prove useful for the generation of ideas that will help to resolve such problems. Diplomatic activity is therefore the first preference. Nonetheless, such efforts may not be enough. Terrorists may attack the United States no matter what this country does. Other preventive measures may inevitably be required.

IN THE REAL WORLD

Use Diplomacy or Not?

During the summer 2007 debates among those vying for the office of President, diplomacy became a heated subject among democratic and republican candidates. Most of those from the left asserted the need to engage enemy nations and find ways to resolve conflict through diplomacy and peaceful foreign policy. Those on the right declared that negotiations with terrorists and governments that support such violence are pointless since they have already stated their desire to attack the United States. One side saw value in diplomatic endeavors while the other affirmed no logical reason to negotiate with well-known enemies. One camp attempts to address root causes through diplomacy while this is discredited by another. Diplomacy with enemy states is a politically contentious issue for sure.

SELF-CHECK

1. Addressing the root causes of terrorism is currently the most used approach to preventing terrorist attacks. True or False?

2. Some people believe that continuing poverty and injustice will augment terrorist attacks against the United States. True or False?

3. Which is not seen as a way to address root causes of terrorism?

    (a) Eliminating the indoctrination of children to hate the United States

    (b) Improving U.S. foreign policy

    (c) Disregarding the rights of Palestinians

    (d) Respecting different cultures around the world

4. Will poverty reduction, human rights, and the expansion of democracy prevent all terrorist attacks? Why or why not?

8.2 POLICY AND LEGISLATION

Another measure that has been taken to deal with the threat of terrorism is to create policies and enact laws which make terrorism illegal or criminal. These policies and regulations that outlaw terrorism may emanate from executive orders (e.g., presidential directives), congressional decisions, or state and local legislative bodies. Although laws can be initiated by different branches and at all levels of government, homeland security has been mostly driven by the President and federal agencies. Some of these laws were implemented before 9/11. Others were created to promote homeland security after this fateful date.

8.2.1 Laws Prior to 9/11

Even though the United States has always been threatened by terrorism, it has only recently begun to address terrorism through policy and legislation. To be sure, the government did prosecute those engaging in terrorism, but it usually did so through laws that dealt with murder, arson, and property destruction. In the mid-1990s, however, this began to change.

One of the first policies to address terrorism directly was Presidential Decision Directive 39 (the US Policy on Counter-terrorism). This policy was issued after major terrorist attacks in Japan and the United States. These two attacks are particularly noteworthy.

On March 25, 1995, the apocalyptic cult, Aum Shinrikyo, punctured plastic bags containing liquid sarin on various subways in Tokyo and elsewhere. The attack killed 12 people and sent 5,500 people to hospitals (although only 1,000 had sustained injuries). On April 19, 1995, Timothy

McVeigh detonated a bomb in Oklahoma City at the Alfred P. Murrah Federal Building. It killed 168 people and injured another 800. Recognizing the seriousness of these events, President Clinton reiterated in his statement that it is the policy of the United States to use all means necessary to defeat terrorism. He vowed that the government would work with friendly nations to pursue terrorists through counter-terrorism operations. He also declared that the government would seek the return of any terrorist who commits acts against the interests of the United States for prosecution. President Clinton assigned terrorism-related roles and responsibilities to many federal organizations including the Department of State, the Department of Defense, the Department of the Treasury, the Department of Energy, the Department of Transportation, the Attorney General, and the Director of the CIA. PDD-39 also separated functions dealing with terrorism into two categories. Crisis management was a law enforcement responsibility focusing on the apprehension and prosecution of terrorists. Crisis management was to be led by the FBI. Consequence management dealt more with preparedness, response, and recovery activities. The Federal Emergency Management Agency was put in charge of these functions.

In the late 1990s and early part of the new millennium, congress also began to recognize the growing threat of terrorism against the United States. It passed a few laws which instituted homeland security as a national and foreign policy goal. From this point on, America would be less concerned with enemy states in comparison to individual terrorists and terrorist organizations. Understanding this emerging threat, House Resolution 1158 permitted the establishment of the National Homeland Security Agency. It was passed on March 21, 2001. House Resolution 1292 allowed the President to create a strategy for homeland security. It was enacted on March 29, 2001. While all of these laws signified substantial change, it was not until 9/11 that most of the legislation dealing with homeland security was initiated.

8.2.2 Legislation After 9/11

USA PATRIOT Act:
A homeland security law which stands for "Uniting and Strengthening America by Providing Appropriate Tools Required to Intercept and Obstruct Terrorism." This law aims to prevent terrorist attacks and enhance law enforcement's ability to investigate and punish offenders.

Shortly after the terrorist attacks on the east coast, President Bush established an Office of Homeland Security in the White House. Executive Order 13228 was issued on October 8, 2001. Tom Ridge was sworn in as the first director of this office. Within a few short weeks, additional homeland security legislation would be passed. These laws would have a profound impact upon the United States.

On October 25, 2001, Congress passed and the President ratified the USA PATRIOT Act. The **USA PATRIOT Act** stands for "Uniting and Strengthening America by Providing Appropriate Tools Required to Intercept and Obstruct Terrorism." Its goal was to prevent terrorist attacks and enhance law enforcement ability to investigate and punish offenders.

This law relaxed restrictions on sharing information among the CIA and FBI, permitted roving wiretaps and increased surveillance over computer communications, and allowed for the detention of suspected terrorists. The PATRIOT Act also mandated new measures to prevent the funding of terrorism, prohibited the harboring of terrorists, and augmented the number of border agents. The PATRIOT Act also eliminated the statute of limitations for terrorist acts, meaning that a person could be tried for attacks regardless of how long ago they occurred. Although highly controversial because of the infringement of rights and liberties, this law enhanced the ability of law enforcement to find, apprehend, and prosecute terrorists.

Transportation Security Act:
A law designed to protect transportation systems in the United States.

A short time later (November 19, 2001), the **Transportation Security Act** was passed. In November, Congress created this law to protect transportation systems in the United States. From this point on, only passengers could enter airport terminals. The federal government also took over airport screening operations and purchased new equipment to detect explosives in carry-on and checked baggage. These activities intended to make it more difficult for terrorists to use airplanes in future attacks.

A number of other important policies and laws were implemented in 2002 and 2003. The first of which was Executive Order 13224. On August 9, 2002, President Bush acknowledged that the government would freeze any assets belonging to terrorists to limit attacks against the United States. Courts have since supported this decision and funds supporting terrorism have been seized in the United States and elsewhere. The Justice Department released a statement noting that "freezing the assets of organizations that bankroll terror is a legitimate and important role in the government's arsenal for fighting the war against terrorism." In the most notable case, the Holy Land Foundation for Relief and Development was indicted for supporting terrorism. It is believed that this organization sent over $1.4 million to Hamas. Their court case began in July 2007 and resulted in a hung jury in October. The government is expected to re-try the case.

Homeland Security Act:
A law passed in 2002 which mandated the creation of the Department of Homeland Security.

Another very significant law was passed on November 25, 2002. President Bush signed the **Homeland Security Act**, which because active on January 24, 2003. This law resulted in the most dramatic reformulation of government in 50 years and led to the creation of the Department of Homeland Security. The Homeland Security Act outlined the mission of the DHS, listed its responsibilities dealing with border security, infrastructure protection, and the like. This law also focused on WMD counter-measures, and explained how the transition to homeland security would take place. The Homeland Security Act has resulted in major challenges for the federal government due to massive organizational realignments, but virtually everyone agrees that more needed to be done to deal with the threat of terrorism.

Figure 8-1

The Seal of the Department of Homeland Security reflects its mission. The eagle's claws represent activities during peace and war. The circles surrounding the eagle's wings symbolize DHS' aims to coordinate with other levels of government.

Comprehensive Home-land Security Act:
A law passed in 2003 containing new regulations for critical infrastructure security, railroad security, and more stringent measures related to border control and weapons of mass destruction.

A final important piece of legislation to be mentioned here, the **Comprehensive Homeland Security Act**, was passed on January 7, 2003. This legislation resulted in many new regulations pertaining to security of critical infrastructure and railroads. It also implemented more stringent measures pertaining to border control and the proliferation of weapons of mass destruction. Other portions of the law deal with improving intelligence gathering and weapons of mass destruction. Funds were likewise released to aid local law enforcement efforts to support homeland security goals.

Additional policies and pieces of legislation have been issued or passed over the past several years. In fact, new laws are being implemented every day. If you are working in homeland security, it will be imperative that you stay on top of new developments. Some laws have been changed or repealed while others are being created at a frantic pace. The government is desperately working to prevent terrorist attacks. Unfortunately, some of these laws have been controversial and hastily put together. Funding has also been misdirected and insufficient at times. It is likely that the challenges confronting legislators will continue into the foreseeable future.

IN THE REAL WORLD

The Comprehensive Homeland Security Act

The Comprehensive Homeland Security Act of 2003 is one of the most important pieces of legislation guiding homeland security activities today. This bill, put forward by Senator Thomas Daschle (D–SD), focuses heavily on a variety of measures to prevent terrorism. It established a task force to protect nuclear power plants from terrorist attacks. The goal of this group is to assess the vulnerability of such structures and outline actions to secure them against terrorist threats. Besides noting concern about terrorist attacks involving radioactive material, the act also mandated a national smallpox vaccination program, promotes ways to foster intelligence dissemination, increased regulations pertaining to the use of hazardous materials, and augmented financial and technical assistance to law enforcement agencies in the United States. This law will have lasting impact upon homeland security for the foreseeable future.

SELF-CHECK

1. Terrorism has always been an important subject of legislation in the United States. True or False?

2. Homeland security was being discussed as a policy before 9/11. True or False?

3. Which terrorist attacks resulted in Presidential Decision Directive 39?

    (a) 9/11 and the Oklahoma City Bombing

    (b) The Tokyo subway attack and Oklahoma City Bombing

    (c) The Tokyo subway attack and 9/11

    (d) The sarin gas attack and 9/11

4. What are some of the features of the Homeland Security Act and Comphrensive Homeland Security Act?

8.3 INTELLIGENCE

Intelligence:
The function of collecting, assessing, and distributing information about an enemy, criminal or terrorist.

One of the best ways to prevent terrorist attacks is to have a sound understanding of the plans of potential terrorists. This brings up the important function of intelligence. **Intelligence** is a word that describes the function of collecting, assessing, and distributing information about an enemy, criminal, or terrorist. Governments have long been concerned about the activities of unfriendly countries. Their desire is to become aware of the threats posed by rival nations so they may take necessary defensive or offensive measures. Law enforcement officials also seek information about citizens who plan to break laws that bring order to society. In this case, detectives attempt to avert the theft, murder, or other crimes and arrest those who are intent on violating the law. In the context of homeland security, intelligence about terrorist intentions is the most important priority. It is imperative to acquire knowledge about potential terrorist attacks in order to prevent their negative consequences of death, damage, and disruption.

8.3.1 The Need for Intelligence

Intelligence has been a major feature of America's national security interests since our birth as a nation. Efforts have always been undertaken to understand the activities of enemy nations and the threat they posed to the United States. This was especially the case after World War II. Intelligence efforts were bound to the Cold War mentality. Although animosity with the former Soviet Union dissipated in the late 1980s, American political and military leaders remained fearful of potential enemy nations. In particular, the United States was spending time and energy on understanding rising powers (i.e., China, North Korea, and Iran) during the 1990s. On the domestic front, law enforcement agencies were giving attention to the war on drugs, the sale or use of illegal weapons, and civil rights violations (e.g., hate crimes). It was under this context that terrorists took America by surprise.

For instance, during President Clinton's tenure in office, the United States witnessed several terrorist attacks against American interests. On February 26, 1993, Middle Eastern terrorists bombed the World Trade Center. High profile attacks also occurred toward the end of the 1990s. Two United States embassies were bombed in the African nations of Tanzania and Kenya on August 7, 1998. Another attack took place against the U.S.S. Cole (a military vessel) in a Yemen port on October 12, 2000. The intelligence community was able to detect and deter one major attack during this period. The **Bojinka plot**—a planned attack on airliners over the Pacific Ocean—was thwarted in 1995. However, in hindsight it appears that not enough was being done to anticipate the growing threat of terrorism.

This trend continued when George W. Bush was elected as President. The CIA and FBI began to collect evidence specifying that Al Qaeda was intent on attacking the United States. One analyst in Phoenix, Arizona, noted in July 2001 that potential terrorist operatives were taking flight training lessons at U.S. schools. On August 6, 2001, President Bush was given a brief entitled "Bin Laden Determined to Strike in U.S." It stated that Al Qaeda was intent on bringing the fight to America and that it was recruiting and operating in places like New York City. In spite of these clues, the

Bojinka plot:
A planned attack on airliners over the Pacific Ocean.

United States appeared to be oblivious to the impending attacks on 9/11. After a careful study of events leading up to that fateful day, the 9/11 Commission (2004) listed several reasons why the attacks were not fully anticipated: an increased number of intelligence reports with insufficient details, an inability to share intelligence across government agencies, and a failure to appreciate the tenacity and creativity of terrorists. Terrorist attacks and government panels revealed that intelligence must be a key feature if homeland security is to be successful.

IN THE REAL WORLD

Detainee Treatment and Interrogation

Although preventing future terrorist attacks is desirable, it can be controversial. While no one wants to see further acts of terrorism, many people are concerned about the treatment of prisoners who may have information about terrorists' plans. Abu Ghraib and waterboarding are examples of this issue. Abu Ghraib is a prison on the west side of Baghdad. At one time, it housed about 7,000 detainees who were believed to have been involved in insurgent attacks against U.S. troops. In April 2004, it was revealed that prisoners were being beaten, raped, and forced to pose naked for pictures in sexually explicit positions. Twelve soldiers have been convicted for their roles in the abuse scandal. The practice of waterboarding has also been decried by human rights watch groups. Waterboarding is a technique used to force victim confessions. It involves immobilizing a person on his or her back, and lifting the lower part of the body in the air. Water is then poured over the persons' face to simulate drowning. This action has been condemned as a cruel form of torture. Those in favor of forceful interrogation techniques argue that confessions may help to prevent future terrorist attacks. However, it is also alleged that that prisoner treatment and interrogation techniques may also result in additional acts of terrorism. There is some evidence that Nicholas Berg, an American businessman in Iraq, was beheaded as a result of the treatment of prisoners in Abu Ghraib.

Intelligence cycle:
A four-step process of gathering, understanding, and synthesizing data, and then sharing it with those who will use it.

8.3.2 The Intelligence Cycle

In an attempt to overcome prior weaknesses, Patrick Duecy (2006) recommends that those involved rely on the **intelligence cycle**. This includes a four step process of gathering, understanding and synthesizing data, and then sharing it with those who will use it.

Intelligence collection:
Activities to gather information about terrorist organizations, their operations, and potential attacks.

OPINT:
Open source intelligence acquired through publicly available materials including academic research, newspaper articles, library books, etc.

SIGINT:
Interception and interpretation of electronic communications such as phone conversations and emails.

IMINT:
Geospatial imagery collected by satellites and aircraft.

MASINT:
Measurement and signature intelligence that looks for the characteristics of certain types of actions (e.g., the presence of nuclear material when one is trying to develop a nuclear weapon).

HUMINT:
Intelligence collected by people from people (and can be done overtly or covertly).

Intelligence analysis:
Efforts to make sense of the voluminous data that is gathered from the field.

Intelligence production:
The creation of written reports, briefings, images, or maps to influence operational decisions.

Intelligence dissemination:
Sharing information with end-users (e.g., policy makers, FBI Special Agents, homeland security personnel, etc.).

1. **Intelligence collection**—activities to gather information about terrorist organizations, their operations and potential attacks. Information may be obtained through a variety of means including:

   - **OPINT**—open source intelligence is acquired through publicly available materials including academic research, newspaper articles, library books, etc.
   - **SIGINT**—interception and interpretation of electronic signal communications such as phone conversations and emails.
   - **IMINT**—geospatial imagery collected by satellites and aircraft.
   - **MASINT**—measurement and signature intelligence looks for the characteristics of certain types of actions (e.g., the presence of nuclear material when one is trying to develop, smuggle or use a nuclear weapon or dirty bomb).
   - **HUMINT**—intelligence collected by people from people (and can be done overtly or covertly).

2. **Intelligence analysis**—efforts to make sense of the voluminous data that is gathered from the field. This is often performed at the headquarters level where individuals and groups process information to determine what is really going on at the field level.

3. **Intelligence production**—the creation of publications, briefings, images or maps to influence policy or operational decisions. Written reports, oral presentations, and supporting documents are examples of this stage of the intelligence cycle.

4. **Intelligence dissemination**—sharing information with end-users to increase agency awareness, warn the public, and take steps to "preempt, disrupt or defeat terrorism" (Kaupi 2006, 423). This may include policy makers, FBI Special Agents, homeland security personnel, the military, etc.

Of course, additional intelligence will be required when collection is incomplete, analysis seeks to "connect the dots," production generates new questions, and dissemination results in the anticipation of future concerns. We may therefore want to add another step to this cycle and label it as **intelligence adjustment**. The intelligence cycle adapts repeatedly based on intelligence shortfalls, insufficient information, changing priorities, and unfolding needs. It requires a great deal of planning and direction with an eye toward the future (Kauppi 2006, 415).

8.3.3 Challenges Facing the Intelligence Community

As can been seen, the intelligence cycle is not a simple linear process. Nor is it exempt from significant challenges. At least four major difficulties have to be overcome. The first problem relates to the types of intelligence

Intelligence adjustment:
Adaptation of the intelligence cycle is required when collection is incomplete, analysis seeks to "connect the dots," production generates new questions, and dissemination results in the anticipation of future concerns.

that are useful for homeland security purposes. During the Cold War, the United States relied heavily upon IMINT and MASINT to detect troop movements and the building of missile sites or bomb bunkers. HUMINT was also utilized during this time by spies and secret agents who understood the language, history, and culture of Russia. The problem with these sources of intelligence is that they are less useful in homeland security (at least as they have traditionally been used). IMINT and MASINT can still be utilized to detect terrorism activities, but they are of reduced value because terrorists are especially adept at operating in stealth.

The HUMINT system built up during the Cold War is also not suited to address today's homeland security needs. Besides needing a substantially larger quantity of agents, the United States must have operatives who understand Arabic languages, Islamic religion, and Middle Eastern cultural practices. This is no small feat when one considers the complexity of these subjects. Even as the American intelligence community re-tools for today's homeland security objectives, it will be extremely difficult to penetrate terrorist groups and cells. Terrorists have close knit relations and they are not likely to allow much infiltration into their organizations. The United States will therefore have to work with Arabs and others around the world that already understand and can assimilate into terrorist goals and activities.

A second problem with the function of intelligence is that it is heavily dependent on technology. Terrorists communicate, plan, and conduct attacks with the use of technology. Cell phones, fax machines, pagers, tele-conferencing, emails, and the Internet are all frequently used by terrorists. This technology allows terrorists to operate with a degree of impunity. FBI Director Louis Freeh stated before a US Senate Commission in March 2000 that "uncrackable encryption is allowing terrorists to communicate without fear of outside intrusion." He further stated, because of this technology "they're thwarting the efforts of law enforcement" (in Thetford 2001, 252). Therefore, the intelligence community must have adequate equipment and training to allow them to operate in the modern world of technology.

A third problem is that there are many organizations that provide intelligence services. Most people have heard of the well-known Central Intelligence Agency (CIA) and Federal Bureau of Investigations (FBI) which operate in international and domestic spheres respectively. You may not have heard about the National Security Agency (NSA), the Defense Intelligence Agency (DIA), the National Geospatial Intelligence Agency (NGA), and the National Reconnaissance Office (NRO). The shear number of federal agencies (which are not mentioned in their totality here) is only eclipsed when we consider those from state and local jurisdictions in the United States. States are developing terrorism intelligence units, and even the City of New York has its own dedicated agency to assess threats against the largest metropolitan area in the United States.

This diversity of organizations obscures intelligence ownership and sometimes discourages collaboration. As an example, before 9/11, the FBI and CIA were prohibited by law from sharing information with each other. Fortunately, new laws have been passed and a Terrorist Threat Integration Center (TTIC), which joins the efforts of the FBI and CIA, has been created to improve cooperation in the federal government. The Department of Homeland Security also aims to collect information on attacks planned against the United States. Efforts have also been undertaken to augment the sharing of intelligence internationally and with lower levels of government in the United States. For instance, **INTERPOL** is an international police organization that is involved in intelligence gathering and sharing. It has 186 member nations that collect and distribute information about terrorists and various forms of criminal behavior. The United States also works with NATO (the North Atlantic Treaty Organization), other friendly nations, and state and local governments.

INTERPOL:
An international police organization that is involved in intelligence.

This brings up a fourth challenge: determining who to share the intelligence with. For instance, while some information is sensitive but unclassified, much of it can be classified. **Classified intelligence** is given only to a very specific and limited number of people to protect sources of acquisition and deny adversaries information that would lead them to alter their communications or operations (Deucy 2006, 401). Classified intelligence is thus only given on a need to know basis and is strictly guarded. Unfortunately, failing to share information with others could prove dangerous as we found out on 9/11. Finding an appropriate balance between safeguarding and sharing intelligence is imperative for success.

Classified intelligence:
Information given only to a very specific and limited number of people to protect sources of acquisition and deny adversaries information that would lead them to alter their communications or operations.

A final problem concerns gathering intelligence about the funding of terrorism. Since 9/11, the government has been very interested in disrupting terrorist finances. Numerous laws have been passed to make it illegal to support terrorism through monetary means. A challenge arises due to the fact that terrorists are very careful about laundering money. **Money laundering** is the process of hiding where money is coming from and what it is being used for. Terrorists are adept at collecting money through legal and illegal means and hiding its sources.

Money laundering:
The process of hiding where money is coming from and what it is being used for.

They may gather funds from legitimate charities and businesses as well as fraudulent companies and organizations. These finances may then be sent through a variety of accounts in banks around the world. This creates significant obstacles for intelligence officers who are trying to cut off the financial lifeblood of terrorist organizations. For this reason, financial institutions are required to report to the government wire transfers and other bank transactions that involve a significant amount of money (usually anything over $10,000).

IN THE REAL WORLD

The Terrorist Threat Integration Center

In light of the information sharing weaknesses made evident on 9/11, the federal government is undertaking measures to increase collaboration across intelligence agencies. On May 1, 2003, the Terrorist Threat Integration Center was formed. According to the government, the Terrorist Threat Integration Center (TTIC) is an interagency body intended "to provide a comprehensive, all-source-based picture of potential terrorist threats to U.S. interests." It is comprised of personnel from many organizations, including the CIA, the FBI and the Department of Homeland Security. Each organization will continue to gather data from their respective areas of specialization: the CIA focusing on terrorists at the international level, the FBI focusing on terrorists at the domestic level, and DHS focusing on ways to reduce vulnerabilities to known threats. The overall objective of the TTIC is to increase information sharing and avert any disconnects relating to intelligence collection and processing. In other words, the FBI, CIA, and DHS can help one another "fill in the blanks" where intelligence is lacking and find ways to "connect the dots" where it is present. When fully staffed, the TTIC will employ between 250–300 U.S. Government employees.

8.3.4 Successes

In spite of notable difficulties, the intelligence community has been fairly successful at uncovering terrorist conspiracies in the United States and around the world. For instance, on August 10, 2006, 24 suspects were arrested in the United Kingdom. These individuals intended to board 10 jets from Britain to California, New York, and Washington, D.C. They wanted to smuggle on board gel explosives in sports drink bottles and detonate them with the use of electronic signals from an iPod or cell phone. Officials in the United States and United Kingdom worked closely to investigate the plot.

On May 8, 2007, six men were arrested for planning to purchase automatic weapons and attack the Fort Dix Army base in New Jersey. The men talked to an employee at a store and wanted him to transfer video footage of them firing weapons to a DVD. The thoughtful citizen promptly notified the FBI and the attack was foiled. In another case, four men were intent on blowing up a terminal building fuel pipelines, and fuel tanks at JFK airport in New York. This plot was thwarted on June 2, 2007, and may have been only days away from implementation.

Such cases indicate the importance of working with other nations, the need for citizen involvement, and anticipatory action. While these and other accomplishments are praiseworthy, the intelligence community must not be complacent. Terrorist leaders have said they are sending suicide bombers to the United States, and many fear it is only a matter of time before these and other attacks occur in the future. It is a common adage that terrorists only have to be successful once, while intelligence officials have to be right 100 percent of the time.

IN THE REAL WORLD

Gathering Intelligence

Information is vital for those involved in gathering intelligence. In order to keep track of potential terrorists, the government is turning to corporations for assistance. Companies such as ChoicePoint and LexisNexis are working closely with homeland security and intelligence officials. They obtain and retain personal data about people including information about homes, relatives, and criminal records. Software has also been developed to find links in the data which would be indicative of terrorist activity. While some people like former Attorney General John Ashcroft argued that these new tools are vital for homeland security, others in the FBI fear that there is not sufficient oversight or restrictions pertaining to corporations collecting information and then sharing it with the government (O'Harrow 2008).

SELF-CHECK

1. There were no clues that the attacks would take place on 9/11. True or False?

2. IMINT is intelligence collected by electronic communication. True or False?

3. Which part of the intelligence cycle is concerned with the creation of briefings and maps?
   (a) Intelligence collection
   (b) Intelligence analysis
   (c) Intelligence production
   (d) Intelligence feedback loop

4. What are some of the challenges facing the intelligence community?

8.4 COUNTER-TERRORISM

Counter-terrorism:
The active pursuit of known terrorists which includes pre-emptive military strikes.

One way of the ways the United States deals with threats to our nation is to engage in counter-terrorism. **Counter-terrorism** is the active pursuit of known terrorists which includes preemptive military strikes or the involvement of law enforcement officials. Counter-terrorism relies heavily on intelligence and may be used before attacks or even while they are taking place. The goal of such activities is to neutralize the terrorist threats before they materialize or rescue hostages and minimize the loss of life afterwards. There are numerous counter-terrorism organizations in the United States and in other nations. Some of their operations illustrate the importance of adequate training. Others provide unique lessons of failed or successful operations.

The United States has several entities that are involved in counter-terrorism operations. This may include covert operatives from the CIA or law enforcement officials from the FBI. The CIA infiltrates enemy organizations and operates on foreign soil. Its main purpose today is to gather intelligence about terrorist activities internationally. However, the CIA may also actively pursue individuals if it is believed they pose a threat to the United States. The FBI is also interested in intelligence issues and it does collaborate with other law enforcement agencies abroad. In fact, the FBI has offices in at least 40 nations around the world. However, and in contrast to the CIA, the FBI is only interested in preventing terrorist attacks at home. FBI Special Agents seek to arrest individuals who threaten or plan attacks in the United States. At times, these measures may turn violent if the alleged criminals or terrorists resist.

Counter-terrorism is also carried out by military forces. Some of the more well-known teams include Delta Force (U.S. Army), Special Warfare Units (U.S. Navy), Special Operations Wing (U.S. Air Force), and the Anti-terrorism Battalion (United States Marine Corps). These teams are sent around the world to stop terrorist organizations. Counter-terrorism forces may work with soldiers in foreign nations, as is the case in the Philippines. Others have been deployed to Afghanistan and Iraq to capture Al Qaeda members or other terrorist insurgents. In several cases, U.S. Special Forces have been highly effective at disrupting terrorists and keeping them on the run. States and local governments are now developing counter-terrorism squads. They work closely with the FBI on Joint Terrorism Task Forces. The City of New York also has intelligence officers staged at home and abroad. It is probably the most proactive jurisdiction outside of the federal government.

IN THE REAL WORLD

Delta Force

Delta Force, or 1st Special Forces Operational Detachment-Delta, is a well-known special forces unit of the United States Army. It was formed in 1977 under Colonel Charles Beckwith and is modeled after the British SAS. Although the Pentagon does not report on its activities, Delta Force is believed to be involved with reconnaissance, hostage rescuing, and fighting against enemy forces. Delta Force is made up of about 1,000 soldiers who have come from the Green Berets and the 75 Ranger Regiment. Candidates seeking to qualify for Delta Force membership are considered on an invitation only policy. They must have been in the military for at least four and a half years, and then must undergo extensive physical and psychological tests. Delta Force members look like ordinary citizens (they can let their hair grow) and often have no markings on uniforms. If accepted, they will be given a M1191 .45 caliber pistol. They are expert marksmen with M14, M21, M25 rifles. Delta Force trains with many other special forces around the world, and they have been deployed in many counter-terrorism operations.

8.4.1 Risky Operations

Counter-terrorism operations can be very risky and may involve a significant loss of life. Two of the most notable problematic counter-terrorism operations are Operation Eagle's Claw and the Moscow Theater crisis. Operation Eagle's Claw occurred on April 24, 1980 after 53 people were taken hostage in the United States Embassy in Teheran, Iran. In an attempt to resolve the situation, two activities were required. First, a staging base would have to be established in Iran. Second, the military units would need to approach the embassy, extract the hostages and take them out of Iran. Unfortunately, things went wrong from the start. Two helicopters got lost in a sandstorm and another suffered mechanical problems. A bus of civilian Iranians also came too close to the staging area and had to be captured to limit U.S. military presence. In light of these problems, President Carter called off the rescue attempt. After the mission was aborted, a helicopter crashed into a C-130 transport plane and eight airmen and marines were killed. This fiasco underscored the need for counter-terrorism funding, better equipment, and improved training and communications.

Another counter-terrorism operation also had deadly results. On October 23, 2002, approximately 40 terrorists entered a Broadway-style theater in Russia with explosives and took about 850 hostages. The terrorists demanded

Figure 8-2

Russian Special Forces were able to kill terrorists at a Russian Theater. Unfortunately, many citizens died in the process. Here, explosives and arms captured in the siege are put on display in Moscow.

the withdrawal of Russian military forces from Chechnya. The Kremlin would not give in to such demands and the situation deteriorated when a girl was shot by the terrorists. After a two and a half day siege, Russian leaders decided to spray Fentanyl (an anesthetic) into the building through the ventilation system which caused everyone to fall asleep. OSNAZ (Russian Special Forces) then entered the building and killed about 30 of the terrorists with gunfire. The hostages were then taken out of the building and laid on the sidewalk. Many of the citizens suffered adverse reactions to the chemicals. Complicating the matter, there were insufficient ambulances, and military leaders did not want to release information about the chemical agent to doctors. It is estimated that about 128 hostages died as a result.

8.4.2 Learning from Other Nations

Because the United States has limited experience in dealing with terrorism, it may want to glean knowledge from countries that have a long history of dealing with this type of activity. According to Cindy Combs (2000, 169–176), Germany, Britain, and Israel are notable examples. A successful counter-terrorism operation can also be witnessed from activities in Peru.

GSG9:
A German counter-terrorism organization, whose name means "border guards, group 9."

The **GSG9** is a German counter-terrorism organization, whose name means "border guards, group 9." The GSG9, which is now part of the federal police, was created after the terrorist attacks during the Olympics in Munich in 1972. Terrorists entered the Olympic village where Israeli athletes were staying. They killed some athletes and took others hostage. The response by the German government was less than desirable because it resulted in the death of law enforcement officials and civilians. Wishing to minimize such problems in the future, this organization has developed specialized training in counter-terrorism operations. Members are extremely proficient in weapons use and equipped with BMWs and BO 105 helicopters. In 1977, the GSG9 was able to enter a hijacked plane (Luftansa Boeing 737) in Somalia and rescue 82 passengers. Four terrorists were killed in the confrontation. The GSG9 has been involved in several operations against the Red Army faction, a left wing terrorist organization in Germany.

Special Air Service (SAS):
A British counter-terrorism organization.

Because Britain has experienced many terrorist attacks from the Irish Republican Army, it also has an acclaimed counter-terrorism organization—the **SAS** or **Special Air Service**. The SAS has developed a great deal of expertise as it has been in existence for nearly 50 years. Those wishing to become members of this group must serve in the military for a minimum of three years. They must then pass rigorous tests of strength and endurance. According to Combs:

> *Out of every 100 men who apply, only about 19 will meet the physical and mental requirements. The initial tests include a series of treks across the Welsh hills, carrying weighted packs. The final trek covers 37 miles, carrying a 55 pound pack, over some of the toughest country in the Brecon Beacons. It must be covered in 20 hours, and it is literally a killer course. Men have died trying to complete it (2000, 173).*

If accepted, SAS recruits will subsequently be trained in hand to hand combat, water warfare, and emergency medicine. They are also experienced with the use of pistols, machine guns, and enemy weapons.

The British SAS carried out a successful counter-terrorism operation in 1980. During the first few days in May, members of the Democratic Revolutionary Movement for the Liberation of Arabistan took over the Iranian Embassy in downtown London. They demanded freedom of their associates who were imprisoned and also wanted to gain possession of oil fields in Iran. After a hostage was killed, officials in the United Kingdom decided to implement Operation Nimrod. In order to move SAS forces into place without detection, they ordered that all airplanes flying into London approach the airport at a much lower altitude than normal. They also had a British utility company work in the area to create as much noise as possible. When the timing was right, the SAS set off a charge in the building and cut the power to the facility. SAS members then swung down from ropes and burst into the windows (after placing explosives on them). As they entered the building, they first set off stun grenades. Within a short period of time, they killed five terrorists and captured the last one remaining. Only one hostage was killed in the incident and the rest were safely escorted from the building.

Of all of the counter-terrorism organizations, none of them are as well-known as the Sarayet Matkal in Israel. Sarayet Matkal is a strike team devoted to finding terrorists before they attack Israeli interests. They were also established after the Munich massacre and shortly thereafter killed the mastermind of this attack (Ali Hassan Salameh) with a car bomb in Beruit. Because of the longstanding threat of terrorism in Israel, this Special Forces group is carefully selected. On a biannual basis, Camp Gibush is held to determine who can join the organization as new recruits. If applicants pass the constant monitoring of military officials, doctors, and psychologists, they then must train for an additional 20 months. This training is rigorous and includes, among other things, basic and advanced infantry training, parachuting, counter-terrorism classes, reconnaissance, and martial arts.

The Sarayet Matkal illustrated its capabilities when a Belgian aircraft was hijacked from Vienna to Tel Aviv on May 8, 1972. While the airplane was on the tarmac in Israel, 16 commandos (who were dressed as airplane technicians) told the terrorists the plane needed servicing. The terrorists let the technicians in disguise approach the plane and the rescue operation ensued. Within 10 minutes, two terrorists were killed and others were taken captive. Three civilians were injured and one died as a result. Benjamin Netanyahu (an Israeli Prime Minister) was a member of Sarayet Matkal at the time.

Peru also has special military forces to deal with the Shining Path and other left-wing and drug-related terrorist organizations. While Peru's special units are not as well-known as those in Germany, Britain, or Israel, they did participate in a successful counter-terrorism operation. On December 17, 1996, 14 members of the Tupac Amaru terrorist organization stormed a Japanese embassy. They took at least 72 people hostage, including President Alberto Fujimori's brother. The Tupac Amaru wanted 400 people released from prison, but the government would not acquiesce to this demand. Instead, counter-terrorism forces smuggled listening devices into the embassy and closely monitored the activities of the terrorists. They noticed that the terrorists would play soccer everyday at 3:00 pm and decided this would be the best time to conduct the raid. For the next several days, the Special Forces implemented Operation Chavin de Huantar (a name referring to Pre-Inca site with secret passages). While loud music was playing nearby, six tunnels were dug into the compound from nearby buildings. On the designated day (April 22, 1997), several explosive charges were detonated. Special Forces then emerged from the ground, entered the embassy and began to exchange gunfire with the terrorists. During the conflict, hostages took cover as they were previously notified to do so through an intelligence agent who posed as a doctor. In the end, each of the 14 members of the Tupac Amaru were killed. In contrast, one hostage and one soldier were killed. Nine others were injured. The operation was hailed as a national success, but international human rights monitors believe some of the terrorists were summarily executed.

8.4.3 Controversy Regarding Counter-terrorism

In spite of the successes and perhaps as a result of notable failures, counter-terrorism is highly controversial. Those supporting counter-terrorism argue that there are many in and outside of the United States that wish to do us harm. They assert that the government has a moral responsibility to protect its citizens and prevent attacks. Others decry counter-terrorism and suggest that it is an immoral undertaking. They fear intelligence operations and oppose the use of preemptive force. While these individuals seem to overlook the enemies that wish to do us harm, they could be right when they note that counter-terrorism may aggravate hostilities and breed additional violence. For these reasons, counter-terrorism will likely remain a contentious and divisive policy option in the future.

IN THE REAL WORLD

Counter-terrorism in Afghanistan

Shortly after 9/11, it was discovered that Osama bin Laden and Al Qaeda were responsible for the attacks against the United States. It was also a well-known fact that the Taliban was providing these terrorists sanctuary in Afghanistan. On January 22, 2002, special U.S. forces flew into the mountains of Kandahar to stop the instruction of terrorists at a training camp (Zaroya 2003). Before arriving at the compound, they launched a grenade to catch the terrorists off guard. They then entered the facility and began shooting at those offering resistance. While searching through the premise, one U.S. soldier was hit over the shoulder with a large stick. He then began to fight the terrorists by hand. The soldier broke his collarbone but prevailed in the altercation. The training, tactics, night vision goggles and other equipment were believed to have been some of the reasons for the success of this counter-terrorism operation. Allies who opposed the Taliban in Afghanistan were also very helpful in this surprise attack.

SELF-CHECK

1. Preemptive military strikes are known as counter-terrorism operations. True or False?

2. The FBI does not have offices in foreign countries. True or False?

3. Which nation has special forces that rescued hostages in the Iranian embassy?

   (a) The United States
   (b) Britain
   (c) Peru
   (d) Germany

4. Are there any drawbacks to counter-terrorism operations?

8.5 BORDER CONTROL

Reducing or eliminating the incursion of terrorists and WMD into the United States is another way to prevent possible terrorist attacks. If the government can control the flow of people and goods into this nation, then there will obviously be less likelihood that enemies from abroad will be able to implement terrorist acts against us. This brings up the important subject of borders and border control.

8.5.1 What Is the Border?

Border:
The territorial boundary of any nation along with its various points of entry.

The **border** is the territorial boundary of any nation along with its various points of entry. Jack Riley, an Associate Director of RAND Infrastructure, Safety and Environment, states people and goods can enter the United States from one of four locations (2006, 587). This includes airports, sea ports, guarded land points, and unguarded land borders and shoreline.

Airports are the transportation hubs where foreigners fly into the United States, where they are allowed or denied entry based on valid passports and visas for business, student, or vacation purposes. Sea ports are also transportation networks that make up portions of the border. They facilitate the movement of people and likewise play a role in commerce due to the trade they facilitate. Guarded land points include border stations where people, vehicles, and trucks are processed for entry. Unguarded land borders are those locations between the United States and its neighboring countries (i.e., Canada to the North and Mexico to the South). These may be protected at times by fences and walls, but are not always secured in other cases. There are also coastlines to the Northeast, East, West, and South of the United States which are considered a part of national borders. The waterways near the Great Lakes, the Atlantic Ocean, Pacific Ocean, and Gulf of Mexico are often open to human movement and maritime shipping with limited or at least minimal oversight. Unfortunately, the openness of our nation is an invitation to those who wish to do us harm.

8.5.2 Our Porous Border

Statistics regarding the size and fluid nature of the border are impressive or overwhelming, depending on your point of view. For instance, there are more than 100 international airports in the United States (Riley 2006, 587). America also has 90,000 miles of coastline (Hoffman 2006, 143) and "more than 1,000 harbor channels and 25,000 miles of inland, intracoastal, and coastal waterways, serving over 300 ports, with more than 3,700 passenger terminals" (Bentzel 2006, 631). These numbers do not include, of course, the hundreds of other foreign airports and seaports around the world that are connected to counterparts in this country. Furthermore, there are also

9,000 miles of land borders (Hoffman 2006, 143). The shear scope of the border is therefore awe-inspiring.

The extent of the border is only dwarfed by the dizzying pace of activity that takes place around it. In a single year, a "half a billion people, 125 million cars, 12 million trucks, and 33 million overseas shipments—including nearly six million shipping containers, 800 million planes, two million railcars, and over 200,000 ships—went through U.S. borders" (Hoffman 2006, 143). There are also thousands or even hundreds of thousands of laborers that enter the country on a daily basis to work in the agricultural sector or in factories called maquiladoras along the U.S.-Mexican border. These numbers do not include those people or goods entering the country illegally. As an example, estimates suggest that between 500,000 and four million people cross the border without permission each year (Knickerbocker 2006). There are many reasons why the border appears so open to trade and attracts so many visitors.

Besides the millions of people who travel here for leisure or business opportunities, there are also millions who come here to seek a better way of life (e.g., economic and educational opportunities). The former group comes from around the world, while the latter is comprised mainly of Mexican nationals and others from Latin America. International commerce has likewise increased substantially in the past few decades due to improvements in transportation and the high demand for foreign goods and services. Corporations also prefer the ability to import products quickly into the United States. "Many manufacturers and retailers now use the 'just-in-time strategy' to reduce the costs of carrying and storing inventory" (Riley 2006, 588). This has boosted international commerce over the past decade.

Politicians on the left and right also prefer an open border. Some want to extend America's freedoms and prosperity to anyone wishing to obtain them. Others desire a constant supply of cheap labor to keep corporate profits high. Finally, the scope and expense of securing our borders is monumental. "Airport officials estimate that less than 10 percent of all this cargo is physically inspected, and most airports lack the equipment to conduct inspections, especially of large containers" (Riley 2006, 593). There is also a shortage of manpower to prevent illegal immigration or quickly process the vast numbers of people and goods that come to the United States on a daily basis.

Regardless of the cause for this substantial degree of movement in and around our borders, citizens and experts alike recognize the potential danger for homeland security. If the border cannot be adequately controlled or regulated, terrorists may be able to enter the United States along with weapons of mass destruction. This situation has already been used to the advantage of those who wish to do us harm on 9/11. Frank Hoffman states that bin Laden "struck at America's Achilles' heel—its porous borders, transportation networks, and vulnerable economic portals" (2006, 142). He also states that "our most daunting domestic challenge is posed by the open nature of America's society: borders" (Hoffman 2006, 143).

8.5.3 Participants Involved in Border Control

There is no single entity involved in border control. Instead, there are a variety of government agencies interested in securing of our border. This includes the Transportation Security Administration, Immigration and Customs Enforcement, and the Coast Guard. Corporations and international organizations also play an important role in securing our border.

The **Transportation Security Administration (TSA)** is a federal agency under the Department of Homeland Security. It was created after 9/11 to protect our transportations systems from terrorist attacks. It includes over 43,000 security officers, inspectors, and air marshals who have the goal of preventing terrorist attacks on airplanes, subways, and rail systems. The TSA screens passengers, checks luggage and cargo for bombs, deters hijackings and other attacks on transportation systems, and works with local law enforcement agencies to protect transportation systems.

Immigration and Customs Enforcement (ICE) is the largest investigative organization within the Department of Homeland Security. It was created in March 2003 by combining the Immigration and Naturalization Service and the U.S. Customs Service. The goal of ICE is to enforce immigration and customs laws. The agents working for ICE specifically attempt to deter illegal immigration and the smuggling of money, drugs, and other

Transportation Security Administration (TSA):
A federal agency under the Department of Homeland Security created to protect our transportation systems from terrorist attacks.

Immigration and Customs Enforcement (ICE):
The largest investigative organization within the Department of Homeland Security which attempts to deter illegal immigration and the smuggling of money and materials that support terrorism.

Figure 8-3

Securing borders is a major priority for the Department of Homeland Security.

materials that support terrorism. In an attempt to protect the homeland, ICE looks for fraudulent passports, investigates employers that hire illegal aliens, and stops the transport of weapons and sensitive military technologies.

United States Coast Guard (USCG):
A military branch within the Department of Homeland Security which is in charge of maritime law, environmental protection of waterways, search and rescue operations at sea, and interdiction of illegal aliens and contraband.

The **United States Coast Guard (USCG)** is a branch of the Department of Homeland Security. It employs over 40,000 people who enforce maritime law, manage vessel traffic, respond to maritime pollution, and participate in search and rescue operations (due to severe weather and sinking or incapacitated boats). In terms of terrorism, the USCG also interdicts illegal aliens and seizes illegal contraband. Because the Coast Guard is a military branch, its employees receive the same pay and benefits as other active and reserve personnel in the other branches of the armed forces.

Besides these agencies in the Department of Homeland Security, others also play a role in border control. For instance, "private companies such as airlines, truckers, container shippers, and manufacturers—as well as companies whose employees travel over these borders—are stakeholders" (Riley 2006, 588). Any attack along the border could have drastic economic consequences for corporations. In addition, Airports Council International helps to set global standards regarding the safety and security of airports. It has taken a more active role since 9/11. The United Nations International Maritime Organization (UNIMO) has rules on piracy and security procedures to prevent the shipment of dangerous goods such as weapons of mass destruction. The UNIMO also establishes rules regarding access issues and security at seaports. The Association of American Railroads works to track and inspect rail shipments. The United States government likewise works closely with other countries to address border control issues around the world. Border security is truly a team effort.

8.5.4 Measures to Secure Borders

Those charged with border control are implementing a number of programs to prevent terrorist attacks against the United States. The most well known programs include US-VISIT, CAPPS II/Secure Flight, the Container Security Initiative, and Customs-Trade Partnership Against Terrorism. The government and citizens are also undertaking other measures to protect the integrity of the border.

United States Visitor and Immigrant Status Indicator Technology (US-VISIT):
A computer database used to screen passengers who wish to travel to the United States.

The **United States Visitor and Immigrant Status Indicator Technology (US-VISIT)** is a computer database created and maintained by the Department of Homeland Security. It contains information about passengers who wish to travel to the United States. Those seeking visas will have their biometric data recorded (e.g., digital finger scans and photographs). When the traveler arrives in the United States, his or her biometric data will then be compared to the information stored on the system and checked against known criminals and terrorists around the world. According to Riley, "the system was first tested in Atlanta in late 2003 and became operational at all 115 international airports on 5 January 2004. Simultaneously, it was introduced at 14 major seaports served by cruise liners" (2006, 592). At least two million people have had their biometric information recorded by US-VISIT. However, citizens of 27 allied countries are excused from this system. This is a major weakness in that some of the terrorists on 9/11 came from these exempted nations.

Computer Assisted Passenger Prescreening System II (CAPPS II):
A former computer program utilized by the TSA to screen passengers against lists of known terrorists and others with criminal records.

The **Computer Assisted Passenger Prescreening System II (CAPPS II)** is another database which ensures that passengers are screened by every airliner and airport that operates within the United States. This system was also implemented after 9/11 and was maintained by the Transportation Security Administration. It included additional information about passengers including date of birth, street address, and telephone numbers. Once collected, this data would then be compared to terrorist or most-wanted lists and federal and state warrants for arrest. A risk score would then be calculated and printed on the boarding pass so airport screeners could be notified. Because potential rights violations, watchdog groups and the General Accounting Offices became very critical of CAPPS II. In the summer of 2004, this program was cancelled. However, a new program is to be implemented as soon as accuracy, privacy, due process, and oversight issues can be resolved. Its replacement, known as **Secure Flight**, is anticipated to be tested in 2008 and fully operational by 2010.

Secure Flight:
The proposed program to replace the Computer Assisted Passenger Prescreening System II.

Container Security Initiative (CSI):
One of the first measures taken by the government to protect maritime trade and ports against terrorism.

The **Container Security Initiative (CSI)** was one of the first measures taken by the government to protect maritime trade and ports against terrorism. Launched in 2004, this program has four components (Hoffman 2006, 145). First, shipments are to be placed in tamper-proof containers to limit the possibility that something can be smuggled into the United States. Second, computers are used to identify potential high-risk containers—those thought to be containing questionable goods such as WMD. Third, high-risk containers are pre-screened to limit the chances that they arrive at the intended location. Finally, hi-tech detection equipment will be used to identify WMD before/during shipment or after arrival. In order to accomplish this goal, U.S. Customs officials are being deployed abroad to push the borders out and speed up the process. Cargo manifests also have to be given to U.S. officials 24 hours before containers are loaded onto ships. Hoffman notes that 18 of the top 20 seaports have agreed to the CSI. These ports represent about 70 percent of all containers shipped to the United States (Hoffman 2006, 145).

Customs-Trade Partnership Against Terrorism (C-TPAT):
An agreement between the public and private sectors to protect international commerce from terrorists attacks.

The **Customs-Trade Partnership Against Terrorism (C-TPAT)** is an agreement between the public and private sectors to protect international commerce from terrorists attacks. As of 2006, it included at least 1,600 importers, manufacturers, carriers (air, rail, and sea), brokers, port authorities, and others involved in international trade. These organizations voluntarily adhere to high standards pertaining to physical security, access controls, personnel security, training and education, manifest procedures, and other requirements relating to trade. Once certified by the government, these businesses are promised fewer and quicker inspections as long as they do not let their support of the agreement lapse. C-TPAT is a novel way to support efforts to prevent terrorist attacks through international trade.

The government is also looking into and implementing other measures to secure our borders and prevent further terrorist attacks. Some officials in the government assert that passports need to be changed to prevent tampering and falsification. Smart lanes and electronic passes (much like toll tags) are being developed to speed up the processing of trucks carrying goods into the United States. Un-manned aerial drones and stationary cameras are being used along the borders to detect locations where people are entering the United States illegally. In order to increase the effectiveness of border agents, the government has opened up a border patrol academy in Artesia, New Mexico. At this school, recruits are taught Spanish, learn about immigration law, practice using weapons, and develop other law enforcement techniques. Patrol of the border has also increased, which has led to the discovery of tunnels and capture of illegal aliens. President Bush and Congress also passed a law that would fund the building of a fence along the U.S.-Mexican border (although it is unclear to what extent this objective is seriously being pursued by the government at this time).

Finally, citizens are becoming more involved in border security. After feeling that the government is not doing enough to protect the United States against the entry of illegal aliens and potential terrorists, a group of concerned individuals in Arizona joined together to form the **Minutemen Project**. People who join the Minutemen Civil Defense Corps lobby local, state, and federal officials to do more about border security. They also organize shifts of volunteers who patrol the border and notify the government when people attempt to cross the border illegally. While the group is having an impact upon politicians' views and deterring those wishing to enter the United States illegally, some fear that this group may aggravate tensions along the border and be unprepared if conflict erupts. Regardless, hundreds of illegal immigrants have been detained as a result of the efforts of the Minutemen.

Minutemen Project: Activities to promote border security carried out by a group of volunteers which founded the Minutemen Civil Defense Corps in Arizona.

IN THE REAL WORLD

Ahmed Ressam

On December 14, 1999, Ahmed Ressam attempted to enter the United States to conduct a terrorist attack known as the millennial plot. Ressam hid explosives in his car and was attempting to travel from Canada to California in order to blow up the Los Angeles International Airport on New Year's Eve. When questioned by a border agent near Seattle, Washington, Ressam became anxious and evaded questioning. He was consequently arrested for his activities along with a colleague from Brooklyn, New York. This case illustrated the importance of observant border patrol agents.

✓✓✓ SELF-CHECK

1. Airports are not considered as part of the territorial boundary of the United States. True or False?

2. It is relatively easy for the United States to oversee the people and goods that enter our country. True or False?

3. Which agency is responsible for investigating companies that hire illegal aliens?

    (a) The Transportation Security Administration
    (b) Immigration and Customs Enforcement
    (c) The United States Coast Guard
    (d) The United Nations International Maritime Organization

4. What are a few of the measures taken by the Department of Homeland Security to prevent illegal immigration?

SUMMARY

Preventing terrorist attacks is one of the main pillars of the national homeland security strategy. If you are to succeed in this area, it is vital that you understand the importance and limitations of addressing the root causes of terrorism. You should promote laws that prohibit terrorism and punish those who support it. Relying on human and other sources of intelligence may help you to apprehend terrorists before they strike. At times, this may also require the involvement of the military in counterterrorism operations. Protecting all points of entry into the United States will also be crucial if acts of terrorism are to be averted. There are countless measures you can take to prevent acts of terrorism against American citizens.

ASSESS YOUR UNDERSTANDING

UNDERSTAND: WHAT HAVE YOU LEARNED?

 Go to **www.wiley.com/college/mcentire** to assess your knowledge of measures to prevent terrorist attacks.

SUMMARY QUESTIONS

1. While appearing on the news on TV one night, a scholar suggests that America must address the root causes of terrorism. What does this mean and will "addressing root causes" eliminate all terrorist attacks?

2. If you were working in homeland security and someone suggested that laws will not help to reduce terrorism, what would you say?

3. A co-worker who just started working with the FBI asserts that the United States should spend more money on SIGINT? Will this type of intelligence provide the most accurate view of terrorist operations? Is there another type that is preferable?

4. As a concerned citizen, you frequently watch the presidential debates broadcast on national television. On one occasion, there was a heated discussion about the merits of counter-terrorism operations. What are the pros and cons of counter-terrorism operations?

5. You have just been appointed to a blue ribbon group to study how best to protect our borders. What are some steps that can be taken to accomplish this goal?

6. Not everyone agrees with the military response to the threat of terrorism. True or False?

7. The United States cannot be held responsible for all of the causes of terrorism. True or False?

8. Policy and legislation may emanate from presidential directives but not congressional decisions. True or False?

9. The USA PATRIOT Act attempts to prevent terrorist attacks by strengthening law enforcement abilities. True or False?

10. The 9/11 terrorist attacks took the United States by surprise because it was operating under a Cold War mentality. True or False?

11. IMINT includes intelligence gathered from academic research and books. True or False?

12. Counter-terrorism can be defined as preemptive military strikes against terrorists. True or False?

13. The SAS is a counter-terrorism force in Israel. True or False?

14. Currently, all airport shipping containers are inspected. True or False?

15. The Container Security Initiative includes tamper-proof containers and pre-screening of cargo. True or False?

16. Which may be considered as a root cause of terrorism that cannot be controlled by the United States?

   (a) The treatment of Muslims around the world

   (b) The upbringing of children in the Middle East in a culture of hate and violence

   (c) American foreign policy

   (d) Respect for culture and religion

17. Which is not a feature of the Comprehensive Homeland Security Act?

   (a) Creation of the Department of Homeland Security

   (b) Protection of nuclear power plants

   (c) Increased border control

   (d) Regulations pertaining to rail security

18. PDD 39 reaffirmed:

   (a) the importance of border control.

   (b) the need for improved intelligence.

   (c) the value of rights and liberties.

   (d) the policy of the United States to defeat terrorism.

19. Which component of the intelligence cycle deals with sharing information with policy makers?

   (a) Intelligence collection

   (b) Intelligence analysis

   (c) Intelligence production

   (d) Intelligence dissemination

20. Intelligence given to specific and limited individuals is known as:

   (a) HUMINT.

   (b) classified intelligence.

   (c) categorized intelligence.

   (d) IMINT.

21. Which counter-terrorism force is the most well-known around the world?

   (a) SAS

   (b) GSG9

   (c) Sarayet Matkal

   (d) Shining Path

22. People and goods can enter the United States from one of:
    (a) two locations.
    (b) three locations.
    (c) four locations.
    (d) five locations.

23. Which organization is in charge of preventing terrorist attacks on airplanes, subways and rail systems?
    (a) TSA
    (b) ICE
    (c) USCG
    (d) CSI

BE A HOMELAND SECURITY PROFESSIONAL

Assignment: Understanding the Intelligence Cycle

Write a two-page paper about the intelligence cycle. Be sure to mention the steps that must be taken to gather intelligence about potential terrorists.

A New Recruit

You have just joined the military and you desire to participate in counter-terrorism operations. What kind of training might you undertake in the future?

Working with the Public Sector

You are the president of an association that represents business interests in port security. You are a signatory to the Customs-Trade Partnership Against Terrorism. You have been asked to testify before congress about ways to protect shipping from terrorist attacks. What would you state in your briefing?

KEY TERMS

Bojinka plot	A planned attack on airliners over the Pacific Ocean.
Border	The territorial boundary of any nation along with its various points of entry.
Classified intelligence	Information given only to a very specific and limited number of people to protect sources of acquisition and deny adversaries information that would lead them to alter their communications or operations.
Comprehensive Homeland Security Act	A law passed in 2003 containing new regulations for critical infrastructure security, railroad security, and more stringent measures related to border control and weapons of mass destruction.
Computer Assisted Passenger Prescreening System II (CAPPS II)	A former computer program utilized by the TSA to screen passengers against lists of known terrorists and others with criminal records.
Container Security Initiative (CSI)	One of the first measures taken by the government to protect maritime trade and ports against terrorism.
Customs-Trade Partnership Against Terrorism (C-TPAT)	An agreement between the public and private sectors to protect international commerce from terrorists attacks.
Counter-terrorism	The active pursuit of known terrorists which includes preemptive military strikes.
GSG9	A German counter-terrorism organization, whose name means "border guards, group 9."
Homeland Security Act	A law passed in 2002 which mandated the creation of the Department of Homeland Security.
HUMINT	Intelligence collected by people from people (and can be done overtly or covertly).
IMINT	Geospatial imagery collected by satellites and aircraft.
Immigration and Customs Enforcement (ICE)	The largest investigative organization within the Department of Homeland Security which attempts to deter illegal immigration and the smuggling of money and materials that support terrorism.
Intelligence	The function of collecting, assessing, and distributing information about an enemy, criminal or terrorist.
Intelligence adjustment	Adaptation of the intelligence cycle is required when collection is incomplete, analysis seeks to "connect the dots," production generates new questions, and dissemination results in the anticipation of future concerns.

Intelligence analysis	Efforts to make sense of the voluminous data that is gathered from the field.
Intelligence collection	Activities to gather information about terrorist organizations, their operations and potential attacks.
Intelligence cycle	A four-step process of gathering, understanding, and synthesizing data, and then sharing it with those who will use it.
Intelligence dissemination	Sharing information with end-users (e.g., policy makers, FBI Special Agents, homeland security personnel, etc.).
Intelligence production	The creation of written reports, briefings, images, or maps to influence operational decisions.
INTERPOL	An international police organization that is involved in intelligence.
MASINT	Measurement and signature intelligence that looks for the characteristics of certain types of actions (e.g., the presence of nuclear material when one is trying to develop a nuclear weapon).
Minutemen Project	Activities to promote border security carried out by a group of volunteers which founded the Minutemen Civil Defense Corps in Arizona.
Money laundering	The process of hiding where money is coming from and what it is being used for.
OPINT	Open source intelligence acquired through publicly available materials including academic research, newspaper articles, library books, etc.
Secure Flight	The proposed program to replace the Computer Assisted Passenger Prescreening System II.
SIGINT	Interception and interpretation of electronic communications such as phone conversations and emails.
Special Air Service (SAS)	A British counter-terrorism organization.
Transportation Security Act	A law designed to protect transportation systems in the United States.
Transportation Security Administration (TSA)	A federal agency under the Department of Homeland Security created to protect our transportation systems from terrorist attacks.
United States Coast Guard (USCG)	A military branch within the Department of Homeland Security which is in charge of maritime law, environmental protection of waterways, search and rescue operations at sea, and interdiction of illegal aliens and contraband.

United States Visitor and Immigrant Status Indicator Technology (US-VISIT)	A computer database used to screen passengers who wish to travel to the United States.
USA PATRIOT Act	A homeland security law which stands for "Uniting and Strengthening America by Providing Appropriate Tools Required to Intercept and Obstruct Terrorism." This law aims to prevent terrorist attacks and enhance law enforcement's ability to investigate and punish offenders.

REFERENCES

9/11 Commission. (2004). *The 9/11 Commission Report: Final Report of the National Commission on Terrorist Attacks Upon the United States.* W.W. Norton and Company, Inc.: New York.

Abu-Amara, Suad. (2002). "Terrorism is a Result of Israel's Denying a People Its Rights." *Dallas Morning News.* Viewpoints, Monday, July 22, 9A.

Benztzel, Carl. (2006). "Port and Maritime Security." Pp. 631–648 in Kamien, David G. (ed.) *The McGraw-Hill Homeland Security Handbook.* McGraw-Hill: New York.

CNN. (2001). "Iranian President: 'Root of Terrorism' Must be Addressed." November 12. http://archives.cnn.com/2001/WORLD/meast/11/12/khatami.interview/index.html (last accessed 12/17/07).

Combs, Cindy C. (2000). *Terrorism in the Twenty-First Century.* Prentice Hall: New Jersey.

Deucy, C. Patrick. (2006). "Intelligence and Information Sharing in Counterterrorism." Pp. 391–412 in Kamien, David G. (ed.) *The McGraw-Hill Homeland Security Handbook.* McGraw-Hill: New York.

Francis, David R. (2002). "Poverty and Low Education Don't Cause Terrorism." The NBER Digest. September.

Hoffman, Frank. (2006). "Border Security: Closing the Ingenuity Gap." Pp. 142–166 in Howard, Russell, James Forest and Joanne Moore. *Homeland Security and Terrorism: Readings and Interpretations.* McGraw-Hill: New York.

Kauppi, Mark V. (2006). "Counterterrorism Analysis and Homeland Security." Pp. 413–430 in Kamien, David G. (ed.) *The McGraw-Hill Homeland Security Handbook.* McGraw-Hill: New York.

Knickerbocker, Brad. (2006). "Illegal Immigrants in the US: How Many are There?" Christian Science Monitor. May 16. Accessed at www.csmonitor.com/2006/0516/p01s02-ussc.html (last accessed 12/17/07).

Lash, Jonathan. (2001). "Dealing with the Tinder as well as the Flint." *Science.* Vol. 294 (5548). www.sciencemag.org/cgi/content/short/294/5548/1789 (last accessed 12/17/07).

Leiter, Kenneth. (2002). "Palestinians Must Remake Their Society Before Peace Can Come." Dallas Morning News. Viewpoints, July 22, 9A.

Lustick, Ian. (2007). "The War on Terror: When the Response is the Catastrophe." Paper presented at FEMA Higher Education Conference, June 5, Emmitsburg, MD.

O'Harrow, Robert. (2008). "Mining Personal Data: One Company Keeps Tabs on the Public in the Name of Post-9/11 Security." Pp. 141–143 in Badey, Thomas J. (ed.). *Annual Editions Homeland Security.* McGraw Hill: Dubuque, IA.

Riley, K. Jack. (2006). "Border Control." Pp. 587–612 in Kamien, David G. (ed.) *The McGraw-Hill Homeland Security Handbook*. McGraw-Hill: New York.

Shakil-ur-Rahman, Mir. (2007). "Root Causes of Terrorism Must be Addressed: PM." The International News. Monday, August 13. www.the-news.com.pk/top_story_detail.asp?Id=5452 (last accessed 12/17/07).

Thetford, Robert T. (2001). "The Challenge of Cyberterrorism." Pp. 238–257 in Hogan, Lawrence J. (ed.). *Terrorism: Defensive Strategies for Individuals, Companies and Governments*. Amlex, Inc.: Frederick, Maryland.

Zaroya, Gregg. (2003). "Inches Divide Life, Death in the Afghan Darkness." *USA Today*, October 19, 4A.

9

PROTECTING AGAINST POTENTIAL ATTACKS

Threat Assessment and Security Enhancement

Do You Already Know?

- How to assess the threat of terrorism
- The advantages of structural and non-structural mitigation
- Ways to increase physical security

For additional questions to assess your current knowledge of protecting against potential attacks, go to **www.wiley.com/college/mcentire**

What You Will Find Out	What You Will Be Able To Do
9.1 The importance of mitigating terrorist attacks	• Assess the threat of terrorism
9.2 The need to build structures with terrorism in mind	• Predict the advantages of structural and non-structural mitigation

INTRODUCTION

To minimize the impact of terrorist attacks, it is imperative that you take steps to protect the nation. One of your primary responsibilities is to assess the threat of terrorism. This entails an evaluation of critical infrastructure, key assets, and other potential targets. It also requires that you work closely with homeland security partners at the federal, state, and local level as well as businesses in the private sector. Once your analysis is complete, you must then improve structural and non-structural mitigation through architectural design, improved construction practices, zoning, and set back requirements, and other security measures. The overarching goal of this process is to make targets less attractive to terrorists and to diminish consequences should deterrence fail.

9.1 ASSESSING THREATS

Because of the nature of terrorism, it will be impossible to prevent every single terrorist attack. For this reason, it will be necessary for you to consider the benefit of strategies to enhance protection. In homeland security, **protection** is proactive activity designed to minimize the possibility and consequences of terrorist events. In other words, protection is an attempt to deny attacks and defend oneself. If terrorists are able to enter the United States or plan attacks that we are not aware of, we must be able to minimize the appeal of anticipated targets and reduce the severity of attacks that do occur.

Protection:
An attempt to deny attacks and defend oneself from terrorism.

Protection activities require a threat assessment of possible attacks that could occur in our nation, states, and communities. A **threat assessment** is a careful study of the targets that might be appealing to terrorists. It is basically the same thing as a hazard and vulnerability analysis in emergency management. A hazard and vulnerability analysis is an assessment of risk—an evaluation of what may occur along with possible consequences. Instead of determining the potential impact of natural or technological disasters, a threat assessment focuses specifically on potential terrorist attacks and their probable impacts. It is an educated guess about what terrorists might do as well as a determination of the outcome of such actions (see figure 9-1).

Threat assessment:
A careful study of the targets that might be appealing to terrorists.

9.1.1 Critical Infrastructure, Key Assets, and Soft Targets

When conducting a threat assessment (or hazard and vulnerability analysis), it is important that you consider both critical infrastructure and key assets. **Critical infrastructure** is defined as interdependent networks comprised of industrial, utility, transportation, and other distribution systems (Pupura 2007, 359). According to Nancy Wong, the Deputy Director of the U.S. Critical Infrastructure Assurance Office, examples of this infrastructure include:

Critical infrastructure:
Interdependent networks comprised of industrial, utility, transportation, and other distribution systems.

- Information and communications systems (computer networks, line-based phone systems, and cell towers)

Figure 9-1

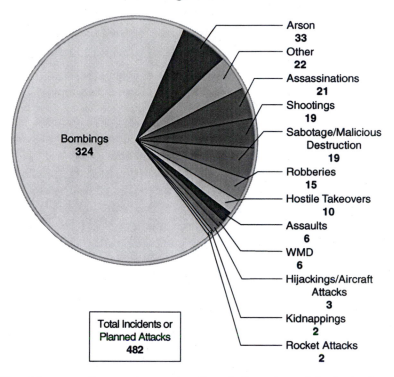

Arson
33

Other
22

Assassinations
21

Shootings
19

Sabotage/Malicious
Destruction
19

Robberies
15

Hostile Takeovers
10

Assaults
6

WMD
6

Hijackings/Aircraft
Attacks
3

Kidnappings
2

Rocket Attacks
2

Bombings
324

Total Incidents or
Planned Attacks
482

Bombings are the most common threats from terrorists, but other attacks are possible and may have even greater consequences.

IN THE REAL WORLD

Threats Facing the United States

Francis Townsend served as the Assistant to the President for Homeland Security. In 2007, she was interviewed about the danger of terrorism. She stated she is particularly concerned about Hezbollah because this group has historically killed more Americans than any other organization. Townsend also noted that terrorists are trying to enter the United States from the Southwest border. She also noted Al Qaeda leaders have clearly stated their desire to acquire and use weapons of mass destruction. In light of this assessment, Townsend believes the nation will see substantial investment in the Secure Border Initiative (HS Today 2007).

- Electrical systems (power plants, step up and step down stations, transformers)
- Transportation systems (airports, highways, bridges, seaports)
- Petro-chemical systems (oil wells, refineries, storage facilities)
- Water systems (dams, sewage treatment plants, distribution lines) (as cited by McEntire, Robinson and Weber 2001, 5)

To this list of vulnerable locations, we may also want to add farms, food processing plants, and food distribution networks. They, too, may be deemed as critical infrastructure.

All of these infrastructure systems are regarded to be "critical" because "their incapacity or destruction would have debilitating impact on the defense or economic security of the United States" (Clinton 1996). For instance, the loss of the Internet or phone systems would limit our ability to conduct business and communicate with others. ATMs and credit card swiping devices would be rendered useless. Disruption of energy systems would prohibit the heating and cooling of homes in the winter or summer, and limit visibility at night. The destruction of

IN THE REAL WORLD

Cyber-Terrorism

The average citizen may not regard computers and the Internet to be included as critical infrastructure. However, our economy and way of life are intricately related to modern technology. Terrorists may employ cyber-terrorism tactics as a way to negatively affect the United States. Cyber-terrorism is the use of computers and the Internet to launch attacks, or it is attacks directed at these modern forms of technology. This may include hacking into computers to control pipeline flow or disable 911 emergency communication systems. Cyber-terrorism may also attempt to produce a denial of service on computers through Trojan horses, viruses, and worms. Trojan horses are programs that are secretly placed on others' computers to destroy important files. Viruses are files placed on one's computer and overload the system through mass reproduction. Worms are similar to viruses, but they are distributed through email and the Internet to other computers. In light of these threats, the United States government has instituted the National Strategy to Security Cyberspace. This program aims to prevent cyber-terrorism or effectively respond with the help computer specialists in the private sector. More information about this program can be obtained at www.whitehouse.gov/pcipb/cyberspace_strategy.pdf.

transportation systems would also have an enormous impact on the movement of goods and services. If petro-chemical plants are taken out of service, many aspects of our lives, including manufacturing and travel, would be in jeopardy. An attack on water and food resources could result in sickness or even death.

It is also imperative that you assess threats against key assets. **Key assets** include "a variety of unique facilities, sites, and structures that require protection" (White House 2003, 71). Examples include banks, financial institutions, major corporations, fire and police stations, hospitals, national monuments, and government property (the White House, Capital Hill, the Supreme Court building, the governor's office, city hall, etc.).

Besides considering critical infrastructure and key assets in your threat assessment, you must also recognize that any location of public assembly could be attacked by terrorists. For instance, sporting venues, fairgrounds, shopping malls, grocery stores, restaurants, bus stations, subways, and train cars are all likely to be attacked. Schools are also likely to be attacked as was witnessed in Beslan, Russia on September 1, 2004. Chechen separatists took over 1,200 adults and children hostage. A few days later, a gun battle broke out and the fighting resulted in the death of 334 people (including 186 children). Such locations are likely to be attacked because they are regarded to be "**soft targets**," meaning they are open and accessible to the public. Soft targets are also extremely vulnerable to attacks due to the high

Key assets:
Facilities, sites, and structures that are believed to require additional protection from terrorist attacks.

Soft targets:
Potential sites of terrorist attacks because they are open and accessible to the public.

IN THE REAL WORLD

The Attractiveness of Certain Targets

On June 2, 2007, Russell Defreitas, a resident of Brooklyn, New York, devised a plot to blow up fuel pipelines leading into J.F.K international airport. According to the U.S. Justice Department, Defreitas stated that the attack would provide "more bang for the buck" because of the anticipated fire as well as economic and psychological consequences. Pipelines such as this one may be attractive targets because it is impossible to protect them due to their length. The loss of pipelines could lead to a fuel shortage and rising prices. For this reason, the security of pipelines is an important priority in the National Infrastructure Protection Plan. The Department of Homeland Security, under direction of Homeland Security Presidential Directive 7, is working with oil and petroleum companies to plan responses to future threats in this area. Many corporations are now taking steps to protect the most vulnerable locations. Improved monitoring and shut-down strategies are making pipelines less appealing targets to terrorists (Kimery 2007).

Figure 9-2

Subways are vulnerable to attacks because they are accessible to terrorists and contain a large number of potential victims.

concentration of people in a single location. The July 7, 2005, attacks on the London subway and bus systems are examples of soft targets. These soft targets are extremely difficult to protect and defend because of the freedom of movement in and around them.

9.1.2 Working with Others to Identify Threats

In order to accurately assess the threat of attacks against critical infrastructure, key assets and soft targets, it will be imperative that you work closely with others. Government agencies, department leaders, and members of the business community have special knowledge and expertise to help you determine the likelihood of an attack along with possible consequences.

At the local and state level, there are also many departments and individuals that can help you assess terrorist threats and risks. The Department of Transportation will have vital information about traffic patterns, key interchanges, and vulnerable bridges. Transportation officials will also possess vital information about subway and bus terminals. River authorities can provide you with data about the age and capacity of dams while utility departments can help you assess the criticality of waste water systems. Engineering departments will have statistics on building age and occupancy rates. Planning and development can help you acquire information about zoning requirements, demographic data, and census numbers. Parks and recreation departments can be contacted to gain knowledge about athletic venues, water parks and large community gatherings. The Chamber of Commerce will likewise help you to identify commercial districts and industrial areas. Public health department can determine the dangers associated with biological terrorist attacks.

The private sector can also be a great partner when you conduct your threat assessment. Businesses are heavily involved with critical infrastructure. In fact, it is estimated that approximately 85 percent of all infrastructure is owned or operated by the private sector (Ewing 2004). Therefore, contacting communication companies, energy producers, and power suppliers can help you to understand the threats posed to phone lines, gas systems, and electrical grids. Manufacturers and the safety managers at petro-chemical plants will also be able to assist you in the threat assessment. They will have knowledge about hazardous materials that could be used in or targeted by a terrorist attack. You can also communicate with hospitals to identify the consequences of major public health emergencies associated with terrorist attacks. Insurance companies are others who can help you to identify the economic losses associated with potential attack scenarios.

There are many other possible partners for your threat assessment. Farmers will have vital information about cattle and agricultural production. Biotechnology research firms may have data about the diseases they are studying in your community. Rail companies and trucking firms are good assets to contact if you want to know what is being shipped through your county. Emergency managers are adept at conducting these types of analyses. They have undertaken such assessments for decades and can be very useful for this purpose. The key point is to recognize that you can and should tap into the expertise of others by networking and collaborating. Without involving specialists in your threat assessment, you will fail to accurately estimate the probability of attacks and their negative potential.

Philip Pupura, the Director of the Security Training Institute and Resource Center, has identified several partners at the federal level that could help you assess risks (2007, 361). Such stakeholders, along with their areas of expertise, include:

- **FBI.** Gathers intelligence about the plans of terrorists which are then filtered down to state and local law enforcement officials. It also works to prevent attacks on computer systems and the Internet.
- **Department of Defense.** Responsible for the physical security of military installations and the defense industrial base.
- **Department of Energy.** Oversees the safeguarding of power plants, energy infrastructure, and nuclear weapons production facilities.
- **Department of Health and Human Services.** In charge of health-care assets.
- **Environmental Protection Agency.** Deals with water and wastewater systems.

- **Department of Agriculture.** Focuses on the need to protect agriculture and food infrastructure.
- **Department of Treasury.** Responsible for banking and financial institutions.
- **Department of the Interior.** Conscientious about the security of national monuments such as the Statue of Liberty, Mount Rushmore, etc.

Finally, the Department of Homeland Security is charged with the protection of numerous sites that could be the target of terrorist attacks. They include telecommunication systems, postal and shipping sectors, emergency services, and transportation systems (in conjunction with the Department of Transportation). DHS also works closely with the Nuclear Regulatory Commission to oversee the security of nuclear reactors and nuclear waste sites. It also collaborates with the Secret Service to oversee special events and the National Cyber Response Coordination Group to monitor cyber security. Another responsibility of DHS is the protection of government facilities. The Federal Protective Service helps DHS to reach this vital goal.

9.1.3 Points of Consideration

As you assess threats and associated vulnerabilities, you should take into consideration many important questions. For instance:

- Are there known groups in your jurisdiction that may desire to carry out a terrorist attack?
- What are the possible targets that they may wish to destroy?
- How easy would it be to carry out an attack against critical infrastructure through sabotage?
- What is the likelihood of key assets being attacked with traditional explosives?
- Which soft targets would permit more fatalities due to the concentration of people in the area?
- Which locations are more likely to be targeted than others?
- Are any measures in place to defend these locations from an attack?
- What are the probable consequences of a terrorist attack at that specific location?
- What types of attacks would have the greatest impact on life, property, the environment, government and corporate operations, and general social disruption?

Answering these questions can lead to very formal and complex threat assessments, which could take months and even years to complete. Of course, there is always difficulty knowing what you should focus on: probability, consequences, or both likelihood and impact. Some attacks may be highly probable but generate limited consequences. As an example, a conventional explosive might fall into this category. Other attacks may be improbable but result in significant impacts. A biological attack is an example of this type of event. It is thus a challenge to know how to weigh each scenario and its resulting severity.

Nevertheless, the process of conducting a threat assessment can be simplified if you put yourself in the position of a terrorist. People playing this

IN THE REAL WORLD

Risk Based Funding Prioritization

In June 2006, the Intelligence and Analysis Office in the Department of Homeland Security released the findings of a study about the risk facing states around the nation. The study examined a number of factors including population size and density, the importance of critical infrastructure, proximity to the border and ports, the presence of hazardous materials, and iconic value among other variables. The results provided one view on how to prioritize homeland security funding around the nation. Below is a list of states and territories in rank order.

1.	California	27.	Mississippi
2.	Texas	28.	Colorado
3.	New York	29.	Connecticut
4.	Florida	30.	Oregon
5.	Illinois	31.	South Carolina
6.	District of Columbia	32.	Oklahoma
7.	Michigan	33.	Iowa
8.	Ohio	34.	Nevada
9.	New Jersey	35.	Arkansas
10.	Pennsylvania	36.	New Mexico
11.	Georgia	37.	Utah
12.	Louisiana	38.	West Virginia
13.	Arizona	39.	Nebraska
14.	Massachusetts	40.	Maine
15.	Washington	41.	Rhode Island
16.	North Carolina	42.	Wyoming
17.	Indiana	43.	North Dakota
18.	Virginia	44.	Hawaii
19.	Kentucky	45.	Vermont
20.	Minnesota	46.	Idaho
21.	Maryland	47.	Delaware
22.	Missouri	48.	Montana
23.	Tennessee	49.	New Hampshire
24.	Kansas	50.	South Dakota
25.	Alabama	51.	Alaska
26.	Wisconsin		

role are known in war games as the "red team" (the "blue team" would include those responding to the actions of the red team). If you were a terrorist, what critical infrastructure, key assets and soft targets would give you maximum publicity for your cause? Which of these targets would be easiest to infiltrate and operate in? How would you implement the attack to have the greatest potential impact? These thoughts are morbid, but are necessary if you are to be successful in assessing threats.

Another method to help you determine threats and vulnerabilities is a risk assessment matrix. David Alexander, a well known scholar of emergency management, has developed a table to determine the risk of natural and technological disasters. It is based on an examination of probability and severity (2002, 57). Adapting this table to the threat of terrorism, different types of events (e.g., assassination, bombings, mass shootings, attacks involving weapons of mass destruction) can be categorized in Table 9-1.

Terrorist attacks placed in low probability and low severity cells are described as having an acceptable level of risk. Attacks listed with a moderate degree of probability and severity is defined as having significant risk. Events described as being frequent and catastrophic are regarded to be of critical risk.

As possible terrorist attack scenarios are being described, you should determine your top priorities (see in the Real World, Catastrophic Scenarios, on next page). The Federal Emergency Management Agency has a publication, *Building Design for Homeland Security*, that discusses how to accurately assess risks. This manual can be accessed at www.fema.gov/library/viewRecord.do?id=1939. It will help you be most concerned about attacks that are deemed to be significant or critical. However, the process of determining risks is subjective and cannot be determined with 100 percent certainty. While risk estimation may include complex mathematical models that incorporate an evaluation of costs and benefits of specific mitigation measures, the unpredictability and adaptability of terrorists make threat assessments problematic at best. Regardless, doing your best to evaluate risk, even when not perfect, is preferable to doing nothing at all.

Table 9-1: Risk Assessment Matrix

Probability of Occurrence				
Severity	Impossible	Improbable	Occasional	Probable	Frequent
Negligible	Acceptable	Acceptable	Acceptable	Acceptable	Acceptable
Marginal	Acceptable	Acceptable	Acceptable	Acceptable	Significant
Moderate	Acceptable	Acceptable	Acceptable	Significant	Critical
Serious	Acceptable	Acceptable	Significant	Critical	Critical
Catastrophic	Acceptable	Significant	Critical	Critical	Critical

IN THE REAL WORLD

Catastrophic Scenarios

In 2004, U.S. homeland security officials identified 15 possible catastrophic scenarios. It is interesting to note that only two of them are natural disasters, even though they are historically more prevalent than terrorist attacks.

Scenario 1: Nuclear Detonation—10-Kiloton Improvised Nuclear Weapon

Scenario 2: Biological Attack—Aerosol Anthrax

Scenario 3: Biological Disease Outbreak—Pandemic Influenza

Scenario 4: Biological Attack—Plague

Scenario 5: Chemical Attack—Blister Agent

Scenario 6: Chemical Attack—Toxic Industrial Chemicals

Scenario 7: Chemical Attack—Nerve Agent

Scenario 8: Chemical Attack—Chlorine Tank Explosion

Scenario 9: Natural Disaster—Major Earthquake

Scenario 10: Natural Disaster—Major Hurricane

Scenario 11: Radiological Attack—Radiological Dispersal Devices

Scenario 12: Explosives Attack—Bombing Using Improvised Explosive Device

Scenario 13: Biological Attack—Food Contamination

Scenario 14: Biological Attack—Foreign Animal Disease (Foot and Mouth Disease)

Scenario 15: Cyber Attack

Figure 9-3

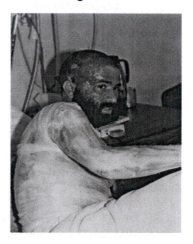

Chemical attacks, which may adversely affect victims such as this one, are one of 15 anticipated attacks against the United States.

IN THE REAL WORLD

Homeland Security Resources

As an employee in homeland security, you may not initially understand the methods to assess the threat of terrorism. Fortunately, there are many resources available to help you fulfill this vital responsibility. Besides working with government officials in emergency management and the Department of Homeland Security, you can also acquire assistance from the private sector. Emergency & Disaster Management, Inc. is one company that can help you assess hazards and vulnerability. It employs unique methodologies to measure risk including blast analysis, entry control point studies, and impact assessments. With this information, Emergency & Disaster Management, Inc. can then help to create and implement effective mitigation strategies based on current anti-terrorism standards. For further information, see www.emergency-management.net/.

SELF-CHECK

1. A threat assessment is a study about what types of attacks could occur and how bad they might be. True or False?

2. Farms and food processing plants are not considered critical infrastructure. True or False?

3. Which of the following is considered a soft target?

   (a) A computer network
   (b) A petro-chemical plant
   (c) A school
   (d) A sewage treatment plant

4. Why is it important to work with others to assess the threat of terrorism?

9.2 STRUCTURAL AND NON-STRUCTURAL MITIGATION

Structural mitigation:
Special construction practices and materials that limit the impact of terrorist attacks.

Protecting against terrorist attacks may require two types of mitigation. **Structural mitigation** involves special construction practices and materials that limit the consequences of terrorist attacks. For instance, installing blast resistant glass on government buildings is an example of structural mitigation.

Non-structural mitigation:
Methods beyond construction that may limit the possibility or consequences of terrorist attacks.

Non-structural mitigation includes other methods (beyond construction) that may limit the possibility or impact of terrorist attacks. Regulations on building location or video surveillance are examples of non-structural mitigation. Both structural and non-structural approaches are vital to homeland security. They can help to reduce injuries and deaths, limit economic losses, and minimize the disruption associated with terrorism.

IN THE REAL WORLD

Four Layers of Defense

The Federal Emergency Management Agency has described four layers of defense against terrorist attacks. These layers include the following:

Deter: Limiting access to a target or countering the weapon or tactic being used. This usually includes perimeter control, fencing, locks, and lighting.

Deny: Designing buildings and infrastructure to withstand blasts or minimize the effects of chemical, biological, or radiological weapons.

Devalue: Finding ways to minimize the consequence of an attack, thereby discouraging the desire of terrorists to attack.

Detect: Gathering intelligence to monitor threats and using security to prevent access to buildings.

9.2.1 Architectural Design and Construction

In the *Reference Manual to Mitigate Potential Terrorist Attacks against Buildings*, the U.S. Department of Homeland Security notes that building design and fabrication plays a large role in the potential impact of terrorist attacks (2003). For instance, "U" or "L" shaped buildings should be avoided since they channel and exacerbate the force of shock waves (see figure 9-4). The use of steel reinforcement in concrete buildings, as well as the number and redundancy of support columns, may also minimize the damage or collapses created by explosive devices. Windows glazed with laminate security film may inhibit or slow down flying shrapnel and other debris. Sprinklers and fire resistant materials can be installed to prevent arson-induced fires from spreading. Ventilation systems can also be protected in certain ways to discourage or stop hazardous materials releases. The great benefit of implementing these structural mitigation measures in light of the threat of terrorism is that they will often be applicable to other types of hazards (e.g., earthquakes, hurricanes, tornadoes, electrical fires, etc.). In fact, it is well known in the emergency management community that these hazards are far more likely to occur than terrorist attacks. Terrorism provides yet another reason why architects and construction companies should take structural mitigation seriously.

Figure 9-4

Shapes that Dissipate Air Blast

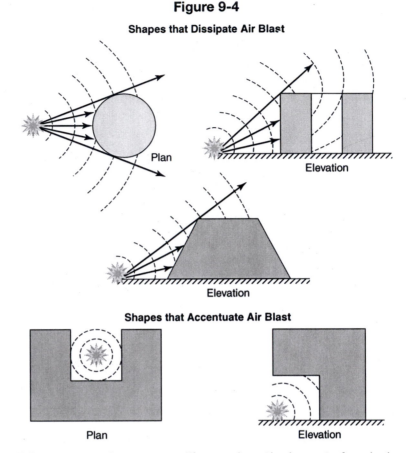

Shapes that Accentuate Air Blast

Building construction may amplify or reduce the impact of explosions.
From Building Design for Homeland Security (FEMA).

9.2.2 Zoning and Set Back Regulations

Zoning:
Regulations that delineate where buildings can be located.

Other ways to protect against terrorist attacks at the local level include zoning and set back requirements as well as unique devices to prevent the movement of people and vehicles. **Zoning** involves regulations that delineate where buildings can be located. Just as you would not want an elementary school located near an industrial plant, you do not want a shopping mall located near a rail yard which transports chemical tankers. In either case, the accidental or intentional release of hazardous materials could injure or kill scores of people, or even hundreds or thousands. Prescribing the best location for businesses, homes, sporting venues, and critical infrastructure could do much to limit the impact of terrorist attacks. Planning with spatial relationships in mind can be extremely beneficial. For instance, if no homes are located in flood plains down stream, terrorists will be less likely to blow up dams and levies. There is minimal incentive to carry out such an attack because the consequences will be less severe. The added benefit of such planning is that repetitive flood losses from excessive precipitation will also

Figure 9-5

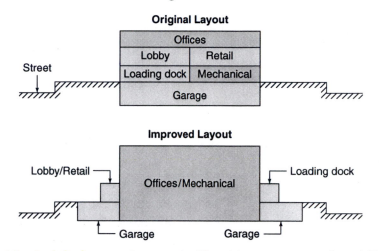

Architectual design may have a significant impact upon vulnerability.
Taken from Building Design for Homeland Security (FEMA).

be minimized as a result. This could save many lives and countless dollars on the part of taxpayers.

Set back requirements:
Laws that describe the proximity of buildings to roads and parking lots.

Set back requirements describe the proximity of buildings to roads and parking lots. Many, if not most, terrorist attacks involve vehicle delivered bombs. Creating fewer vehicle access points near a building, avoiding parking lots beneath structures, and moving parking sites away from edifices will dampen the effects of explosive detonations (see figure 9-5). For instance, if the driveway leading next to the Murrah Federal Building in Oklahoma City were eliminated, the impact of Timothy McVeigh's 1995 bomb would have logically been minimized. A bomb half a block away will produce far less damage to a building and its occupants than an explosive device placed within several yards of the structure. Stand-off zones can be a great defense against acts of terrorism.

9.2.3 Other Security Measures

There are countless other mitigation measures that can be taken to reduce the probability and consequences of terrorist attacks. Pupura (2007) and Kelly (2006) have identified several of them:

Bollards:
Metal or concrete posts installed into the earth or cement to keep vehicles from entering restricted areas.

- **Bollards,** which are metal or concrete posts installed into the earth or cement, can be used to keep vehicles from entering restricted areas. They make it difficult for cars or trucks to come closer to buildings.

- Trees and vegetation may be planted around buildings to limit the blast from explosives. They serve as a natural barrier during terrorist attacks.

- Walls, fences, and barbed wire can be employed around critical infrastructure and key assets to maintain a secure perimeter. While these devices can be broken or cut, they are a vital layer in security.

- Proper lighting can create a psychological deterrent for terrorists and enable detection if they attempt to carry out attacks at night. Terrorists might seek a location that has no lighting or they risk apprehension.

- Guards and guard dogs can help patrol facilities and control employee and visitor traffic. They can sense when behavior is suspicious and take appropriate actions.

- Gates and doors should have locks (whether mechanical or electromagnetic). This will prevent unauthorized access into the building or its rooms.

- Metal detectors and X-ray scanners may used to detect weapons and explosives. Such devices are essential at courthouses and other key assets.

- Background checks can be conducted on prospective employees to determine who should be hired. This will prevent terrorism from internal sources.

- ID badges and access cards and allow or restrict movement into sensitive areas. This will help to ensure that authorized employees are only permitted to roam freely in certain locations.

- Pin numbers and biometric identifiers (e.g., fingerprint or retinal scans) are other means to permit or confine movement of employees. They are useful to gain or restrict access to mission critical areas.

IN THE REAL WORLD

Mass Transit Targets

Recent terrorist attacks in Israel, Britain, Spain, and Russia have been directed at mass transit systems. Recognizing the potential of this threat in the United States, the Department of Homeland Security is working with the American Public Transportation Association (APTA) and others in mass transit, freight rail, trucking, and bus services to develop a plan for attacks on mass transit systems. Private companies and the federal government are assessing vulnerabilities, and they recognize that the openness of transit systems makes them an easy target. There is now more emphasis on employee training, police presence, the use of dogs, and closed-circuit television to monitor what is happening in transportation areas. Efforts are also being taken to "harden" transportation infrastructure. Trace detection portals are being evaluated to determine how effective they are at identifying explosive material. It is hoped that these steps can deter attacks or increase response effectiveness (McCarter 2007).

Figure 9-6

Bollards like these can prevent vehicle delivered bombs from
reaching their intended targets.

- Special attention should be given to security in lobbies, loading docks, and mail rooms. These are logical locations where terrorists might attack.
- Cameras, alarms, and intrusion systems (e.g., motion detectors) are valuable tools to monitor physical security. They can help to warn of unusual activity or solve questions of who was responsible for terrorist attacks.

When key leaders and dignitaries (e.g., CEOs and the President) are to be present at a specific location, physical security becomes even more vital. Areas may need to be "sniffed" in advance for bombs, and access to the building or area carefully controlled. Additional security guards, body guards, snipers, and secret service or special force teams may need to be used to protect such officials.

Where possible and when required, it would also be wise to hire someone to be in charge of security measures at any given location. According to the U.S. Government Accountability Office, "having a chief security officer position for physical assets is recognized in the security industry as essential in organization with large numbers of mission-critical facilities" (2005, 43–44). This person should be familiar with the American Society of Industrial Security, which has additional information about physical security. He or she might also want to "visit a local airport, jail, or courthouse to see the levels of complexity in equipment, operations and management of security systems" (Evans 2001, 96). However, the security specialist should not be viewed as the only one in charge of security. Everyone must take more interest in security if terrorist attacks are to be minimized. This includes anyone working in the public and private sectors as well as the public at large. Attacks have been prevented by citizens who saw something out of the ordinary and reported suspicious behavior.

IN THE REAL WORLD

Virginia Protects Itself

After 9/11, the State of Virginia felt a need to increase security at water treatment plants, power facilities, and tunnels—all potential targets for terrorist attacks. State officials determined that these locations are extremely vulnerable and that employees could take advantage of this risk-laden situation if they had ill-intent. For this reason, it was decided that background checks would be performed on employees applying for sensitive jobs. The Cooperative Extension Service will also verify that employees in the agricultural sector are legal residents of the United States. These are only a few of the vital measures that can be taken to mitigate terrorist attacks.

SELF-CHECK

1. ID cards and pin numbers are examples of structural mitigation. True or False?

2. The shape of buildings can reduce or exacerbate the blast waves from explosions. True or False?

3. The proximity of buildings to roads and parking lots pertains to:

    (a) zoning.

    (b) set back requirements.

    (c) structural mitigation.

    (d) bollards.

4. What special measures need to be taken to protect dignitaries?

SUMMARY

Because it may be impossible to prevent terrorism, it will also be necessary to protect locations against possible terrorist attacks. For this reason, it is important that you understand the benefits of mitigation practices. You will need to work with others to assess the threats posed to critical infrastructure, key assets, and soft targets. You must understand the difference between structural and non-structural mitigation. In particular, you should promote the design and construction of buildings that take terrorism into account. You will likewise need to consider zoning and set back requirements as well as a variety of other measures to augment security. While no single measure will be foolproof, a strong system of self defense will diminish the possibility and effects of terrorism.

ASSESS YOUR UNDERSTANDING

UNDERSTAND: WHAT HAVE YOU LEARNED?

 Go to **www.wiley.com/college/mcentire** to assess your knowledge of mitigation.

SUMMARY QUESTIONS

1. After mentioning to your neighbor that you are studying homeland security, he says that there is no point in trying to figure out where terrorists will attack next. He believes they are too unpredictable. What would you say to him about the benefit of threat assessments?

2. As an employee working in homeland security, you have been asked to conduct a threat assessment looking specifically at the private sector. How could companies help you with your responsibility?

3. As an emergency manager in your community, you have just received word that the city council has approved your request to relocate the emergency operations center. What structural, zoning, and set back measures could help protect it against terrorist attacks?

4. As an expert in homeland security, you have been asked to be interviewed about effective security procedures in buildings. What would you say in your remarks?

5. It is possible to prevent all terrorist attacks from occurring. True or False?

6. A threat assessment is an evaluation of anticipated targets of terrorist attacks. True or False?

7. Infrastructure is regarded to be "critical" if its destruction would have a severe impact upon the well-being of the United States. True or False?

8. The Department of the Interior can help you assess the threat of terrorism posed to power plants and nuclear facilities. True or False?

9. An important question to consider when assessing threat is: Are there any measures in place to deter terrorism from occurring at that location? True or False?

10. Structural and non-structural mitigation may reduce death, economic losses, and disruption caused by terrorist attacks. True or False?

11. Walls and fences may inhibit the ability of terrorists to launch attacks. True or False?

12. It might be wise for any location deemed to be a likely target for attack to hire a security specialist. True or False?

13. A threat assessment is similar to:

    (a) a structural mitigation technique.

    (b) a hazard and vulnerability analysis.

    (c) a key asset target.

    (d) a set back requirement.

14. Which is not considered to be included in critical infrastructure?

    (a) Transportation systems

    (b) Electrical systems

    (c) The White House

    (d) Information and communication systems

15. Which of the following is believed to be a soft target?

    (a) Restaurants

    (b) Police stations

    (c) An oil refinery

    (d) The Supreme Court building

16. What organization could help you assess threats posed against dams?

    (a) The FBI

    (b) The Department of the Interior

    (c) Parks and Recreation

    (d) River authorities

17. A metal pole placed in the ground to prevent movement of vehicles is best known as:

    (a) structural mitigation.

    (b) a bollard.

    (c) non-structural mitigation.

    (d) a set back requirement

18. Which measure would help to prevent someone from bringing a weapon into a building?

    (a) Fences

    (b) Background checks

    (c) Metal detectors

    (d) Cameras

BE A HOMELAND SECURITY PROFESSIONAL

Meeting with the FBI

You are an official in the Department of Homeland Security. It is your responsibility to assess potential targets around the nation. The FBI has requested that you meet with them to discuss the consequences of an attack against transportation systems. They fear that a domestic terrorist organization is intent on carrying out such an attack. What would you say about the vulnerability and criticality of transportation systems?

Assignment: Things to Consider When Assessing Threats

Write a two-page paper discussing the concerns you might need to address if you were to complete a threat assessment. Be as thorough as possible.

Hired as a Security Specialist

You have just been hired as a security specialist for a major industrial firm. You have been tasked with the responsibility of ensuring the safety and security of employees. What measures can you take to reduce the possibility of an attack against your facility?

KEY TERMS

Bollards	Metal or concrete posts installed into the earth or cement to keep vehicles from entering restricted areas.
Critical infrastructure	Interdependent networks comprised of industrial, utility, transportation, and other distribution systems.
Key assets	Facilities, sites, and structures that are believed to require additional protection from terrorist attacks.
Protection	An attempt to deny attacks and defend oneself from terrorism.
Non-structural mitigation	Methods beyond construction that may limit the possibility or consequences of terrorist attacks.
Set back requirements	Laws that describe the proximity of buildings to roads and parking lots.
Soft targets	Potential sites of terrorist attacks because they are open and accessible to the public.
Structural mitigation	Special construction practices and materials that limit the impact of terrorist attacks.
Threat assessment	A careful study of the targets that might be appealing to terrorists.
Zoning	Regulations that delineate where buildings can be located.

REFERENCES

Alexander, David. (2002). *Principles of Emergency Planning and Management*. Oxford University Press: New York.

Clinton, William J. (1996). "Critical Infrastructure Protection: Executive Order 13010." *Federal Register* 61.

U.S. Department of Homeland Security. (2003). *Reference Manual to Mitigate Potential Terrorist Attacks against Buildings*. FEMA: Washington, D.C.

Evans, Richard J. (2001). "Public Works and Terrorism." Pp. 95–100 in Hogan, Lawrence J. (Ed.). *Terrorism: Defensive Strategies for Individuals, Companies and Governments*. Amlex, Inc.: Washington, D.C.

Ewing, L. (2004). "The Missing Link in the Partnership." *Homeland Security*, 1.

HS Today. (2007). "Assessing the Threat." *HS Today: Insight and Analysis for Homeland Security Decisionmakers*. 4 (2): 18–24.

Kelly, Ronald J. (2006). "Role of Corporate Security." Pp. 745–765 in Kamien, David G. (ed.). *The McGraw-Hill Homeland Security Handbook*. McGraw-Hill: New York.

Kimery, Anthony. (2007). "Petrojihad: The Next Front?" *HS Today: Insight and Analysis for Homeland Security Decisionmakers*. 4 (9): 36–42.

McCarter, Mickey. (2007). "Mass Safety for Mass Transit." *HS Today: Insight and Analysis for Homeland Security Decisionmakers*. 4 (7): 20–24.

McEntire, David A., Robie Jack Robinson and Richard T. Weber. (2001). "Managing the Threat of Terrorism," *IQ Report* 33 (12), International City/County Management Association: Washington, D.C.

Purpura, Philip P. (2007). *Terrorism and Homeland Security: An Introduction with Applications*. Butterworth-Heinemann: Burlington, MA.

U.S. Government Accountability Office. (2005). *Homeland Security: Actions Needed to Better Protect National Icons and Federal Office Buildings from Terrorism*. www.gao.gov/cgi-bin/getrpt?GAO-050681 (last accessed 12/17/07).

White House. (2003). "The National Strategy for the Physical Protection of Critical Infrastructure and Key Assets." www.whitehouse.gov/pcipb/physical.html (last accessed 12/17/07).

PREPARING FOR THE UNTHINKABLE
Readiness for Terrorism

Do You Already Know?

- The importance and nature of preparedness
- The role of an advisory council
- How to write an emergency operations plan
- The benefit of training and community education

 For additional questions to assess your current knowledge of preparedness, go to **www.wiley.com/college/mcentire**

What You Will Find Out	What You Will Be Able To Do
10.1 The importance of preparedness measures	• Evaluate the different roles of federal and state governments
10.2 The role of an advisory council	• Compose a city emergency management ordinance
10.3 The requirement of budgets and grants	• Write an emergency operations plan
10.4 The benefit of training and community education	• Design and conduct terrorism exercises

INTRODUCTION

One of your important roles in homeland security is to anticipate and prepare for possible acts of terrorism. In order to accomplish this objective, you must understand the concept and nature of preparedness. It is also vital that you are aware of federal and state preparedness activities as well as steps that must be taken for readiness at the local level. In particular, you must establish a preparedness council, designate and equip an emergency operations center, and plan for possible terrorist attacks. By undertaking these measures, you will enhance your community's capability to deal with the negative effects of terrorist attacks.

10.1 THE IMPORTANCE AND NATURE OF PREPAREDNESS

No matter what steps are taken to prevent terrorist attacks or mitigate their adverse impacts, it is always possible that terrorism will occur anyway. A common saying is that homeland security is similar to the game of soccer. Goalies and homeland security officials have to be effective 100 percent of the time to reach their objectives. In contrast, forwards and terrorists only have to be successful once to accomplish theirs. This reality poses an enormous challenge for those working in the field. There is simply too much vulnerability in comparison to the resources and capacity we have at hand at any given period of time.

For instance, if our intelligence officers are able to intercept one communication stream, terrorists will switch to another. If counter-terrorism forces close down a training camp in one location, it is likely that a new one will emerge elsewhere. If the United States is able to control legal entry through passports and visas, terrorists will find ways to cross the border illegally. If we spend time and energy protecting dams, national monuments, and government buildings, terrorists will simply attack schools, churches, and shopping malls. Prudence therefore dictates that our nation takes adequate, but not over-zealous, measures to prepare for potential terrorist attacks.

The concept of preparedness is not simple or straight forward. Even though it has been the subject of attention in emergency management for years, there is no agreement on a single definition (Kirschenbaum 2002). Godschalk views preparedness as "actions taken in advance of an emergency to develop operational capabilities to facilitate an effective response" (1991, 136). Gillespie and Streeter (1987) suggest that preparedness includes numerous actions taken to improve the safety and effectiveness of a community's response during a disaster. While these views seem to down play the relation of preparedness to recovery, the Department of Homeland

Security believes it is related to all aspects of dealing with terrorism. According to the DHS, preparedness is "the range of deliberate, critical tasks, and activities necessary to build, sustain, and improve the operational capability to prevent, protect against, respond to and recover from domestic incidents" (DHS 2004, 134). For the purposes of this book, **preparedness** assumes terrorist attacks will occur and therefore promotes concerted efforts to improve response and recovery capabilities. In contrast, prevention and protection are more concerned about avoidance, deterrence, denial, and mitigation. Preparedness is thus necessary for more effective post-terrorism operations. It is often driven by policy and activity at the federal and state levels.

Preparedness:
Concerted efforts to improve response and recovery capabilities.

10.1.1 Federal and State Initiatives

Responsibility for national preparedness falls to the federal government in general, and the Department of Homeland Security and Federal Emergency Management Agency in particular. However, in an attempt to ready the nation for terrorist attacks, the President often issues policies to encourage improved preparedness programs. As an example, on May 4, 2007, President Bush issued Homeland Security Presidential Directive (HSPD) 20. It establishes continuity of operation requirements for all executive departments and agencies. **Continuity of operation** deals with the maintenance of government functions after terrorist attacks through the identification of leader succession, alternate work sites, and resumption of operational practices. The idea is the government must continue to serve the American people if its leaders, departments, and missions fall victim to terrorism. While continuity of operations plans existed among some federal entities before HSPD 20, this directive clarified their purpose and mandated further compliance.

Continuity of operation:
The maintenance of government functions after terrorist attacks through the identification of leader succession, alternate work sites, and resumption of operational practices.

Congress also passes many laws to enhance our nation's preparedness for terrorist attacks. Such pieces of legislation started in the 1990s and have become more frequent over time. Examples of such laws are numerous and include:

- The National Defense Authorization Law was passed after the World Trade Center bombing in 1993. It specified that FEMA and other federal agencies should devote more attention to planning for future terrorist attacks.

- The Anti-terrorism and Effective Death Penalty Act of 1996, which required additional training for first responders and provided funds to accomplish this goal.

- The Defense Against Weapons of Mass Destruction Act (also known as the Nunn, Lugar and Domenici Act) was also approved in 1996. It mandates improved preparedness measures in 120 cities around the United States regarded to be vulnerable to terrorist attacks.

- The Public Health Security and Bio-terrorism Preparedness and Response Act of 2002 provided local and state governments $4.6 billion to improve public health readiness around the nation.
- The Comprehensive Homeland Security Act of 2003 recommends improvement in the area of interoperable communications for first responders.

There are additional laws that deal more specifically with preparedness for all types of disaster scenarios. One important example is the Robert T. Stafford Disaster Relief and Emergency Assistance Act which was passed November 23, 1988 (see www.fema.gov/pdf/about/stafford_act.pdf). This law describes federal responsibility to prepare the nation for disasters as well as various programs to help state and local governments when they occur. The Stafford Act recommends that plans be developed and reviewed annually. It also discusses federal financial and technological assistance to state and local governments. Although the Stafford Act has been amended periodically, it serves as the cornerstone of emergency management in the United States.

After the numerous failures witnessed in the response to Hurricane Katrina, senators and representatives also proposed ways to strengthen the ability of the United States to deal with all types of disasters. Known as the

IN THE REAL WORLD

Target Capabilities List (TCL)

In light of the threat of terrorism and other catastrophes, the President and Congress recently advocated the creation of an improved national preparedness system. The vision proposed by the National Preparedness Guidelines is "A nation prepared with coordinated capabilities to prevent, protect against, respond to, and recover from all hazards in a way that balances risk with resources and need." This objective will require a consensus approach among all of the relevant homeland security stakeholders in order to build capabilities. These capabilities include common functions such as planning and communications; prevention capabilities such as intelligence gathering, counter-terrorism, and law enforcement; protection capabilities such as food and agricultural safety and epidemiological surveillance; response capabilities such as incident and EOC management, search and rescue, and warning and evacuation; and recovery capabilities such as damage assessment and lifeline (utility) restoration. Everyone involved in homeland security and emergency management is encouraged to work toward the building of capabilities in these and other areas. For more information, see www.llis.dhs.gov/getFile.cfm?id=26724.

Post-Katrina Emergency Management Reform Act:
A law which specifies ways to avert the slow and disjointed federal response to the catastrophe in New Orleans, Louisiana.

Post-Katrina Emergency Management Reform Act, this law (signed in October 2006) specifies ways to avert the slow and disjointed federal response to the catastrophe in New Orleans, Louisiana. For instance, after being severed when the Department of Homeland Security was created, the close organizational ties that once existed between the Director of FEMA and the President were reinstated. Some of the national preparedness programs were returned to the Federal Emergency Management Agency (after being integrated elsewhere into DHS and the FB). FEMA's budget was also enhanced substantially since much of its funding was diverted for DHS start up costs. The Reform Act also points out ways to enhance the nation's ability to cope with chemical and radiological incidents. It is significant and will likely have a positive impact on preparedness for terrorism and all types of disasters. This is particularly important since terrorists may attack during or after natural and other types of disasters.

National Incident Management System (NIMS):
A comprehensive national approach for incident management in the United States.

National laws do not always prove to be beneficial, however. There is disagreement about the benefit of policies and legislation at the federal level. One of the strategies developed after 9/11 was the **National Incident Management System (NIMS)**. NIMS is defined as a comprehensive national approach for incident management (see www.fema.gov/pdf/emergency/nims/nims_doc_full.pdf). It was initiated after it was illustrated that police and fire units could not or would not operate jointly in New York City when the World Trade Center was attacked. NIMS consequently specified the procedures and structures to improve interoperable communications and collaboration among responding organizations. It also gives guidelines for resource management and promotes compatible technologies. NIMS helps to standardize expectations in disasters and it will likely improve communication ability in disasters. Nevertheless, NIMS might focus excessively on technological solutions to coordination problems and it may prove too rigid in the dynamic conditions of disasters. It may not always be applicable because of the politics of response operations and it may have trouble relating to mitigation and recovery activities (Buck, Trainor and Aguiree 2006).

National Response Plan (NRP):
A document that describes the procedures for responding to all-types of hazards with a multi-disciplinary perspective.

Similar charges have been made against the Department of Homeland Security's National Response Plan. In December 2004, DHS created this planning document. The **National Response Plan (NRP)** described national procedures for responding to all-types of hazards with a multidisciplinary perspective (see www.dhs.gov/xlibrary/assets/NRPbaseplan.pdf). It listed 15 vital post-disaster functions such as transportation, mass care, and search and rescue and divides those responsibilities among primary and support agencies. The goal of the NRP was to define what federal agencies and all other actors are to do when terrorism or disasters occur. While the intentions were laudable, critics argue that the plan focuses too heavily on terrorism and that it was far too complicated (Tierney 2006). The fact that the existing plan (the Federal Response Plan) was not simply revised and that FEMA's concerns about the National Response Plan were overlooked has led to quite a controversy. Many of the individuals and agencies that reviewed the initial drafts of the NRP found it unwieldy. This is because the relationship between the NRP and NIMS is at times unclear. The complexity of the NRP was also faulted, in part, for the poor response to Hurricane Katrina. Fortunately, the NRP is being revised at the time of this book's writing. Its successor is the National Response Framework.

National Response Framework (NRF):
The successor to the National Response Plan; a document that describes the principles, roles and structures of response and recovery operations.

The **National Response Framework (NRF)** is a document that describes the principles, roles, and structures of response and recovery operations. It is written for all elected and appointed leaders at the federal, state, and local levels of government. The NRF is based on five key principles:

- **Engaged partnerships.** Leaders at all levels must communicate and support one another in times of crisis.

- **Tiered response.** Incidents are managed at the lowest level of government and supported by others when needed.

- **Flexible operational capabilities.** Management activities will change to meet the size, scope, and complexity of events.

- **Unified command.** Clear understanding of the roles of others is required as is collaboration.

- **Readiness to act.** Individuals, families, community organizations, and all levels of government must prepare to deal with incidents of national significance.

While the exact contents and nature of the document are in question, it is anticipated that it will clarify the roles and responsibilities, describe what must be done to improve response and recovery operations, and explain how concepts and structures are applied to incident management objectives. FEMA's Regional Advisory Boards are providing feedback on the NRF and other preparedness initiatives. If the NRF includes the comments from the emergency management and homeland security communities, it will become an important plan at the national level.

In addition to the federal government, states are also heavily involved in preparedness activities. State homeland security departments are being established around the nation. Focus groups in these political jurisdictions are meeting to consider important policy decisions. Laws are being passed to better protect infrastructure and key assets. Tax revenues are being used to improve security, law enforcement, and emergency management functions. States are also working together to improve post-disaster operations. In 1996, Congress approved the state initiative, the **Emergency Management Assistance Compact (EMAC)**. The Emergency Management Assistance Compact is an agreement among states to render assistance to one another in time of need. The goal is to establish guidelines for the sharing of material resources, and to resolve in advance legal questions about personnel (e.g., who will pay overtime or death benefits). It has been deployed in several disasters and is

Emergency Management Assistance Compact (EMAC):
An agreement among states to render assistance to one another in time of need.

National Emergency Management Association:
A professional association of state emergency management agencies.

Emergency Management Accreditation Program:
A standard-based assessment and certification initiative for local and state emergency management agencies.

administered by the National Emergency Management Association. The **National Emergency Management Association** is a professional association which is comprised mainly of officials from state emergency management agencies. It was initiated in 1974 when the state directors of emergency management desired to discuss common concerns around the nation. It has been a key organization for the development of the Emergency Management Assistance Compact (an inter-state mutual aid agreement) and the **Emergency Management Accreditation Program** (a standard-based assessment and certification initiative for local and state emergency management agencies).

As has been noted, it is vital that the federal government be fully involved in emergency management activities throughout the nation. The federal government provides policy direction and financial resources which can have a significant impact upon national preparedness. However, it is imperative that state governments are prepared to respond as well since they are likely to be on their own for at least 72 hours after a disaster. After Hurricane Katrina struck Louisiana, it took nearly a week before sufficient help arrived. The same principle applies to local governments. Cities and counties should take increased responsibility to be ready for any type of event, including terrorist attacks. Local governments will be impacted most by terrorism and may be on their own for several days before outside assistance arrives. For this reason, it is imperative that you promote local government preparedness.

IN THE REAL WORLD

The Emergency Management Accreditation Program

After a conference presentation on the importance of standards in emergency management in 1997, the National Emergency Management Association began to discuss the need to establish recommendations for emergency management programs around the nation. In time, the Emergency Management Accreditation Program was developed and implemented. EMAP is a voluntary accreditation initiative which attempts to improve emergency management capabilities around the nation. It is based on the National Fire Protection Association's Standard on Disaster/Emergency Management and Business Continuity Programs which encourages norms regarding laws and authorities, program management, mutual aid, training, and many other preparedness activities. Emergency management officials who desire accreditation must write a self-assessment document and invite a team of independent assessors to review their program. Based on the findings of the review committee, the EMAP commission may accredit state and local programs. Accreditation implies that the jurisdiction is in compliance with widely accepted preparedness guidelines. An added benefit is that external reviews will point out weaknesses that can be corrected in the future.

SELF-CHECK

1. Preparedness deals more with improving response and recovery capabilities rather than avoidance and deterrence. True or False?

2. There is a large consensus on the benefits of federal policies and legislation, such as the National Incident Management System. True or False?

3. The successor of the National Response Plan is the:
   (a) Emergency Management Assistance Compact.
   (b) Comprehensive Homeland Security Act of 2003.
   (c) National Response Framework.
   (d) Post-Katrina Emergency Management Reform Act.

4. Why is it essential that local governments take responsibility to prepare for acts of terrorism?

10.2 SETTING THE FOUNDATION

In order to foster local preparedness for terrorist attacks, it will be imperative that you work closely with key stakeholders, establish legal guidelines, and obtain financial resources. You will therefore need to organize a preparedness committee, draft ordinances, and seek funding through budgets or grants. When this has been accomplished, you should also consider if your community needs an emergency operations center.

10.2.1 Preparedness Councils

Preparedness council:
A group of individuals who provide recommendations for policy and assist with program administration.

Because homeland security is very interdisciplinary, it will be necessary for you to create a preparedness council. A **preparedness council** is a group of individuals that provide recommendations for policy and assist with program administration. Such councils may be comprised of representatives from law enforcement, public health, public works, hospitals, key businesses, the American Red Cross, and volunteer groups among others. The goal is to ensure that many diverse viewpoints and areas of expertise are incorporated into the preparedness council. It is also wise to make sure that there are sufficient members to get the work done, but avoid excessive numbers because that may prove overwhelming and unmanageable.

Local Emergency Planning Committees (LEPCs):
Preparedness councils promoted in the 1980s to help communities prepare for hazardous materials releases.

Local Emergency Planning Committees (LEPCs) are one type of preparedness council. LEPCs were promoted in the 1980s to help communities prepare for hazardous materials releases (Lindell 1994). During this decade, there was a desire on the part of government leaders to avoid some of the mistakes being made in disasters associated with industrial accidents. For instance, doctors had major problems responding to the toxic gas release in Bhopal, India in 1984. The failure to identify the chemical that was released and treat victims resulted in nearly 3,000 deaths. LEPCs were seen as a way to identify hazardous materials concerns and help the jurisdiction anticipate how best to deal with fires and deadly toxins.

It should be noted that there will likely be multiple committees to assist with preparedness at the federal, state, and local levels. One might focus on weapons of mass destruction while another is geared toward natural disasters. Some committees are in charge of public health emergencies, and others deal with security and preparedness at a community sporting event. Thus, in reality, there will likely be various preparedness committees instead of a single preparedness council. It is also probable that the emergency manager will be the leader of these preparedness networks. An **emergency manager** is a local government official in charge of disaster mitigation, preparedness, response, and recovery. Emergency managers have been leading preparedness councils for decades and should be recognized among homeland security officials for their expertise.

Emergency manager:
A local government official in charge of disaster mitigation, preparedness, response, and recovery.

IN THE REAL WORLD

Local Emergency Planning Committees

Well-known disaster scholar, Michael Lindell, has conducted several important studies on local emergency planning committees. His research illustrates that LEPCs are comprised of representatives from fire departments, environmental protection agencies, hospitals, and corporations from the petro-chemical industry (1994). Lindell notes that LEPCs are beneficial in that they promote collaboration among organizations involved in preparedness. LEPCs are also advantageous in that they help to acquire additional funding, foster risk assessment, and rely on the expertise of highly committed members. Each jurisdiction should ensure that they have developed an advisory committee that focuses on terrorism and other types of disasters.

10.2.2 Ordinances

Ordinance:
An authoritative order or law issued by a government.

Passing local laws pertaining to the preparedness aspect of homeland security and emergency management will also be necessary. An **ordinance** is an authoritative order issued by a government. In terms of homeland security or emergency management, an ordinance will justify the need for community preparedness for terrorism and other types of disasters. It will specify the creation of an office or department to deal with these threats and permit the appointment of an official to help the community build capabilities for such events. Duties of this employee will be outlined in the ordinance along with powers that may be granted to him or her in time of crisis. In some cases, mutual aid will be addressed in ordinances. **Mutual aid** is a collaborative agreement between jurisdictions when external help is warranted. Promises are made to assist one another when internal resources prove insufficient. Other issues, including penalties for failure to comply with local laws, may be discussed in ordinances.

Mutual aid:
A collaborative agreement between jurisdictions when external help is warranted.

Sample ordinances can be obtained from other jurisdictions, and states may have recommended templates for those working in homeland security and emergency management. The input of political leaders (e.g., the mayor) and members of the preparedness council will be helpful in the creation of ordinances. Drafts must be run approved by the city attorney since these are legal documents. The important point to remember is that ordinances dictate what should be done (and what must be avoided) when preparing for terrorism and other types of disasters.

10.2.3 Budgets and Grants

Every organization will need resources if it is to survive and accomplish its mission. This is also the case with homeland security and emergency management offices. Without people and monetary support, it will be impossible to prepare a city for terrorist attacks. Resources can be acquired from local budgets as well as state and federal grants.

If you work at the local level, you will be asked to submit a proposed budget to the mayor and city council each year. This budget may include money needed to fund your position and that of your co-workers and staff. Estimated costs for office supplies, computers, phone lines, and other expected expenses will need to be outlined in your recommendation. The city manager and budget office can help you understand the rules that must be followed in your jurisdiction.

Once your budget draft is completed, you will probably need to present your proposal to city leaders. Concise communication, with supporting evidence and documentation, will help you to get as much money for your preparedness program as possible. Because you will be competing for funds with many other departments, you will probably not get everything you desire. However, persuasive argument, accountability for existing funds, and visible activity in your program will enable you to increase your budget over time.

Grants:
Funds given to local governments to support or enhance homeland security and emergency management programs.

Since local funds are limited, it may be advisable for you to seek grants from federal or state governments. **Grants** are funds given to local governments to support or enhance homeland security and emergency management programs. They may provide monies for personnel costs and material resources. There are numerous grants that can be obtained by local jurisdictions. For instance:

- Emergency Management Performance Grants help to fund emergency manager's positions and their general office expenses.
- Assistance to Fire Fighters Grants provides money to purchase equipment to fight fires.
- Public Safety Interoperable Communications Grants are awarded to acquire and utilize improved communication equipment.
- Homeland Security Grant Program gives financial assistance to help local jurisdictions prepare to deal with terrorism involving weapons of mass destruction.
- Infrastructure Protection Program shares money to improve security at sea ports, rail stations, bus terminals, and other transportation hubs and networks.
- Citizen Corps Support Program provides money to help train civilians teams to prepare for terrorist attacks and other disasters.
- Law Enforcement Terrorism Prevention Program gives resources to police departments to gather intelligence and share information about possible terrorists and criminals.
- Metropolitan Medical Response System Program funds public health organizations to response effectively to bio-terrorism attacks and cope with mass fatality incidents.

IN THE REAL WORLD

Urban Area Security Initiative (UASI)

The most recognized government grant program in homeland security is the Urban Area Security Initiative (UASI). The purpose of UASI is to help local governments build capabilities to deal with terrorist attacks and catastrophic disasters. Funds are directed toward large and dense metropolitan areas that are considered to be vulnerable targets of future terrorist attacks. Those applying for the grants must take a regional approach towards planning. In other words, cities will only be eligible for funds if they collaborate with nearby jurisdictions. UASI grants can be used to purchase equipment, train responders, and conduct exercises. Monies are also given to help prevent and protect against the use of weapons of mass destruction. The UASI program is multi-disciplinary, and supports numerous organizations working in preparedness, warnings, public health, search and rescue, triage, mass care, fire fighting, fatality management, etc. UASI is funded by the federal government and managed by the state. More information can be obtained at: www.ojp.usdoj.gov/odp/docs/fy2006hsgp.pdf.

There are also grants for hospital and school planning, urban search and rescue teams, and chemical stockpile emergency preparedness.

These and other grants are awarded on a competitive basis. That is to say, there are a fixed number of grants and they will be given to those jurisdictions that put together the best applications. As a result, it is imperative that you carefully read the grant instructions and ensure that you have met all requirements in the application documents. Clear writing is key, and it is wise to have the budget or grant office help you prepare your application. Another important consideration is to illustrate your ability to manage the grant. In some cases, your city will need to help fund the program you are proposing and match government monies. If you receive the grant, you will need to work closely with your grant team to accomplish all of the goals that were identified in the proposal. Documentation of expenses must be meticulous and reported on a periodic basis (depending on the type of grant). Failure to follow up on required paper work and use funds as outlined could result in termination of the grant or even imprisonment.

10.2.4 EOC

Emergency Operations Center (EOC):
A location from which disaster response and recovery activities can be overseen and managed.

Another foundational step toward preparedness is to establish an **Emergency Operations Center (EOC)**. An EOC is a location from which disaster response and recovery activities can be overseen and managed. While not every city has a designated EOC, they are becoming the norm for large

Figure 10-1

EOCs are equipped locations to help you manage response and recovery operations.

jurisdictions around the nation. In these EOCs, government and other community leaders will coordinate all of the functions that have to be performed after terrorist attacks or other disasters. This may include members of the preparedness council and others who have specialized knowledge and skills required in case of an emergency.

Emergency operations centers may include a large office space with tables, phones, computers, white boards, and TV monitors. At times, EOCs may be a designated area adjoined to other rooms (for top officials, media briefings, a break area, rest rooms, etc.). In other cases, it will be quickly set up when an incident occurs. In either case there is no standard layout for emergency operations centers. It could be set up by department, function, or any other organizational arrangement. The important point to remember is that you will need desks for many organizations as well as common office supplies (e.g., pencils, paper, copy and fax machines, computers, etc.). You will also need to develop procedures for activating the EOC. For instance, you will want to determine when you will open the EOC and how you will contact participants to report to it (e.g., a phone call or page).

While temporary EOCs can be established in training rooms, most communities now prefer to build permanent facilities. Designated EOCs have the advantage of being ready at a moment's notice whereas temporary EOCs take time to establish and activate. Controlling access to EOCs and having a back up facility is a good idea. On 9/11, New York City's EOC was disabled and later destroyed due to the terrorist attacks and collapse of the World Trade Center. As a result, the city had to quickly set up a temporary EOC at a pier on the Hudson River. It is also possible that EOCs could be intentionally selected as targets by terrorist organizations in order to add to the chaos and disruption associated with attacks. They should be carefully guarded as a key asset.

SELF-CHECK

1. Local Emergency Planning Committees are a type of a preparedness council. True or False?

2. Ordinances justify the need for community preparedness for terrorism and other types of disasters. True or False?

3. Who in the community is predominantly in charge of disaster mitigation, preparedness, response, and recovery?
   (a) Mayor
   (b) Emergency manager
   (c) City manager
   (d) Preparedness council

4. What is needed to have a well-equipped emergency operations center?

10.3 PLANNING

Emergency Operations Plan (EOP):
A document that describes what may be anticipated in terms of homeland security and emergency management and how to best to react.

One of the central priorities of preparedness is writing an emergency operations plan. An **Emergency Operations Plan (EOP)** is a document that describes what may be anticipated in terms of terrorism and how to best to react. The plan may note what types of terrorist attacks or disasters may occur in a community. It also provides an educated guess on the types of issues that will arise and how they will be met. The EOP outlines who will be in charge of specific post-event functions (outlined in Chapters 11 and 12). For this reason, plans help to foster coordination and speed up response and recovery operations.

Writing an EOP can be a lengthy and technical task. Fortunately, guidance for writing plans can be obtained from homeland security and emergency management personnel in neighboring jurisdictions or from the state. FEMA has also provided details about planning in SLG 101 (see www.fema.gov/pdf/plan/slg101.pdf). This document describes the importance of plans and value to the community. It also discusses the format and content of plans so you will be able to help your community prepare for terrorism and other disasters.

Basic plan:
An overview of the entire emergency operations plan.

Annexes:
A portion of the emergency operations plan that discusses specific hazards or functions that will need to be addressed if an event takes place.

EOPs are divided into three sections. The **basic plan** is an overview of the entire document. It describes the general strategy for dealing with response and recovery operations. The **annexes** discuss specific hazards or functions that will need to be addressed if an event takes place. The basic plan and annexes often contain at least six sections:

- **Authority.** The first section of the plan often mentions the federal, state, and local laws pertaining to homeland security and emergency management. The goals of the document are taken from the Stafford Act, the National Response Plan, state mandates, and local ordinances.

- **Purpose.** This portion of the plan covers the objectives of the plan. It may mention, among other things, the need to protect life, reduce property loss, minimize societal disruption, and promote coordination among participating organizations.

- **Situation and assumptions.** The third part of the plan examines the context of terrorism and other hazards in the community. The potential for attacks and disasters is mentioned along with expected impacts. This portion of the plan is vital for the understanding of what response and recovery functions will have to be performed.

- **Concept of operations.** The fourth component of plans typically identifies, in brief fashion, what organizations are in charge of specific functions. It often notes that departments will respond based on daily activities and areas of expertise.

- **Organization and assignment of responsibilities.** The segment of the plan describes in detail the roles of each responding organization. It is far more explicit than the concept of operations section.

- **Direction and control.** The final section of the plan is concerned with the management of the entire post-event operation. It gives highest attention to top officials in the EOC and their decision making and oversight duties.

Appendices:
Additional information at the end of the emergency operations plan which includes resource and contact lists, maps, standard operating procedures, and checklists.

The third section of plans—the **appendices**—contain additional information to support the plan including resource and contact lists, maps, standard operating procedures, and checklists.

When putting together an EOP, several principles should be kept in mind. First, it is vital that you do not plan alone! Be sure to work with others to develop the plan as it will help you generate a better game plan for anticipated response and recovery operations. Your preparedness council, city manager, and legal offices can help you develop a useful and logical document. Second, your plan should be as comprehensive as possible. It should include all types of events (e.g., terrorism and other disasters) and all actors involved in homeland security and emergency management (e.g., those from the public, private and non-profit sectors). Third, your plan should be reviewed and updated annually. Failing to do so may result in the plan being outdated, incomplete, or obsolete. Fourth, your plan must ensure that the government is, itself, preparing for disaster. Known as continuity of operations plans, these documents specify how to keep the government functioning in time of crisis as well as a line of succession. Finally, you must remember that writing the plan is only one aspect of preparedness. Far too many jurisdictions write a plan and assume they are ready to react in an effective manner. Known as the **paper plan syndrome**, this attitude implies

Paper plan syndrome:
An attitude that assumes that having a plan ensures you are prepared to deal with terrorism and other types of disasters.

FOR EXAMPLE

The Paper Plan Syndrome

Public officials sometimes comment that they are prepared for any terrorist attack because "we have a plan." Writing an emergency operations plan is necessary since it describes what could happen, and how response and recovery functions are to be performed. Planning also helps to clarify roles and therefore increases effectiveness and efficiency of service delivery. While planning is important, it should not be regarded as a panacea. Planning is a process, not a check list that is completed once and never revisited. Concentrating on plans ignores the greatest challenge in emergency management—developing capabilities to enhance your ability to react successfully in a crisis situation. Preparedness cannot be pursued without planning, but writing an emergency operations plan does not ensure you are ready for a terrorist attack. It is imperative that those working in homeland security and emergency management do not fall into the paper plan syndrome.

that having a plan ensures you are prepared (Auf der Heide 1989). Nothing could be further from the truth! Don't be fooled into thinking that your compliance with state and federal planning mandates is sufficient. Dwight D. Eisenhower once stated "in preparing for battle, I have always found that plans are useless. But planning is indispensable!" Planning is vital, but should not overshadow other preparedness activities to build community capacity.

SELF-CHECK

1. Writing an emergency operations plan ensures that a local government is ready for a terrorist attack. True or False?

2. The appendices in an EOP discuss specific hazards or functions that will need to be addressed if an event takes place. True or False?

3. Which of the following is not one of the principles for putting together an EOP?

   (a) The plan should be as comprehensive as possible.
   (b) The plan should be created by one person.
   (c) The plan should be reviewed and updated annually.
   (d) The plan must be considered as only one aspect of preparedness.

4. What are the usual sections contained within the basic plan and annexes of an EOP?

10.4 OTHER MEASURES

Preparedness entails much more than those activities described above (McEntire and Myers 2004). Training, exercises, and community education are vital if a jurisdiction is to be ready to deal with terrorism. Training helps police, fire, and other personnel to respond in a safe and effective manner. Exercises identify weaknesses in the plan and illustrate room for improvement. Community education enlists the support of citizens since response and recovery require a joint effort with the populous.

10.4.1 Training

Training:
Information sharing in classroom or field settings to help familiarize people with protocol.

According to the well-known disaster sociologist, E. L. Quarantelli, training is a vital component of community preparedness (1984, 29). **Training** includes information sharing in classroom or field settings to help familiarize people with protocol. Training helps all of those involved in response and

First responders:
The first official government responders in the field including police, fire fighters, and emergency medical technicians.

recovery to anticipate what could happen and how best to react. It may be focused on **first responders**, such as police, fire fighters, and emergency medical technicians to save lives and better communicate one with another. Training can help the directors of public works and the water department to know their roles when terrorist attacks occur. Mayors and city managers can also be taught how to seek state and federal assistance. Everyone—regardless of position or department—should have some training about terrorism and how to deal with it.

Training courses are provided by FEMA as well as the FBI, the Department of Defense, the Environmental Protection Agency, the Department of Transportation, and other federal agencies. State agencies, including public health, public safety, and emergency management departments, often provide training on a variety of subjects pertaining to terrorism and on a rotating basis. Emergency management associations and regional council of government organizations will also be aware of training opportunities for you and your jurisdiction.

If you are responsible for training, make sure you recognize that it must be continual. New employees will be hired. People will take on new positions in city government. Everyone can forget what they have learned in the past. New policies and procedures will be instituted by federal and state officials. A training program will be incomplete and limited in impact if it is not repeated and updated over time.

10.4.2 Exercises

Exercises:
Drills and mock events that test the knowledge and skills of those in charge of reacting to attacks.

Table top exercises:
Informal discussions about hypothetical scenarios that occur in an office setting.

Functional exercises:
Practice scenarios that explore one or a few of the annexes in the plan.

Full-scale exercises:
Major scenarios that test many functions or the entire response system.

Because disasters and terrorist attacks are infrequent, experience in dealing with them is generally limited. For this reason, homeland security and emergency management officials should develop and participate in exercises. **Exercises** are drills and mock events that test the knowledge and skills of those in charge of reacting to attacks. They are the semi-realistic methods to evaluate and test the validity of the emergency operations plan (Daines 1991). Exercises indicate where planning and training fall short so they can be remedied in the future.

There are three types of exercises. **Table top exercises** are informal discussions about hypothetical scenarios. They occur in an office setting and often involve the key leaders of each department. Table top exercises are useful to help decision makers reflect upon how they would respond should a terrorist attack occur. **Functional exercises** are drills that explore one or a few of the annexes in the plan. Such exercises may include a field component as well as equipment and a mild degree of stress. **Full-scale exercises** are major scenarios that test many functions or the entire response system. They often have an EOC and field component and explore the interaction of the broad array of responding agencies. Full-scale exercises may include realistic props, "moulaged" victims, and most department leaders from the community.

The City of Denton, Texas, has participated in each of these types of exercises. The emergency manager frequently invites his preparedness council to review how they would respond to different scenarios. These table top exercises are a great way to contemplate what you might do in a difficult situation. At other times, the city has tested its ability to decontaminate victims that resulted from a school bus crashing into a tanker truck carrying hazardous materials. Functional exercises can test any operation that might be needed after a terrorist attack. On a final occasion, many city departments responded to a mock bombing at a utility company headquarters. This full scale exercise involved communications, emergency medical care, law enforcement, and the emergency operations center.

In order to develop an exercise program, it is first necessary to identify the potential weaknesses in the plan or emergency management system. Once you have determined what areas need improvement, an exercise scenario can then be developed with the help of an exercise design team (probably the members of your preparedness council). The scenario may include some contextual information about the event as well as specific injects from participants who act out certain roles (e.g., a victim calling 911, a fire fighter in the field, or an emergency manager from a neighboring jurisdiction). As the scenario is being developed, you should also schedule the date and location of the exercise and notify all of the participants. Be sure to assign evaluators to determine the success or shortcomings in responding to the mock event.

IN THE REAL WORLD

TOPOFF Exercises

In order to prepare for anticipated terrorist attacks, the federal government has instituted an exercise program known as TOPOFF. TOPOFF stands for "top officials," and therefore has the purpose of assessing how key government leaders and others respond to fictitious terrorist attacks. The most recent TOPOFF exercise, which took place on October 15–19, 2007, focused on intelligence gathering and analysis, victim decontamination, coordination with the military, and the implementation of large-scale recovery activities. Thousands of federal, state, and local participants played roles in this exercise. The lessons learned from such events are vital in that they can facilitate national preparedness for future terrorist attacks.

During the exercise, a controller will make sure the scenario is unfolding at a logical pace. Those responding to the event will then react according to the plan, their training, and the specific nature of the scenario. While there are many "right" ways to react to terrorist events, it is important that evaluators look for major errors so they can be corrected in the future. Mistakes may include safety violations, failure to communicate and coordinate with others, and general ineffectiveness in dealing with the problems presented to them.

When the exercise is over, evaluators should write up findings so follow up can occur. Many emergency management organizations fail to address weaknesses which can make the exercise a useless waste of time, energy, and tax payer dollars. You will also need to submit paperwork to state and federal officials on exercise findings and your actions to address weaknesses. Failure to do so may result in you losing grants or good standing among your peers.

10.4.3 Community Education

Because the government is not the only one involved in response and recovery activities, it is vital that you educate businesses, churches, volunteer groups, and citizens about terrorism. These non-official partners can be of great assistance to you if you harness their potential and

Figure 10-2

The Red Cross can help you educate your community about terrorist attacks and other disasters.

channel their efforts in constructive ways. Alternatively, if you ignore or neglect these groups and individuals, your response and recovery operations can be more problematic. For instance, they may visit the scene of attacks out of curiosity and put themselves at risk. They may also donate goods and supplies that really are not needed after most terrorist attacks and disasters. Educating others about terrorism, homeland security, and emergency management is a great way to foster compliance and effectiveness.

There are many ways to share information with the public. Community education may include speeches at schools, booths at fairs and other community gatherings, and the distribution of pamphlets and related information about homeland security and emergency management. Developing a useful Web site can also help people acquire information about what they should do to be prepared for the threat of terrorism. For

IN THE REAL WORLD

Citizen Corps

Citizen Corps is a network of a variety of volunteer associations. Its mission is to "harness the power of every individual through education, training, and volunteer service to make communities safer, stronger, and better prepared to respond to the threats of terrorism, crime, public health issues, and disasters of all kinds." Besides CERT, Citizen Corps include Neighborhood Watch, Volunteers in Police Service, Medical Reserve Corps, and the Fire Corps. According to the Citizen Corps Web site (www.citizencorps.gov/councils/), Local Citizen Corps Councils will:

- *promote and strengthen the Citizen Corps programs at the community level, such as Volunteers in Police Service programs, CERT teams, Medical Reserve Corps units, and Neighborhood Watch groups;*
- *provide opportunities for special skills and interests;*
- *develop targeted outreach for the community, including special needs groups;*
- *provide opportunities of training in first aid and emergency preparedness;*
- *organize special projects and community events; encourage cooperation and collaboration among community leaders;*
- *capture smart practices and report accomplishments; and create opportunities for all residents to participate.*

instance, the Department of Homeland Security has a Web site (www. ready.gov) which helps individuals and families develop their own plans, anticipate needed supplies, and become more self-sufficient until further help arrives. Since most people rely on the computer to acquire information today, it is imperative that your Web site be as user friendly as possible.

Community Emergency Response Team (CERT):
A group of citizens who receive basic training response operations.

Another excellent way to educate your citizens is to develop a **Community Emergency Response Team (CERT)**. A Community Emergency Response Team is a group of citizens who receive basic training response operations. They are taught general information about terrorism and disasters and learn how to perform small scale fire fighting, search and rescue, and medical functions. CERT members also gain knowledge about shutting off gas valves and helping victims with emotional distress. Having multiple CERTs in your jurisdiction will augment preparedness beyond normal levels. Establishing CERTs is one of many important ways to promote preparedness in your community.

While there is no single or correct way to educate your community, there are probably some mistakes to avert. For instance, assuming some one else will share vital information about terrorism with the public is incorrect and problematic. Also, failing to coordinate your public education campaign with others will result in conflicting and contradictory information. Finally, educating the public on a one time basis will ensure that citizens forget what is relayed, which will halt preparedness activity. Avoiding these mistakes will go a long way to ensure your community is ready to deal with terrorist attacks.

IN THE REAL WORLD

KnoWhat2Do

In 2007, the North Central Texas Council of Governments produced a public education campaign to reach out to millions of people in the 16-county region surrounding the Dallas-Fort Worth metropolitan area. Funded by a grant from the Department of Homeland Security, the KnoWhat2Do initiative included the distribution of calendars, playing cards, DVDs, and brochures to help citizens understand what to do in case of a terrorist attack or other type of disaster. A Web site, accessed at www.KnoWhat2Do.com, has also been created to help people anticipate possible hazards/threats and take measures to protect themselves from harm. KnoWhat2Do is a creative example of reaching out to the community for the purpose of preparedness.

SELF-CHECK

1. A training program does not need to be repeated in order to be complete. True or False?
2. The first step in developing an exercise program is to identify weaknesses in the plan or emergency management system. True or False?
3. Which of the following is the best example of a first responder?
    (a) Mayor
    (b) City manager
    (c) Police officer
    (d) Governor
4. How do Community Emergency Response Teams help increase preparedness beyond normal levels?

SUMMARY

Preparing for terrorism is one of your central responsibilities in homeland security. In order to help your community become ready for possible terrorist attacks, you will need to comprehend the executive orders and legislation issued by the president and congress. You should also set the foundation for preparedness by creating an advisory council, passing ordinances, acquiring monetary resources, and establishing an EOC. Writing plans and promoting training, exercises and education are other ways to improve the degree of preparedness in your jurisdiction. Preparedness is vital if you are to effectively respond to and recover from the effects of terrorism.

ASSESS YOUR UNDERSTANDING

UNDERSTAND: WHAT HAVE YOU LEARNED?

 Go to **www.wiley.com/college/mcentire** to assess your knowledge of preparedness.

SUMMARY QUESTIONS

1. As an emergency manager, it is important that you organize a preparedness council. Who could you get to participate on the council?

2. As an emergency manager, you need to submit a proposed budget to the mayor and city council. What can you do to get as much money as possible for your preparedness program and, over time, increase your budget?

3. As a homeland security expert, you have been asked to talk with local governments about the importance of community education. What reasons would you give in support of a strong community education program?

4. As an emergency manager, you have just completed a full-scale exercise. What steps could you take to properly follow up on the exercise?

5. National preparedness is particularly the responsibility of the Department of Homeland Security and the Federal Emergency Management Agency. True or False?

6. The National Emergency Management Association is mainly composed of emergency management offices from city governments. True or False?

7. Grants always cover the full financial need of a proposed program. True of False?

8. An important justification for preparedness councils is the interdisciplinary nature of homeland security. True or False?

9. Assistance with writing an emergency operation plan can be sought from homeland security and emergency management personnel in neighboring jurisdictions or from the state. True or False?

10. A paper plan syndrome occurs when a plan provides a false assurance of effective preparation. True or False?

11. Training is meant only for first responders. True or False?

12. It is important to educate the public only once to ensure adequate preparation. True or False?

13. The process by which government functions are maintained after terrorism is best known as:

(a) preparedness.

(b) continuity of operation.

(c) prevention.

(d) mitigation.

14. Which law serves as the cornerstone of emergency management in the United States?

(a) The Robert T. Stafford Disaster Relief and Emergency Assistance Act

(b) The National Defense Authorization Law

(c) The Comprehensive Homeland Security Act of 2003

(d) The Anti-terrorism and Effective Death Penalty Act of 1996

15. A collaborative agreement between jurisdictions when external help is warranted is best known as:

(a) an ordinance.

(b) mutual aid.

(c) annexes.

(d) an emergency operations plan.

16. Which of the following is not one of the three sections of an emergency operations plan?

(a) Annexes

(b) Basic plan

(c) Appendices

(d) NFPA 1600

17. Training about terrorism and how to deal with it should be provided for:

(a) city managers and mayors.

(b) emergency managers.

(c) first responders.

(d) everyone.

18. Functional exercises are best described as:

(a) major scenarios that test the entire response system.

(b) informal discussions about hypothetical situations.

(c) practice scenarios that explore one or a few annexes in a plan.

(d) scenarios that are studied in an office setting.

BE A HOMELAND SECURITY PROFESSIONAL

Presentation to the City Council

You are the emergency manager for a local community that is not well prepared for a terrorist attack. In order to accomplish your office's mission of increasing the city's level of preparedness, you need more people and monetary support. The city council is considering an increase in your budget, but first you must persuade them that such a step is an important and effective use of the taxpayers' money. When you are asked by the council about why preparedness is important, how could you respond?

Assignment: Federal and State Governments

Write a one-page paper comparing and contrasting the roles of federal and state governments in preparedness. Be as thorough as possible.

Creating Ordinances

You are the emergency manager for a local government. Ordinances are a necessary component in justifying and executing measures aimed at increasing preparedness. Such regulations indicate what should and should not be done in preparing for terrorism. As an emergency manager, you have an important role in the creation of ordinances. What methods could you utilize to facilitate the development of ordinances?

KEY TERMS

Annexes	A portion of the emergency operations plan that discusses specific hazards or functions that will need to be addressed if an event takes place.
Appendices	Additional information at the end of the emergency operations plan which includes resource and contact lists, maps, standard operating procedures, and checklists.
Basic plan	An overview of the entire emergency operations plan.
Community Emergency Response Team (CERT)	A group of citizens who receive basic training response operations.
Continuity of operation	The maintenance of government functions after terrorist attacks through the identification of leader succession, alternate work sites, and resumption of operational practices.
Emergency Management Accreditation Program	A standard-based assessment and certification initiative for local and state emergency management agencies.
Emergency Management Assistance Compact (EMAC)	An agreement among states to render assistance to one another in time of need.
Emergency manager	A local government official in charge of disaster mitigation, preparedness, response, and recovery.
Emergency Operations Center (EOC)	A location from which disaster response and recovery activities can be overseen and managed.
Emergency Operations Plan (EOP)	A document that describes what may be anticipated in terms of homeland security and emergency management and how to best to react.
Exercises	Drills and mock events that test the knowledge and skills of those in charge of reacting to attacks.
First responders	The first official government responders in the field including police, fire fighters, and emergency medical technicians.
Full-scale exercises	Major scenarios that test many functions or the entire response system.
Functional exercises	Practice scenarios that explore one or a few of the annexes in the plan.
Grants	Funds given to local governments to support or enhance homeland security and emergency management programs.

Local Emergency Planning Committees (LEPCs)	Preparedness councils promoted in the 1980s to help communities prepare for hazardous materials releases.
Mutual aid	A collaborative agreement between jurisdictions when external help is warranted.
National Emergency Management Association	A professional association of state emergency management agencies.
National Incident Management System (NIMS)	A comprehensive national approach for incident management in the United States.
National Response Framework (NRF)	The successor to the National Response Plan; a document that describes the principles, roles and structures of response and recovery operations.
National Response Plan (NRP)	A document that describes the procedures for responding to all-types of hazards with a multi-disciplinary perspective.
Ordinance	An authoritative order or law issued by a government.
Paper plan syndrome	An attitude that assumes that having a plan ensures you are prepared to deal with terrorism and other types of disasters.
Post-Katrina Emergency Management Reform Act	A law which specifies ways to avert the slow and disjointed federal response to the catastrophe in New Orleans, Louisiana.
Preparedness	Concerted efforts to improve response and recovery capabilities.
Preparedness council	A group of individuals who provide recommendations for policy and assist with program administration.
Table top exercises	Informal discussions about hypothetical scenarios that occur in an office setting.
Training	Information sharing in classroom or field settings to help familiarize people with protocol.

REFERENCES

Auf der Heide, Erik. (1989). *Disaster Response: Principles for Preparation and Coordination.* C.V. Mosby: St. Louis, MO.

Buck, Dick A., Joseph E. Trainor and Benigno E. Aguirre. (2006). "A Critical Evaluation of the Incident Command System and NIMS." *Journal of Homeland Security and Emergency Management* 3 (1): 1–27.

Daines, Guy E. (1991). "Planning, Training, and Exercising." Pp. 161–200 in Drabek, Thomas E. and Gerard G. Hoetmer (Eds.) *Emergency Management: Principles and Practices for Local Government.* International City/County Management Association: Washington, D.C

Department of Homeland Security. (2004). National Incident Management System. www.dhs.gov (last accessed 12/17/07).

Gillsepie, David F. and Calvin L. Streeter. (1987). "Conceptualizing and Measuring Disaster Preparedness." *International Journal of Mass Emergencies and Disasters* 5 (2): 155–176.

Godschalk, David R. (1991). "Disaster Mitigation and Hazard Management." Pp. 131–160 in Drabek, Thomas E. and Gerard G. Hoetmer (Eds.) *Emergency Management: Principles and Practices for Local Government.* International City/County Management Association: Washington, D.C.

Kirschenbaum, Alan. (2002). "Disaster Preparedness: A Conceptual and Empirical Reevaluation." *International Journal of Mass Emergencies and Disasters* 20 (1): 5–28.

Lindell, Michael K. (1994). "Are Local Emergency Planning Committees Effective in Developing Community Disaster Preparedness?" *International Journal of Mass Emergencies and Disasters* 5 (2): 137–153.

McEntire, David A. and Amy Myers. (2004). "Preparing Communities for Disasters: Issues and Processes for Government Readiness." *Disaster Prevention and Management* 13 (2): 140–152.

Tierney, Kathleen J. (2006). "Recent Developments in U.S. Homeland Security Policies and Their Implications for the Management of Extreme Events." PP. 405–412 in Rodrigues, Havidan, Enrico L. Quarantelli, and Russell R. Dynes (Eds.) *Handbook of Disaster Research.* Springer: New York.

Quarantelli, E. L. (1984). *Organizational Behavior in Disasters and Implications for Disaster Planning.* Federal Emergency Management Agency: Washington, D.C.

RESPONDING TO ATTACKS
Important Functions and Coordination Mechanisms

Do You Already Know?

- The concepts of convergence and emergence
- How to perform warning and evacuation functions
- How to coordinate responses to terrorist attacks

 For additional questions to assess your current knowledge of response operations, go to **www.wiley.com/college/mcentire**

What You Will Find Out	What You Will Be Able To Do
11.1 How the concepts of convergence and emergence relate to safety, search and rescue, emergency medical care, decontamination, and investigation	• Predict what types of activities will take place after terrorist attacks and evaluate the effectiveness of investigative practices
11.2 The importance of warnings, evacuations, and sheltering	• Perform warning and evacuation functions
11.3 How to coordinate responses to terrorist attacks	• Set up incident command and EOC coordination mechanisms

INTRODUCTION

When terrorist attacks occur, it is vital that you know how to respond successfully. This entails understanding that resources will arrive on the scene of an attack along with the behavior of altruistic citizens. You will also need to fulfill many priorities including site security, search and rescue, emergency medical care, decontamination, and investigation. Where possible or when required, you may also need to warn citizens of impending attacks or evacuate them away from harm. Because so many organizations are involved in these functions, you may need to rely on various coordination mechanisms. The incident command system and emergency operations centers are two tools that can help deal with negative terrorism effects in an effective manner.

11.1 MAJOR PRIORITIES

When a terrorist attack occurs, both first responders and citizens will assist with post-incident operations. In the vast majority of cases, official governmental first responders will arrive after they are notified by citizens who call emergency numbers (e.g., 911). In this sense, the title of first responder is somewhat of a misnomer. It is ordinary people who will typically be present on the scene before police, fire, and emergency medical personnel. Citizens are almost always first to arrive because they are located everywhere—at home, in their cars, at work, in the shopping mall, at the movie theater, in the sports stadium, running errands in government offices, etc. They will generally see or hear of the event, and then do what they can to help victims. Their behavior has been described by sociologists as "convergence" and "emergence."

Convergence:
The flow of people and resources to the scene of an emergency or disaster.

Convergence is the flow of people and resources to the scene of an emergency or disaster (Kendra and Wachtendorf 2003). When others have been impacted by a major incident, bystanders will stop what they are doing and go to the location of the attack. In some cases, they will bring needed supplies with them (e.g., a fire extinguisher, a first aid kit, or any other resource that might be useful). Their goal is to come to the focal point of the incident to provide assistance to those in need. This brings up another important concept: emergence. **Emergence** is the appearance of altruistic behavior that is unfamiliar to the participants (Drabek and McEntire 2002). In emergency or disaster situations, people will take on new roles and interact cooperatively with strangers. They will also develop new relationships that often end when emergency needs have been addressed.

Emergence:
The appearance of altruistic behavior that is unfamiliar to the participants.

The terrorist attacks on 9/11 provide vivid examples of convergence and emergence. For instance, people from around the nation and world sent supplies for first responders and monetary support for the victims' families. Also, occupants from different floors in the World Trade Center worked together to evacuate the disabled or injured. Carrying someone down stairs is something people don't normally do, but in a disaster citizens will take on new responsibilities.

To be sure, the activities of every day citizens and official responders will vary significantly, depending on the type of attack that occurs. For instance, an arson event may require fire fighters from multiple stations. A biological attack will necessitate the involvement of public health officials. A mass shooting will necessitate heavy police involvement and tactical EMS. **Tactical emergency medical services** is the name given to a team of paramedics that are armed and trained in weapons use. Tactical emergency services teams have been given greater attention since the mass shootings at Columbine High School and Virginia Tech. Since the vast majority of attacks in the United States and around the world involve explosives, it is also imperative that you understand how to respond to them effectively.

11.1.1 Safety and Security

Bombings will produce property destruction, injury, and death. For these reasons, there will be a strong inclination for people to rush into the area to help victims. It is important, however, that everyone resist this temptation— at least initially. The first priority is to assess the situation to determine what has occurred and how to respond safely. The process of evaluating the nature of the attack site is known as a **size up**. This quick assessment is imperative because the location of terrorist attacks is inherently dangerous. Citizens and first responders can be injured by glass, twisted metal, falling debris, unstable buildings, broken gas lines that result in fire, and many other hazards. Knowing what type of conditions you will be dealing with is central to your safety and that of others.

There are other potential dangers that you must be concerned about as well. It is possible that terrorists may detonate other bombs **(secondary devices)** to add to the disruption and fear. By setting off additional explosions, terrorists attempt to kill those who are trying to aid initial victims. This only adds to the casualty count and creates compounded problems for those trying to react to the mayhem. Eric Rudolph, a terrorist who opposed abortion, used secondary devices when he attacked an abortion clinic in 1998. **Dirty bombs**, or explosives combined with hazardous materials (e. g., chlorine or nuclear material), have been used in Iraq and could be utilized in the United States in the future. While the blast area is generally limited to a certain geographic area, chemical fumes can be transported by wind far from the scene of an attack. Someone should therefore be given the task of monitoring safety concerns and air quality. Known as **situational awareness**, this is vital under dangerous working conditions. You should expect that terrorists will do all they can to hinder response operations.

There are at least three principles to remember to keep first responders out of harms way at the scene of a terrorist attack (FEMA 1999). First, those responding to a terrorist event should not stay at the location for any extended length of time. There may be hazardous agents that can do physical harm to people. Besides dangerous materials, fatigue resulting from extensive work

Tactical emergency medical services:
The name given to a team of paramedics that are armed and trained in weapons use.

Size up:
The process of evaluating the nature of the attack site.

Secondary devices:
The detonation of other bombs to add to the disruption and fear of the initial attack.

Dirty bombs:
Explosive devices laden with dangerous chemicals or radioactive material.

Situational awareness:
Continual monitoring of safety concerns at the scene of a terrorist attack.

Figure 11-1

The scene of a terrorist attack can be extremely dangerous.

periods at the location can lead to many accidents and injuries. Second, keeping a distance between you and the site of the attack or harmful chemicals will enhance your safety. While this is not always feasible for those involved in response operations, the goal should be promoted where possible. Finally, if you must enter a dangerous area, be sure you have the proper personal protective equipment. Fire gear and hazardous materials suits may be needed to ensure your survivability in hostile conditions. Time, distance, and shielding are central ways to keep you safe when responding to terrorist attacks.

In addition to these recommendations, there is also the need for site security. As soon as is feasible, first responders should gain control over the scene. This may include the use of squad cars to block off roads as well as barricades, fences, and police or National Guard units on foot patrol. The main priority is to prevent further attacks so that additional lives can be spared and response can take place without further constraints. While site security is essential, the scene must not be impermeable. Other responders, public works employees, and contractors may need to enter the area to accomplish vital post-disaster missions. For this reason, a check-in system can be established by locating tables, chairs, and personnel at the site entrance. The intentions, legitimacy, and qualifications of those wishing to enter the scene can then be determined by checking ID cards, reviewing licenses, or making phone calls. Any donations coming into the area should also be carefully checked to ensure they do not include bombs or WMD. This can limit the probability of secondary attacks and protect your safety.

11.1.2 Search and Rescue

Search and Rescue (SAR):
Response activities undertaken to find disaster victims and remove them from danger or confinement.

While safety and site security issues are major priorities, they are means to an end. Safety and security will enhance your ability to care for the victims, which is your ultimate goal after a terrorist attack. One of the first steps you will need to take is to participate in search and rescue operations. **Search and Rescue (SAR)** is defined as "response activities undertaken to find disaster victims and remove them from danger or confinement" (McEntire 2007, 142). There are many different types of search and rescue ranging from swift water to wildland contexts. In relation to terrorism, search and rescue includes finding the victims under rubble and extracting them to a safe location.

Search and rescue will be undertaken initially by emergent groups. Later on, fire fighters, who have specialized knowledge for this important function, will take over. Fire fighters have personal protective equipment and tools such as helmets, goggles, dust masks, and other gear (e.g., saws and jacks) to reach and retrieve victims. Local fire departments may be insufficient however. In major events, national Urban Search and Rescue (USAR) teams may be required. FEMA has nearly 30 such teams made up of fire fighters, engineers, doctors, and paramedics. They can be activated within hours and transported by C-130 aircraft or bus to the scene of an attack. USAR teams are especially valuable when destroyed areas are extensive or when search and rescue operations will last long periods. Such teams can be rotated periodically to keep them fresh, alert, and productive. USAR teams were used extensively after the Oklahoma City Bombing and after the 9/11 attacks on the World Trade Center.

11.1.3 Medical Care and Triage

As victims are extracted from or around damaged buildings, it will be necessary to provide them medical care. Much of the medical attention will be provided by citizens (similar to those engaged in search and rescue operations). When fire fighters and paramedics arrive, they will take over. They have expertise and supplies that citizens will not possess. Treatment will vary depending on the nature and extent of injuries.

Some individuals may suffer from minor cuts and bruises to smoke inhalation. Others will have broken bones or life threatening injuries (e.g., damaged internal organs). If the number of injuries is limited, first responders will be able to handle the load easily. They will stop bleeding, provide oxygen, or immobilize fractures. If there are many or serious casualties, the emergency medical system can be severely taxed. In this case, triage may need to be implemented.

Triage:
The assessment, sorting, and treatment of the injured in such a way as to maximize limited resources.

Triage is the assessment, sorting, treatment, and transportation of the injured in such a way as to maximize limited medical resources (Mayer 1997). Because there may be a large number of victims in comparison to

Figure 11-2

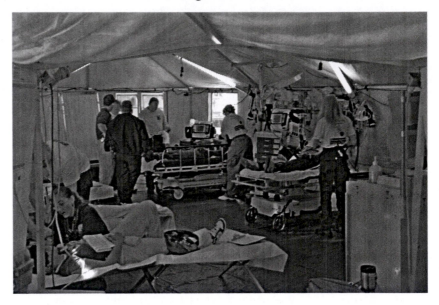

An important priority after a terrorist attack is emergency medical care. Here, New Orleans Disaster Media Assistance Team (DMAT) members tend to patients in an acute care tent.

paramedics, choices will have be made about who will receive care. For instance, those with minor injuries and those with fatal injuries will be treated last or not at all. Attention will be given to those who require immediate help and have a strong chance of survival. The practice of triage sounds cruel or inhumane, but the reality of terrorist attacks often dictates the extent to which medical personnel can assist everyone. Difficult choices have to be made to do the most good for the most number of people.

Another major advantage of triage is that it limits the number of people who go to the hospital for further treatment. In most disasters (terrorist attacks included) people will be taken to the hospital by friends, co-workers, and neighbors. That is to say, they are **self-referred**, walking wounded, or ambulatory, meaning they arrive at the hospital whether they require immediate care or not. This often clogs the hospital with patients who may not always have critical injuries. Triage ensures that only those who need further treatment are sent to hospitals, thereby limiting the chance that nurses and doctors will be overwhelmed with patients.

Self-referred:
Patients who arrive at the hospital whether they require immediate care or not.

11.1.4 Decontamination

Regardless of how patients arrive at the hospital, it may be necessary to clean them before they receive additional treatment. Patients may be covered in hazardous materials that could result in harming themselves, fire fighters, paramedics, and medical staff in hospitals. If a hospital receives contaminated patients or even contaminated gurneys, its operations could be jeopardized. **Decontamination**, or the removal of hazardous materials from victims through clothing removal and the washing of bodies, must be performed at the scene, at a field hospital, or before entering a permanent medical facility. If victims are not decontaminated, the chemicals on them may adversely impact physicians and nurses as was the case after the Tokyo sarin gas attacks in 1995.

Decontamination:
The removal of hazardous materials from victims through clothing removal and the washing of bodies.

The process of decontamination is technical and must be followed meticulously. When responding to a terrorist incident involving hazardous materials, three zones should be identified near the attack site. A **hot zone** is the area which has been contaminated by the terrorist attack. A **warm zone** is the location where victims are washed. A **cold zone** is the uncontaminated area. It is where responders and victims may enter and leave the area. When setting up and cordoning off these zones, it is important that wind direction be taken into consideration. The zones should be set up in such a way that wind blows toward the hot zone. This will ensure that hazardous materials are not sent in the direction of responders and decontaminated individuals.

Hot zone:
The area contaminated by the terrorist attack.

Warm zone:
The location where victims are washed. It is located between the hot and cold zones.

Cold zone:
The uncontaminated area where responders and victims may enter and leave.

Decontamination in the warm zone must take into account several important factors. Those involved in decontamination must have the proper protective gear and training. Inadequate hazardous materials suits, incorrect breathing apparatus, and mistakes in operations can lead to the loss of further lives. Another important priority is to protect the privacy of those being decontaminated. Decontamination tents or colored plastic sheeting can be hung to shield undressing, washing, and dressing areas. In order to properly clean victims, water, a mild soap, and brushes can be used. Contaminated run off can be captured in children's plastic swim pools or other devices made especially for this purpose. Affected clothing or gurneys with hazardous residues should also be properly disposed. Dirty liquids can then be treated in an environmentally sensitive way. When finished with the decontamination process, new clothing or medical gowns can be given to victims. At this point, victims can be transported, receive further medical treatment, or admitted into hospitals. Responders should also be decontaminated in the same manner before they leave the scene. This will ensure their safety as well. Remediation teams and the Environmental Protection Agency may need to be involved after attacks to determine the impact on the environment and what can be done to clean up hazardous chemicals.

11.1.5 Investigation

Another major priority after a terrorist attack is to begin the process of investigation (McEntire, Robinson and Weber 2001). As life safety issues are being addressed, attention can also be shifted toward law enforcement activities (i.e., investigation). In order to apprehend or prosecute terrorists, evidence must be collected. It is necessary that you remember that anything at the scene of a terrorist attack—debris, a body, or anything else—may provide evidence. For this reason, responders should be aware that the scene of an attack should be protected to the fullest extent possible. Unauthorized people should not be allowed to enter the area, or they should operate with minimal disruption in mind. Evidence should be meticulously recorded and stored for future court proceedings. Photos can also be taken of the scene and maps can be drawn to assist with the investigation. Other measures, including information gathering from witnesses, can help you piece together critical facts and data.

All of these measures could help you identify who committed the attacks, prevent further terrorist acts, and facilitate successful prosecution. Cases have been solved because of seemingly insignificant clues. For instance, the serial numbers of blown up vehicles have helped law enforcement officials track down the terrorists who rented or owned them. A 2007 terrorist plot in London was thwarted when a terrorist parked a car illegally. When police went to move the vehicle they detected explosives and were able to track down the people involved in the diabolical plan. Alternatively, cases may be lost on a technicality because evidence has not been carefully collected and recorded with a clear chain of custody. An investigation is one of the things that separate terrorism from other types of disaster operations.

IN THE REAL WORLD

9/11

The attacks on the World Trade Center in New York illustrate the variety of functions that have to be performed when terrorism occurs. Ground Zero and the area surrounding it was a dangerous area due to fires, unstable debris piles, broken glass, and twisted metal. This situation required additional equipment and instructions be given to first responders. Because a secondary attack by terrorists could not be ruled out, anyone wishing to enter the area had to be carefully screened. Only those with legitimate reasons for entering Ground Zero were permitted to do so once they were approved and given proper identification documents. Urban Search and Rescue teams arrived from around the nation to find the injured and deceased. September 11 also produced the largest crime scene in America. Evidence from more than a 16 block area had to be collected by numerous agencies. One of the major concerns was the presence of hazardous materials (e.g., dust, soot, dangerous chemicals). First responders were adversely affected by breathing the contaminated air around Ground Zero. Many required long-term medical care to treat their symptoms. The major lesson from 9/11 is that those working in homeland security and emergency management will be preoccupied with many responsibilities after terrorist attacks occur.

SELF-CHECK

1. Usually, the very first people to help out with a post-disaster operation are not first responders, but rather ordinary citizens. True or False?

2. Emergence is the flow of people and resources to the scene of an emergency or disaster. True or False?

3. The process of assessing and evaluating the initial situation at an attack site is best known as:

   (a) triage.
   (b) search and rescue.
   (c) situational awareness.
   (d) a size up.

4. Why should responders be aware that the attack scene should be protected to the fullest extent possible?

11.2 OTHER CRUCIAL FUNCTIONS

There are many other important functions that will need to be addressed when terrorist attacks occur. If possible, warnings should be issued and information must be shared with the public. People must be evacuated out of dangerous areas and sheltered if required. These measures can keep citizens safe and minimize the impact of terrorism.

11.2.1 Warning, Intelligence, and Public Information

Warnings:
Notifications sent out to the public so they can take protective measures.

Warnings are notifications sent out to the public so they can take protective measures. Warnings have been issued several times since 9/11. Warnings were given due to possible attacks against the financial district in New York as well as when terrorists attempted to smuggle explosives on airliners crossing the Atlantic Ocean from England to the United States. Unfortunately, most terrorist attacks will not allow advanced warning. Terrorists often make threats against their enemies but they rarely explain exact details about what they intend to do. The element of surprise is one of their greatest strengths. It is true that intelligence officers may at times intercept communications and obtain terrorist plans. However, this information may be sketchy, incomplete and require corroboration. In addition, there is always the difficulty of knowing what and how much to share with the public.

On the one hand, the intelligence community may wish to avoid sharing sensitive information in a warning because it may compromise the safety of their agents or make terrorists aware of their tracking methods. This, in turn, will harm future intelligence efforts. On the other hand, sharing information with the public could help avert attacks or capture terrorists. For instance, if terrorists threaten to attack airports, relaying this information to the public could help them be more aware of the activities taking place around them. While this dilemma may never be completely resolved, authorities should use their best judgment about what to do. The particulars of the situation will probably dictate which course of action to follow.

Regardless of whether or not a warning is possible or desirable, it is imperative that officials in emergency management and homeland security communicate often to the public after a terrorist attack. Citizens will want to know:

- What happened?
- Who was responsible for the attack?
- What are the impacts?
- Are they in danger?
- What steps should they take to protect themselves?
- What is the government doing?
- What should they do if they need assistance?

Weather radios:
Electronic devices that receive information from the National Weather Service to warn people of approaching severe weather.

Emergency alert system:
An announcement that interrupts TV and radio programs and relays information about what is taking place and what people should do for protection.

Reverse 911 systems:
Computerized messages sent over phone lines rapidly to anyone in a designated area.

To notify people of impending attacks or to answer their questions, emergency management and homeland security officials should rely heavily on existing warning systems (McEntire 2007). **Weather radios** are electronic devices that receive information from the National Weather Service to warn people of approaching severe weather. If needed, they could be used to relay information about terrorist attacks. Alternatively, the **emergency alert system** can be activated. It interrupts TV and radio programs, and provides an announcement about what is taking place and what people should do for protection. The drawback of these systems is that not everyone has a weather radio, is watching TV, or listening to the radio.

Some cities have **reverse 911 systems**, which are essentially computerized phone messages sent rapidly to people in a designated area. Reverse 911 is useful because it can relay detailed information to thousands of citizens and businesses within a specific area code or zip code. It allows you to target a specific group of people with a detailed message. The drawback of reverse 911 systems is that they are expensive, require constant updating and data entry, and are not always applicable to cell phones.

The most common method of communicating with the public is through the media. Before and after terrorist attacks, emergency management and homeland security officials should interact frequently with reporters representing the television, radio, Internet, and print media. Press conferences can be held periodically to make sure information is getting to the public. Because the media wants lots of information, it is vital that you meet their requests. Failing to do so will likely result in them seeking

Figure 11-3

The media can share vital information to help your community respond successfully to a terrorist attack.

knowledge elsewhere or reporting inaccurate information. Anytime you hear anything that is incorrect, it should be brought to the attention of reporters and clarified. The rule is to provide clear, consistent, and repeated information by a credible authority (Quarantelli 1990). Anytime this rule is not followed, public information will be ineffective and even counterproductive. A **public information officer**, a city employee who specializes in working with the media, can help you share information successfully to the media and the citizens you are trying to inform.

Public information officer: The person who gathers information for the incident commander(s) and shares information with the media, or a city employee who specializes in working with the media.

11.2.2 Evacuation and Sheltering

Depending on the consequences of the attack, you may need to evacuate your citizens and shelter them in safe locations. Terrorist attacks will result in burnt down buildings or unstable structures. A bomb may release toxic chemicals into the atmosphere. A dirty bomb, an explosive device laden with radiation, could contaminate the environment for an extended period of time. The detonation of a nuclear device would level a large city and leave it inhabitable for decades. Those victims that survive would need to leave or risk radiation contamination. For these reasons, you may need to evacuate the citizens in your community.

Evacuation:
The movement of people away from hazardous areas or situations.

Evacuation is the movement of people away from hazardous areas or situations. When attacks threaten the lives or well-being of individuals, an evacuation request should be made. This decision should not be taken lightly since "unnecessary evacuations are expensive, disruptive, and unpopular" (Baker 1990, 3). However, evacuation for short or long-periods may be required before or after terrorist attacks. It is therefore important that you notify people of the need to evacuate, and provide clear instructions about when and how they should leave. In addition, after a major attack you may need to make transportation arrangements for those without vehicles. Buses, trains, and planes can help you evacuate large numbers of people. As neighborhoods or communities are evacuated, you will want to have sufficient law enforcement personnel to help monitor and direct traffic. Contraflow plans—reversing the flow of transportation arteries as is done before hurricane landfall—can help to speed up the evacuation process. This will enable a quicker and safer exit from the location of the terrorist attack.

If people are leaving their homes and neighborhoods, they will logically require a place to go. Some individuals and families will stay in hotels while others will locate with friends and families in other areas. Some people will not have financial resources or supportive networks. In other cases, the number of evacuees is so large that this puts an extreme burden on receiving communities. In these cases, sheltering elsewhere will be required.

Sheltering:
The location of individuals in places of safety and refuge.

Sheltering is the location of individuals in places of safety and refuge (Mileti, Sorensen and O'Brien 1992). It includes not only a roof overhead but other life sustaining activities. There are a number of factors that need to be considered when opening shelters:

- The number of evacuees versus the number of shelters needed to house them
- Occupancy rates in relation to the size of the buildings or rooms
- Electrical supply
- Sleeping arrangements (e.g., beds, cots, sleeping bags, pillows, blankets)
- Food and water (i.e., mass care arrangements)
- Bathroom and shower facilities
- Medical care
- Law enforcement presence
- Records of who was staying in the shelter

Churches and organizations like the American Red Cross and Salvation Army are frequently involved in sheltering operations. Faith based agencies and volunteer groups can help you understand what else needs to be taken into account when establishing and running shelters.

When possible, you will want to encourage those in the shelter to find temporary or permanent housing (e.g., apartments or homes). The time frame of this may depend largely on whether or not evacuees can return home or start a new life elsewhere. Because some individuals and families will lack resources, the transition from an evacuee status to a returned or permanent resident can be long and challenging. You may need to provide government assistance or financial support from non-profit organizations.

IN THE REAL WORLD

Sheltering First Responders

When sheltering is discussed by the public, the impression is given that it is directed toward the victims of terrorist attacks and disasters. While this is undoubtedly true, it ignores the fact that those responding to the event may also need a place to stay. After the terrorist attacks on 9/11, hundreds of emergency workers had to be sheltered in the Jacob Javits Convention Center in New York City. Cots and bedding had to be acquired for this purpose. Shower facilities and food were also required to care for those responding to the terrorist attack. The sheltering operations at the Javits Center went on for an extended period of time, and were vital to the success of the recovery activities at Ground Zero.

SELF-CHECK

1. Most terrorist attacks will not allow advanced warning. True or False?

2. The most common method of communicating with the public is the emergency alert system. True or False?

3. The movement of people away from hazardous areas or situations is best known as:
   (a) a warning.
   (b) sheltering.
   (c) an evacuation.
   (d) the emergency alert system.

4. Why is there a dilemma in the intelligence community about whether or not to share sensitive information?

11.3 COORDINATION MECHANISMS

As can be seen, there are numerous activities that have to be performed after terrorist attacks. They range from site security and medical care to search and rescue and sheltering. Because of this wide array of responsibilities, there are countless organizations involved in response operations. Besides first responders, public works will be involved in damage assessment and debris removal. Public information officers will work closely with the media to provide information to citizens. Public health may assist with medical needs along with hospitals. State and federal government officials will arrive to provide security and investigate. Businesses can provide resources and nonprofit organizations will assist with sheltering. There are countless people involved after terrorist attacks.

Coordination:
Cooperative efforts to pursue common goals in the wake of terrorist attacks.

Due to this disparate set of activities and actors, coordination becomes imperative. **Coordination** is defined as cooperative efforts to pursue common goals in the wake of terrorist attacks. Such goals may include protecting life, assisting victims, investigating leads, and minimizing social disruption. Coordination helps to identify who will be in charge of vital functions, what collective problems exist, and how they will be overcome. These joint endeavors help to limit gaps in service, and promote efficiency and effectiveness in response operations. Conversely, the lack of coordination may result in "an inability to determine priorities, misunderstanding among organizations, failure to fully utilize equipment and personnel, overly-taxed organizations, delays in service, omission of essential tasks, duplication of effort, safety problems, and counterproductive activity among other things" (McEntire 2007, 293).

IN THE REAL WORLD

Jack Bauer to the Rescue

Many people are familiar with the popular television show *24*. This TV series on Fox depicts the heroic activities of Jack Bauer. Jack (portrayed by Kiefer Sutherland) is a character affiliated with a fictitious government agency—the Los Angeles Counter Terrorist Unit. While the show is correct to note that government officials are involved in counter- and anti-terrorism efforts, the series is misleading in some ways. Jack Bauer always seems to save the day! Reality is very different. One person cannot successfully deal with the threat of terrorism. Instead, there are numerous participants involved in homeland security and each of them plays important roles in dealing with terrorism. While Jack Bauer is fun to watch on *24*, no individual is able to prevent or respond to terrorism without the help of others.

11.3.1 The Incident Command System

Incident Command System (ICS):
A set of personnel and procedures which helps facilitate coordination among first responders.

One of the best ways to promote coordination among field level personnel is to employ the **Incident Command System (ICS)**. The Incident Command System is "a set of personnel, policies, [and] procedures . . . integrated into a common organizational structure designed to improve emergency response operations of all types and complexities" (Irwin 1989, 134). It was developed in California after responses to forest fires witnessed several problems including poor communications, lack of joint planning, and inadequate resource management. ICS helps to overcome these challenges and manage organizations involved in response operations.

The ICS is based on an incident commander and various supporting officers. It also includes four organizational sections and a number of widely accepted principles. While ICS can help promote coordination, first responders must be aware of its potential weaknesses if response operations are to be successful.

Incident command:
The on-scene leader or leaders in the incident command post.

Under the strategy of ICS, the position of incident command will be established. **Incident command** is the on-scene leader or leaders for field operations. When a terrorist attack occurs, incident command will be established by the first person on the scene and later taken over by those with more expertise or higher authority. Incident command may also include

Figure 11-4

If approached correctly, incident command can facilitate coordination among those responding to the impact of terrorist attacks.

more than one commander. In other words, a variety of individuals may meet to make decisions about response priorities and methods.

IN THE REAL WORLD

GEDAPER

When you or the incident commander(s) arrive on scene, you should take several steps to accurately assess the situation. The National Fire Academy recommends the acronym GEDAPER (FEMA 1999, 43). GEDAPER includes:

Gathering information about the event
Estimating potential impact of the attack
Determining response goals
Assessing tactical options and resources at hand
Planning and implementing response actions
Evaluating progress
Reviewing results

By following these recommendations, you will be more likely to protect yourself and successfully respond.

Public Information officer:
The person who gathers information for the incident commander(s) and shares information with the media, or a city employee who specializes in working with the media.

Safety officer:
The person who evaluates the dangers at the scene and makes sure everyone is operating according to safety policies.

Liaison officer:
The person who serves as the link between the incident commander(s) and other organizations.

The incident commander/commanders work(s) closely with three officers. These officers are attached laterally to incident command, and include the **public information officer**, the safety officer, and the liaison officer. The public information officer gathers information for the incident commander/commanders and shares information with the media. The **safety officer** evaluates the dangers at the scene and makes sure everyone is operating according to safety policies. The **liaison officer** serves as the link between the incident commander/commanders and other organizations. Together, the incident commander/commanders and officers oversee the entire field response operation.

The incident commander/commanders and officers do not have to do everything however. They have four organizational sections below them to assist them in responding to terrorist attacks. These sections include planning, operations, logistics, and finance/administration. Each section may include one person or scores of people to fulfill important pre-planning and post-event functions.

- **Planning** is the section in charge of collecting information about the terrorist attack, including operational priorities given to them by the incident commander. It determines what has happened, what may occur, and identifies a strategy to accomplish response goals.

Planning
The section under ICS in charge of collecting information about the terrorist attack, including operational priorities.

Operations:
The name given to the section under ICS that is in charge of implementing the strategy created by those in planning.

- **Operations** is the name given to the section that is in charge of implementing the strategy and tactics to satisfy the objectives of the incident commander and the planning section. It includes a number of activities ranging from fire suppression and triage to search and rescue and decontamination.

- **Logistics** is the section that supports operations. It acquires people, equipment, and other resources needed by those responding to the attack.

- **Finance/administration** is the final section under ICS. This section tracks the expenses associated with response operations and logistics.

As can be seen, ICS helps to organize key functions in response operations. It also promotes coordination and effectiveness because it is based on commonly accepted principles. ICS encourages people to use common terminology when communicating with others; jargon and "ten" codes (e.g., 10-4) are avoided. ICS likewise allows for expansion of the organizational structure based on the nature and scope of the incident; it may be very simple or include additional layers (e.g., divisions, branches, and strike teams). ICS tries to integrate communications; frequencies are assigned and clearly identified. Unity of command is promoted under ICS; this implies that each person reports to one supervisor only. Unified command is also an important priority in ICS; all major organizations may be involved in joint decision making. Another principle is consolidated incident action plans; written documents help guide operations on a 12-hour period. Three other principles are a manageable span of control, designated incident facilities, and comprehensive resource management. Span of control implies that each supervisor should have between 3–7 people to manage and oversee. Designated incident facilities refer to desire to make everyone aware of the incident command post, staging areas, camps, helibases, etc. Comprehensive resource management suggests that all resources, whether human or material, must be checked in and carefully tracked during response operations. Such principles are believed to help promote coordination among field personnel.

11.3.2 Strengths and Weaknesses of ICS

The incident command system has advantages and disadvantages (McEntire 2007, 329). On the one hand, ICS may help promote collaboration among key leaders, increase safety among responders, and enhance communication among many organizations. Realistic management processes and improved use of resources are other benefits of ICS. On the other hand, ICS may not resolve all of the challenges inherented in response operations and it can even exacerbate some (Dynes 1994; Neal and Phillips 1995). Critics argue that incident command may be too rigid for the dynamic nature of post-disaster operations and it may fail to appreciate the need for collaboration and not control. Some feel that first response organizations do not work well with other organizations and that ICS becomes less important in larger terrorist attacks. Regardless of this controversy, ICS remains the principle system for field response operations. Those working under ICS will be more successful if they are aware of the potential pitfalls (e.g., the dangers of focusing too much on technological solutions instead of addressing organizational communication problems, or the problems of stressing who should be in charge vs. how can organizations work together harmoniously).

11.3.3 Using Emergency Operations Centers

Because terrorist incidents will most likely include more than a field response, other organizational layers will be required. This is especially true when terrorist attacks are large and have significant consequences. ICS is helpful for dealing with field operations at a specific location (e.g., search and rescue, medical care, and decontamination). Incident command activities will also be needed to oversee the larger picture of terrorist attacks. This may result in the establishment of **area command** (which supervises several incident command posts) and **Multi-Agency Coordination Centers** (or **MACCs**, which supervises incident command across several jurisdictions). If national assets are required, a **Joint Field Office (JFO)** will be established. The JFO is an incident command organization with federal personnel (and state and local officials on certain occasions). Their purpose is to provide resource support to incident command teams at lower levels. Area command, multi-agency coordination centers, and joint field offices are known in emergency management as emergency operations centers.

Area command:
An ICS organization that supervises several incident command posts.

Multi-Agency Coordination Centers (MACCs):
An ICS organization level that supervises incident command across several jurisdictions.

Joint Field Office (JFO):
An incident command organization with federal personnel (and state and local officials on certain occasions).

In contrast to incident command posts, EOCs are more concerned with the broader issues pertaining to incident response and disaster recovery. They will be activated in the jurisdiction, in neighboring communities, in regional organizations, at the state level, and even among numerous federal government agencies. Multiple EOCs can therefore be running and even interacting at the same time. EOCs are the locations where information is gathered, processed, and acted upon by key decision makers.

When working in an EOC, you must ensure that numerous organizations are represented. This may include police, fire, and emergency medical departments. However, EOCs will also incorporate all major city departments and even major businesses and non-profit organizations. These participants will assist all community-wide response operations such as public information, evacuation, and sheltering. In terrorist attacks, public health and intelligence officials should be given presence in EOCs. This will aid with bio-terrorism response and investigation processes.

IN THE REAL WORLD

Responsibilities of Local Departments and Organizations

When responding to a terrorist attack, it is imperative that you are aware of the other important participants. In cities and counties, this may include several organizations as noted in the following chart:

Dept/Organization	Roles and Responsibilities
Fire	• Isolate impact area and set up perimeter • Position equipment and responders upwind, uphill and upstream from the incident site • Assess downwind hazards and implement evacuation or shelter in place decisions • Identify agenda and adjust scene layout if required • Respond to victim needs with appropriate PPE • Decontaminate all victims, responders, and equipment as needed
EMS	• Implement mass casualty triage procedures • Provide medical treatment as dictated by the incident • Transport victims to definitive care facilities • Determine mental health impact and treat accordingly
Police	• Share preliminary intelligence data with incident command and the EOC • Notify and interact with the FBI • Deploy law enforcement personnel, including bomb squads and tactical operations teams • Assure incident security for first responders • Collect and control evidence • Apprehend and assume custody of suspects at the scene

(Continued)

(Continued)

Dept/Organization	Roles and Responsibilities
Hospitals	• Implement lock-down of facility to ensure security • Decontaminate and triage all arriving patients • Track patients, including their symptoms, and communicate with public health officials • Decide where to treat patients (internally or externally) • Treat as dictated by nature of injuries
Public Health	• Conduct surveillance for evidence of epidemics • Identify and control hazardous agent • Determine and implement protective measures for the population, including immunizations or prophylactic medicines • Work with police to implement quarantines if needed
Coroners	• Receive human remains • Safeguard personal property • Identify the deceased and notify next of kin • Prepare and complete file for each decedent • Photograph, fingerprint, and collect DNA specimens as appropriate • Provide death certificates • Coordinate and release remains for final disposition

Source: Adapted from Ronald W. Perry, 2003, "Municipal Terrorism Management in the United States" *Disaster Prevention and Management* 12 (3): 190–202.

11.3.4 Managing EOCs

One of your major priorities in the EOC is to acquire and manage resources. For instance, if the incident commander and logistics section requests additional body bags, the EOC may be tasked with the responsibility of obtaining and shipping them to the right location. E. L. Quarantelli notes that EOCs also help determine response policies, host visitors, and keep records (1979).

Because EOCs are in charge of so many functions, they can be very noisy and stressful. The nature of response operations is also dynamic and the impacts of terrorism can unfold quickly. For these reasons, it may be necessary to have everyone stop what they are doing every few hours and report on they key issues they are dealing with. This is similar to the planning function of ICS. In both cases, such briefings will ensure that everyone is up to speed on what is taking place and what yet needs to be done.

Those working in EOCs may be required to work long hours under emotionally draining circumstances. Breaks should be taken periodically and healthy food should be supplied to keep energy levels up. Shifts should be designated so that employee burn out does not occur. When shift transitions take place, transfer of command briefings should be given to the fresh crew. These same principles must also be applied to those working in field response.

SELF-CHECK

1. In the Incident Command System (ICS), incident command is always a single on-scene leader. True or False?

2. There is only one EOC operating during a terrorist attack. True or False?

3. Under the strategy of ICS, who serves as a link between incident command and other organizations?

   (a) The information officer
   (b) The safety officer
   (c) The liaison officer
   (d) The emergency manager

4. Why is coordination an important aspect in responding to attacks?

SUMMARY

Successful response operations after a terrorist attack are no accident. They require you to be familiar with convergent and emergent behavior. In addition, effective reactions to terrorist attacks involve many functions such as the protection of first responders and the decontamination of the victims of terrorist attacks. At times, you may also need to warn citizens before an attack or evacuate them to safer areas after terrorism occurs. To help you with your responsibilities, the incident command system and emergency operations centers can be relied upon. By anticipating your responsibility after a terrorist attack, you will be better able to protect life, prosecute terrorists, and collaborate effectively with others.

ASSESS YOUR UNDERSTANDING

UNDERSTAND: WHAT HAVE YOU LEARNED?

 Go to **www.wiley.com/college/mcentire** to assess your knowledge of response operations.

SUMMARY QUESTIONS

1. As a homeland security expert, you have been asked to speak at a first-responder seminar on the importance of safety in responding at a terrorist attack site. What could you say about the importance of a size up?

2. As a homeland security expert, you have been asked to speak at a press conference on responding to attacks. One reporter asks you about the process and importance of decontamination. How could you respond?

3. While serving as an emergency manager after an attack, you are concerned with communicating with the public. How could you effectively utilize the media for this goal?

4. As an emergency manager, you will have to deal with sheltering in the case of an evacuation. What are some factors that you would need to be considered if sheltering was required?

5. In emergency or disaster situations, people will take on new roles and interact cooperatively with strangers. True or False?

6. When providing medical care at an attack site, those with minor or fatal injuries are treated last or not at all. True or False?

7. Triage is the process by which harmful chemicals are removed from victims' clothes and bodies. True of False?

8. Sheltering is the location of people to places of safety and refuge. True or False?

9. Weather radios can be used to relay information on terrorist attacks in addition to approaching severe weather. True or False?

10. The ICS is the principle system for field response operations. True or False?

11. EOCs have a narrower scope in disaster response than ICS. True or False?

12. Logistics is the ICS section that supports operations by acquiring people, equipment, and other needed resources. True or False?

13. Initial search and rescues are usually undertaken by:

(a) firefighters.

(b) Urban Search and Rescue teams.

(c) emergent groups.

(d) police officers.

14. An important way to prevent clogs at hospitals after a terrorist attack is best known as:

(a) triage.

(b) situational awareness.

(c) a size up.

(d) decontamination.

15. All of the following are drawbacks of reverse 911 systems, except that such systems:

(a) are not always applicable to cell phones.

(b) call only homes and not businesses.

(c) require constant updating.

(d) are expensive.

16. To better share information with the media after an attack, it could be most helpful to obtain communication assistance from:

(a) an emergency manager.

(b) a public information officer.

(c) a homeland security official.

(d) a preparedness committee.

17. Under the strategy of ICS, who evaluates the dangers at an attack scene?

(a) The information officer

(b) The liaison officer

(c) The safety officer

(d) The emergency manager

18. The cooperative effort to pursue common goals in the wake of a terrorist attack is best known as:

(a) ICS.

(b) logistics.

(c) planning.

(d) coordination.

BE A HOMELAND SECURITY PROFESSIONAL

Advising a Local Government

You are a consultant on emergency management. A local government has asked you for suggestions on how to keep their first responders safe in the event of a terrorist attack. What recommendations could you provide?

Assignment: Convergence and Emergence

Write a two-page paper describing the concepts of convergence and emergence and how these processes factor into the response to terrorist attacks. Be as thorough as possible.

Managing an EOC

You are an emergency manager. Your office has recently created an emergency operations center. When an EOC opens up to respond to a disaster, the work environment is often noisy, fast-paced, and exhausting. What management strategies could you use to maintain high levels of communication and staff energy in the event your EOC responds to an attack?

KEY TERMS

Area command	An ICS organization that supervises several incident command posts.
Cold zone	The uncontaminated area where responders and victims may enter and leave.
Convergence	The flow of people and resources to the scene of an emergency or disaster.
Coordination	Cooperative efforts to pursue common goals in the wake of terrorist attacks.
Decontamination	The removal of hazardous materials from victims through clothing removal and the washing of bodies.
Dirty bombs	Explosive devices laden with dangerous chemicals or radioactive material.
Emergence	The appearance of altruistic behavior that is unfamiliar to the participants.
Emergency alert system	An announcement that interrupts TV and radio programs and relays information about what is taking place and what people should do for protection.
Evacuation	The movement of people away from hazardous areas or situations.
Hot zone	The area contaminated by the terrorist attack.
Incident command	The on-scene leader or leaders in the incident command post.
Incident Command System (ICS)	A set of personnel and procedures which helps facilitate coordination among first responders.
Joint field office (JFO)	An incident command organization with federal personnel (and state and local officials on certain occasions).
Liaison officer	The person who serves as the link between the incident commander(s) and other organizations.
Multi-agency coordination centers (MACCs)	An ICS organization level that supervises incident command across several jurisdictions.
Operations	The name given to the section under ICS that is in charge of implementing the strategy created by those in planning.
Planning	The section under ICS in charge of collecting information about the terrorist attack, including operational priorities.
Public information officer	The person who gathers information for the incident commander(s) and shares information with the media, or a city employee who specializes in working with the media.

Reverse 911 systems	Computerized messages sent over phone lines rapidly to anyone in a designated area.
Safety officer	The person who evaluates the dangers at the scene and makes sure everyone is operating according to safety policies.
Search and Rescue (SAR)	Response activities undertaken to find disaster victims and remove them from danger or confinement.
Secondary devices	The detonation of other bombs to add to the disruption and fear of the initial attack.
Self-referred	Patients who arrive at the hospital whether they require immediate care or not.
Sheltering	The location of individuals in places of safety and refuge.
Situational awareness	Continual monitoring of safety concerns at the scene of a terrorist attack.
Size up	The process of evaluating the nature of the attack site.
Tactical emergency medical services	The name given to a team of paramedics that are armed and trained in weapons use.
Triage	The assessment, sorting, and treatment of the injured in such a way as to maximize limited resources.
Warm zone	The location where victims are washed. It is located between the hot and cold zones.
Warnings	Notifications sent out to the public so they can take protective measures.
Weather radios	Electronic devices that receive information from the National Weather Service to warn people of approaching severe weather.

REFERENCES

Baker, Ear J. (1990). "Evacuation Decision Making and Public Response in Hurricane Hugo in South Carolina." *Quick Response Research Report #39*. Natural Hazards Research and Applications Information Center, University of Colorado: Boulder, CO.

Drabek, Thomas E. and David A. McEntire. (2002). "Emergent Phenomena and the Sociology of Disaster: Lessons, Trends and Opportunities from the Research Literature." *Disaster Prevention and Management* 12 (2): 97–112.

Dynes, Russell R. (1994). "Community Emergency Planning: False Assumptions and Inappropriate Analogies." *International Journal of Mass Emergencies and Disasters* 12 (2): 141–158.

FEMA. (1999). *Emergency Response to Terrorism*. Independent Study Course. Washington, D.C.

Irwin, Robert L. (1989). "The Incident Command System." Pp. 133–161 in Auf der Heide, Erik. *Disaster Response: Principles of Preparedness and Coordination*. C.V. Mosby Company: St. Louis, MO.

Kendra, James M. and Tricia Wachtendorf. (2003). "Reconsidering Convergence and Converger Legitimacy in Response to the World Trade Center Disaster." Pp. 97–122 in Clarke, Lee (ed.) *Terrorism and Disaster: New Threats, New Ideas*. Research in Social Problems. 11. Elsevier: New York.

Kendra, James M. and Tricia Wachtendorf. (2003). "Creativity in Emergency Response to the World Trade Center Disaster." Pp. 121–146 in Monday, Jacquelyn (ed.) *Beyond September 11th: An Account of Post-Disaster Research*. Natural Hazards Research and Information Applications Center, University of Colorado: Boulder, CO.

Mayer, Thom A. (1997). "Triage: History and Horizons." *Topics in Emergency Medicine*. 19 (2): 1–11.

McEntire, David A. (2007). *Disaster Response and Recovery: Strategies and Tactics for Resilience*. Wiley: New York.

McEntire, David A., Robie J. Robinson and Richart T. Weber. (2001). "Managing the Threat of Terrorism." *IQ Report* 33 (12). International City/County Management Association: Washington, D.C.

Mileti, Dennis S., John H. Sorensen and Paul W. O'Brien. (1992). "Toward an Explanation of Mass Care Shelter Use in Evacuations." *International Journal of Mass Emergencies and Disasters* 10 (1): 25–42.

Neal, David M. and Brenda D. Phillips. (1995). "Effective Emergency Management: Reconsidering the Bureaucratic Approach." *Disasters* 19 (4): 327–337.

Quarantelli, E. L. (1979). "Studies in Disaster Response and Planning." *Disaster Research Center*, University of Delaware: Newark, DE.

Quarantelli, E. L. (1990). "The Warning Process and Evacuation Behavior: The Research Evidence." *Preliminary Paper #148*. Disaster Research Center, University of Delaware: Newark, DE.

CHAPTER 12

RECOVERING FROM IMPACTS
Short-term and Long-term Measures

Do You Already Know?

- How to assess damages resulting from terrorism
- How to deal with debris and mass fatalities
- How to assemble an effective relief operation

 For additional questions to assess your current knowledge of recovery activities, go to **www.wiley.com/college/mcentire**

What You Will Find Out	What You Will Be Able To Do
12.1 The importance of disaster declarations	• Assess damages resulting from terrorism
12.2 The need to deal with debris and mass fatalities	• Propose the justification for outside disaster assistance and support the emotionally traumatized
12.3 Types of assistance available after terrorist attacks	• Assemble an effective relief operation

INTRODUCTION

Reacting to terrorist attacks includes much more than initial life saving measures. If you work in homeland security or emergency management, you should also be aware of the steps that must be taken for recovery. For instance, you should understand the importance of assessing damages and how to declare a disaster. You must be able to deal with mass fatalities, debris, and psychological issues resulting from terrorist attacks. You should likewise be aware of the different types of assistance that can be provided to both governments and citizens. Applying novel approaches during recovery can also help you community rebound quickly from the consequences of terrorist attacks.

12.1 INITIAL STEPS

If you are to promote recovery after a terrorist attack you will need to understand the impact of the event. You may also need to seek help from the state or federal government by acknowledging your shortfalls in dealing with the event. Assessing damages and declaring a disaster are the initial steps to helping you recover from a terrorist attack.

12.1.1 Assessing Damages

Damage assessment:
A survey of physical destruction, economic losses, deaths, social disruption, and recovery needs.

Rapid assessment:
A quick survey of impacts designed to gain an appreciation of the scope of the attack.

Preliminary Damage Assessment (PDA):
A more detailed assessment of impacts that typically takes place within days or weeks of the event; it determines possibility and extent of outside assistance.

Technical assessment:
A survey of damages that points out methods and costs for rebuilding.

One of the first things you will need to do to recover is to assess the effects of an attack. While the emergency period begins to wane and you have addressed urgent response operations, you must also begin to think about long-term issues. In order to comprehend what needs to be done, you will carry out an evaluation of damages. **Damage assessment** is a survey of physical destruction and economic losses. It may also look at the number of deaths and amount of social disruption caused by terrorists. In some cases, it will identify major needs (e.g., debris removal, housing, crisis counseling, etc.). The assessment of impacts is really your first priority for fostering recovery (Oaks 1990, 6). Without an assessment, you will not be able to help your community overcome the negative consequences of terrorist attacks.

There are typically three types of damage assessments as well as different ways of completing them (McEntire 2002). A **rapid assessment** is a quick survey of impacts. It is designed to gain an appreciation of the scope of the attack so immediate needs can be met and additional help can be summoned. It is undertaken by local government officials. A **Preliminary Damage Assessment (PDA)** is a more detailed assessment of impacts that typically takes place within days or weeks of the event. The goal of this assessment is to determine if state and federal help is warranted and in what ways. It is performed by the affected community as well as state and federal officials. A **technical assessment** points out alternative methods and anticipated costs for rebuilding. It identifies what materials and labor will be required for demolition and/or reconstruction. It is completed by engineers, insurance agents, contractors, and FEMA employees.

These damage assessments are not completed in the same fashion. The rapid assessment may be completed by driving near the attack site to view damages or flying overhead to gain an aerial perspective. In other cases, the damaged area will be toured by foot. Walkthroughs are most likely to be used for preliminary and technical damage assessments. At times, it may also be necessary to talk to victims, impacted businesses, and community leaders to tally deaths, economic losses, and societal disturbance. The important point to remember is that the goals of the assessment will determine how it is conducted. Safety should also be a top priority.

12.1.2 Damage Assessment Concerns and Procedures

When completing damage assessments, it will be imperative that you recognize the extreme danger of the attack site. Sharp glass and twisted metal may be present from bombings. Fires and unstable structures are also associated with explosions. Hazardous materials may be located in and around the area of the terrorist attack. There are many more variables that could cause injury or death to those who are involved in damage assessment. For these reasons, access to the area should be carefully controlled and safety should be the top priority. You should also do all you can to ensure that the damage assessment is accurate and complete. Recovery will be slowed down if your evaluation is incorrect or performed in a partial manner.

In order to ensure that your damage assessments are successful, it is a good idea to hold a meeting to discuss who will evaluate the site of the attack and how it will be accomplished. Participants can be trained in safety precautions and given assignments based on geographic location (e.g., building floor or city block) or type of damage to look for (e.g., structural integrity or leaks in gas lines). Protective equipment and communication devices can also be distributed at this meeting. Cameras and forms should likewise be given to those assessing damages along with guidelines on when reports are to be turned in.

At the scene of the attack, you will need to determine if buildings are safe, sanitary, and secure. Depending on the degree of damage, you may need to categorize them in one of three ways. Buildings designated as "green" are habitable and occupants are allowed to return. "Yellow" structures have known or unknown safety concerns, and should only be entered by well-trained and properly equipped individuals. Buildings labeled as "red" are unsafe and should be condemned and destroyed. Once the assessments are completed, they should be reviewed for accuracy, compiled, and then given to state and federal authorities. Such officials will also help you to determine your top priorities and options for recovery.

12.1.3 Declaring a Disaster and Seeking Help

Disaster declaration:
An acknowledgement of the severity of the event and that outside response and recovery assistance is required.

Depending on the findings of your damage assessment, you might need to issue a statement acknowledging that you have experienced an emergency or disaster. If the needs are greater than your resources, you should declare a state of disaster. A **disaster declaration** is an acknowledgement of the severity of the event and that outside response and recovery assistance is required. It is one of the many requirements for obtaining state or federal funds for rebuilding.

In many or even most cases, the damage and impact of a terrorist attack may be so obvious that the President of the United States will recognize the event as such and begin to take measures to deal with the situation at the federal level (e.g., by deploying personnel to the area and sending needed material resources). However, not all situations may require this top down initiation. For this reason, you should know the process of declaring a disaster at the local level.

Figure 12-1

Political leaders are often present when a disaster is declared.

After an attack occurs, you will initiate your response and recovery operations. You will determine the negative consequences of the event along with your ability to handle them. If the municipal and county governments determine that the event will overstretch their abilities, a disaster is declared. This usually includes a formal statement recognizing the death and damages, societal impact, economic losses, and the need for outside assistance. Disaster declarations may also discuss if the damage is covered by insurance, if the attack has traumatized the community, and if it results in unemployment or evacuation and sheltering. At this point, the state will contact you to discuss the situation and may send representatives to verify impact. If the state feels it may also be unable to deal with the consequences effectively, it will also declare a disaster and relay this information to the FEMA regional office responsible for their area. If the officials in the regional office concur with the state's assessment, the declaration will be forwarded to the FEMA director and to the President. A large or significant event will result in a Presidential disaster declaration. This action will free up funds and mobilize the federal government to the aid of the affected community. If the event is minor, the process of declaration could theoretically be stopped at any point. However, because of the political nature of terrorism and homeland security, it is likely that the federal government will be involved in any and all attacks against our nation. This should not discount the fact that there will be many functions that will require the attention of local governments.

IN THE REAL WORLD

Declaring a Disaster

When Timothy McVeigh blew up the Murrah Federal Building in Oklahoma City, first responders initially thought the explosion was a result of a broken gas line. A short time later, it became apparent that the devastation was the outcome of an intentional attack. After consulting with local officials, the governor of Oklahoma called the regional director of FEMA in Denton, Texas. The regional director then notified James Lee Witt, the director of FEMA in Washington, D.C. By that afternoon, President Clinton was made aware of the terrorist attack in Oklahoma. He addressed the nation publicly and declared a state of emergency. This freed up funds, personnel and federal resources so the government could support the response operations at and around the Murrah Federal Building. Declaring a disaster is often the first step toward getting the help you need.

SELF-CHECK

1. A survey of physical destruction and economic losses is known as a damage assessment. True or False?

2. A rapid assessment is generally undertaken by federal officials. True or False?

3. In assessing damage, the color "red" indicates:

   (a) the building is safe.
   (b) the building is sanitary and secure.
   (c) the building is completely destroyed or beyond repair.
   (d) the building should be entered with caution.

4. An acknowledgement of the severity of an event or that outside response and recovery assistance is required is best known as:

   (a) a rapid assessment.
   (b) a preliminary damage assessment.
   (c) emergence.
   (d) a disaster declaration.
   (e) a windshield assessment.

12.2 KEY FUNCTIONS

Besides assessing damages and declaring a disaster, there are many other steps that will have to be taken if you are to promote recovery for your community. You may have to deal with mass fatalities, clean up debris, and address emotional issues. These are some of the major priorities during recovery operations.

12.2.1 Mass Fatality Management

Terrorism may produce a large quantity of deaths. Small attacks around the world may result in several fatalities. Israel has been experiencing this situation for decades, and Iraq is now plagued with similar events. Larger ones, such as Al Qaeda's bombings in Africa on August 7, 1998, claim even more lives. In Nairobi, 212 people died when the U.S. embassy was blown up with explosives in cars parked near the building. On October 12, 2002, over 200 people died when Jemaah Islamiyah initiated three bombings in the tourist area of Bali, Indonesia. On April 19, 1995, 168 people died when Timothy McVeigh parked a Ryder Truck laden with explosives near the Murrah Federal Building. And, on September 11, 2001, an appalling 2,974 people died when 19 terrorists hijacked planes and flew them into the World Trade Center, the Pentagon, and a field in Pennsylvania. These numbers are significant, but experts anticipate greater losses in the future if terrorists use nuclear or biological weapons. It is no exaggeration to suggest that terrorist events could result in thousands, hundreds of thousands, and even millions of fatalities.

Because of these significant numbers and the possibility of even greater attacks down the road, it will be imperative for you to understand challenges of and recommendations for dealing with a mass fatality incident. A **mass fatality incident** is an attack that creates so many deaths that the processing of remains stretches or is beyond the ability of local government. In other words, the large number of deceased is greater in comparison to the resources that are needed to collect, identify, and bury them. Besides the large quantity of dead, there are other challenges associated with mass fatality incidents. While dead bodies do not normally pose a threat to public health, a terrorist attack involving weapons of mass destruction can complicate mass fatality management. Some of the bodies may be contaminated and can adversely affect those trying to bury them. In addition, well-intentioned citizens may move bodies in an attempt to help public officials (Scanlon 1998). This may hinder investigation and record keeping (because they are not located at the scene of the attack). A third problem deals with the heavy emotions of survivors. Family members may be distraught over their losses, and those working in mass fatality management should be sensitive to the situation. Finally, it is also possible that remains may not be identified. Some bodies can be obliterated in attacks and be beyond recognition. After 9/11, searchers found 19,893 separate body parts. However, the remains of 1,268 individuals have never been found (Hampson and Moore 2003). DNA can help determine who people are, but it is not 100 percent successful as we discovered after the World Trade Center attacks.

In order to process large numbers of bodies for burial or cremation, several steps must be taken (Hooft, Noji and Van de Voorde 1989):

1. If possible, the location of bodies should be recorded. This will help with investigation. ID tags and maps can assist with this objective.

2. Bodies should be stored for processing. This may occur at hospitals or county morgues. Innovative ideas can help you when bodies outstrip storage facilities. Bodies have been stored in unmarked refrigerated trucks or even at ice skating rinks.

3. Clothing, jewelry, and other items (e.g., wallets or berets) should be removed and saved for family members. The height, weight, gender, and other identifying features (e.g., tattoos, mustaches, dentures, and cavities) must be recorded. Fingerprints and pictures of the body should also be taken to facilitate body identification.

4. After bodies have been identified, they can be returned to families for burial. If bodies are not claimed, they can be buried in recorded graves.

5. Respect for the wishes of the surviving family members (e.g., cultural burial practices) should be ensured.

Mass fatality incident: An attack that creates so many deaths that the processing of remains is beyond the ability of local government.

Disaster Mortuary Operations Response Team (DMORT):
A group of private citizens from around the nation who may be activated by the federal government to assist with mass fatality incidents.

Should mass fatality incidents warrant substantial outside involvement, a **Disaster Mortuary Operations Response Team (DMORT)** can be requested. A DMORT is a group of private citizens from around the nation who may be activated by the federal government to assist with mass fatality incidents. They include funeral directors, medical examiners, coroners, pathologists, and medical record technicians. Their purpose is to recover bodies and issue death certificates. They can be sent to any location and can assist communities with their portable morgue units.

12.2.2 Debris Management

Because of the nature of most terrorist attacks (i.e., bombings), there will be a great deal of rubble that will have to be cleaned up. This will include concrete, glass, metal, wood, wiring, and other construction materials. The quantity of debris can be overwhelming. For instance, when the Murrah Federal Building was demolished after the Oklahoma City bombing, an average of 800 tons of debris was removed on a daily basis. The amount of debris at the World Trade Center is even more noteworthy. As many as 10 major buildings were destroyed, which left behind 1.2 million tons of debris (McEntire, Robinson and Weber 2003, 451). It took several months working around the clock to remove this large quantity of debris. This brings up the important concept of debris management. **Debris management** is the removal, storage, disposal, or recycling of rubble produced from terrorist attacks. It is an extremely important function to facilitate recovery.

Debris management:
The removal, storage, disposal, or recycling of rubble produced from terrorist attacks.

Debris management after a terrorist attack sounds simple in theory, but it is actually a very complex and complicated issue. There are a variety of factors that must be considered when dealing with rubble. First, trained personnel with adequate heavy equipment will be needed to remove debris. People may not be able to help if they do not have gloves, hard hats, steel toed boots, shovels, back hoes, or dump trucks. Debris can also pose a danger to those working in it and trying to remove it. After the Oklahoma City bombing, a large piece of concrete broke lose from an upper floor and fell on a nurse who was helping with search and rescue operations. She was killed as a result. There are numerous cases where debris created injuries among those trying to clean it up. Cuts, bruises, and crushing from debris are all possible at the site of a terrorist attack. Safety should be a top priority when removing debris.

Debris management operations are also made problematic in that debris may contain evidence as well as human remains. Sorting of debris must be painstakingly careful. Law enforcement and coroners/medical examiners may need to be involved in the debris removal process. Another challenge relates to where to take the debris. Because of the large quantity, debris may need to be stored somewhere temporarily until it can be recycled or buried. This will require a large holding area or a designated landfill. The location

Figure 12-2

Debris is an important, but neglected, function that must be addressed after a terrorist attack.

and disposal of debris brings up another difficulty. The expense associated with moving and burying debris can be enormous. Local governments may need to seek federal assistance for debris management. They will also need to monitor contractors to make sure they are being honest. Some companies involved in debris management have defrauded the government for their services. Continual oversight will be needed. As you deal with debris after a terrorist attack, organizations like the Federal Emergency Management Agency and the Environmental Protection Agency can assist you.

12.2.3 Emotional Issues

Terrorism may create a great deal of emotional distress (McEntire, Robinson and Weber 2001). The victims of terrorism and all other witnesses to it recognize the toll of attacks in terms of injuries, fatalities, and economic disruption. Resulting disabilities, the death of a loved one, and monetary losses are unbearable for certain individuals. But many people are troubled by the fact that terrorism is an intentional act undertaken to instill fear. It is violence that is often directed against the most vulnerable: ordinary citizens. A common response is "why and how could someone do this?" This brings up a major function that you should address during recovery.

Crisis counseling:
The treatment of psychological problems that may arise from the stress produced by terrorism.

Critical incident stress (CIS):
Trauma experienced while on the job that is so severe it inhibits coping among emergency service personnel.

Post-Traumatic Stress Disorder (PTSD):
The clinical diagnosis for individuals who become depressed due to a traumatic event in their lives.

Crisis counseling is the treatment of psychological problems that may arise from the stress produced by terrorism. It includes active listening, sympathetic understanding, and emotional support (both direct and indirect) for the victims of terrorism. These victims may include first responders who experience critical incident stress. **Critical Incident Stress (CIS)** is defined as trauma experienced while on the job that is so severe it inhibits coping among emergency service personnel. For instance, a fire fighter may do all he/she can to save a child after a terrorist attack, but ultimately be unsuccessful. This experience, along with the sights, smells and sounds at the attack site, may be emotionally burdensome over time.

Alternatively, citizens may suffer from symptoms of **Post-Traumatic Stress Disorder (PTSD)**. PTSD is the clinical diagnosis for individuals who become depressed due to a traumatic event that they personally witness or experience indirectly in their lives. As seen after 9/11, terrorism certainly constitutes such an experience. Many people were psychologically disturbed by the terrorist attacks on that day.

Victims experiencing CIS or PTSD may exhibit a number of symptoms. Besides depression, they may gain or lose weight, become angry, use alcohol and drugs, have headaches, and experience mood swings. Twitches, social withdrawal, sleeplessness, and flashbacks are also common signs that someone has been affected psychologically. If a person has difficulty coping with everyday stress and does not have a strong support network, they are considered to be vulnerable to CIS or PTSD.

When a terrorist attack occurs, homeland security and emergency management personnel may set up a clinic to help those affected psychologically. There are two strategies for dealing with the emotional problems created by terrorism. A **defusing** is a short, unstructured meeting to allow a person to discuss an experience as soon as it takes place. It is commonly provided to first responders as they wrap up at the scene so they can vent and unload frustration among colleagues and peers. A defusing is one way to relieve pent-up stress and reduce their compounding effects over time. A **debriefing** is a recurring and more in-depth discussion designed to redirect harmful thinking and develop improved coping mechanisms. Therapists reiterate normal reactions to disappointing events and offer practical suggestions for stress management. The goal is to allow people to talk after the event and help them find ways to deal with and overcome negative psychological impacts.

Defusing:
A short, unstructured meeting to allow a person to discuss an experience as soon as it takes place.

Debriefing:
A recurring and more in depth discussion designed to redirect harmful thinking and develop improved coping mechanisms.

The success rate of defusings and debriefings is debated among scholars (Mitchell 1988; Barnett-Queen and Bergmann 1989). Some research seems to indicate that crisis counseling helps people recover more quickly, but other evidence suggests that repeated exposure to a traumatic event through discussion could be counter-productive. While this issue remains to be resolved, you can seek the most appropriate help for your first responders and citizens. Fire departments and the American Red Cross are organizations that have experience in dealing with CIS and PTSD. They can help your community recover from terrorist attacks.

IN THE REAL WORLD

Debris from the WTC

The terrorist attacks on 9/11 resulted in the collapse of the World Trade Center towers. When these buildings came down, at least eight other buildings were completely destroyed or substantially damaged. The pile of rubble that was produced was equivalent to 1.2 million tons of debris. In order to deal with this large amount of debris, the government divided the 16-acre World Trade Center site into quadrants. It then assigned a number of contractors to remove, ship, and dispose of debris. Cranes, trucks, and even barges were used in the process. A special challenge was the sorting of debris in order to search for and collect evidence and personal belongings. In spite of the monumental undertaking, debris was removed much quicker than initially anticipated. By May 2002, Ground Zero was emptied of steal beams, broken concrete, and other demolished building materials.

SELF-CHECK

1. Experts anticipate that, in the future, there will be less loss of life from terrorist attacks. True or False?
2. Defusing is a recurring and in depth discussion to improve coping mechanisms for those suffering from emotional problems after an attack. True or False?
3. The removal, storage, and disposal of rubble produced by a terrorist attack is best known as:
   (a) defusing.
   (b) debriefing.
   (c) rapid assessment.
   (d) debris management.
4. What challenges are associated with mass fatality incidents?

12.3 THE IMPORTANCE OF DISASTER ASSISTANCE

As individual victims and the community as a whole begin the process of recovery after a terrorist attack, aid will arrive from unofficial and official sources. Unofficial sources include volunteers and donations from concerned citizens. Official sources of assistance will come from organizations like the Federal Emergency Management Agency. In either case, it will be your responsibility to harness these resources and implement innovative strategies to promote recovery.

12.3.1 Volunteer and Donation Management

After a terrorist attack, people will experience a deep and sincere interest in helping victims and the impacted jurisdiction. A study of volunteer behavior after 9/11 reveals that people will sympathize with those affected and desire to find ways to assist them in coping with the aftermath. For instance, a woman who wanted to donate blood after the WTC towers came down stated "there needs to be some positive that comes out of it, and the only way it's positive is if I and other people make it positive" (Lowe and Fothergill 2003, 299). This strong feeling will motivate hundreds or even thousands to volunteer their time, talent, and energy for altruistic causes.

On 9/11, spontaneous volunteers arrived at the WTC to participate in search and rescue operations, provide basic first aid, cheer on first responders, serve food to those removing debris, and give massages to tired workers. Others offered translation services or were willing to perform any other duty that might be required after such a devastating event (e.g., clerical duties, crisis counseling, transportation, etc.). In events such as 9/11, it is not uncommon for there to be hundreds or even thousands of volunteers. While not everyone was able to assist because of the dangerous conditions, the arrival of so many volunteers can be truly impressive.

The influx of significant quantities of volunteers is only matched by the amount of donations that pour into a community after a terrorist attack. The recovery efforts after the Oklahoma City bombing provide a good case in point (ODCEM 1996). Southwestern Bell donated cell phones and a cell tower to help those responding to the event. Fast food companies brought in meals to feed emergency workers. Clothing, pharmaceuticals, water, and other supplies and equipment arrived from around the state, region, nation, and world. Besides these **in-kind donations**, money was also sent to Oklahoma City. Hundred of thousands of dollars were sent to care for the victims and their families.

In-kind donations:
Physical donations including food, water, clothing, supplies, and equipment.

This mass assault of volunteers and donations, as it has been described by Thompson and Hawkes (1962), can create several problems for those working in emergency management and homeland security. For example, there can be too many volunteers in comparison to the number of individuals needed to manage them effectively. Some may be untrained or lack the skills you require after a terrorist attack. Another difficulty is keeping them safe in spite of the dangerous attack location. Others may become frustrated if you do not put them to work immediately or if they are given tasks that they feel are not "making a difference."

Volunteer management:
The harnessing of volunteers to take advantage of their potential contributions while averting potential negative consequences.

Volunteer registration center:
The location where citizens fill out forms noting their skills and other information which can help you when making assignments.

In order to overcome the challenges associated with those wanting to help out, you should implement a coherent strategy for volunteer management. **Volunteer management** is the harnessing of volunteers to take advantage of their potential contributions while averting potential negative consequences. Successful volunteer management often requires a volunteer management center. A **volunteer registration center** is a location where citizens fill out forms noting their skills and other information which can help you when making assignments. When giving responsibilities to volunteers, it is wise to review some basic safety rules and briefly train them on what they will be doing. You will then need to evaluate their progress and care for them as needed (e.g., provide food, water, or safety equipment). Without ensuring the safety and well-being of volunteers, injury and death can result. In addition, liability will be increased if volunteers are not carefully supervised. Although too many uncoordinated volunteers can be a headache, their strength in numbers and desire to serve can have a dramatic and positive impact upon recovery operations.

Donations management:
The collection, sorting, and distribution of goods and money for the benefit of victims of terrorist attacks.

The problems resulting from excessive and unrequested donations may also be addressed through effective donations management (Neal 1994). **Donations management** is the collection, sorting, and distribution of goods and money for the benefit of victims of terrorist attacks. It entails recognizing your needs after an attack and relaying your specific requests to the public through the media. Once received at designated areas (e.g., a

Figure 12-3

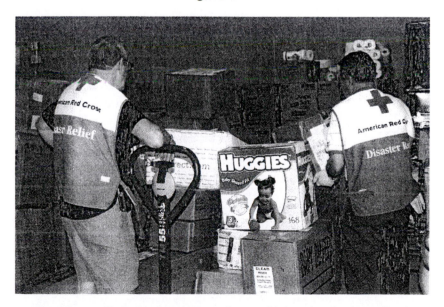

People are likely to donate supplies and labor for the benefit of victims after a terrorist attack.

warehouse), you will need to have a team in place to help receive and disperse needed items. Church groups and non-profit organizations can be very helpful in this respect. Tracking donations with the use of computers can also help you determine what you need, what is coming in, and where it is going.

An even better way to avoid the hassle of donations is to request monetary contributions. This prevents unwanted items from arriving, eliminates some of the labor needed to deal with them, speeds up assistance, and helps the local economy (if goods and services are purchased in the affected or nearby areas). If in-kind and monetary donations are not getting to the appropriate individuals, an unmet needs committee may be established. An **unmet needs committee** is a group of concerned citizens and community leaders who work together to collect donations and address long-term needs of victims (Wedel and Baker 1998). They play a positive role in recovery operations.

Unmet needs committee: A group of concerned citizens and community leaders who work together to collect donations and address long terms needs of victims.

12.3.2 Individual and Public Assistance

If a terrorist attack results in a Presidential declaration, citizens and communities alike may receive federal disaster assistance. There are two types of disaster assistance. **Individual assistance** provides relief to citizens and businesses impacted by terrorist attacks. **Public assistance** makes aid available to government entities which have been affected by terrorism. Both types of assistance have special programs and requirements.

Individual assistance: Relief programs for citizens and businesses impacted by terrorist attacks.

Public assistance: Relief programs that make aid available to government entities which have been affected by terrorism.

Individual assistance includes loans at low interest rates as well as grants that don't have to be repaid. Some of the loans are directed towards homeowners and renters who have lost personal property. In this case up to $200,000 can be provided for primary residences and $40,000 to replace personal property. Other loans are for businesses. These loans provide up to $1,500,000 can be obtained to repair or replace structures and machinery. If the business has suffered economic hardship because of the attack, another $1,500,000 can be acquired. Small grants, up to $27,000 can also be obtained by individuals and families who do not qualify for loans. This money can be used to provide temporary housing in mobile homes, help with hotel/motel stays, or repair or replace destroyed property.

Individuals and families may also obtain needed services after a terrorist attack. Federal and state assistance can help victims understand the types of assistance that are available, file and settle insurance claims, protect against price gouging and fraud, and obtain counseling from attorneys regarding legal issues and contracts. Food stamps, unemployment assistance, and social security and veterans benefits can all be given to victims of terrorist attacks.

In order to obtain individual assistance, victims of terrorism should call the National Processing Service Center at 1 (800) 621-FEMA. The

National Processing Service Center:
A FEMA office set up to help victims apply for federal assistance programs.

Disaster Recovery Center (DRC):
A temporary facility near the attack location where victims can seek information about federal assistance programs.

National Processing Service Center is a FEMA office set up to help victims apply for federal assistance programs. Call takers will input information about the victim's needs into a computer. Alternatively, the victim may go to a Disaster Recovery Center for help. A **Disaster Recovery Center (DRC)** is a temporary facility near the attack location where victims can seek information about federal assistance programs. It includes phone and Internet access to federal disaster programs. The selection of the location of the DRC is a local and state responsibility. It is usually set up in a building that can accommodate tables, chairs, phones, fax machines, and parking. Federal officials will help to publicize and run the DRC. Regardless of how citizens apply for assistance, the information will be reviewed and verified by FEMA employees and contractors. Eventually, decisions will be made about loans, grants, services, and benefits.

If a local or state government, Indian tribe or private non-profit organization is adversely impacted by a terrorist attack, they may qualify for public assistance. Public assistance is divided into two types: emergency assistance and permanent assistance. **Emergency assistance** is financial help given to local governments to take care of immediate needs. It may include monetary and technical support for debris removal and safety precautions. **Permanent assistance** is financial aid for the repairing of publicly owned critical infrastructure and key assets. It may include the help to reconstruct roads, bridges and lights; dikes, levies and dams; public buildings and equipment; water, gas and sewage systems; or parks, airports and recreational facilities.

Emergency assistance:
Financial help given to local governments to take care of immediate needs such as debris removal or safety precautions.

Permanent assistance:
Financial aid for the repairing of publicly owned critical infrastructure and key assets.

Kickoff meeting:
A gathering of local, state, and federal officials for the purpose of explaining public assistance programs in detail.

If individual or public assistance is required, community leaders will need to declare a disaster and share damage assessment findings with federal officials. If assistance is deemed as justified, a kickoff meeting will be held. A **Kickoff meeting** is a gathering of local, state and federal officials for the purpose of explaining public assistance programs in detail (e.g., application materials and deadlines). This meeting will help answer questions about public assistance and begin the process of obtaining outside aid to promote recovery.

The oversight of federal public assistance programs will take place in a **Joint Field Office (JFO)**. The JFO is an established but temporary office that includes local, state, and federal representatives who will manage the paperwork regarding public assistance. Those working in the DFO will ensure that recovery projects are being completed, check for fraudulent activities, and consider the special circumstances surrounding historic buildings, environmental concerns, and rebuilding with mitigation in mind.

12.3.3 Novel Approaches

As can be seen there are many aspects associated with recovery operations. But performing the functions listed above will not necessarily ensure that long-term issues will be successfully addressed. Innovative ideas are needed to help the community rebound quickly from terrorist attacks. One exemplary case is from Manchester, England (Bathos, Williams and Russell 1999).

On June 15, 1996, the Irish Republican Army called officials in this city and advised them of a bomb that would be detonated shortly. A warning was issued and efforts were made to evacuate the area of approximately 80,000 people. About forty minutes later, a 3,000 lb. fertilizer bomb in an illegally parked Ford Van exploded. Fortunately, no one was killed in the bombing but over 200 people were injured. At least 12 buildings were damaged and many of these had such severe structural problems that they had to be demolished. As a result, 672 businesses were displaced and nearly 50,000 square meters of office space was lost. Residents in the area were forced to leave their homes due to fears about the effects of infrastructure damage. The event provided both a test for responders and an opportunity for those involved in recovery.

When the emergency period of fire suppression and life saving activities ended, attention soon focused on long-term concerns. In accordance with the community disaster plan, the area was cordoned off. This "protected people from physical danger, helped preserve criminal evidence at the disaster scene, and [was central to] the city-councils re-occupancy strategy" (Bathos, Williams and Russell 1999, 222). On the next day, a task force made up of the city council, police officials, and representatives from the private sector toured the area and devised a methodical strategy to help the community recover.

The City's architectural department was put in charge of assessing damages and determining what could be done to make the area safe enough for further recovery activities (e.g., demolition of buildings). As structures were deemed or made safe, business owners and citizens were allowed back into the structures to retrieve belongings and resume normal activities. Over the next several days, police presence diminished and companies hired their own security staff to monitor the destroyed buildings. The cordoned-off area was reduced to five buildings.

During the first week, a major challenge for city officials were the 5,000–10,000 people who arrived at city hall wanting information or assistance after the bombing. At first, there was no system in place to address citizen concerns. In time, however, meetings were held for owners and occupants in different geographic areas. This helped to provide information about getting back into damaged buildings and the process of recovery.

City council also helped large businesses relocate to available property of the private sector so they could resume normal operations. A massive media campaign was initiated to help citizens understand what was taking place and how they could assist in the recovery efforts. By the end of the first month, the city had created a committee to oversee the rehabilitation of the area. Three priorities became evident.

First, the Mayor established a fund and asked people to donate to it to help those experiencing hardship from the attack. Over £2.5 million was raised for victims over an 18 month period. Second, the Deputy Prime Minister announced an international urban planning competition in July to generate a vision and plan for recovery. The decision on the wining design was made public 16 weeks later. Finally, an organization, the Manchester Millennium Task Force, was created to oversee the rebuilding of the area. It was put in charge of recovery activities until they were completed in the spring of 2000.

A review of the reaction to this bombing reveals a number of positive features. Prior planning and training helped to ensure a quick response to the event. The oversight of post-attack functions was also successful due to the use of a designated emergency operations center. Police were effective in evacuating most people out of the area and maintaining security presence after the attack occurred. Although determining who should have access to the area was problematic, the City Architect Department was soon made responsible for issuing passes to the area. The leadership and innovation of city officials helped to channel resources and ideas to facilitate recovery. While the rehabilitation of the area was not problem free, the Manchester bombing illustrates the benefit of organizations working together to overcome post-attack problems. Partnerships and cooperation among various parties were cited as reasons for a speedy recovery.

FOR EXAMPLE

Unmet Needs After the Oklahoma City Bombing

Because the terrorist attack on the Murrah Federal Building produced so many deaths and injuries, there was an almost overwhelming sense of responsibility for the victims and their families. Within a short time, the community shifted from short-term emergency needs to long-term concerns. A committee was formed with the participation of city, business, and non-profit organizations (Wedel and Baker 1998). Its goal was to collect monetary and in-kind donations, and ensure that the donations were directed to those in need. Cars, tuition scholarships, and many other resources were given to those in need. The unmet needs committee also tracked relief assistance to make sure that it was not duplicated by other organizations or abused by disaster victims. The superb handling of donations and the treatment of victims was labeled the "Oklahoma Standard."

SELF-CHECK

1. A gathering of local, state, and federal officials for the purpose of explaining public assistance programs in best known as a kickoff meeting. True or False?

2. Contributions of money to help out victims of a terrorist attack are also known as in-kind donations. True or False?

3. Financial aid for repairing publicly owned critical infrastructure and key assets is best known as:

   (a) permanent assistance.
   (b) emergency assistance.
   (c) individual assistance.
   (d) in-kind donations.

4. What problems can volunteers create in the recovery process?

SUMMARY

You will need to fulfill a variety of recovery measures after terrorist attacks in your jurisdiction. After assessing damages, you will need to declare a disaster or state of emergency. You will also need to be involved in mass fatality management, dispose of debris, and provide emotional support for those who have been psychologically impacted by the event. As you begin to address long term issues, you will want to seek public and individual assistance. If you manage the impacts of terrorist attacks successfully, you will speed up the time it takes for recovery and help your community rebound from disturbing events.

ASSESS YOUR UNDERSTANDING

UNDERSTAND: WHAT HAVE YOU LEARNED?

 Go to **www.wiley.com/college/mcentire** to assess your knowledge of recovery activities.

SUMMARY QUESTIONS

1. As a homeland security expert, you are asked by a local government official about the process by which a municipality can obtain federal assistance after a terrorist attack. How could you respond?

2. When having lunch with friends, you mention that you are studying emotional issues related to terrorist attacks in your homeland security class. They are curious about how authorities deal with the stress faced by first responders. How could you answer their question?

3. As a homeland security expert, a local government has asked you about the potential assistance that may become available for their community in the event of a terrorist attack. They are curious about the different types of disaster assistance. How could you respond?

4. As an emergency manager, you have been asked by your organization to come up with some strategies for volunteer management in case of a terrorist attack. What are some recommendations that you could provide?

5. A preliminary damage assessment is a quick survey of attack-related impacts undertaken by local government officials. True or False?

6. A technical assessment identifies what materials and labor will be required for demolition and/or construction. True or False?

7. If a local government declares a disaster, the federal government must provide aid. True of False?

8. If an attack causes so many deaths that a local government is unable to collect, identify, and bury all of the deceased, it is called a mass fatality incident. True or False?

9. DNA is generally, but not always, 100 percent successful in helping to identify remains after an attack? True or False?

10. The Environmental Protection Agency is one of the organizations that can assist local governments in debris management. True or False?

11. After a terrorist attack, people are afraid and usually not many will want to volunteer to help out. True or False?

12. Only local or state governments can qualify for public assistance after a terrorist attack. True or False?

13. If a mass fatality incident warrants substantial outside help in dealing with remains, then a request can be made for:

(a) a Disaster Mortuary Operations Response Team.

(b) tactical emergency medical services.

(c) crisis counseling.

(d) defusing.

14. Critical incident stress is best described as:

(a) the process of determining which buildings are safe after an attack.

(b) a clinical diagnosis for individuals suffering from depression.

(c) the inability of first responders to cope with trauma from work.

(d) a treatment for psychological problems associated with attacks.

15. A short, unstructured meeting to allow a first responder to discuss job-related experiences and reduce emotional stress is best known as:

(a) a damage assessment.

(b) defusing.

(c) debriefing.

(d) decontamination.

16. The oversight of federal public assistance programs after a terrorist attack takes place in a:

(a) National Processing Service Center.

(b) Joint Field Office.

(c) Disaster Recovery Center.

(d) volunteer registration center.

17. Financial help given to local governments for immediate needs, such as debris removal, is best known as:

(a) permanent assistance.

(b) in-kind donations.

(c) individual assistance.

(d) emergency assistance.

18. Relief provided to citizens and businesses affected by terrorist attacks is best known as:

(a) permanent assistance.

(b) emergency assistance.

(c) individual assistance.

(d) public assistance.

BE A HOMELAND SECURITY PROFESSIONAL

Planning for Debris Management

You are an emergency manager with a local government. In the event of a terrorist attack, there could be a large quantity of debris that needs to be removed, stored, disposed, or recycled. You have been asked to prepare a report on this aspect of recovery in case of an attack. What concerns would you address in your report on debris management?

Assignment: Damage Assessments

Write a two-page paper discussing the concerns you might want to address if you were to complete a damage assessment. Explain factors that must be considered.

Addressing Donations Management

You are an employee in an emergency management office. In order to be prepared for recovery in case of a terrorist attack, the office should be ready to handle the large influx of donations that usually accompanies such an event. Without proper management, donations can become excessive or irrelevant. What recommendations could you provide on how to effectively manage donations?

KEY TERMS

Crisis counseling	The treatment of psychological problems that may arise from the stress produced by terrorism.
Critical incident stress (CIS)	Trauma experienced while on the job that is so severe it inhibits coping among emergency service personnel.
Damage assessment	A survey of physical destruction, economic losses, deaths, social disruption, and recovery needs.
Debriefing	A recurring and more in depth discussion designed to redirect harmful thinking and develop improved coping mechanisms.
Debris management	The removal, storage, disposal, or recycling of rubble produced from terrorist attacks.
Defusing	A short, unstructured meeting to allow a person to discuss an experience as soon as it takes place.

Disaster declaration	An acknowledgement of the severity of the event and that outside response and recovery assistance is required.
Disaster Mortuary Operations Response Team (DMORT)	A group of private citizens from around the nation who may be activated by the federal government to assist with mass fatality incidents.
Disaster Recovery Center (DRC)	A temporary facility near the attack location where victims can seek information about federal assistance programs.
Donations management	The collection, sorting, and distribution of goods and money for the benefit of victims of terrorist attacks.
Emergency assistance	Financial help given to local governments to take care of immediate needs such as debris removal or safety precautions.
Individual assistance	Relief programs for citizens and businesses impacted by terrorist attacks.
In-kind donations	Physical donations including food, water, clothing, supplies, and equipment.
Kickoff meeting	A gathering of local, state, and federal officials for the purpose of explaining public assistance programs in detail.
Mass fatality incident	An attack that creates so many deaths that the processing of remains is beyond the ability of local government.
National Processing Service Center	A FEMA office set up to help victims apply for federal assistance programs.
Permanent assistance	Financial aid for the repairing of publicly owned critical infrastructure and key assets.
Post-traumatic stress disorder (PTSD)	The clinical diagnosis for individuals who become depressed due to a traumatic event in their lives.
Preliminary Damage Assessment (PDA)	A more detailed assessment of impacts that typically takes place within days or weeks of the event; it determines possibility and extent of outside assistance.
Public assistance	Relief programs that make aid available to government entities which have been affected by terrorism.
Rapid assessment	A quick survey of impacts designed to gain an appreciation of the scope of the attack.
Technical assessment	A survey of damages that points out methods and costs for rebuilding.
Unmet needs committee	A group of concerned citizens and community leaders who work together to collect donations and address long terms needs of victims.
Volunteer management	The harnessing of volunteers to take advantage of their potential contributions while averting potential negative consequences.
Volunteer registration center	The location where citizens fill out forms noting their skills and other information which can help you when making assignments.

REFERENCES

Barnett-Queen, Timothy and Lawrence H. Bergmann. (1989). "Counseling and Critical Incident Stress." *The Voice* (August/September): 15–18.

Bathos, Stuart, Gwyndaf Williams and Lynne Russell. (1999). "Crisis Management to Controlled Recovery: The Emergency Planning Response to the Bombing of the Manchester City Centre." *Disasters* 23 (3): 217–233.

Hampson, Rick and Martha T. Moore. (2003). "Two Years After Sept. 11, NYC Couple to Bury Son." *USA Today*. Thursday, September 4, 1A–2A.

Hooft, Peter J., Eric K. Noji and Herman P. Van De Voorde. (1989). "Fatality Management in Mass Casualty Incidents." *Forensic Science International* 40: 3–14.

Lowe, Seana and Alice Fothergill. (2003). "A Need to Help: Emergent Volunteer Behavior after September 11th." Pp. 293–314 in Monday, Jacquelyn L. (Ed.) *Beyond September 11th: An Account of Post-Disaster Research*. Natural Hazards Research and Applications Information Center, University of Colorado: Boulder, CO.

McEntire, David A. (2002). "Understanding and Improving Damage Assessment." *IAEM Bulletin* (May): 9, 12.

McEntire, David A., Robie J. Robinson, Richard T. Weber. (2001). "Managing the Threat of Terrorism." *IQ Report* 33 (12). International City/County Management Association: Washington, D.C.

McEntire, David A., Robie J. Robinson, Richard T. Weber. (2003). "Business Responses to the World Trade Center Disaster: A Study of Corporate Roles, Functions and Interaction with the Public Sector." Pp. 431–457 in Monday, Jacquelyn L. (Ed.) *Beyond September 11th: An Account of Post-Disaster Research*. Natural Hazards Research and Applications Information Center, University of Colorado: Boulder, CO.

Mitchell, James K. (1988). "Stress: The History, Status and Future of Critical Incident Stress Debriefings." *JEMS* 13 (11): 47–52.

Neal, David M. (1994). "The Consequences of Unrequested Donations: The Case of Hurricane Andrew." *Disaster Management* 6 (1): 23–28.

Oaks, Sherry D. (1990). "The Damage Assessment Process: An Overview." Pp. 6–16 in Bolin, Robert (Ed.). *The Loma Prieta Earthquake: Studies of Short-Term Impacts*. Program on Environment and Behavior Monograph #50. Institute of Behavioral Science, University of Colorado: Boulder, CO.

Oklahoma Department of Civil Emergency Management. (1996). Donations Management Case Study of the Alfred P. Murrah Federal Building Bombing, 19 April 1995 in Oklahoma City, Oklahoma: Summary and Lessons Learned. Oklahoma City, OK.

Scanlon, Joseph. (1998). "Dealing with Mass Death after a Community Catastrophe: Handling Bodies after the 1917 Halifax Explosion." *Disaster Prevention and Management* 7 (4): 288–304.

Thompson, J. and Hawkes, R. (1962). "Disaster Community Organization and Administrative Process." Pp. 268–300 in Baker, G. and D. Chapman (Eds.). *Man and Society in Disaster*. Basic Books: New York.

Wedel, Kenneth R. and Donald R. Baker. (1998). "After the Oklahoma City Bombing: A Case Study of the Resource Coordination Committee." *International Journal of Mass Emergencies and Disasters* 16 (3): 333–362.

LOOKING TOWARD THE FUTURE

Forthcoming Challenges and Opportunities

Do You Already Know?

- The challenges facing homeland security in the future
- The dangers of radiological and nuclear weapons
- Ways to respond to biological and chemical weapons
- The need for accountability in homeland security

For additional questions to assess your current knowledge of the future of homeland security, go to **www.wiley.com/college/mcentire**

What You Will Find Out	What You Will Be Able To Do
13.1 Anticipated challenges facing homeland security in the future	• Predict new threats confronting the United States
13.2 The dangers of radiological weapons	• Estimate the outcome of dirty bombs
13.3 The potential impact of nuclear weapons	• Evaluate the consequences of nuclear terrorism
13.4 What to do about biological weapons	• Select ways to respond to biological attacks
13.5 The types of chemical weapons	• Plan how to respond to chemical weapons
13.6 The need for accountability in homeland security	• Critique prior problems in homeland security and devise new strategies for dealing with terrorism

INTRODUCTION

If you are to prevent terrorist attacks and minimize their consequences, you must anticipate future challenges and be prepared to embrace potential opportunities. You must be aware of the probability of terrorist attacks which involve radiological, nuclear, biological, and chemical weapons. Understanding the threat they pose, the ability of terrorists to acquire such weapons, and the effects of their use will be imperative. In addition, you must take a number of measures to prevent their use or react effectively should attacks occur anyway. Another important obligation you have is to promote accountability in homeland security. Success can only be achieved when policies are based on sound principles, when resources are used wisely, and when those involved in homeland security work diligently to accomplish goals.

13.1 THE FUTURE OF TERRORISM AND WMD

There are innumerable concerns about the future of terrorism. There are new terrorist groups appearing each day and their motivation for attacks is becoming more ingrained and intense. For instance, domestic terrorist groups remain a constant threat, in spite of the fact that they do not get much publicity or attention from the media. In contrast, some environmental groups play a much greater role in terrorism than was the case in the past. Terrorism may also take on new forms in the future. Cyber-terrorism attacks are expected to grow in quantify and sophistication. There is also the chance of suicide bombings or mass shootings in crowded public areas. All of these threats have implications for homeland security policy and programs.

IN THE REAL WORLD

Al Qaeda and WMD

Research illustrates that terrorists are taking many measures to acquire and use weapons of mass destruction. Dunn's study (2008) reveals that Al Qaeda is working diligently to obtain weapons of mass destruction. For instance, it is believed that Al Qaeda operatives attempted to purchase radiological material in Russia and elsewhere. Hard evidence suggests that Al Qaeda contacted scientists in Pakistan to learn more about nuclear weapons. Training manuals seized in Afghanistan reveal that labs were beginning to develop ricin and botulinum toxin. Al Qaeda ran experiments to test the impact of cyanide on dogs in 2001. Dunn believes that Al Qaeda would not think twice about using WMD if it is successful in acquiring and testing them.

Of course, the main area of focus right now is on radical Islamic terrorists. These individuals and groups have vowed to bring the fight again to the United States. They are growing discontent with simply fighting American troops in Afghanistan and Iraq. Their desire is to affect the West directly by launching attacks on our own soil. Countries, including Iran and Syria, are increasing their support of terrorism (financially and in other ways). For instance, Iran trains terrorists within its borders, has funded operations in Lebanon and Israel, and sends soldiers and weapons into Iraq to be employed against American soldiers. More worrisome yet, is the fact that Iran is developing nuclear technology. While the leaders of this country maintain they are taking this course of action to meet future energy needs, it is also possible that highly enriched uranium could be used for belligerent purposes. If this occurs, Israel or the United States could be targeted or blackmailed by Iran. It is also possible that Iran could share nuclear materials or weapons with terrorist organizations. This would theoretically make it more difficult to prevent attacks or trace responsibility to Iran. In any case, Iran is regarded by many to be a major threat in the Middle East and toward the United States. Its leaders have clearly stated their desire to attack us. Should diplomacy fail to bring about desired results, sanctions and all-out war are possible retaliatory measures in the future.

The threat of nuclear materials being developed in Iran brings up the most pressing future concern in homeland security: weapons of mass destruction.

Figure 13-1

Leaders in Iran have claimed their right to develop their country's nuclear capabilities, but they have also stated in the past their desire to act violently against America and others.

Weapons of Mass Destruction (WMD):
Weaponry that will create major injuries, carnage, destruction, and disruption when utilized.

As noted in earlier chapters, **Weapons of Mass Destruction (WMD)** are weaponry that will create major carnage, destruction, and disruption when utilized. WMD is not only possible, but probable in the future. Virtually all scholars and policy experts agree that prospective attacks will likely involve weapons of mass destruction in the future. There are numerous reasons why this is the case. *America's Achilles Heal*, a study by three terrorism experts, Falkenrath, Newman, and Thayer (1998, 5–6), reveals that terrorists may seek and use weapons of mass destruction for the following reasons:

- **Massive casualties.** Weapons of mass destruction may result in an overwhelming number of injuries and fatalities. Over 5,000 people sought medical care after the 1995 sarin gas attack on a Tokyo subway in Japan. Hundreds of thousands or even millions of people could be adversely impacted by weapons of mass destruction.

- **Degraded response capabilities.** Terrorism involving weapons of mass destruction will have at least three consequences for first responders. First, countless police, fire and emergency medical technicians will be numbered among the victims of these types of attacks. Second, first responders will be overwhelmed by the demands placed upon them by the other victims. Third, responding to WMD attacks will require a great deal of knowledge and skill. Unfortunately, this expertise may not currently be available among all first responders due to the technical nature of WMD and insufficient training or funding programs.

- **Contamination.** The use of WMD has a significant negative consequence on the environment. Because of the dangers associated with weapons of mass destruction, the impacted area may require remediation. In certain cases, the location of the attack may be uninhabitable for days, weeks, months, and years. The accidental release of radiation in Chernobyl illustrates this potential in vivid manner. Decades after the incident, the area is still considered hazardous and is therefore declared uninhabitable.

- **Economic damage.** An attack involving weapons of mass destruction will have extensive financial consequences. Direct financial losses will include the loss of buildings, property and the infrastructure as well as the costs associated with response and recovery. Indirect economic losses could result from disruptions in business transactions, astronomical insurance payouts or unsettled claims, and resulting unemployment. The terrorist attacks on 9/11 cost at least $40 billion; future costs could be unimaginable.

- **Psychological impact.** Because the outcome of any WMD attack is likely to be significant in so many ways, victims and others witnessing this type of terrorism may feel intense fear. Anxiety, sleeplessness, stress and other emotional tolls are likely. While most people are resilient after major events, terrorism adds psychological distress because it is intentionally caused.

IN THE REAL WORLD

WMD Identifiers

When responding to terrorist attacks, you should pay special attention to WMD identifiers. FEMA has identified several of them (1999, 25–26):

Biological
- Unusual numbers of sick or dying people or animals
- Dissemination of unscheduled and unusual sprays, especially outdoors and/or at night
- Abandoned spray devices with no distinct odors

Nuclear
- Presence of Department of Transportation placards and labels
- Monitoring devices

Incendiary
- Multiple fires
- Remains of incendiary devices
- Odors of accelerants
- Heavy burning
- Fire volume

Chemical
- Massive onset of similar symptoms in a large group of people
- Mass fatalities
- Hazardous materials or lab equipment that is not relevant to the occupancy
- Exposed individuals reporting unusual odors and tastes
- Explosions dispersing liquids, mists, or gasses
- Explosions that destroy a package or the bomb devise alone
- Unscheduled dissemination of an unusual spray
- Abandoned spray devices
- Numerous dead animals, fish, and birds
- Absence of insect life in a warm climate
- Mass casualties without obvious trauma
- Distinct pattern of casualties and common symptoms
- Civilian panic in potential target areas, e.g., government buildings, public assemblies, subway systems, etc.

Explosive
- Large-scale damage to a building
- Blown-out windows
- Scattered debris
- Victims with shrapnel-induced trauma
- Appearance of shock-like symptoms
- Damage to eardrums

- **Political change.** The use of WMD could result in significant governmental changes. The freedoms we enjoy could be seriously curtailed in an attempt to respond effectively after an attack occurs. Isolationism or vengeance in foreign policy is another possibility if terrorists use WMD. The organizational and policy changes after 9/11 are indicative of how societies can change after major terrorist attacks.

Of course, not all types of WMD will have each of these impacts to the same degree. This is because weapons of mass destruction may range from crude bombs made out of common household cleaning products as well as more elaborate and large scale explosives comprised of fuel and fertilizers acquired from commercial outlets. However, the most feared WMDs include radiological, nuclear, biological, and chemical weapons. For this reason, each of these will be discussed in turn.

SELF-CHECK

1. Cyber-terrorism is expected to decline in frequency in the future. True or False?

2. Scholars and practitioners are increasingly fearful of WMD use in the future. True or False?

3. WMD produces injuries and deaths, but not social disruption. True or False?

4. Responding to WMD attacks is difficult because:

   (a) responders are likely to be victims.
   (b) there will be a large number of victims.
   (c) responses to WMD require technical expertise.
   (d) all of the above.

5. Discuss three reasons why terrorists may use WMD in future attacks.

13.2 RADIOLOGICAL WEAPONS

Radiological weapons:
Weapons that spread dangerous radiological material but do not result in a nuclear explosion. Radiological weapons are also known as radiological dispersion devices (RDDs) or dirty bombs.

Radiological weapons spread dangerous radiological material but do not result in a nuclear explosion. Instead, these Radiological Dispersion Devices (RDDs) are made out of a combination of conventional explosives and nuclear materials. RDDs are commonly known as dirty bombs. Terrorism involving radiological material can also occur by simply exposing it to people and the environment. In other words, terrorists could place a container with radiological material in a subway and then remove the lid. This would affect all those in the immediate vicinity. As you will soon learn, the alpha, beta, and gamma radiation in these bombs generate additional complications beyond more routine terrorist activities.

Radioactive substances are not readily available to the average person. However, they can be obtained from hospitals, industrial facilities, and elsewhere (e.g., the black market or smugglers). Philip Purpura, a well-known security expert, asserts that radiological materials are used for various commercial purposes, including food sterilization and the treatment of cancer (2007, 74). Unfortunately, the sources for dirty bombs or radiological dispersion devices are not always secure. "Since 1999 . . . federal investigators have documented 1,300 cases of lost, stolen, or abandoned radiological material" in the United States (Purpura 2007, 74). There are also over 100 countries that have not adequately controlled radiological substances. The ease of access (in comparison to other types of WMD) as well as their potential negative impacts makes radiological weapons inviting to terrorists.

IN THE REAL WORLD

Radiological Terrorism

Terrorism involving radiological material is not a theoretical proposition, but an empirical reality. Gavin Cameron (1998), an expert at the Centre of Military and Strategic Studies, observes that radiological terrorism is more common than one might think. In 1974, a man called police and noted that he had placed a non-lethal amount of Iodine-131 on a train bound to Rome. The material was stolen as it was being shipped to a hospital. The man took this action due to his grievance about the treatment of mentally ill patients in Austria. In 1985, a man sent a letter to the Mayor of New York demanding the release of a prisoner. If the city failed to respond adequately, plutonium tricholride would be placed in reservoirs serving New York. Although there was no proof that the threat was acted upon, the U.S. Department of Energy did find elevated levels of plutonium in the water. In 1993, a Moscow businessman was killed when the Russian Mafia placed gamma-ray emitting pellets in his office. In 1996, three men attempted to kill officials of the Republican Party by placing radium in the victims' cars, food, and toothpaste. One man was found unfit to stand trial (on grounds of insanity) and the other two were sentenced for their participation in the attack. In 1995, the Chechen guerrilla leader, Shamyl Basayev, placed radioactive material in Ismailovo Park. Russian authorities were able to find the Cesium 137 wrapped in a yellow plastic bag and contained in a case. In 2001, Ivan Ivanov, a Bulgarian businessman, told British officials that he was asked by bin Laden's associates to obtain radiological material. He was also offered $200,000 to acquire fuel rods from the Kozlodui nuclear power plant in Bulgaria.

Surprisingly, radiological weapons have not been used frequently in the past. Nevertheless, there have been confirmed attempts or actual uses of radiological weapons. Jose Padilla, a U.S. citizen trained by Al Qaeda in Afghanistan, was arrested for plotting to use a radiological dispersion device in Chicago. In another incident, Ceisum-137 was left in a Moscow park by Chechen separatists (Falkenrath, Newman, and Thayer 1998, 42). Although a gram of this radiological material was not enough to harm the population, it did generate a significant amount of media interest. Since instilling fear in others is a major motivator for terrorists, the recognition gained by radiological dispersion devices make them attractive weapons. For these reasons, it is highly likely that radiological weapons will be employed in the future.

If used, radiological weapons could pose health hazards to humans. The length of exposure will determine the extent of injuries and deaths. Those who are exposed for a brief time may not suffer any notable consequences. However, a strong dose or prolonged exposure could lead to immediate fatalities or cancer that develops over time. In addition, radiological weapons could contaminate geographic locations for an extended period. Even if the amount of radiological material dispersed is insignificant, the presence of such substances could create social disruption and concern. People will not want to live or work in an area that has been exposed. This could lead to major evacuations, housing shortages, and economic decline around the nation.

The theft of radioactive material from a medical clinic in Brazil illustrates the potential negative outcome of dirty bombs. In 1987, scavengers entered an abandoned medical facility and came across a container with radiological material. They broke the source open, thereby releasing the radioactive material into the environment. As a result, "four people died, more than 100,000 others had to be monitored for contamination, and cleanup costs amounted to tens of millions of dollars" (Ferguson and Lubenau 2008, 139).

In order to prevent the use of radiological weapons, it will be imperative to secure the sources of this material. For instance, each year, 50 radioactive gauges are stolen from the oil industry in Nigeria (Ferguson and Lubenau 2008, 141). If such thefts are to be prevented, the material will have to be held under lock and key or protected by armed guards. The issuing of licenses (allowing the legal use of radiological materials) should also be carefully controlled. As an example, Stuart Lee Adelman posed as a professor in 1996 and successfully obtained radiological material. He pled guilty to this fraud and was sentenced to five years in prison (Ferguson and Lubeanu 2008, 143). Terrorists may also seek radiological materials through such deception. Records should therefore be carefully kept and shipments should also be meticulously monitored. Homeland security personnel should ensure that steps are taken to prevent terrorists from acquiring radiological material.

If radiological weapons are used by terrorists, it will be imperative to rely on the expertise of highly trained individuals. Normally, this will require military personnel or others who have knowledge and understanding of how to isolate and clean up radiological material. The Department of Defense has 55 **Civil Support Teams** around the nation, with more on the way. These teams can be quickly activated and mobilized to respond to this type of event anywhere in the country. They assist local and state governments in identifying hazardous agents (including radiological dispersion devices), determining consequences and appropriate response techniques, and requesting additional support if required. Other military

Civil Support Teams:
Specialized military units that assist local and state governments that have been affected by weapons of mass destruction.

Figure 13-2

Civil Support Teams can help local jurisdictions deal with attacks involving weapons of mass destruction.

personnel, from U.S. NORTHCOM (Northern Command), may also be activated to assist when circumstances warrant their assistance. Medical personnel and coroners will also be needed to treat the injured. A major priority is to wash those affected by the radiation and "purge inhaled or ingested materials" (Purpura 2007, 305). The disposal of deceased must be completed in the proper manner (assuring that others are not contaminated in the process).

In order to be prepared for terrorism involving radiological materials, monitoring devices should be strategically placed around cities to detect their presence. This is especially important in that radiological dispersion devices may or may not have an obvious and associated explosion. The lack of forewarning or the desire to avert drawing attention to this type of attack means that these weapons can be employed covertly. In addition, radiological materials cannot be detected by the senses because they are colorless and odorless. The only way to know that they have been used at times is through constant monitoring of the environment. Having adequate equipment will also be necessary for those responding to radiological dispersion devices. This may include Geiger counters, personal protective clothing covering the entire body, and breathing apparatus. Keeping a safe distance from the radiological materials or limiting time of exposure is another recommendation when responding to this type of terrorist attacks.

IN THE REAL WORLD

Treating Radiation Poisoning

Three medical experts in the Dallas/Fort-Worth area, Elvin Adams, Ira Nemeth, and John White, assert that Radiological poisoning can be minimized in some cases. If a person has been exposed to radioactive U-235, an antidote of baking soda and water can be administered to eliminate the radioactive isotope from the body. If Cesium has been used in an attack, the pigment Prussian blue can bind the cesium and carry it out in the stool. If Iodine 131 is present in the environment, the administration of Potassium Iodide will help. Large doses are required to saturate the thyroid in order to block exposure to radioactive I-131. If given to the victim quickly, some forms of cancer can be prevented. The most critical method to prevent dangerous internal exposure is to prevent ingestion of a radiological agent. Use of an N-95 mask will prevent inhaling of the agent. When drinking is required, using a straw to prevent ingestion of materials on the lips will significantly reduce the amount of radioisotopes taken into the body.

SELF-CHECK

1. Examples of radiological weapons include dirty bombs and radiological dispersion devices. True or False?

2. There have been no cases of radiological weapons use in the past. True or False?

3. Which country illustrates the potential deaths and economic impact of radiological terrorism?
   - (a) Nigeria
   - (b) Brazil
   - (c) Colombia
   - (d) Iran

4. What experts will be needed to react effectively to radiological terrorism?

13.3 NUCLEAR WEAPONS

Nuclear weapons:
Weapons that produce massive explosions due to the release of vast amounts of energy through fission or fusion.

Suitcase bomb:
Portable nuclear weapons.

Nuclear weapons also contain radiological material as dirty bombs or RDDs do. However, **nuclear weapons** produce massive explosions due to the release of vast amounts of energy through the process of nuclear fission or fusion. Most nuclear weapons are placed in the tip of rockets and cruise missiles. However, portable nuclear weapons are also possible. In fact, many experts in homeland security fear the use of a **suitcase bomb**.

Nuclear weapons are possessed by major powers including China, France, Great Britain, Russia, and the United States. India, Israel, North Korea, and Pakistan also have nuclear weapons, and it is believed that Iran is actively seeking to develop them. While it would be difficult for terrorist organizations to acquire highly enriched material for nuclear bombs, it is not impossible to rule out their success in obtaining them. Theft, blackmail and bribery are all potential ways of acquiring plutonium or other nuclear material. Once obtained, any organization with sufficient knowledge and technological sophistication may build nuclear weapons. Information on their construction is accessible in scientific journals, academic books, or even on the Internet. It is also true that states possessing nuclear weapons may also simply give them to known terrorists. This is why the United States and others are currently concerned about Iran and other countries that oppose the United States and the West.

Should nuclear weapons be acquired and used in a terrorist attack, the impacts are almost unimaginable. The devastation produced by the nuclear weapons at the end of World War II was impressive. America's use of the A-bomb killed approximately 130,000 and 65,000 in Hiroshima and Nagasaki respectively. But today's technology is far superior. The explosion of a nuclear weapon produces a mushroom cloud that can be seen from miles and miles away. In the blink of an eye, people and property in the immediate area (perhaps a 15 mile radius or greater) would simply be vaporized. Those on the outskirts would be killed by the intense heat, injured by flying debris, or blinded by the extreme light produced in the explosion. Sickness and death from radiological poisoning would also take place, requiring a major medical and mass fatality response. The infrastructure would be severely damaged and the environment would be contaminated for decades. Living near the blast or fallout zone would be impossible due to the health consequences of radiation. Due to the loss of businesses and impact on the stock market, serious economic repercussions would be inevitable. Government would cease to exist or function in the immediate area, and nearby jurisdictions would be severely hampered. The results truly bring up images of Armageddon.

In order to prevent the use of nuclear weapons by terrorists, those involved in homeland security must work closely with intelligence officials, foreign governments, military agencies and multi-lateral institutions to avert proliferation. **Proliferation** is the acquisition, sharing, and spread of nuclear weapons and materials to those who do not currently possess them. The **Non-Proliferation Treaty (NPT)** is an international regime designed to prevent nuclear states from providing nuclear weapons or materials to those who do not possess them. It was initiated in 1968 due to the Cold War, and has been signed by over 180 governments around the world. It is administered by the **International Atomic Energy Agency (IAEA)**.

Unfortunately, not everyone has signed the NPT and others may not adhere to IAEA requirements. As an example, Iran has disregarded the wishes of the NPT and hindered the activities of the IAEA and others. Furthermore, terrorist organizations are not signatories of the treaty because they are not nation-states. In addition, one radical Saudi cleric states that it would be morally permissible to use a nuclear bomb against the United States as a way to stop American actions against Muslims (Bunn and Wier 2008, 125). The loopholes in the NPT and desire of others to acquire nuclear materials and technology limit 100 percent compliance.

Bunn and Wier's chapter in *Weapons of Mass Destruction and Terrorism* dispels seven myths pertaining to nuclear terrorism:

- Some terrorists do want to use nuclear weapons against the United States and others. Osama bin Laden has declared this to be a major priority.

- Acquiring nuclear material is not impossible. Bribery and theft are only two of the many ways terrorists may acquire highly enriched uranium or plutonium.

- Building a nuclear weapon is not improbable. The U.S. Office of Technology Assessment asserts that a small group of individuals could build such a device if they were sufficiently committed.

- Setting off a nuclear weapon is not as unlikely as is commonly believed. Some of the older weapons in the possession of Russia do not have permissive action links (electronic locks requiring coded access).

Proliferation:
The acquisition, sharing, and spread of nuclear weapons and materials to those who do not currently possess them.

Non-Proliferation Treaty (NPT):
An international regime designed to prevent nuclear states from giving nuclear weapons or materials to those who do not possess them.

International Atomic Energy Agency (IAEA):
The international organization responsible for the enforcement of the non-proliferation treaty.

- State sponsorship in obtaining nuclear weapons is not a requirement. As long as nuclear materials can be acquired, individuals and groups will be able to manufacture nuclear weapons independently.

- Smuggling a nuclear device into the United States is likely to be achieved. It would be very difficult for border officials to prevent the delivery of a nuclear weapon or its component parts because of the vast quantity of goods that enter our nation each day through legal and illegal means.

- A strong military offensive will not stop terrorists from using nuclear weapons. Counter-terrorism operations have not prevented terrorist attacks in the past and there is no reason to believe they will be 100 percent successful in the future.

For these and other reasons, it is essential to prepare for a terrorist attack involving a nuclear weapon. Preparing for this scenario is likely to be undertaken especially by the military and medical communities. Personnel in the armed forces have special training on nuclear weapons in addition to personnel protective gear and radiological monitoring devices. Doctors, nurses, and paramedics will also be needed to care for the injured. Those exposed to radiation will lose hair and experience the destruction of cells that are vital for the brain, heart, and other internal organs. There is no way to reverse the effects of this type of radiation exposure, although symptoms can be relieved through various medical treatments.

Because of the dangers of radiation, government leaders will also need to plan on ways to evacuate hundreds of thousands of people from the impacted area. Such an evacuation could take place if a credible threat is issued or after a nuclear detonation has occurred. Doing so would require detailed evacuation plans that take into account all exit routes and all methods of transportation. Contra-flow strategies with the use of countless law enforcement personnel would be needed along with others to monitor vehicle breakdowns and fuel shortages. However, many vehicles will be rendered useless due to the electro-magnetic pulse associated with nuclear weapons.

Any mass evacuation will also necessitate large quantities of sheltering and housing. Hurricane Katrina resulted in one of largest evacuations in U.S. history (the California wildfires of 2007 were another exception). The destruction of New Orleans and surrounding cities caused over one million people to migrate to other locations. Every state received evacuees. This led to the need for short term shelters operated by organizations like the American Red Cross. The integration of evacuees into long-term residential housing will also be required after terrorist attacks, which will lead to severe shortages in the housing market and place significant burdens on the construction industry. This is to say nothing about the need to help evacuees find schools, obtain jobs, and gain a sense of belonging in their new community. Evacuation is a short-term action that has long-term consequences for those involved in homeland security.

FOR EXAMPLE

Future Possibilities of Nuclear Terrorism

Research reveals differing opinions about the future possibility of nuclear terrorism (Maerli, Schaper, and Barnaby 1998). Some assume that terrorists will attack a U.S. city as soon as they are able to acquire nuclear weapons. Others assert that other types of WMD are more likely to be employed due to the technical requirements associated with developing nuclear weapons. While the risks of nuclear terrorism may be low, the unimaginable consequences should warn us about complacency or a false sense of security. If terrorists cannot obtain nuclear weapons from supporting governments, they may be able to make crude weapons such as those that destroyed Hiroshima and Nagasaki during World War II. If terrorists are able to obtain nuclear material, says one nuclear-weapons physicist, "even a high school kid could make a bomb in short order" (Alvarez in Maerli, Schaper and Barnaby 1998, 115).

SELF-CHECK

1. The only threat of nuclear terrorism comes from missiles and rockets. True or False?

2. Pakistan currently possesses a nuclear weapon. True or False?

3. Which of the following is not associated with nuclear weapons?

   (a) Radiation sickness
   (b) Vaporization of people in the immediate detonation area
   (c) Immunity through vaccination programs
   (d) Injuries due to fires and flying debris

4. What is the Non-Proliferation Treaty?

13.4 BIOLOGICAL WEAPONS

Biological weapons:
Living organisms, or agents produced by living organisms, that may be used in terrorist attacks.

Another major concern among those in homeland security is biological weapons. **Biological weapons** are living organisms, or agents produced by living organisms, that may be used in terrorist attacks. There are three types of biological agents that can be converted into weapons of mass destruction:

Bacteria:
A single cell organism that causes disease in plants, animals, and humans.

- **Bacteria** are single cell organisms that cause disease in plants, animals and humans. Anthrax is an example of such pathogens that can be reproduced on their own.

Virus:
A microscopic genetic particle that infects the cells of living organisms but cannot multiply outside a host cell.

Toxin:
A poison that is produced by plants or animals.

- A **virus** is a microscopic genetic particle that infects the cells of living organisms. It lives inside a host cell and cannot multiply outside of this location. Ebola, small pox and AIDS are well-known viruses.
- A **toxin** is a poison that is produced by plants or animals. They vary in strength, but can destroy blood cells, tissues, and the central nervous system. Ricin is frequently mentioned as a toxin.

Developing and using biological weapons in attacks is ironically straightforward and difficult at the same time (Falkenrath, Newman, and Thayer 1998). On the one hand, converting biological agents into weapons is relatively simple. A seed stock of the agent must be acquired and then it must be produced in bulk. Information to accomplish this objective is widely available in the scientific literature and medical community. Equipment to reach this goal is also present in many locations because of numerous research or commercial enterprises engaged in bio-engineering. On the other hand, it is admittedly more challenging to store, transport, and disseminate biological weapons. For instance, there are significant technical hurdles inhibiting the development of aerosol dissemination, unless the perpetrator is willing to utilize less effective methods for spreading the biological agent.

IN THE REAL WORLD

The 2001 Anthrax Crisis

Shortly after the 9/11 attacks, an unknown person or group sent four envelopes containing powdered anthrax spores from Trenton, New Jersey (Thomas 2003). The first victim was a photo editor who worked with the National Enquirer. Over the next several weeks, 21 others became ill. Four of these individuals succumbed to the effects of inhalation anthrax. Because antibiotics can stop infection and treat anthrax disease, the government implemented an aggressive prophylactic treatment; 32,000 people were given antibiotics for 10 days. Of these, 10,000 were also given a 60-day treatment. Although it was impossible to tell who was infected, public health officials and the CDC believed that this measure saved countless lives. As the emergency period ended, focus shifted to other issues. The post office and other buildings had to be cleaned of any remaining anthrax. These facilities had to be shut down for an extended period of time until they were believed to be free of any remaining biological agent. The FBI initiated a massive manhunt to determine who was involved in the attacks. By the end of 2007, no one had been charged for the attacks. The anthrax crisis in 2001 illustrates the deadly and disruptive potential of bio-terrorism along with the difficulty of prosecution.

Category A agents:
Biological weapons that pose a serious risk to people because they are easily transmitted to others and they result in high mortality rates.

Category B agents:
Biological weapons that have a moderate chance of contagion and generally result in lower morbidity rates than Category A agents.

Category C agents:
Biological weapons that could be used for mass dissemination and high morbidity if engineered for that purpose.

The impacts of biological weapons will vary dramatically, depending on the type of agent used and the method of distribution. **Category A agents** pose a serious risk to people because they are easily transmitted to others and they result in high mortality rates. Small pox is an example of these types of biological weapons. **Category B agents** have a moderate chance of contagion and generally result in lower morbidity rates than Category A agents. Typhus fever is an example of Category B agents. **Category C agents** could theoretically be used for mass dissemination and high morbidity if engineered for that purpose. An example of this type of agent is hantavirus.

	Category A Agents	Category B Agents	Category C Agents
Example	Plague	Viral encephalitis	West Nile Virus
Transmissibility	High	Moderate	Low
Mortality Rates	High	Moderate	Low

Bio-terrorism:
Terrorism that employs biological weapons.

The effects of **bio-terrorism**—terrorism that employs biological weapons—will also be dependent on whether it is absorbed through cracks in the skin, ingestion, or inhalation. Depending on the agent used, extent of exposure, and health of the victim, symptoms may appear quickly or over time. They may include fever, respiratory distress, vomiting and diarrhea, painful lesions, blackened fingers and toes, shock, paralysis, and death in certain cases. Ricin is one example of a biological agent. It is a toxin that is produced by plants and can be very deadly. While ricin may kill only those who have been directly exposed to it, other types of biological weapons could kill countless people. Respiration (e.g., coughing) or physical contact (e.g., touching pustules) are factors in contagion. The ease of travel today may also spread diseases around the nation and world within days. In 2007, an infected passenger traveled from Europe to the United States even though he was known to have been diagnosed with tuberculosis. In another case, Severe Acute Respiratory Syndrome (SARS) spread rapidly in Canada and Hong Kong as people travel within cities or to distant locations.

It is vital to recognize that humans may not be the only target of biological attacks however. David Franz, the Director of the National Agricultural and Biosecurity Center, notes that hoof and mouth disease could easily be used in a terrorist attack (1998, 190). It is readily available in the natural environment, it does not pose a risk to humans, and it would easily spread through the livestock population. **Agro-terrorism**, or terrorism against farming industries and products, must therefore be taken into consideration as well.

Agro-terrorism:
Terrorism against farming industries and products.

Preventing bio-terrorism or agro-terrorism is similar to efforts to inhibit terrorism involving radiological or nuclear weapons. That is to say, the proliferation of biological agents among states and non-state actors should be strongly opposed by the international community.

Biological Weapons Convention (BWC):
An international treaty designed to prevent the proliferation of biological agents around the world.

The **Biological Weapons Convention (BWC)** has this purpose, but it also suffers from the weaknesses of the NPT. As an example, Iraq successfully hid its anthrax program from the United Nations until after the first Gulf War. For this reason, George W. Bush's administration observed that the BWC was "inherently unverifiable" in 2001 (Chyba and Greniger 1998, 1999).

Minimizing the threat of bio-terrorism will likewise require the close monitoring of biological agents in other ways. Efforts, including security and verification of legitimate use, should be taken to limit access to qualified medical personnel and researchers only. Protecting air intakes of buildings and using high efficiency particulate air (HEPA) filters in large occupancy buildings are other methods minimize the possible use or impact of bio-terrorism. Recurring evaluation of herds and crops should also be a top priority of those trying to prevent agro-terrorism. Those involved in the agricultural and ranching sectors must maintain situational awareness at all times. If cattle and agricultural produce appear to have been tainted in any way, they should be reported to the proper authorities immediately. This may include the U.S. Department of Agriculture, the Federal Bureau of Investigation, or the Department of Homeland Security.

Effective responses to a bio-terrorism attack will require a great deal of collaboration among doctors, nurses, public health officials, emergency managers, the National Disaster Medical System (NDMS), and the Center for Disease Control (CDC). It will also necessitate quick distribution of medicines through the strategic national stockpile to state and local governments. The **Strategic National Stockpile (SNS)** is a cache of medicines in secret locations that can be quickly sent to affected locations around the country. This includes 14 push pack components such as antibiotics that can easily fill a 747 aircraft. Medicines can also be obtained from the Vendor Managed Inventory (VMI), which includes drugs manufactured and distributed by large pharmaceutical companies. The goal is to break these pallets of supplies down and send them to the Point of Distribution (PODs) as soon as possible. PODs may be set up at government buildings, schools, churches, or any location that can handle large numbers of people. Victims should be given appropriate shots or pills within as little as 48 hours.

Strategic National Stockpile (SNS):
A cache of medicines in secret locations that can be quickly sent to affected locations around the nation.

In some cases, vaccines can be administered to prevent the agent from impacting victims. For instance, small pox vaccinations have been given to medical personnel and first responders around the nation. If a biological attack does take place, the general population may also be given necessary antibiotics, respiratory treatments, or other forms of prophylaxis. This obviously assumes that the biological agent is identified early enough and that medicines are readily available to be dispersed. Unfortunately, it may take days or weeks to identify a bio-terrorism outbreak and some medicines can only be created long after the proper strain of the pathogen has been identified.

Planning activities must take into consideration the important process of resource distribution. Preparedness measures must also find ways to involve the public. For example, the washing of hands is the single most effective way of reducing the spread of disease. Home nursing care, work-at-home programs, and even quarantines may need to be implemented after a biological terrorist attack. Steps must be taken to isolate infected people and animals from others. Unfortunately, we lack sufficient information on the best methods and effectiveness of quarantines. The last time they were used extensively was during the Spanish Flu outbreak in the early 1900s. More studies of how to deal with bio-terrorism will be required in the future.

IN THE REAL WORLD

Terrorist Attacks vs. Other Types of Disasters

Responding to a terrorist attack involving WMD is similar, in some ways, to other types of disasters. All events may require emergency medical care, media relations, and donations management. However, there are also some significant differences between WMD events and natural disasters. For instance, there may be no warning for a terrorist attack whereas some events like hurricanes provide advanced notification. Debris removal should be handled with care after a terrorist attack since destroyed buildings may contain evidence and can be deadly. There may be greater demand for crisis counseling after a terrorist attack because it has been caused by humans. It is also possible that terrorist attacks involving biological weapons could kill millions of people. People may overrun hospitals because they do not know if they have been affected or not. It is important to be able to compare and contrast the impact of terrorist attacks and other types of disasters so your actions will be appropriate for the situation at hand.

SELF-CHECK

1. Health impacts of biological weapons may include fever, vomiting, paralysis, and death. True or False?

2. A Category B agent is more deadly than a Category A agent. True or False?

3. Which type of biological weapon is a poison produced by plants or animals?
   (a) Bacteria
   (b) Toxin
   (c) Virus
   (d) Category C agents

4. What is the National Strategic Stockpile?

13.5 CHEMICAL WEAPONS

Chemical weapons:
Lethal man-made poisons that can be disseminated as gasses, liquids, or aerosols.

Nerve agents:
Chemical weapons that prevent the transmission of electrical signals in the nervous system.

Vesicants:
Blister agents that produce chemical burns.

Blood agents:
Chemical weapons that prevent the flow of oxygen in the blood.

Choking agents:
Chemical weapons that cause respiratory distress.

Irritants:
Agents that lead to allergic reactions.

Terrorists may also attempt to access and use chemical weapons in the future. Lethal man-made poisons that can be disseminated as gasses, liquids, or aerosols are known as **chemical weapons** (Falkenrath, Newman and Thayer 1998, 17). Chemical weapons are divided into five categories:

- **Nerve agents** prevent the transmission of electrical signals in the nervous system. An example of nerve agent is soman.
- **Vesicants** are blister agents that produce chemical burns on the body. Lewisite is a type of vesicant.
- **Blood agents** prevent the flow of oxygen in the blood. Cyanide is an example of a blood agent.
- **Choking agents** inhibit the pulmonary system. Phosgene falls into the category of choking agents.
- **Irritants** are agents that lead to allergic reactions (e.g., tearing, runny nose, or respiratory distress). Mace is a common example of an irritant.

Chemical Weapons	Example	Impacts
Nerve Agents	Sarin	Convulsion of muscles
Vessicants	Mustard gas	Burns/blisters on the skin
Blood Agents	Cyanide	Depletion of oxygenated blood
Choking Agents	Chlorine	Suffocation
Irritants	Pepper spray	Allergic reactions

Many countries used chemical weapons during World War I. Today, many countries have eliminated their stockpiles, but could produce them in a moments notice. Others, including Iran and Syria, are believed to be current possessors of chemical weapons. Thus, it is possible that terrorists could obtain chemical weapons from governments around the world. Theft and bribery are, again, possible ways for terrorists to obtain chemical weapons.

Virtually any individual or organization could produce chemical weapons since their precursor materials are available from legitimate commercial suppliers (Falkenrath, Newman, and Thayer 1998, 103). It is estimated that the United States produces 300,000 metric tons of cyanide to be used in electroplating, dyeing, printing, and the production of plastics (Tucker 2008, 217). Ordinary household chemicals or supplies from mail-order companies could also be used to acquire chemical weapons.

For instance, terrorist organizations like Aum Shinrikyo have developed chemical weapons in the past. Aum Shinrikyo is a quasi-Buddhist sect which was comprised of disillusioned intellectuals from Japan and Russia during the late 1980s (Tucker 2008, 214). Led by Shoko Asahara, this terrorist organization was able to acquire a net worth of $1 billion through legitimate and illegitimate practices. With this money, it desired to instigate a major war between the United States and Japan by using chemical weapons. Scientists were subsequently hired to develop this type of weaponry within the organization's "Ministry of Science and Technology." In time, these technicians were successful in producing sarin, which was later tested on sheep on a remote ranch in Australia. In the mid-1990s, Aum Shinrkyo then used sarin to kill three judges in Matumoto. Seven others were later killed with the use of aerosolize sarin during an attack on a subway in Tokyo. Fortunately, the sarin gas in this latter attack was diluted and not as potent as it could have been.

Chemical weapons may be comprised of conventional explosives that disperse hazardous materials into the atmosphere (e.g., a bomb that disperses chlorine). Alternatively, chemical weapons may be employed by simply releasing chemicals that are normally stored in protective containers (e.g., opening up a valve on a chlorine tanker). Opening a lid or using a spray device to impact others are various means to distribute

Figure 13-3

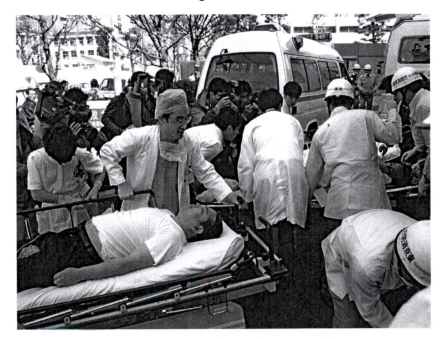

Chemical weapons are both deadly and disruptive
as we witnessed in Japan in 1995.

chemical agents. For instance, chemical weapons could be introduced into a heating, ventilation, and air conditioning (HVAC) system inside a building. Product tampering, injection with a syringe, and the sending of letters or packages with powdery substances are other ways to deliver chemical weapons. Jonathan Tucker, a senior fellow at the Center for Non-Proliferation Studies, provides a list of three more types of chemical weaponry:

- Distribution of military-grade chemical warfare agent into the air.
- Use of toxic agents to contaminate water or food supplies.
- Assassination of a specific individual or group with chemical agents (2008, 213).

In conjunction with the type of attack, the impact of chemical agents could vary significantly. Some chemicals are persistent (meaning that they evaporate slowly) while others dissipate quickly. Certain chemical agents may lead to minor medical problems while others lead to immediate death. Depending on the type of chemical agent used and environmental conditions (i.e., temperature, humidity, and wind speed), results could include physical annoyance, long-term respiratory or central nervous system damage, and widespread mortality. Environmental problems are also likely consequences of chemical weapons. Water and soil can remain contaminated long after a chemical agent has been used in a particular geographic area.

Much like radiological, nuclear or biological weapons, the development of chemical weapons can be minimized by carefully controlling the manufacturing, use, transportation and storage of hazardous materials. Suppliers can also ensure that those requesting chemicals have legitimate and peaceful purposes. Nevertheless, it will be impossible to prevent the acquisition of chemical weapons. Materials and knowledge to make them are everywhere. Known state possessors could also give them to terrorist organizations. Even industry and transportation methods can be used against us. A bomb could release dangerous chemicals at a manufacturing plant. A tanker truck or rail car could also be penetrated, thereby releasing toxic materials in the air near a school, business district or residential area.

The possibility of chemical weapons suggests that much more attention should be given to detection, decontamination, emergency medical response, and environmental reclamation. Planning with the Metropolitan Medical Response System, the Department of Health and Human Services, and the National Disaster Medical System needs to be improved. More paramedics, doctors and nurses will be required to treat the victims of chemical weapons. Training of these individuals should focus on ways to identify chemical weapons and respond effectively. For instance, people should be aware that the FBI has labs to help you to identify what agent is being used. In addition, atropine may need to be administered quickly to victims if their lives are to be spared. Military personnel and some paramedics may have MARK I auto-injector kits for this purpose. MARK I is a spring-loaded injector that has been developed by the military. It contains atropine and an oxime, which can help treat patients affected by nerve agents. MARK I kits and other drugs may only help to save those with moderate exposure however. Also, such medicines will certainly be lacking in a major attack. For instance, only 29 percent of hospitals that responded to a survey had sufficient medicines to care for 50 victims (Tucker 2008, 222). Some larger jurisdictions do have Chempack antidotes strategically placed across the city, but it is unclear if funding is adequate to replace them when the drugs reach their expiration date. Organizational resources, including the Disaster Medical Assistance Teams and environmental restoration companies, will need to be deployed quickly after a chemical attack takes place. Chemical weapons, along with other types of weapons of mass destruction, are all likely to be used by terrorists in the future. It will be crucial that homeland security personnel take measures now to prevent their use or be ready to respond if that cannot be averted.

FOR EXAMPLE

Chemical Terrorism

Between 1960 and 2001, there were only 125 incidents of terrorists using chemical weapons (Tucker 2008). Most of these were small in scope and were committed by a wide range of terrorists (e.g., nationalists, religious extremists, anti-abortion or environmental groups, left-wing and right-wing organizations). However, it is anticipated that the number of chemical weapons attacks will rise in the future. One case in Russia illustrates how easy it is for scientists to develop chemical weapons. A man named Valery Borzov was fired from the Moscow Scientific Research Institute of Reagents in 1997. In order to maintain an income, the 40-year-old chemist started to develop blister agents in his own clandestine laboratory. His desire was to sell vials of the poisonous substance for $1,500 to the Russian mafia or other criminal organizations. When arrested, investigators found recipe books, equipment, and 50 liters of dangerous products in his home. Borzov was found incompetent to stand trial and he was committed to a mental institution. Police were fortunate to interdict his efforts to make money at the expense of others' lives.

SELF-CHECK

1. Chemical weapons are disseminated as liquids only. True or False?

2. Responding to chemical weapons may involve decontamination, emergency medical response, and environmental reclamation. True or False?

3. Which type of agent prevents the transfer of electrical signals in the body?

   (a) Blood agents
   (b) Vesicants
   (c) Irritants
   (d) Nerve agents

4. Why are attacks involving chemical weapons increasingly likely in the future?

13.6 ACCOUNTABILITY AND POLICY IN HOMELAND SECURITY

Those working to counter terrorist activities and minimize their impacts may have some—but not complete—control of the acquisition and use of weapons of mass destruction. However, homeland security officials certainly have the power over the administration of prevention, protection, and preparedness initiatives. National leaders can also shape the direction of policy in the areas of response and recovery in the future.

Unfortunately, it appears that limited vision and poor management have been glaring weaknesses among those responsible for or involved in this national priority. Since its inception, homeland security has suffered continual problems. The leaders and employees of homeland security have at times created and/or ignored innumerable challenges:

- The burial of FEMA within a massive department which focuses almost exclusively on security or law-enforcement concerns jeopardized natural hazard mitigation, terrorism preparedness, and response coordination. The overarching focus on terrorism in this organization and the movement of different programs away from FEMA has hurt the nation's ability to deal with all types of crisis events.

- The structural changes resulting from the creation of DHS also resulted in the loss of ties between the FEMA Director and the President. The lack of communication between Michael Brown and President Bush was readily apparent after Hurricane Katrina struck the United States in 2005. This weakness can be directly traced to the layers of bureaucracy that have been added to emergency management in recent years.

- The rejection of emergency operations plans that proved to be effective in prior disasters and terrorist attacks resulted in unclear expectations for subsequent response activities. The new strategies of the National Response Plan were too complex, convoluted and unclear. Time will tell if the National Response Framework will correct these mistakes.
- The introduction of the Homeland Security Advisory System (HSAS) has lessened the credibility of the government to issue warnings. The HSAS was not based on the scientific literature on how to most effectively notify people of impending harm.
- The distribution of millions of dollars for communications equipment has not led to any real improvement in interoperability. Jurisdictions now have more communications equipment, but the lack of concrete national standards may continue to limit the ability to coordinate with each other.
- A portion of the billions of dollars of financial resources appears to have been squandered on questionable projects or spent in unscrupulous ways. Homeland security funds have been spent on baseball caps and leather bomber jackets instead of on major prevention, protection, or preparedness initiatives as intended.
- The failure to protect U.S. borders against outside infiltration has been one of the most glaring weaknesses of homeland security. In spite of the growing threat of terrorism around the world, it seems as if little has been done to prevent people from simply walking across national boundaries into the United States.

It appears, therefore, that many of the troubles we are currently facing are a result of incorrect planning assumptions as well as ineffective government oversight and follow through. This is not to deny the significant threat of terrorism or the major trials of undertaking the most sweeping reform of government in history. Problems are to be expected when cunning enemies are present and anytime a reorganization of this magnitude takes place. The criticisms against homeland security are not meant to diminish the important roles of the military, intelligence, and law enforcement communities either. Fighting against terrorism would be impossible without these important partners. It is also necessary to note that many of the aforementioned problems are being corrected under the Post-Katrina Emergency Management Reform Act. For example, the President now has closer ties to the FEMA director and some of the preparedness programs have been put back into this important disaster organization.

Accountability:
The expectation of being responsible for decisions and activities.

Nevertheless, accountability seems to be lacking in homeland security. **Accountability** is the expectation of being responsible for decisions and activities that impact citizens in democratic nations. It includes being answerable for failed policies, misused resources, and incomplete goal attainment. In other words, accountability includes constant review of goals and programs in order to overcome mistakes and capitalize on successes. Accountability in homeland security should be a major priority for the future. But accountability will not resolve all of the problems as evidenced in the past.

Perhaps one of the reasons why homeland security programs have failed at times is because our nation does not have a coherent policy for homeland security. Without a definitive statement of the goals of homeland security and methods of attaining them, our efforts to deal with terrorism will continue to flounder aimlessly. For this reason, it is vitally important that you also consider policy issues in homeland security.

As this book reveals, the objectives of homeland security are surprisingly straightforward. The goals of those working in this field are two-fold: 1). reduce the probability of terrorism and, 2). minimize the consequences of attacks that do occur. Put differently, homeland security attempts to limit both the possibility and impact of terrorist attacks. Such intentions will require not only prevention and protection measures, but preparedness, response, and recovery activities as well. Emergency management must therefore be viewed as an equal partner in the homeland security process.

Although clarifying the purpose of homeland security is imperative, this does not necessarily illustrate the means for implementing the desired priorities. For this reason, you might want to consider two proposed concepts to help guide your work in homeland security. These principles are liability reduction and capacity building (McEntire 2005; McEntire 2004).

Liability reduction:
A strategy that attempts to address the factors that result in or permit terrorist attacks.

The means for reducing the *probability* of terrorism is policy that focuses on liability reduction. **Liability reduction** is the name given to the strategy that attempts to address the factors that result in or permit terrorist attacks. This includes both proactive actions and defensive measures. Examples include:

- Understanding what motivates terrorists and working to alleviate root causes.
- Enhancing national security while protecting personal liberty.
- Reducing the permeable nature of the borders.
- Guarding vulnerable infrastructure and key assets.
- Stopping the proliferation of weapons of mass destruction.

Capacity building:
A strategy that attempts to enhance the ability of the nation, states, and communities to effectively deal with potential or actual terrorist attacks.

The way to effectively deal with the *consequences* of terrorism is to enhance response and recovery capabilities. It is known as capacity building. **Capacity building** is a strategy that attempts to enhance the ability of the nation, states, and communities to effectively deal with potential or actual terrorist attacks. This includes:

- Establishing laws and ordinances in homeland security and emergency management.
- Meeting with an advisory council to plan how to best react to terrorist attacks.
- Training responders on important functions including warning, evacuation, sheltering, decontamination, search and rescue, and emergency medical care.
- Helping leaders to understand their roles in disaster declarations, EOC activities, debris management, and individual and public assistance programs.
- Conducting exercises and educating the community about how to prepare for terrorist attacks and other disasters.

While liability reduction and capacity building have thus far been treated as isolated strategies, the reality is that these processes are inherently intertwined. Minimizing liabilities necessitates the development of additional capacities. For instance, surprise attacks can only be averted by augmenting human intelligence. Strengthening capabilities can likewise limit liabilities. As an example, the provision of additional training for first responders could promote increased safety at the scene of attack.

Other complicated relationships among liability reduction and capacity building are also possible. Counter-terrorism activities could aggravate additional terrorist attacks if they result in the death of innocent people, while well-justified offensive operations could increase our ability to protect life and freedoms. In another example, media reports may intensify terrorist behavior unless reporters are made aware of the potential negative impact of their portrayals of terrorism. Failing to understand how terrorists operate will likewise result in future attacks, although improved understanding of the dynamic nature of terrorism can augment readiness for unprecedented violence. Liability reduction and capacity building should thus be seen as mutually reinforcing policies for an effective homeland security apparatus.

Future success in homeland security will largely be dependent upon the ability of DHS and national leaders to formulate a logical mission, identify major priorities, and craft appropriate policies. Support and monitoring of necessary programs as well as the intentional adaptation of a coherent strategy will also be required if we are to successfully deal with terrorism. In short, the threat of future attacks is real and menacing. It is up to you and others involved in homeland security to meet this challenge and do so in a successful manner.

IN THE REAL WORLD

DHS Performance

On September 6, 2007, Paul A. Schneider, the Under Secretary for Management in the Department of Homeland Security, testified before the U.S. Senate Committee on Homeland Security and Governmental Affairs. After reviewing 24 performance expectations dealing with emergency preparedness and response, he revealed that DHS has produced mixed results since it was established. The department succeeded in five areas including grant funding, exercise programs, and the development of a national incident management system. However, DHS was unsuccessful in 18 other areas. Risk assessments, planning, training programs, and interoperable communications were regarded to be unsatisfactory. Other problems included the lack of an inventory of federal capabilities, unclear national goals, and a failure to provide assistance to individuals and communities during emergency events. The Government Accountability Office and other government oversight organizations have also been highly critical of the activities of the Department of Homeland Security. Fortunately, recommendations are being made to correct prior problems. They include improved strategic planning, sharing information with key stakeholders, partnering with other agencies, and integrating DHS' management functions. It is anticipated that progress will be made in these areas.

SELF-CHECK

1. Poor management has been one of the glaring weaknesses in homeland security. True or False?

2. Some of the money devoted to homeland security has been misspent or used in fraudulent purposes. True or False?

3. Correcting problems and ensuring policies are effective may be labeled as:

    (a) accountability.
    (b) adaptability.
    (c) flexibility.
    (d) command and control.

4. Explain how the concepts of liability reduction and capacity building could improve homeland security in the future.

SUMMARY

As a participant in homeland security, it is imperative that you anticipate the future. It will be necessary for you to comprehend the impacts of dirty bombs and radiological dispersion devices. You must recognize the possible devastation that may result if nuclear weapons are acquired by terrorists. Preparing for biological or chemical weapons should be one of your top responsibilities. In addition, it is advisable that you promote accountability in homeland security. The goals of preventing attacks, limiting their negative consequences, and reacting to them effectively can only be achieved if you work intelligently and diligently to counter the deadly intents of terrorists. The concepts of liability reduction and capacity building may help to direct your actions.

ASSESS YOUR UNDERSTANDING

UNDERSTAND: WHAT HAVE YOU LEARNED?

 Go to **www.wiley.com/college/mcentire** to assess your knowledge of the future of homeland security.

SUMMARY QUESTIONS

1. WMD is described as a major possibility in future attacks. List three reasons why terrorists are anticipated to use weapons of mass destruction.

2. Some of the weapons of mass destruction are similar in certain respects. Explain the different between a radiological dispersion device and a nuclear weapon.

3. If you were working in the public health field, you might hear comments about the different types of biological agents. Describe the difference between Category A, B, and C agents.

4. Terrorism with the use of chemical weapons is a major concern in the future. What steps can be taken to prevent or respond to terrorism involving chemical weapons?

5. Define the word "accountability" and discuss its relation to homeland security.

6. Theft of radiological material has been a problem in recent years. True or False?

7. The International Atomic Energy Agency is not responsible for the Non-Proliferation Treaty. True or False?

8. The nature and extent of impact from biological weapons is dependent on the type of agent used as well as health of the victim and extent of exposure. True or False?

9. Irritants are the most deadly type of chemical agent. True or False?

10. The creation of new response plans has only complicated responses to terrorist attacks and other disasters in the nation. True or False?

11. Agro-terrorism has no relation to biological agents. True or False?

12. The IAEA is in charge of preventing the spread of chemical weapons. True or False?

13. Liability reduction implies a strategy to minimize the probability of terrorist attacks. True or False?

14. Radiological agents:

    (a) can be obtained from hospitals, industrial facilities, and the black market.

    (b) are not used in dirty bombs.

    (c) never pose health threats to humans.

    (d) do not necessitate the involvement of the military or expert medical physicians.

15. Which of the following causes the least concern among terrorism experts?

    (a) A suitcase bomb

    (b) A declared nuclear possessor giving nuclear weapons or material to a terrorist organization

    (c) Iran developing nuclear weapons

    (d) The U.S. losing one of its nuclear weapons

16. Which type of biological agent is comprised of a single cell organism that causes diseases in plants, animals, and humans?

    (a) Toxin

    (b) Virus

    (c) Bacteria

    (d) Category A agents

17. Which of the following helps to prevent the spread of biological weapons?

    (a) IAEA

    (b) NPT

    (c) BWC

    (d) NTW

18. Which type of chemical weapon damages the pulmonary system?

    (a) Nerve agents

    (b) Vesicants

    (c) Blood agents

    (d) Choking agents

19. Many of the shortcomings in homeland security result from a failure of:

    (a) action.

    (b) imagination.

    (c) accountability.

    (d) effort.

20. Which of the following is representative of capacity building?

    (a) Launching a pre-emptive strive against known terrorists

    (b) Sealing off the borders so terrorists cannot enter the United States

    (c) Planning, training and exercises

    (d) Promoting tolerance among different religions

BE A HOMELAND SECURITY PROFESSIONAL

Nuclear Proliferation

Write a paper on the proliferation of nuclear weapons and how it relates to terrorism. Be sure to explain who is responsible for halting the spread of nuclear weapons around the world.

Bio-terrorism

As a seasoned analyst in the Center for Disease Control, you have been asked to identify the risk of bio-terrorism. Be sure to explain why bio-terrorism is both likely and unlikely.

Accountability in Homeland Security

Review some of the government reports on the status of homeland security in the United States. Explain whether or not you think the Department of Homeland Security has been effective or ineffective in its responsibilities.

KEY TERMS

Accountability	The expectation of being responsible for decisions and activities.
Agro-terrorism	Terrorism against farming industries and products.
Bacteria	A single cell organism that causes disease in plants, animals, and humans.
Biological weapons	Living organisms, or agents produced by living organisms, that may be used in terrorist attacks.
Biological Weapons Convention (BWC)	An international treaty designed to prevent the proliferation of biological agents around the world.
Bio-terrorism	Terrorism that employs biological weapons.
Blood agents	Chemical weapons that prevent the flow of oxygen in the blood.
Capacity building	A strategy that attempts to enhance the ability of the nation, states, and communities to effectively deal with potential or actual terrorist attacks.
Category A agents	Biological weapons that pose a serious risk to people because they are easily transmitted to others and they result in high mortality rates.
Category B agents	Biological weapons that have a moderate chance of contagion and generally result in lower morbidity rates than Category A agents.
Category C agents	Biological weapons that could be used for mass dissemination and high morbidity if engineered for that purpose.
Chemical weapons	Lethal man-made poisons that can be disseminated as gasses, liquids, or aerosols.
Choking agents	Chemical weapons that cause respiratory distress.
Civil Support Teams	Specialized military units that assist local and state governments that have been affected by weapons of mass destruction.
International Atomic Energy Agency (IAEA)	The international organization responsible for the enforcement of the non-proliferation treaty.
Irritants	Agents that lead to allergic reactions.
Liability reduction	A strategy that attempts to address the factors that result in or permit terrorist attacks.
Nerve agents	Chemical weapons that prevent the transmission of electrical signals in the nervous system.

Non-Proliferation Treaty (NPT)	An international regime designed to prevent nuclear states from giving nuclear weapons or materials to those who do not possess them.
Nuclear weapons	Weapons that produce massive explosions due to the release of vast amounts of energy through fission or fusion.
Proliferation	The acquisition, sharing, and spread of nuclear weapons and materials to those who do not currently possess them.
Radiological weapons	Weapons that spread dangerous radiological material but do not result in a nuclear explosion. Radiological weapons are also known as radiological dispersion devices (RDD) or dirty bombs.
Strategic national stockpile (SNS)	A cache of medicines in secret locations that can be quickly sent to affected locations around the nation.
Suitcase bomb	Portable nuclear weapons.
Toxin	A poison that is produced by plants or animals.
Vesicants	Blister agents that produce chemical burns.
Virus	A microscopic genetic particle that infects the cells of living organisms but cannot multiply outside a host cell.
Weapons of Mass Destruction (WMD)	Weaponry that will create major injuries, carnage, destruction, and disruption when utilized.

REFERENCES

Bunn, Matthew and Anthony Wier. (2008). "The Seven Myths of Nuclear Terrorism." Pp. 125–137 in Howard, Russell D. and James J. F. Forest (Eds.). *Weapons of Mass Destruction and Terrorism*. McGraw-Hill: New York.

Cameron, Gavin. (2008). "Nuclear Terrorism: Reactors & Radiological Attacks after September 11." Pp. 148–166 in Howard, Russell D. and James J. F. Forest (Eds.). *Weapons of Mass Destruction and Terrorism*. McGraw-Hill: New York.

Chyba, Christopher F. and Alex L. Greninger. (2008). Pp. 198–211 in Howard, Russell D. and James J. F. Forest (Eds.). *Weapons of Mass Destruction and Terrorism*. McGraw-Hill: New York.

Dunn, Lewis A. (2008). "Can Al Qaeda Be Deterred from Using Nuclear Weapons?" Pp. 295–316 in Howard, Russell D. and James J. F. Forest (Eds.). *Weapons of Mass Destruction and Terrorism*. McGraw-Hill: New York.

Falkenrath, Richard A., Robert D. Newman, and Bradley A. Thayer. (1998). *America's Achilles' Heel: Nuclear, Biological and Chemical Terrorism and Covert Attack*. MIT Press: Cambridge, MA.

FEMA. (1999). *Emergency Response to Terrorism*. Independent Study Course. Washington, D.C.

Ferguson, Charles D. and Joel O. Lubenau. (2008). "Securing U.S. Radiological Sources." Pp. 139–166 in Howard, Russell D. and James J. F. Forest (eds.) *Weapons of Mass Destruction and Terrorism*. McGraw-Hill: New York.

Maerli, Morten Breme, Annette Schaper and Frank Barnaby. (1998). "The Characteristics of Nuclear Terrorist Weapons." Pp. 100–124 in Howard, Russell D. and James J. F. Forest (Eds.). *Weapons of Mass Destruction and Terrorism*. McGraw-Hill: New York.

McEntire, David A. (2004). "Tenets of Vulnerability: Assessing a Fundamental Disaster Concept." *Journal of Emergency Management* 2(2): 23–29.

McEntire, David A. (2005). "Why Vulnerability Matters: Illustrating the Need for a Modified Disaster Reduction Concept." *Disaster Prevention and Management* 14(2): 206–222.

Purpura, Philip P. (2007). *Terrorism and Homeland Security: An Introduction with Applications*. Butterworth-Heinemann: Burlington, MA.

Thomas, Patricia. (2003). *The Anthrax Attacks*. The Century Foundation's Homeland Security Project Working Group on the Public's Need to Know. The Century Foundation: New York.

Tucker, Jonathan B. (2008). "Chemical Terrorism: Assessing Threats and Responses." Pp. 213–226 in Howard, Russell D. and James J. F. Forest (Eds.). *Weapons of Mass Destruction and Terrorism*. McGraw-Hill: New York.

GLOSSARY

9/11
The terrorist attacks involving hijacked planes against the United States that occurred on September 11, 2001.

Absolute poverty
State in which people lack so many resources that they cannot even meet basic necessities such as food, clothing, and shelter.

Abu Musab al-Zarqawi
A Sunni terrorist responsible for many atrocities in Iraq, including the beheading of American businessman Nicolas Berg.

Abu Sayef
An Islamic separatist group in the Philippines that desires an independent state in Mindanao.

Accountability
The expectation of being responsible for decisions and activities.

Affect dimension
Specific emotions that are generated in conjunction with an ideology.

Agro-terrorism
Terrorism against farming industries and products.

Al Jazeera
A TV station based in Qatar that is popular in the Middle East and used to disseminate terrorist information.

Al Qaeda
An extreme Islamic fundamentalist terrorist organization.

Al Qaeda
A well-known terrorist organization whose name refers to the "base"—the location from which its supporters attacked the Soviet Union to free Afghanistan.

Anarchists
Those opposing specific governments or all governments.

Animal Liberation Front
A terrorist organization that opposes cruelty to animals.

Annexes
A portion of the emergency operations plan that discusses specific hazards or functions that will need to be addressed if an event takes place.

Appendices
Additional information at the end of the emergency operations plan which includes resource and contact lists, maps, standard operating procedures, and checklists.

Area command
An ICS organization that supervises several incident command posts.

Armed Forces of National Liberation (FALN)
A Puerto Rican terrorist organization seeking liberation of Puerto Rico from the United States.

Arousal hypothesis
Media reports on terrorism can increase people's interest in acting aggressively.

Asymmetrical warfare
Terrorist attacks on the part of the militarily weak against those who are powerful.

Bacteria
A single cell organism that causes disease in plants, animals, and humans.

Basic plan
An overview of the entire emergency operations plan.

Biological Weapons Convention (BWC)
An international treaty designed to prevent the proliferation of biological agents around the world.

Biological weapons
Living organisms, or agents produced by living organisms, that may be used in terrorist attacks.

Bio-terrorism	Terrorism that employs biological weapons.
Black Panthers	An organization comprised of African Americans to revenge the actions of the KKK and other white supremacists.
Black September	An operational unit of the Al-Fatah terrorism organization that initiated the terrorist attacks on Israeli athletes at the Munich Olympic games in 1972.
Blood agents	Chemical weapons that prevent the flow of oxygen in the blood.
Bojinka plot	A planned attack on airliners over the Pacific Ocean.
Bollards	Metal or concrete posts installed into the earth or cement to keep vehicles from entering restricted areas.
Border	The territorial boundary of any nation along with its various points of entry.
Built-in escalation hypothesis	More deadly and visible attacks are required to get equal media coverage in the future.
Capacity building	A strategy that attempts to enhance the ability of the nation, states, and communities to effectively deal with potential or actual terrorist attacks.
Category A agents	Biological weapons that pose a serious risk to people because they are easily transmitted to others and they result in high mortality rates.
Category B agents	Biological weapons that have a moderate chance of contagion and generally result in lower morbidity rates than Category A agents.
Category C agents	Biological weapons that could be used for mass dissemination and high morbidity if engineered for that purpose.
CBRNE	Acronym for chemical, biological, radiological, nuclear, or explosive devices.
Cell	A terrorist branch or unit operating in locations away from the organization's headquarters.
Censorship	The withholding, banning, or altering of information the media shares with the public.
Chemical weapons	Lethal man-made poisons that can be disseminated as gasses, liquids, or aerosols.
Choking agents	Chemical weapons that cause respiratory distress.
Civil defense	The government's initiative to prepare communities and citizens to react effectively to a nuclear exchange during the Cold War.
Civil Support Teams	Specialized military units that assist local and state governments that have been affected by weapons of mass destruction.
Classified intelligence	Information given only to a very specific and limited number of people to protect sources of acquisition and deny adversaries information that would lead them to alter their communications or operations.
Cognitive dimension	The knowledge and beliefs of the ideology.
Coherence	The internal logic of an ideology.
Cold zone	The uncontaminated area where responders and victims may enter and leave.
Communism	An ideology that sympathizes with the poor and downtrodden and attempts to do away with private property.

Community Emergency Response Team (CERT)	A group of citizens who receive basic training in response operations.
Comprehensive Homeland Security Act	A law passed in 2003 containing new regulations for critical infrastructure security, railroad security, and more stringent measures related to border control and weapons of mass destruction.
Computer Assisted Passenger Prescreening System II (CAPPS II)	A former computer program utilized by the TSA to screen passengers against lists of known terrorists and others with criminal records.
Conflict disaster	A socially disruptive and divisive event that involves a riot or some type of warfare.
Consensus disaster	A socially disruptive event such as an earthquake that brings the community together.
Consequence management	An emergency management function that stresses planning, emergency medical response and public health, disaster relief, and restoration of communities.
Container Security Initiative (CSI)	One of the first measures taken by the government to protect maritime trade and ports against terrorism.
Continuity of operation	The maintenance of government functions after terrorist attacks through the identification of leader succession, alternate work sites, and resumption of operational practices.
Convergence	The flow of people and resources to the scene of an emergency or disaster.
Coordination	Cooperative efforts to pursue common goals in the wake of terrorist attacks.
Corporatist model	A model that stresses the integration of various components of society into the state government.
Counter-terrorism	The active pursuit of known terrorists which includes preemptive military strikes.
Crazy	A terrorist that is regarded to be psychologically disturbed (e.g., Ted Kaczynski).
Criminal justice	A discipline and profession interested in intelligence gathering, terrorist investigation, prosecution, border control, and other security measures.
Criminal	A terrorist that seeks personal gain through illegal means (e.g., drugs or crime).
Crisis counseling	The treatment of psychological problems that may arise from the stress produced by terrorism.
Crisis management	A law enforcement function that concentrates on identifying, anticipating, preventing, and prosecuting those involved in terrorism.
Critical incident stress (CIS)	Trauma experienced while on the job that is so severe it inhibits coping among emergency service personnel.
Critical infrastructure	Interdependent networks comprised of industrial, utility, transportation, and other distribution systems.
Crusader	A terrorist that promotes high moral goals (e.g., Islamic fundamentalists).
Crusades	Wars between 1100 and 1300 @C endorsed by the Pope to recapture the Holy Land of Jerusalem from the control of Muslims.
Culture	The lifestyle of groups, including their shared history, language, religion, and moral system.
Customs-Trade Partnership Against Terrorism (C-TPAT)	An agreement between the public and private sectors to protect international commerce from terrorists attacks.

Cyber-terrorism	The use of computers to plan or launch attacks.
Damage assessment	A survey of physical destruction, economic losses, deaths, social disruption, and recovery needs.
Daniel Pearl	A reporter with the *Wall Street Journal* who was killed by terrorists in Karachi, Pakistan.
Debriefing	A recurring and more in depth discussion designed to redirect harmful thinking and develop improved coping mechanisms.
Debris management	The removal, storage, disposal, or recycling of rubble produced from terrorist attacks.
Decontamination	The removal of hazardous materials from victims through clothing removal and the washing of bodies.
Defusing	A short, unstructured meeting to allow a person to discuss an experience as soon as it takes place.
Department of Defense (DOD)	The government agency responsible for the military.
Department of Homeland Security (DHS)	A newly created organization which aims to prevent terrorist attacks or react to them effectively.
Department of State (DOS)	The government agency in charge of diplomatic relationships among nations.
Dirty bombs	Explosive devices laden with dangerous chemicals or radioactive material.
Disaster declaration	An acknowledgement of the severity of the event and that outside response and recovery assistance is required.
Disaster Mortuary Operations Response Team (DMORT)	A group of private citizens from around the nation who may be activated by the federal government to assist with mass fatality incidents.
Disaster Recovery Center (DRC)	A temporary facility near the attack location where victims can seek information about federal assistance programs.
Disinhibition hypothesis	Violence portrayed by the media may weaken the inhibition of others to participate in terrorism.
Domestic terrorism	Terrorism that occurs within a single country.
Donations management	The collection, sorting, and distribution of goods and money for the benefit of victims of terrorist attacks.
Dynastic assassination	The murder of the head official in government.
Earth Liberation Front	A terrorist organization that opposes environmental degradation.
Economic class model	A model that suggests a division of society based on the amount of wealth one possesses.
Emergence	The appearance of altruistic behavior that is unfamiliar to the participants.
Emergency alert system	An announcement that interrupts TV and radio programs and relays information about what is taking place and what people should do for protection.
Emergency assistance	Financial help given to local governments to take care of immediate needs such as debris removal or safety precautions.
Emergency Management Accreditation Program	A standard-based assessment and certification initiative for local and state emergency management agencies.

Emergency Management Assistance Compact (EMAC)	An agreement among states to render assistance to one another in time of need.
Emergency management	A discipline and profession that addresses how to prevent or react successfully to various types of disasters.
Emergency manager	A local government official in charge of disaster mitigation, preparedness, response, and recovery.
Emergency Operations Center (EOC)	A location from which disaster response and recovery activities can be overseen and managed.
Emergency Operations Plan (EOP)	A document that describes what may be anticipated in terms of homeland security and emergency management and how to best to react.
Enlightenment	A period in history when a new way of looking at social, political, and economic structures emerged.
Evacuation	The movement of people away from hazardous areas or situations.
Exercises	Drills and mock events that test the knowledge and skills of those in charge of reacting to attacks.
Extensiveness	How many people share a particular ideology.
Fascism	An ideology which promotes the uniting of citizens in support of the state.
Fatwa	A religious edict.
Federal Bureau of Investigation (FBI)	The government agency that concentrates on the enforcement of United States law.
Federal Emergency Management Agency (FEMA)	The national organization in charge of disaster management.
First responders	The first official government responders in the field including police, fire fighters, and emergency medical technicians.
Focused terror	Terrorism directed toward a specific group of people deemed as the enemy.
Freedom of religion	People cannot be denied their right to worship according to the dictates of their own conscience.
Freedom of speech	People are allowed to express their opinions, even when they criticize the government.
Full-scale exercises	Major scenarios that test many functions or the entire response system.
Functional exercises	Practice scenarios that explore one or a few of the annexes in the plan.
Geneva Conventions	A set of internationally accepted laws pertaining to the conduct of war.
George Habash	Founder of the militant Popular Front for the Liberation of Palestine (PFLP) and a terrorist who opposes Israel. He sponsored many airline hijackings in the 1970's and 1980's.
Grants	Funds given to local governments to support or enhance homeland security and emergency management programs.
Group competition model	A model of politics that asserts that interest groups interact with or counteract one another in their attempt to sway government policy.
GSG9A	German counter-terrorism organization, whose name means "border guards, group 9."

Guerilla	Spanish term for little war which is an armed protest of occupying forces.
Gunpowder Plot	An attempted terrorist attack in 1605 against King James I and other leaders of Parliament to reinstate Catholic involvement in England.
Hamas	The name for the Islamic Resistance Movement, an offshoot of the Muslim Brotherhood founded to denounce the national borders drawn up by colonial powers in Europe.
Hazard(s)	The physical or other agent(s) that may trigger or initiate disaster events and processes.
Holocaust	The extermination of Jews by the Nazi regime during World War II.
Homeland Security Act	A law passed in 2002 which mandated the creation of the Department of Homeland Security.
Homeland Security Advisory System (HSAS)	The nation's method for warning the population of potential and unfolding terrorist attacks.
Homeland security	A concerted national effort to prevent terrorist attacks within the United States, reduce America's vulnerability to terrorism, and recover from and minimize the damage of attacks that do occur.
Hot zone	The area contaminated by the terrorist attack.
HUMINT	Intelligence collected by people from people (and can be done overtly or covertly).
Ideology	A set of beliefs related to values, attitudes, ways of thinking, and goals.
IED	Acronym for improvised explosive device.
IMINT	Geospatial imagery collected by satellites and aircraft.
Immigration and Customs Enforcement (ICE)	The largest investigative organization within the Department of Homeland Security which attempts to deter illegal immigration and the smuggling of money and materials that support terrorism.
Incident Command System (ICS)	A set of personnel and procedures which helps facilitate coordination among first responders.
Incident command	The on-scene leader or leaders in the incident command post.
Individual assistance	Relief programs for citizens and businesses impacted by terrorist attacks.
In-kind donations	Physical donations including food, water, clothing, supplies, and equipment.
Input functions	Activities that influence priorities in the political system.
Intelligence adjustment	Adaptation of the intelligence cycle is required when collection is incomplete, analysis seeks to "connect the dots," production generates new questions, and dissemination results in the anticipation of future concerns.
Intelligence analysis	Efforts to make sense of the voluminous data that is gathered from the field.
Intelligence collection	Activities to gather information about terrorist organizations, their operations and potential attacks.
Intelligence cycle	A four-step process of gathering, understanding, and synthesizing data, and then sharing it with those who will use it.
Intelligence dissemination	Sharing information with end-users (e.g., policy makers, FBI Special Agents, homeland security personnel, etc.).
Intelligence production	The creation of written reports, briefings, images, or maps to influence operational decisions.

Intelligence	The function of collecting, assessing, and distributing information about an enemy, criminal or terrorist.
Intensiveness	The strength of attachment to an ideology.
International Atomic Energy Agency (IAEA)	The international organization responsible for the enforcement of the non-proliferation treaty.
International relations	A discipline and profession that deals with the conflicts among nation states and non-state actors (e.g., why terrorism occurs and what governments are doing about it).
International terrorism	Terrorism that spans two or more nations.
INTERPOL	An international police organization that is involved in intelligence.
Iran	A state in the Middle East that denounces the United States, promotes anti-western propaganda, and has a long history of participation in terrorism.
Irritants	Agents that lead to allergic reactions.
Islamic fundamentalists	Individuals or groups of Muslims that violently oppose Israel and the United States.
Japanese Red Army (JRA)	A left-wing terrorist organization that emerged in the 1960s to protest U.S. military presence in Japan after World War II, the war in Vietnam, and capitalism.
Jihad	Literally means an internal struggle to pursue righteousness or a war of self-defense, but has been used by terrorists to denote an offensive attack.
Joint field office (JFO)	An incident command organization with federal personnel (and state and local officials on certain occasions).
Key assets	Facilities, sites, and structures that are believed to require additional protection from terrorist attacks.
Kickoff meeting	A gathering of local, state, and federal officials for the purpose of explaining public assistance programs in detail.
Ku Klux Klan (KKK)	A white supremacist group that has been involved in terrorism in the United States since the Civil War.
Liability reduction	A strategy that attempts to address the factors that result in or permit terrorist attacks.
Liaison officer	The person who serves as the link between the incident commander(s) and other organizations.
Libya	A country in Northern Africa that heavily supported terrorism in the 1980s.
Local Emergency Planning Committees (LEPCs)	Preparedness councils promoted in the 1980s to help communities prepare for hazardous materials releases.
Lone-wolf terrorists	Individual terrorists who act alone.
Madrasahs	Schools in Pakistan and elsewhere that at times indoctrinate students in extreme Islamic thought.
Maintenance	The feedback function of the political system.
MASINT	Measurement and signature intelligence that looks for the characteristics of certain types of actions (e.g., the presence of nuclear material when one is trying to develop a nuclear weapon).
Mass fatality incident	An attack that creates so many deaths that the processing of remains is beyond the ability of local government.

Mass terror	Terrorism by the government in power against its own citizens.
Minutemen Project	Activities to promote border security carried out by a group of volunteers which founded the Minutemen Civil Defense Corps in Arizona.
Mitigation	Activity that attempts to avoid disasters or minimize negative consequences.
Molly Maguires	A group of Irish citizens that joined together to dispute the treatment of coal mine workers in the United States.
Money laundering	The process of hiding where money is coming from and what it is being used for.
Multi-agency coordination centers (MACCs)	An ICS organization level that supervises incident command across several jurisdictions.
Muslims	People who follow the prophet Muhammad and adhere to the religion of Islam.
Mutual aid	A collaborative agreement between jurisdictions when external help is warranted.
National Emergency Management Association	A professional association of state emergency management agencies.
National Incident Management System (NIMS)	A comprehensive national approach for incident management in the United States.
National Processing Service Center	A FEMA office set up to help victims apply for federal assistance programs.
National Response Framework (NRF)	The successor to the National Response Plan; a document that describes the principles, roles and structures of response and recovery operations.
National Response Plan (NRP)	A document that describes the procedures for responding to all-types of hazards with a multi-disciplinary perspective.
Nationalist movements	Efforts on the part of a group or nation to obtain political independence and autonomy.
NBC	Acronym for nuclear, biological, and chemical weapons.
Nerve agents	Chemical weapons that prevent the transmission of electrical signals in the nervous system.
Non-Proliferation Treaty (NPT)	An international regime designed to prevent nuclear states from giving nuclear weapons or materials to those who do not possess them.
Non-structural mitigation	Methods beyond construction that may limit the possibility or consequences of terrorist attacks.
Nuclear weapons	Weapons that produce massive explosions due to the release of vast amounts of energy through fission or fusion.
Operation Mongoose	An attempt by the United States to kill Cuban leader Fidel Castro with a poisoned cigar.
Operations	The name given to the section under ICS that is in charge of implementing the strategy created by those in planning.
OPINT	Open source intelligence acquired through publicly available materials including academic research, newspaper articles, library books, etc.
Ordinance	An authoritative order or law issued by a government.
Output functions	Activities emanating from the political system.

Paper plan syndrome	An attitude that assumes that having a plan ensures you are prepared to deal with terrorism and other types of disasters.
Permanent assistance	Financial aid for the repairing of publicly owned critical infrastructure and key assets.
Pervasiveness	How long an ideology has been in existence.
Planning	The section under ICS in charge of collecting information about the terrorist attack, including operational priorities.
Political elite model	A model in which the leaders are ruling over the masses.
Political system	A governing process that operates in a self-contained environment (e.g., a national territory).
Politics	The authoritative allocation of values and resources in society.
Post-Katrina Emergency Management Reform Act	A law which specifies ways to avert the slow and disjointed federal response to the catastrophe in New Orleans, Louisiana.
Post-traumatic stress disorder (PTSD)	The clinical diagnosis for individuals who become depressed due to a traumatic event in their lives.
Preliminary Damage Assessment (PDA)	A more detailed assessment of impacts that typically takes place within days or weeks of the event; it determines possibility and extent of outside assistance.
Preparedness	Readiness measures in anticipation of a disaster.
Preparedness council	A group of individuals who provide recommendations for policy and assist with program administration.
Preparedness	Concerted efforts to improve response and recovery capabilities.
Prevention	Counter-terrorism operations such as intelligence gathering and preventive strike activity.
Program dimension	Conjure up the plans and actions to support the goals of an ideology.
Programs dimension	The plans and actions to support goals.
Proliferation	The acquisition, sharing, and spread of nuclear weapons and materials to those who do not currently possess them.
Protection	Anti-terrorism operations such as improved building design, enhanced security, and infrastructure protection.
Protection	An attempt to deny attacks and defend oneself from terrorism.
Public administration	A discipline and profession that directs attention to the formation policy and the best organization to deal with difficult societal problems.
Public assistance	Relief programs that make aid available to government entities which have been affected by terrorism.
Public health	A discipline and profession that concentrates on understanding diseases and how to treat them (e.g., identifying how to react from a medical standpoint to the use of nuclear, biological, chemical, or radiological weapons).
Public information officer	The person who gathers information for the incident commander(s) and shares information with the media, or a city employee who specializes in working with the media.
Radiological weapons	Weapons that spread dangerous radiological material but do not result in a nuclear explosion. Radiological weapons are also known as radiological dispersion devices (RDD) or dirty bombs.

Random terror	An attack on large numbers of people wherever they gather.
Rapid assessment	A quick survey of impacts designed to gain an appreciation of the scope of the attack.
Recovery	Long-term activities to rebound after disasters or terrorist attacks.
Red Scare	Senator McCarthy's fear of communist infiltration into the United States.
Reign of Terror	A period during the French Revolution where an estimated 20,000 persons were killed by France's Committee of Public Safety.
Relative poverty	State where some people are less wealthy than their fellow citizens or peers in other countries.
Religion	The beliefs and practices espoused by those sharing a common spiritual faith.
Response	The immediate reaction to an emergency situation, like a terrorist attack.
Reverse 911 systems	Computerized messages sent over phone lines rapidly to anyone in a designated area.
Right to assemble	People are permitted to join in politically motivated gatherings.
Right to bear arms	Guns can be purchased and owned without government interference.
Risk	A measure of probability and consequences.
Safety officer	The person who evaluates the dangers at the scene and makes sure everyone is operating according to safety policies.
Scope	The subjects covered by an ideology.
Search and Rescue (SAR)	Response activities undertaken to find disaster victims and remove them from danger or confinement.
Secondary devices	The detonation of other bombs to add to the disruption and fear of the initial attack.
Secure Flight	The proposed program to replace the Computer Assisted Passenger Prescreening System II.
Self-censorship	Media control over their reporting of news to the public.
Self-referred	Patients who arrive at the hospital whether they require immediate care or not.
Set back requirements	Laws that describe the proximity of buildings to roads and parking lots.
Sheltering	The location of individuals in places of safety and refuge.
SIGINT	Interception and interpretation of electronic communications such as phone conversations and emails.
Situational awareness	Continual monitoring of safety concerns at the scene of a terrorist attack.
Size up	The process of evaluating the nature of the attack site.
Social base dimension	The individuals or groups that espouse an ideology.
Social learning theory	Observing terrorist attacks in the news may generate similar type of behavior among others.
Soft targets	Potential sites of terrorist attacks because they are open and accessible to the public.
Special Air Service (SAS)	A British counter-terrorism organization.
Strategic national stockpile (SNS)	A cache of medicines in secret locations that can be quickly sent to affected locations around the nation.

Structural mitigation	Special construction practices and materials that limit the impact of terrorist attacks.
Structure	The organizational relationships within the political system.
Suitcase bomb	Portable nuclear weapons.
System requirements	Functions that must be established to maintain operation of a political system.
Table top exercises	Informal discussions about hypothetical scenarios that occur in an office setting.
Tactical emergency medical services	The name given to a team of paramedics that are armed and trained in weapons use.
Tactical terror	The use of attacks against the government for revolutionary or other purposes.
Taliban	The name of the government which provided a safe haven for Al Qaeda.
Technical assessment	A survey of damages that points out methods and costs for rebuilding.
Terrorism	The use or threat of violence to support ideological purposes.
Theocracy	A government run by clerics in the name of God.
Theodore "Ted" Kaczynski	Terrorist known as the "Unabomber" who opposed technological advances.
Threat assessment	A careful study of the targets that might be appealing to terrorists.
Toxin	A poison that is produced by plants or animals.
Training	Information sharing in classroom or field settings to help familiarize people with protocol.
Transportation Security Act	A law designed to protect transportation systems in the United States.
Transportation Security Administration (TSA)	A federal agency under the Department of Homeland Security created to protect our transportation systems from terrorist attacks.
Triage	The assessment, sorting, and treatment of the injured in such a way as to maximize limited resources.
United States Coast Guard (USCG)	A military branch within the Department of Homeland Security which is in charge of maritime law, environmental protection of waterways, search and rescue operations at sea, and interdiction of illegal aliens and contraband.
United States Visitor and Immigrant Status Indicator Technology (US-VISIT)	A computer database used to screen passengers who wish to travel to the United States.
Unmet needs committee	A group of concerned citizens and community leaders who work together to collect donations and address long terms needs of victims.
USA PATRIOT Act	A homeland security law which stands for "Uniting and Strengthening America by Providing Appropriate Tools Required to Intercept and Obstruct Terrorism." This law aims to prevent terrorist attacks and enhance law enforcement's ability to investigate and punish offenders.
Valuation dimension	The norms and judgments of an ideology.
Vesicants	Blister agents that produce chemical burns.
Virus	A microscopic genetic particle that infects the cells of living organisms but cannot multiply outside a host cell.

Volunteer management	The harnessing of volunteers to take advantage of their potential contributions while averting potential negative consequences.
Volunteer registration center	The location where citizens fill out forms noting their skills and other information which can help you when making assignments.
Vulnerability	A high degree of disaster proneness and/or limited disaster management capabilities.
Wahhabism	A stringent and legalistic movement that attempts to ensure the purity of the Muslim faith with no deviations whatsoever.
Warm zone	The location where victims are washed. It is located between the hot and cold zones.
Warnings	Notifications sent out to the public so they can take protective measures.
Weapons of Mass Destruction (WMD)	Weaponry that will create major injuries, carnage, destruction, and disruption when utilized.
Weather radios	Electronic devices that receive information from the National Weather Service to warn people of approaching severe weather.
WMDs	Acronym for weapons of mass destruction.
Writ of habeas corpus	A law protecting citizens from unlawful imprisonment.
Zoning	Regulations that delineate where buildings can be located.

INDEX

327

PHOTO CREDITS

CPSIA information can be obtained at www.ICGtesting.com
Printed in the USA
BVOW04n0056050815

411006BV00013B/5/P